Fingerweaving Basics

Written and Illustrated by: **Gerald L Findley**

Published by:
Crazy Crow Trading Post
P.O. Box 847 Pottsboro, Texas 75076-0847

903-786-2287 • FAX: 903-786-9059

www.crazycrow.com • info@crazycrow.com

ISBN NO.
1-929572-0805

© 2005 by Gerald L Findley
Hermon, New York

All rights reserved. No part of this publication may be reproduced or transmitted in any form or any means, electronic or mechanical, including photocopying, recording or any information storage and retrieval system, without written permission from the publisher.

INTRODUCTION

Fingerweaving is the art of producing useful textiles without the use of a loom. Various forms of fingerweaving are found throughout the world. This book, however, will deal only with two forms of fingerweaving commonly found among the people of the first nations of North America: warpface weaving and openface weaving.

Each person who does fingerweaving seems to develop their own style. Therefore, you will find people who do things differently than what is presented in this book. The fact that they do things differently does not mean they are wrong. It only means they are different. Observe the differences, they may work for you.

The presentations in this book rely on graphics to illustrate what is happening to the strands as the weaving is done. As you are weaving, concentrate on what is happening to the strands and the patterns of movement of the strands. The hand positions shown in the illustrations are only relative and are intended only to clarify the positioning of the strands.

It makes no difference if you are left-handed or right-handed, you will need to use both hands. The first two fingers and the thumb of each hand are used to manipulate the strands. The remaining fingers of each hand are used primarily to hold the strands and apply the needed tension to the strands.

No attempt will be made to associate a particular pattern or style of fingerweaving with a cultural group or historical period. That debate will be left to the historians and archaeologists.

Table of Contents

PART 1: GETTING STARTED 4

PART 2: WARPFACE WEAVING 8

    Diagonal Pattern: Over/under Weave 9
    Chevron Pattern: Over/under Weave 14
    Reversed Chevron: Over/under Weave 21
    Double Chevron: 27
        Double Chevron: W Pattern 27
        Double Chevron: M Pattern 29
    Chevron Pattern: Over Two/Under Two 32
    Reversed Chevron: Over Two/Under Two 36
    Lightning Pattern: 40
    Double Lightning Pattern 47
    Arrowhead Pattern: Over/Under Weave
        (Point Down) 53
    Arrowhead Pattern: Over/Under Weave
        (Point Up) 64
    Arrowhead Pattern: Over Two/Under Two
        (Point Down) 72
    Changing Direction: Over Two/Under Two 78
    Arrowhead Pattern: Over Two/Under Two
        (Point Up) 78

PART 3: OPENFACE WEAVING 85

    Plain Weaving 86
    Joining Bands 93

    Borders 98
    Adding Bead Accent 105
        Diamond Pattern: Carrier Strands 109
        Over/under Only 109
            Three Bead Diamond Mesh 109
            Six Bead Diamond Mesh 110
            Six Bead Zigzag 111
            Four Bead Diamond Mesh 112
    Colored Strands Accent 113
        With Bead Accent Carrier Strand 116
        With Bead Accent: Over/Under Weave 118
    Diamond Design 117
    Twining 119
        Twining and Beads Combined 125
    Warp Accent 126
        Warp Accent With Beads 131

PART 4: FRINGES 132

    Tied Fringe 133
    Braided Fringe 135
        Bead Accented 138
    Twisted Fringe 139

GLOSSARY 141

INDEX 141

PART 1: GETTING STARTED

Materials and Tools
    yarn
    scissors
    tape measure
    measuring board
    safety pins
    1/4"* 6" dowels (headsticks)

Type of yarn
The type and size of yarn used to do finger weaving affects the appearance of the finished product. 2 or 3-ply tightly spun wool yarn was the traditional yarn.

The photographs in this book are mostly of work examples created with 4-ply acrylic yarn. This is a good yarn to start with. It is inexpensive, and can be bought in almost any department or craft store.

After you have learned the basic technics, you may wish to use lighter 3-ply yarn. Lighter yarn requires more strands to obtain the same size pattern element as was obtained with 4-ply yarn. The use of more strands increases the clarity of the pattern.

Length of yarn
The length of the strands needed to complete a piece of finger weaving can be estimated by determining the desired length of the woven portion and the desired length of the fringe. Calculate the total length of the woven part and the fringe, then add 20% to this length (some of the length of the strands is used as the weaving is done and the fringe is being made)

Example:
Belt with 36-inch fringe.
    waist size --------- 32-inches
    fringe length (36-in.)* 2 =
            --------------72-inches
    finished length =104-inches
    ----
    finished length * 20% =
            ---- 20.8-inches
    ----
    finished length --- 104-inches
    20% --------------- 20.8-inches
    total length   = 124.8-inches

Number of strands of yarn
The number and color of the strands needed is determined by the pattern and the desired width of the finished article. Warpface weaving in 4-ply acrylic yarn uses about 22 strands per inch of width.

Example:
5-inch wide chevron belt.
    width ----------- 5-in.
                times
    22 strands per inch
    Total number of strands
            = 110 strands

[NOTE]
For 2 color bands of the same width, use 1/2 the total number of strands for each color (55 strands of each color).

Measuring
Setup two up rights so that they are 1/2 the total length of the strands apart and wind the required number of strands around them. Any thing can be used, stakes in the ground, chairs, clamps on the edge of a table, or you can make and use a measuring board as shown here.

Measuring Board
Making board
Use a piece of 1-in. by 4-in. lumber that is several inches longer than 36-inch. Lay out and drill 1/2-in. holes as shown in the following illustration. Insert 6-in. long 1/2-in. dowel rods in each hole.

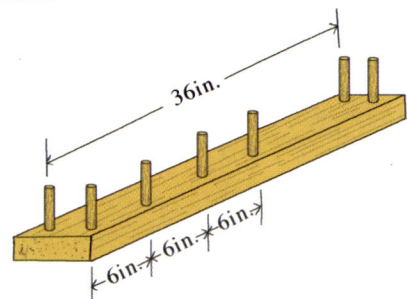

Using board
[STEP 1]
Tie off yarn.

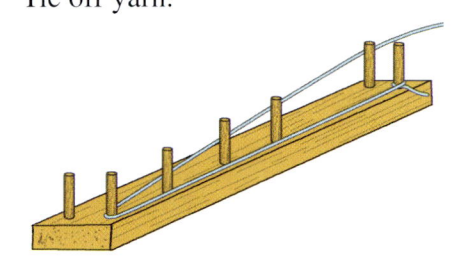

[STEP 2]
Choose a wrapping pattern that will give the desired length. Following the wrapping pattern, wrap the desired number of strands of each color around the pegs.

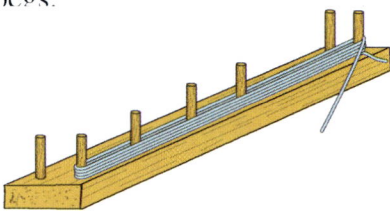

[STEP 3]
About 6 inches from the middle of the bundle of yarn, use short pieces of yarn to tie off each side of the yarn bundle.

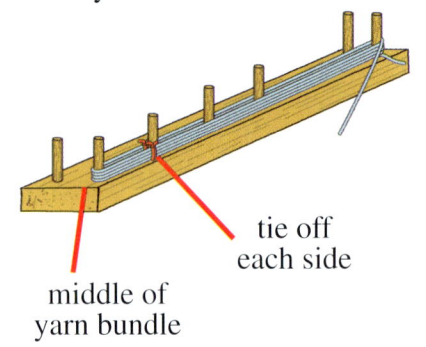

[STEP 4]
After tying off, cut the strands apart.

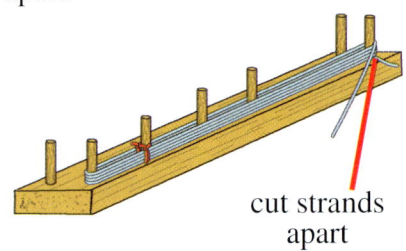

[4]

Casting on
The middle of each strand is secured to a headstick with a clove hitch.

Headstick
The headstick is used to arrange and secure the strands when starting a fingerwoven project. The procedure for securing the strands to the headstick can be done in several different ways. The method shown here uses a clove hitch to secure each strand to the first headstick and then two additional headsticks to set up the over/under pattern for starting the weaving.

Small pencil sized sticks (1/4-inch) of any kind may be used for the first headstick. Smaller diameter sticks may be used for the additional head sticks.

[STEP 1]
Place middle of yarn bundle over index finger of left hand.

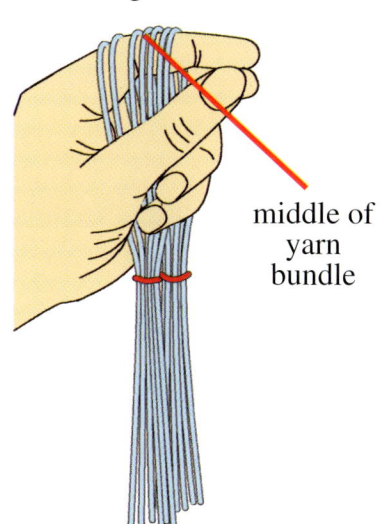

middle of yarn bundle

[STEP 2]
Start a clove hitch by grasping a strand as shown.

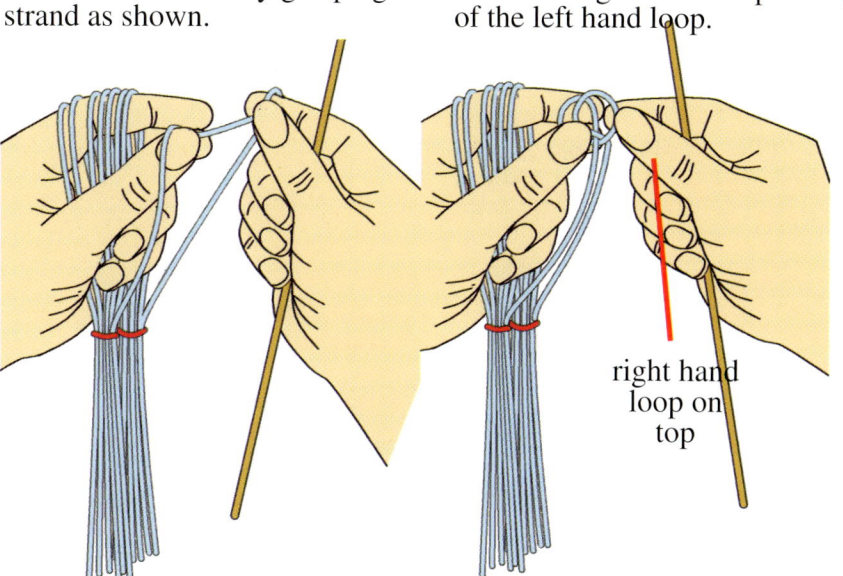

[STEP 3]
Twist the strand to form two underhand loops at its center.

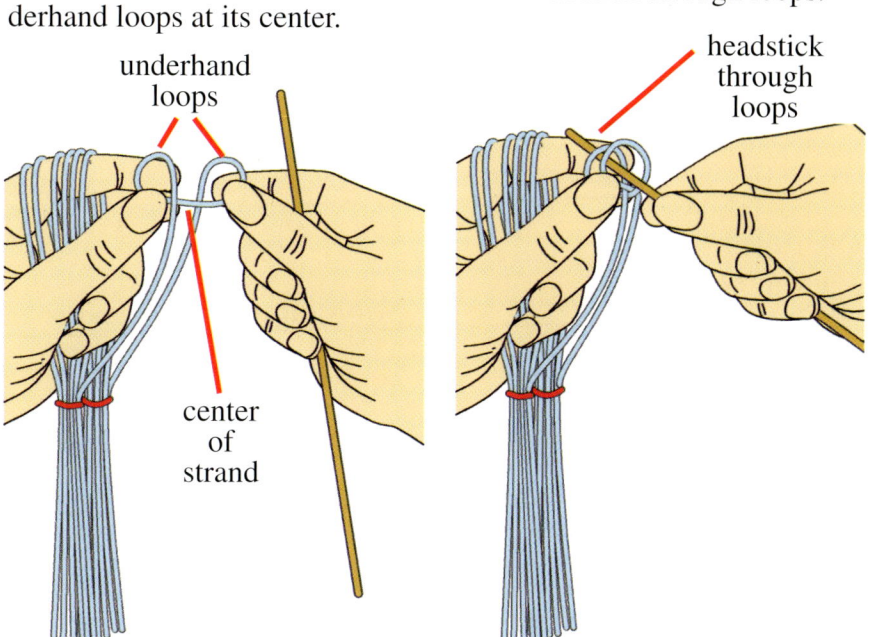

underhand loops

center of strand

[STEP 4]
Place the right hand loop on top of the left hand loop.

right hand loop on top

[STEP 5]
Pass headstick through loops.

headstick through loops

[STEP 6]
Pull clove hitch tight.

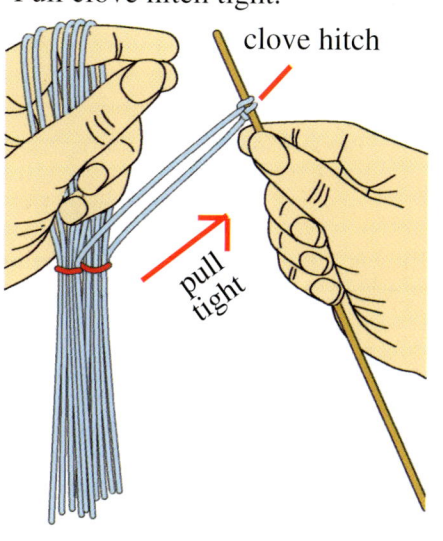

clove hitch

pull tight

[STEP 7]
Repeat steps 2 through 5 for each strand.

[5]

Anchoring

The work piece must be anchored to something so that the proper tension can be applied to the strands for each step of the weaving.

The anchor can be anything that the work piece can be fastened to. For example a chair, a hook in the wall, a door knob, what ever is handy. For portability, pin the work to a pillow or use a clipboard. A small backpack works well also.

I personally anchor my work to a small pack basket. The pack basket not only makes a good anchor but it also allows me to easily carry all my materials and tools with me.

[6]

Setting up the Shed

After the strands are cast on and the work piece is anchored, weave two additional headsticks across the warp strands to set up the over/under pattern of the shed.

[NOTE]
The **shed** is the open space formed between the two layers of warp strands when the over/under pattern is established.

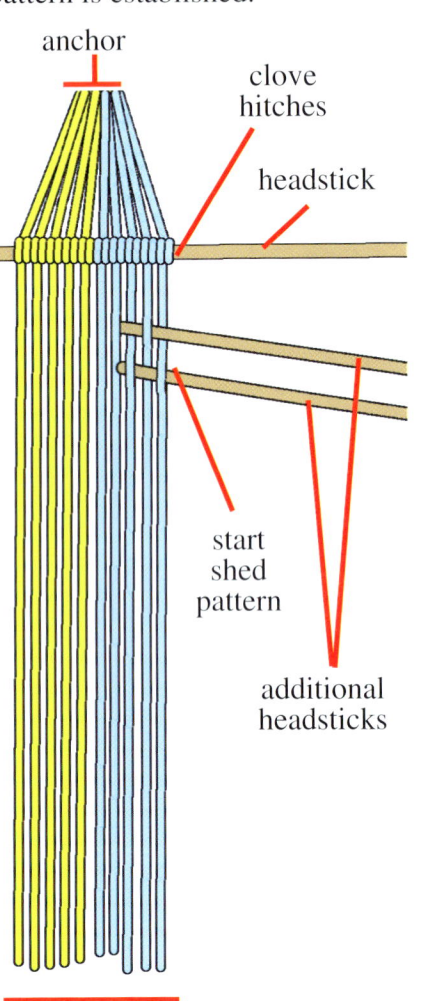

Picking up the Shed

When the over/under pattern of the shed has been established, get ready for weaving by picking up the shed so that the two layers are separated by the index finger.

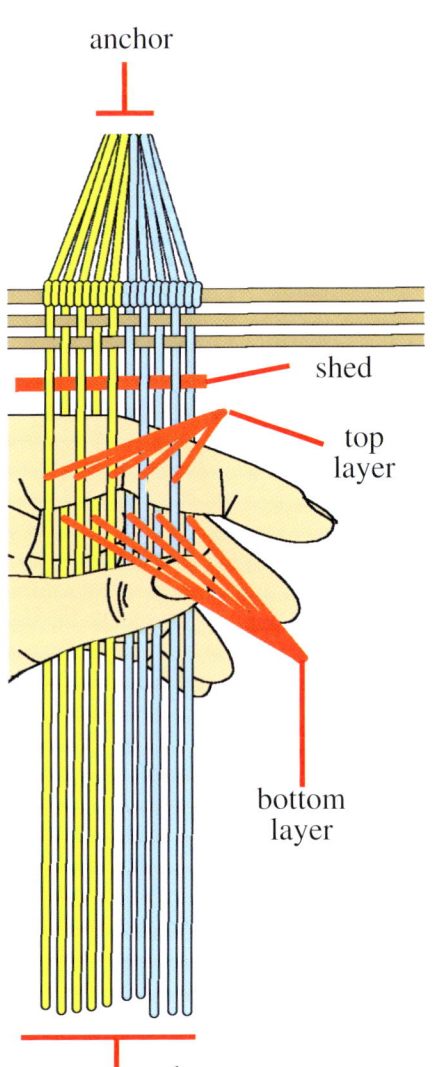

[NOTE]
The **top layer** of warp strand starts under the headstick or weft strand and then goes over the index finger.

The **bottom layer** of warp strands starts above the headstick or weft strand and then goes under the index finger.

Keeping an Open Shed
As you weave, the open shed is maintained by keeping the two layers separated by the index fingers.

When you wish to stop weaving for a while, a spring-loaded hair clip or a clothes pin can be used to hold one layer of the shed till you are ready to start work again.

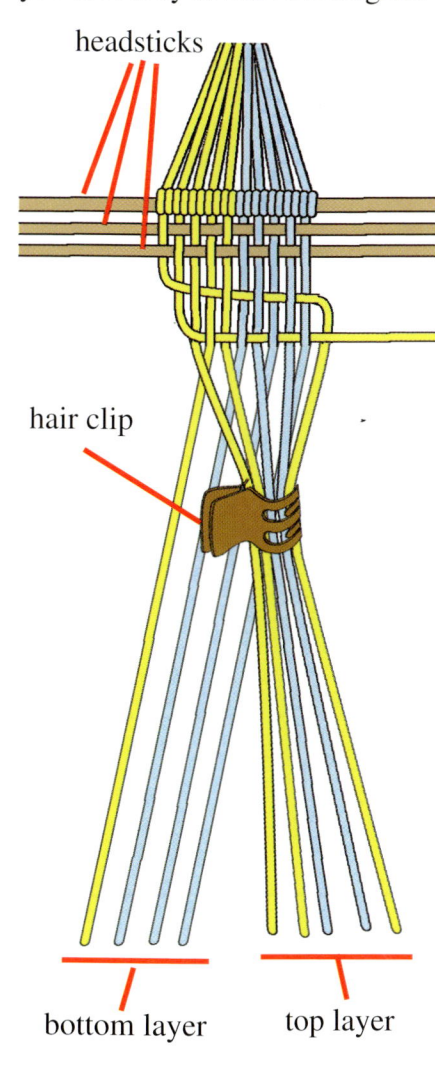

Securing a Weft Strand
After a row is woven, hook the weft strand over the headstick to hold it in place.

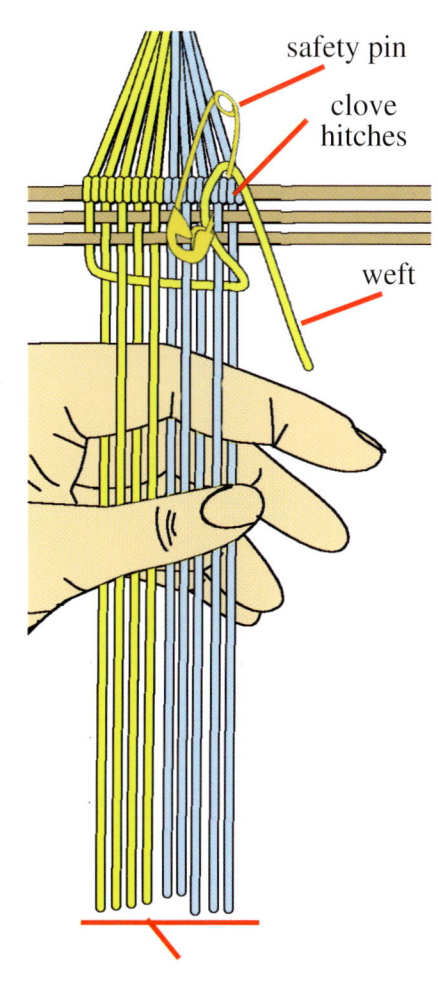

[NOTE]
Hooking the weft strand around a safety pin that has been fastened to the headstick is a more efficient way of holding the weft strand in place than just hooking it over the headstick.

Adding Accent Beads
Accent beads can be woven into warp face weaving. They are usually placed at the edge of a color to emphasize the contrast between two colors or to emphasize a particular part of a pattern. When adding beads to warp face weaving the beads are usually strung on the same type yarn that is used for the rest of the weaving. The size of the yarn depends on the size of the bead.

Yarn and Bead Size
3-ply acrylic yarn is the best size yarn to use for most designs that are decorated with bead work. #8 beads can be easily slid along 3-ply yarn and placed where required.

4-ply yarn could be used but it is difficult to slide #8 beads along the strands and #5 beads are large and require that the weaving be left loose so that the beads can fit between the strands.

Preparing Yarn
Reduce the size of the end of the yarn by scraping it with a dull knife.

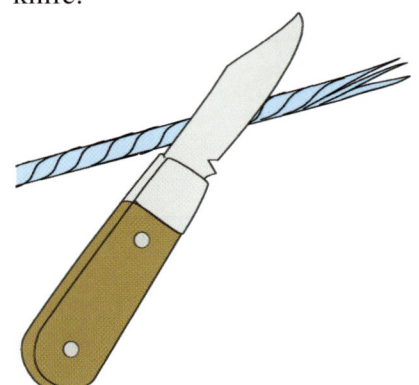

Wax the end of the yarn by holding it firmly against a block of beeswax and pulling the yarn across the wax block several times.

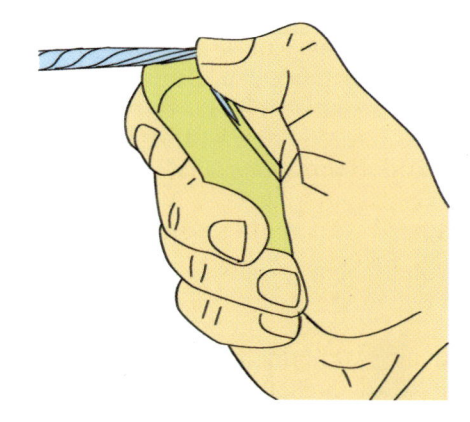

Roll the waxed yarn between the fingers to produce a tapered point.

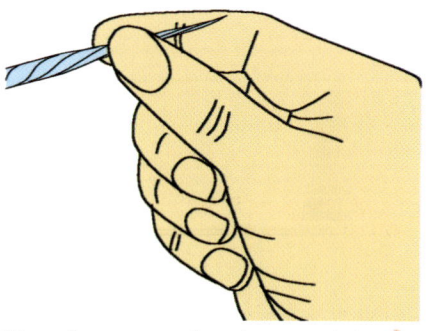

Use the tapered point to pick up the beads.

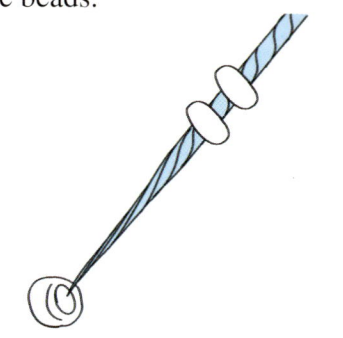

[7]

PART 2: WARPFACE WEAVING

In warpface weaving, only the warp strands show on the face of the finished product. The different patterns are achieved by the way the colored yarn strands are arranged and by changing which strands are visible on the face of the work.

The following photographs show examples of the four basic patterns that are presented in this part of the book. Additional patterns can be produced by combining and modifying these basic patterns.

Diagonal　　Chevron　　Lightning　　Arrowhead

Diagonal Pattern Over/under Weave

The diagonal pattern is named for the diagonal stripes that develop when two or more colors are used.

The setup for the diagonal pattern requires that the strands are made up of two or more colors. The number of strands of each color is not important. See (Part 1: Getting Started).

[STEP 1]
Cast the required number of strands of yarn on to headstick. Use clove hitches to tie the yarn in place. See (Part 1: Getting Started).

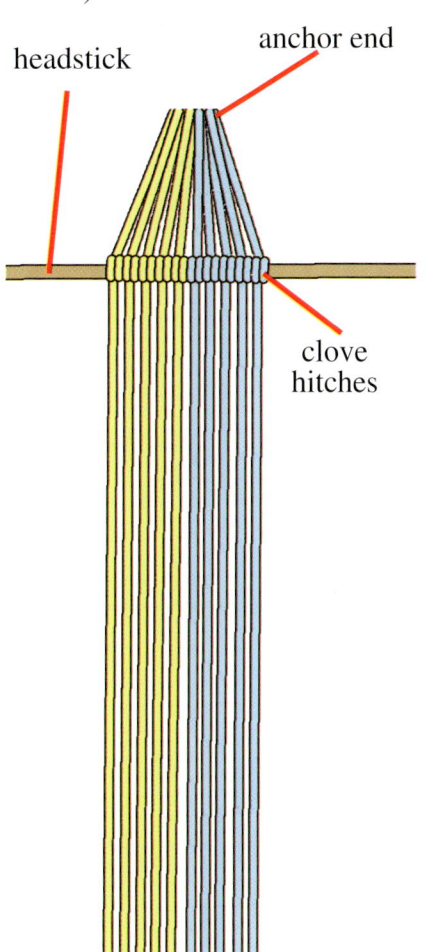

headstick
anchor end
clove hitches

[STEP 2]
Set up the over/under weaving pattern of the shed with two smaller sticks.

headsticks
pattern of shed
warp

[STEP 3]
Pick up the shed on the index finger of the left hand.

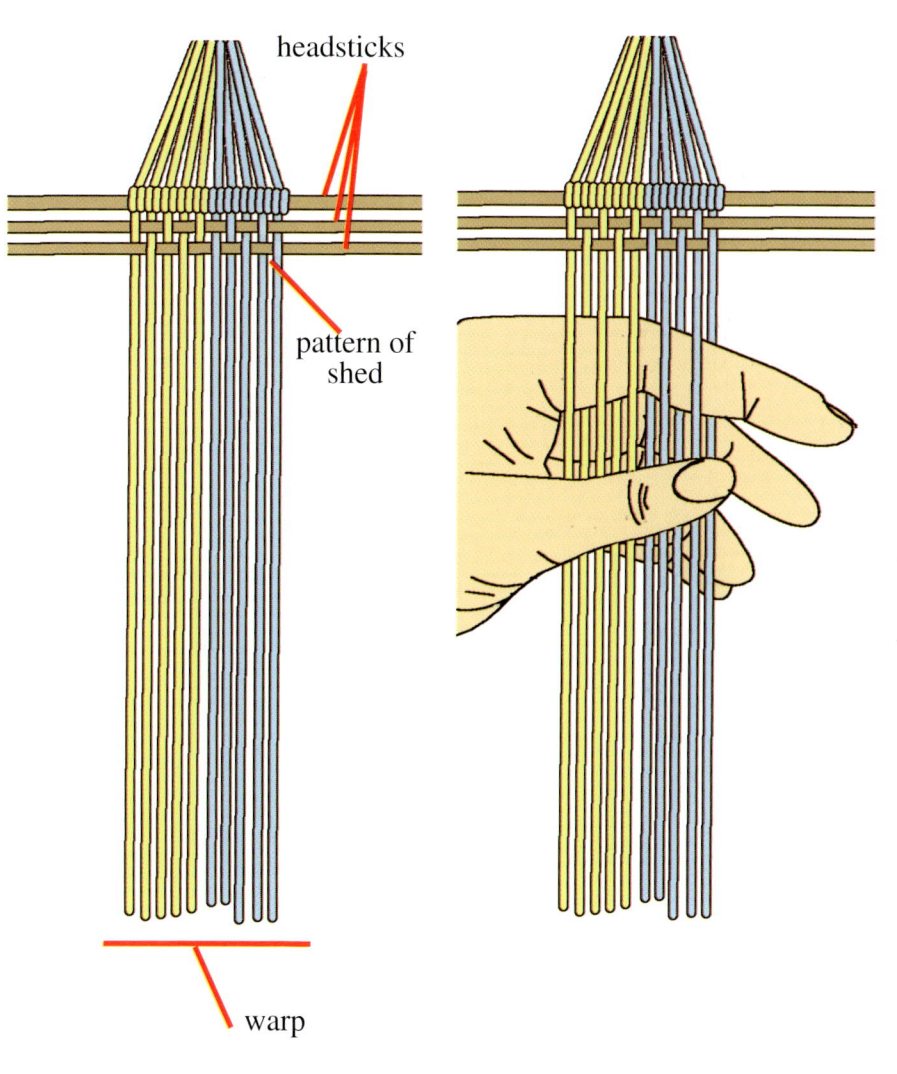

[NOTE]
Shed --- the open space between the two layers of warp strands.

[9]

[STEP 4]
Use the right hand to pull the first warp strand on the left through the open shed. This action changes the first warp strand into the first weft strand.

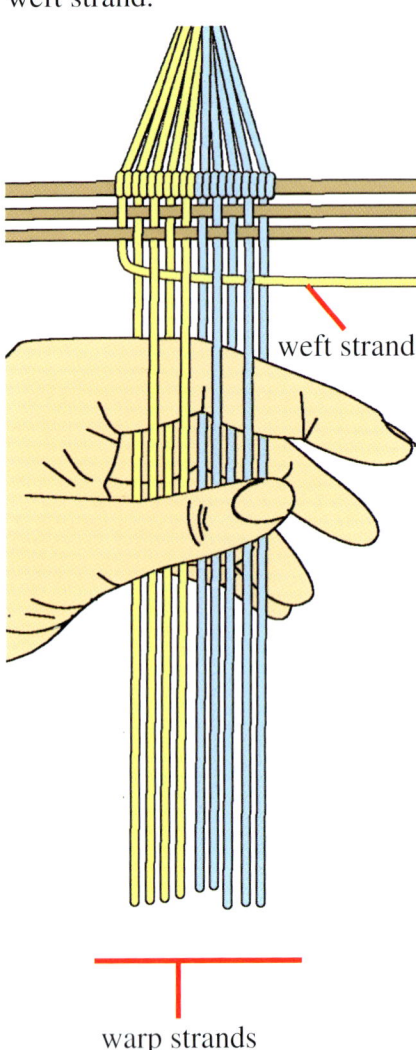

weft strand

warp strands

[STEP 5]
Hook the weft strand over the headstick to hold it in place.

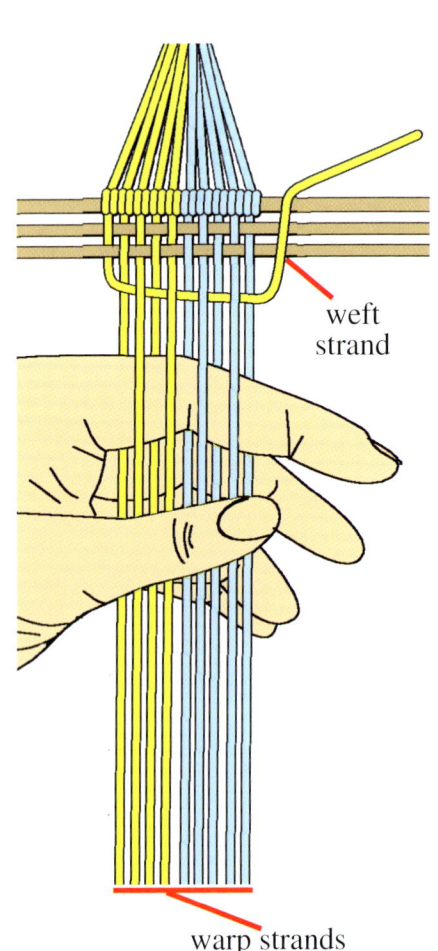

weft strand

warp strands

[NOTE]
Hooking the weft strand around a safety pin that has been fastened to the headstick is a more efficient way of holding the weft strand in place than just hooking it over the headstick., See (Part 1: Getting Started).

[STEP 6]
Reverse the shed by transferring the warp strands one at a time to the left index finger so that the warp strands that were up in the shed are down and the warp strands that were down in the shed are up.

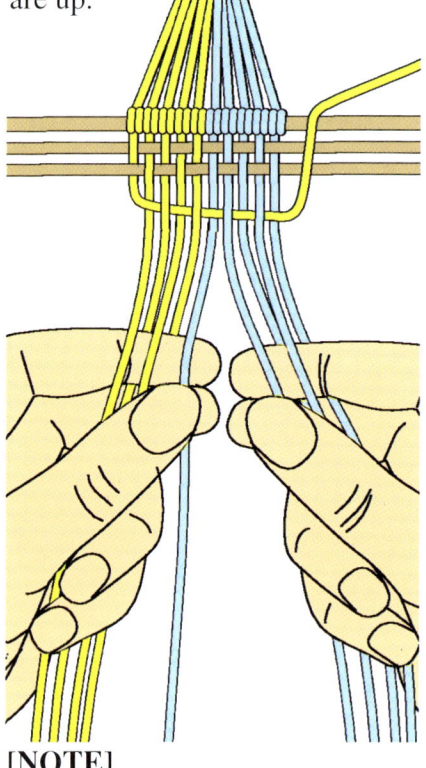

[NOTE]
The reversing of the shed can be done either from the left to the right as shown or right to left. The choice of direction is up to you.

[NOTE]
As each warp strand is transferred to the other hand, check that the proper strand has been selected by observing its position as it crosses the weft strand.

[STEP 7]
Set the weft strand in place by pulling the two layers of the shed in opposite directions.

[NOTE]
Check to see if all strands are properly tightened.

[STEP 8]
Use the right hand to pull the second weft strand through the open shed.

second weft

[STEP 9]
Turn the first weft strand down. The first weft strand is now a warp strand again.

first weft
second weft

[STEP 10]
Hook the weft strand over the headstick to hold it in place.

weft
warp strands

[NOTE]
Hooking the weft strand around a safety pin that has been fastened to the headstick is a more efficient way of holding the weft strand in place than just hooking it over the headstick. See (Part 1: Getting Started).

[STEP 11]
Reverse the shed by transferring the warp strands one at a time to the left index finger so that the warp strands that were up in the shed are down and the warp strands that were down in the shed are up.

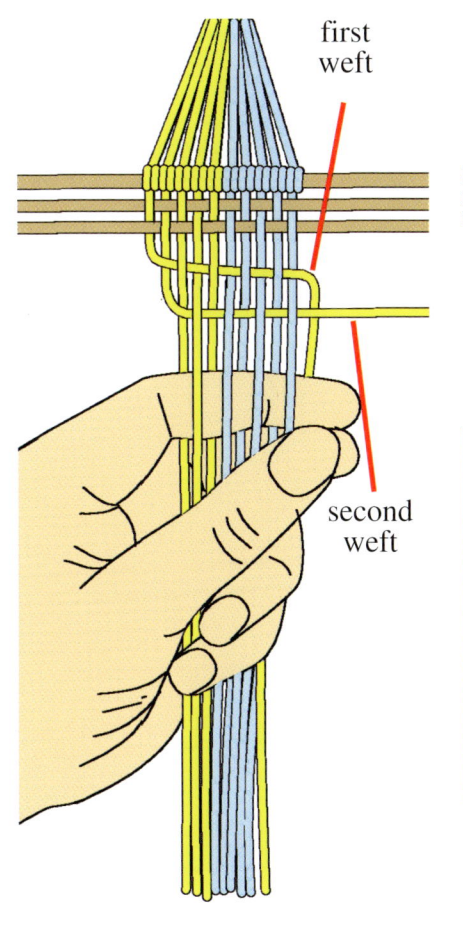

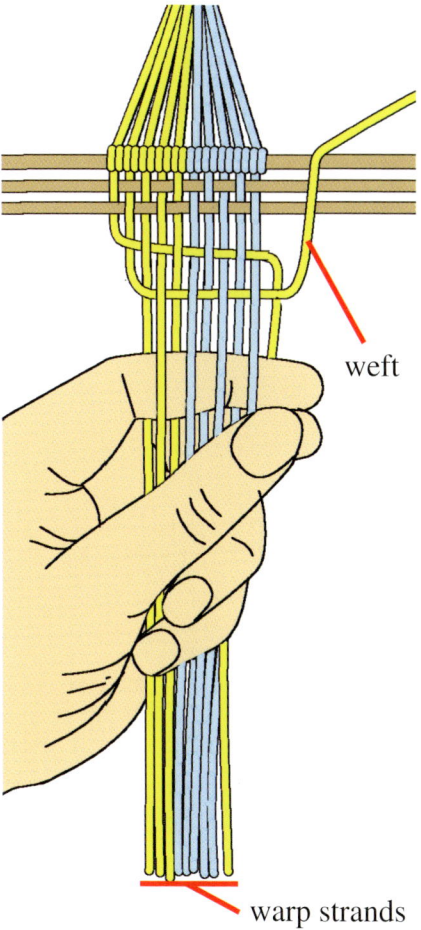

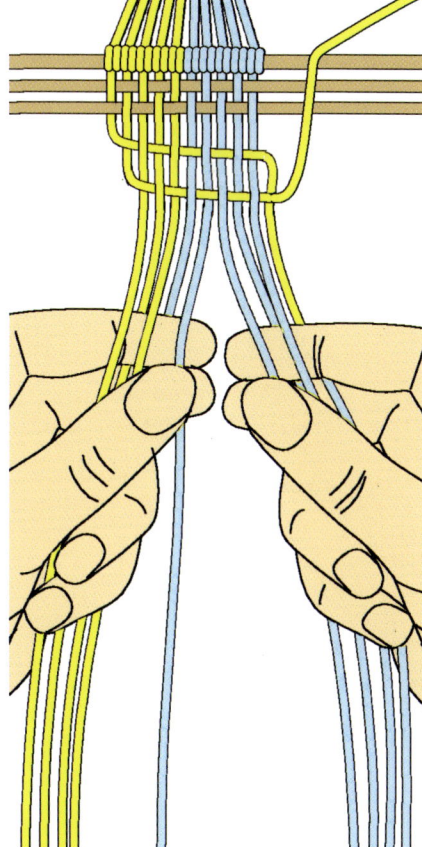

[NOTE]
As each warp strand is transferred to the other hand, check that the proper strand has been selected by observing its position as it crosses the weft strand.

[11]

[STEP 12]
Set the weft strand in place by pulling the two layers of the shed in opposite directions.

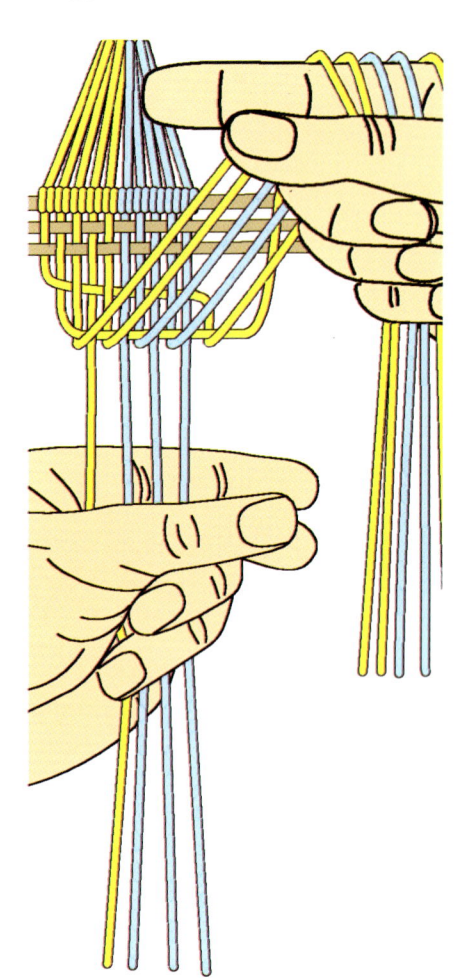

[NOTE]
Check to see if all strands are properly tightened.

[12]

[STEP 13]
Continue to weave in this manner until the desired length is reached.

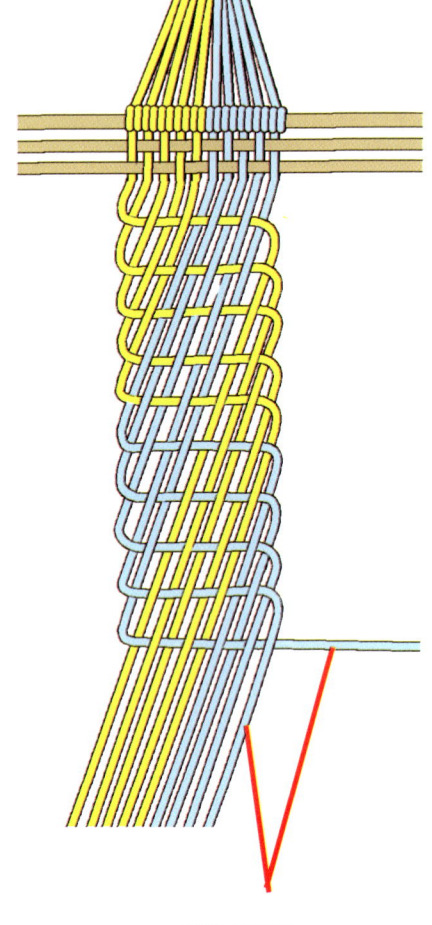

[NOTE]
The weaving may be ended by tying a square knot in these two strands.

[STEP 14]
Turn work piece around (same side up) and anchor the end.

anchor end

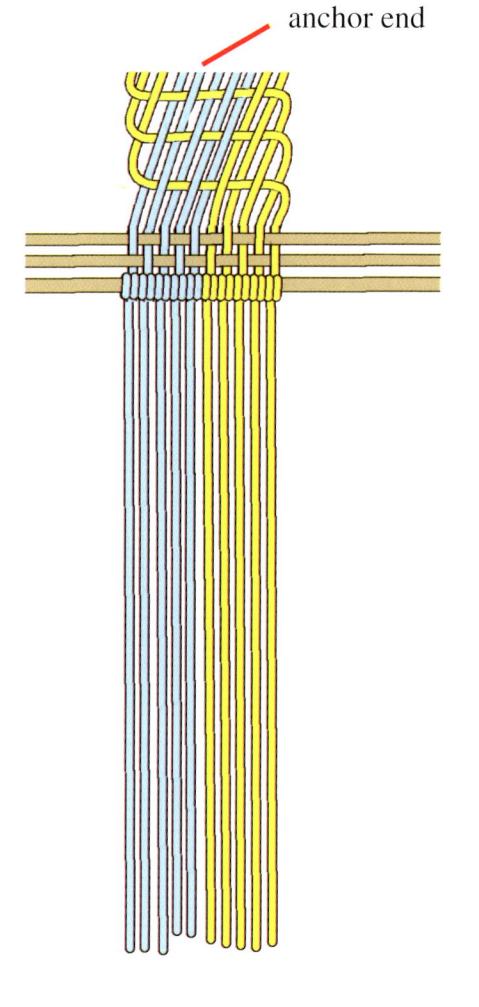

[STEP 15]
Remove headsticks.

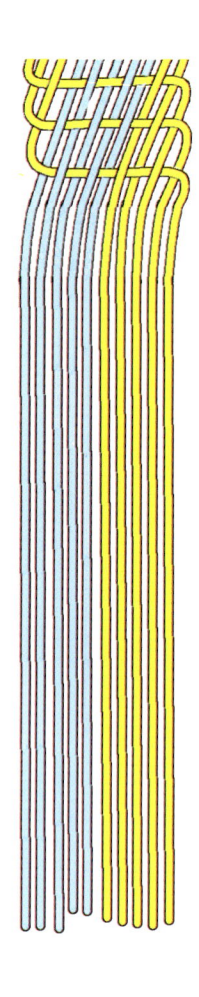

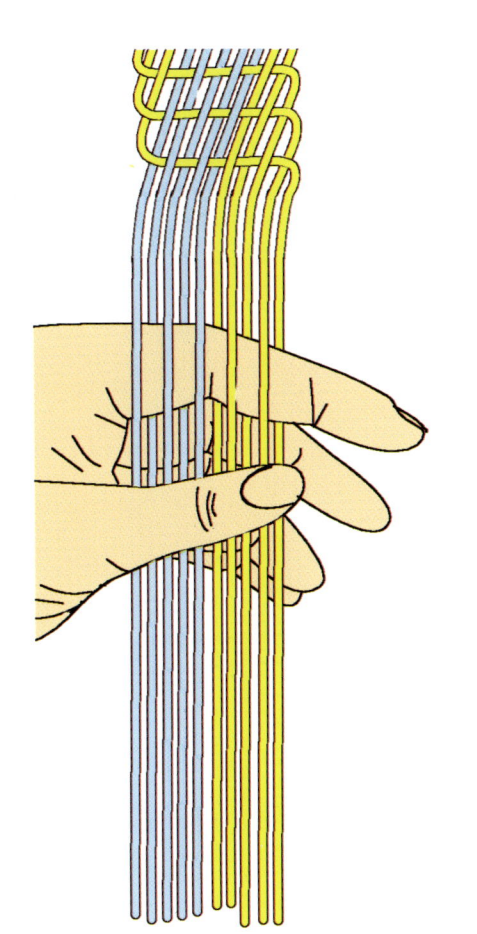

[STEP 16]
Pick up shed.

[STEP 17]
Set the weft strand in place by pulling the two layers of the shed in opposite directions.

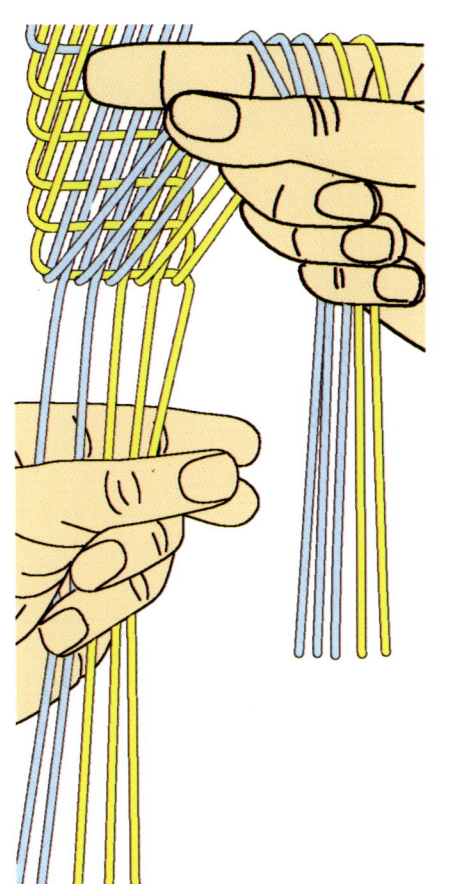

[STEP 18]
Use the first warp strand on the left as a weft strand; pull it to the right through the open shed.

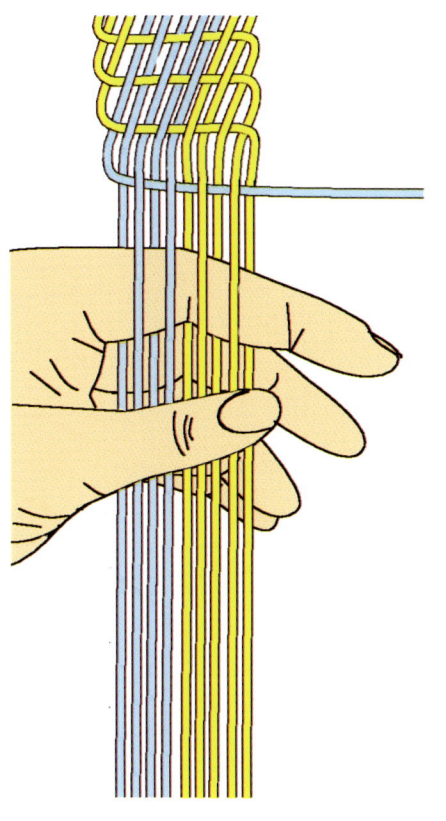

Diagonal Pattern Example:

[STEP 19]
Continue weaving as before until the desired length is reached.

[13]

Chevron Pattern Over/under Weave

The chevron pattern is named for the "V" shaped pattern that develops when two or more colors are used.

The setup for the chevron pattern uses two or more colors. There must be an even number of strands of each color. The strands are arranged so that the two sides are mirror images of each other.

The chevron pattern is made by combining two diagonal patterns that are worked in opposite directions. One to the left and one to the right.

[STEP 1]
Cast the required number of strands of yarn on to headstick. Use clove hitches to tie the yarn in place. See (Part 1: Getting Started).

anchor
clove hitches
headstick
equal number of strands on both sides of the middle
the two side are mirror images of each other

[STEP 2]
Set up the over/under weaving pattern of the shed with two smaller sticks.

headsticks
pattern of shed

[STEP 3]
Pick up the shed on the index finger of the left hand.

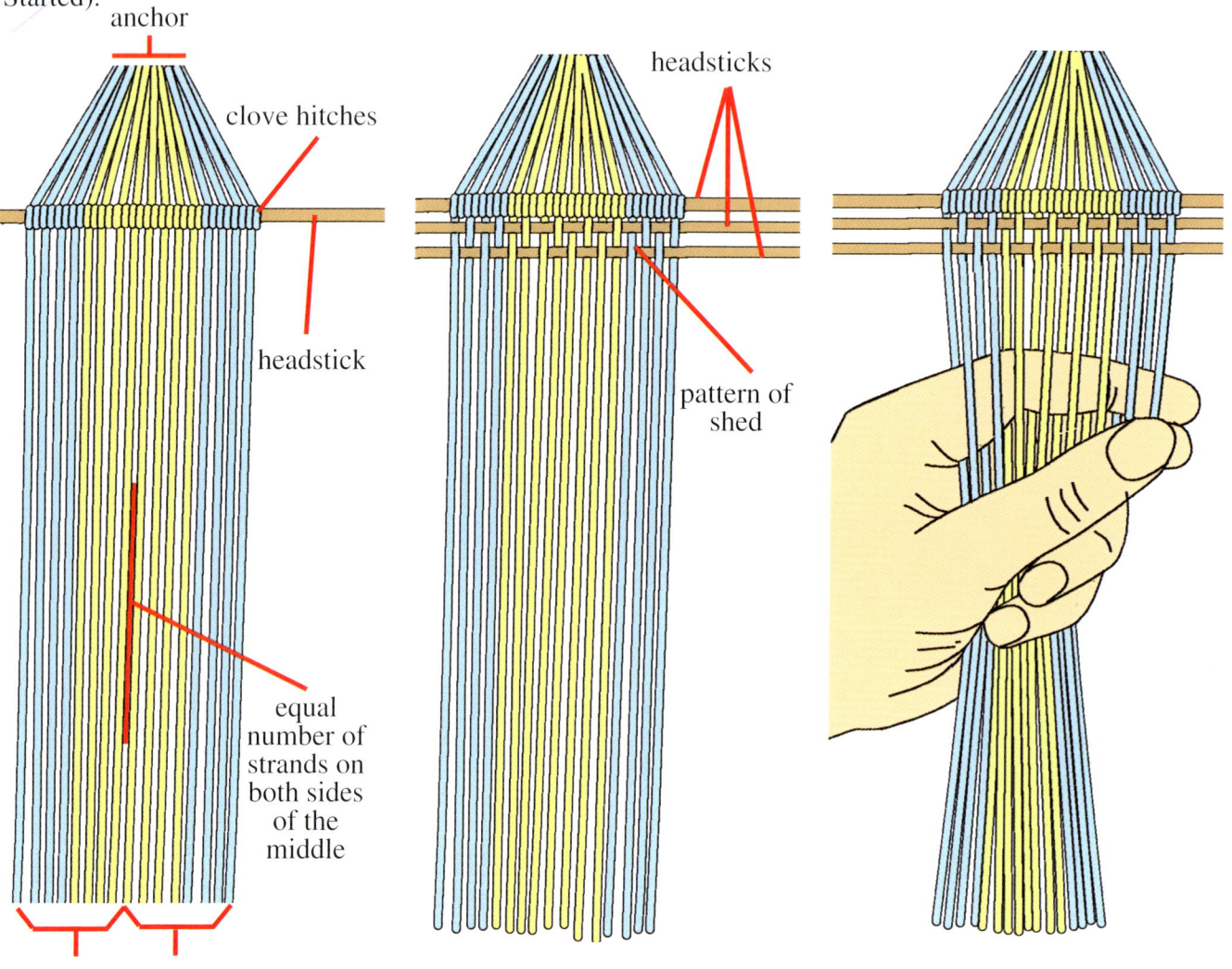

[14]

[STEP 4]
The first warp strand to the left of the middle becomes a weft strand when it is pulled to the right through the open shed and hooked over the headstick to hold it in place.

middle

first weft strand

[STEP 5]
Transfer the open shed to the right hand.

[STEP 6]
The first warp strand to the right of the middle becomes a weft strand when it is pulled to the left through the open shed and hooked over the headstick to hold it in place.

second weft strand

[STEP 7]
Reverse the shed by transferring the warp strands one at a time to the left index finger so that the warp strands that were up in the shed are down and the warp strands that were down in the shed are up.

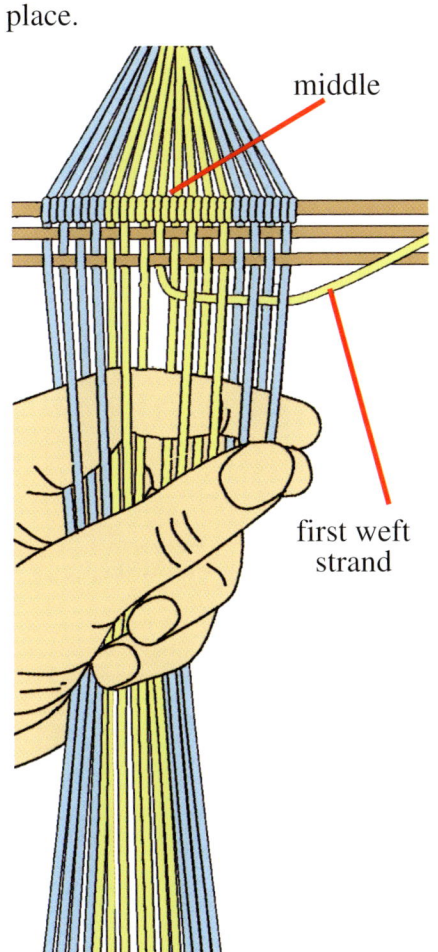

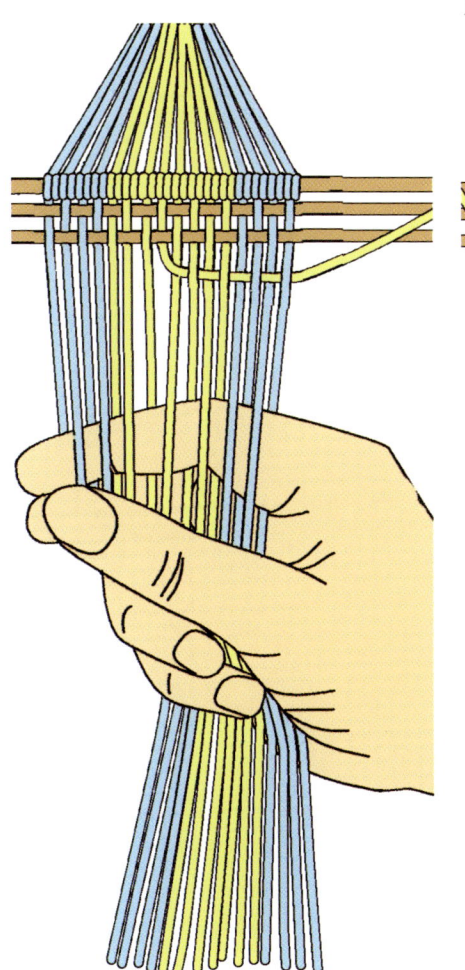

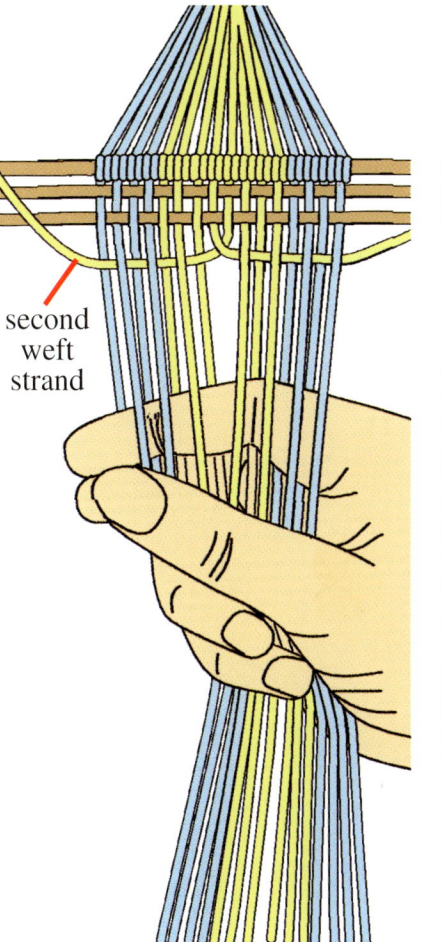

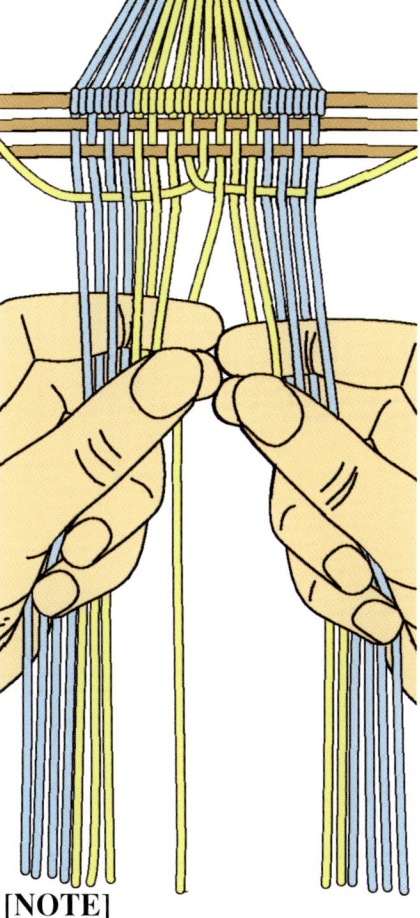

[NOTE]
As each warp strand is transferred to the other hand, check that the proper strand has been selected by observing its position as it crosses the weft strand.

[15]

[STEP 8]
Set the weft strands in place by pulling the two layers of the shed in opposite directions.

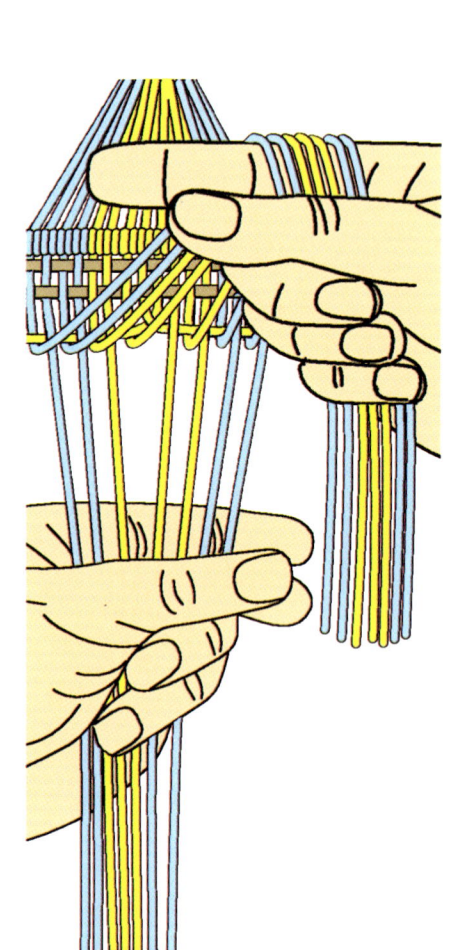

[STEP 9]
Again the first warp strand to the left of the middle becomes a weft strand when it is pulled to the right through the open shed and placed over the headstick to hold it in place.

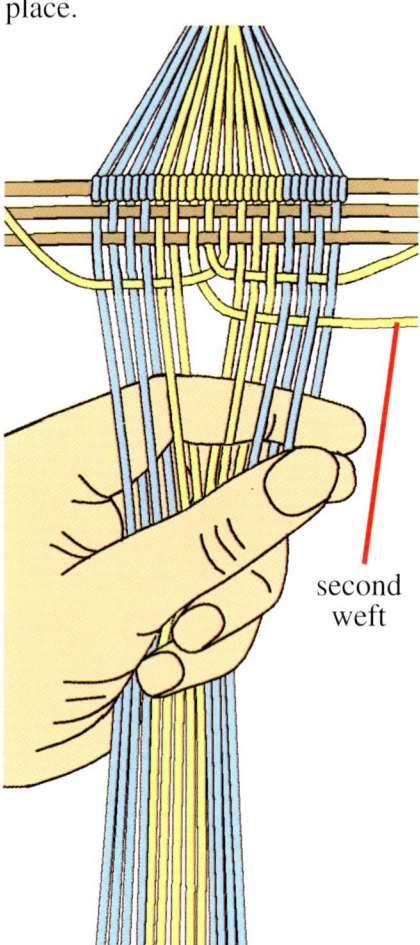

[STEP 10]
Turn the first weft strand of the previous row down. This strand is now a warp strand again.

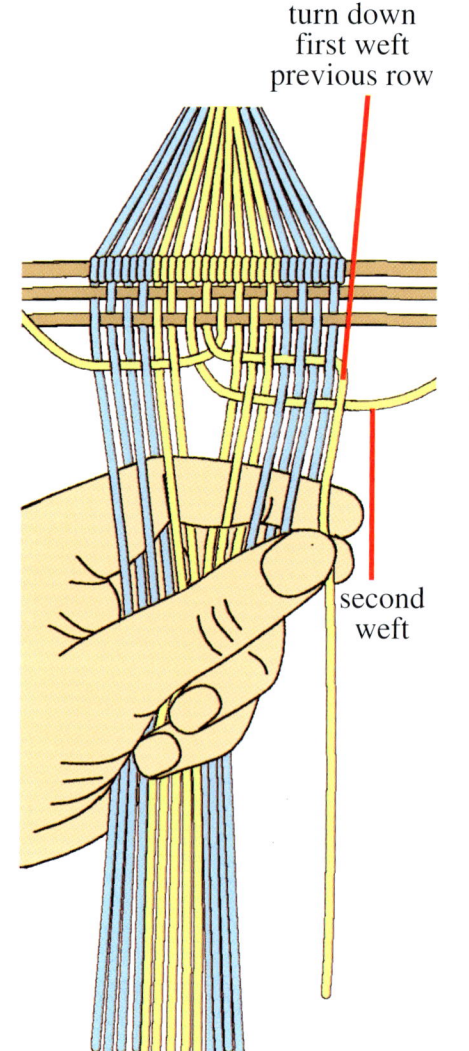

[STEP 11]
Again the first warp strand to the right of the middle becomes a weft strand when it is pulled to the left through the open shed and hooked over the headstick to hold it in place.

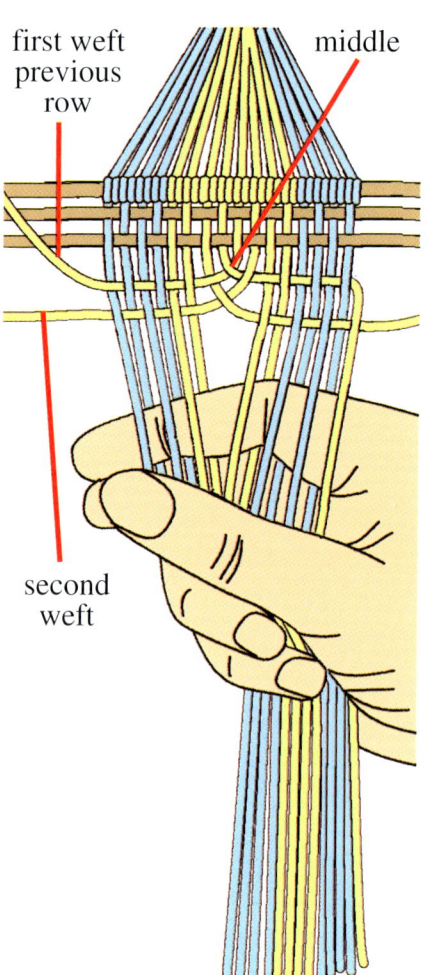

[NOTE]
Check to see if all strands are properly tightened.

[16]

[STEP 12]
Turn the second weft strand of the previous row down. This strand is now a warp strand again.

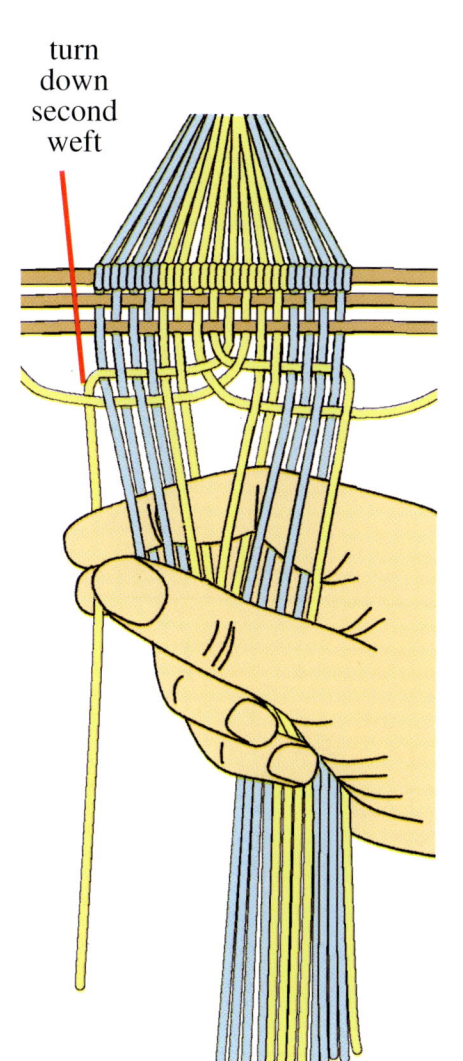

turn down second weft

[STEP 13]
Reverse the shed by transferring the warp strands one at a time to the left index finger so that the warp strands that were up in the shed are down and the warp strands that were down in the shed are up.

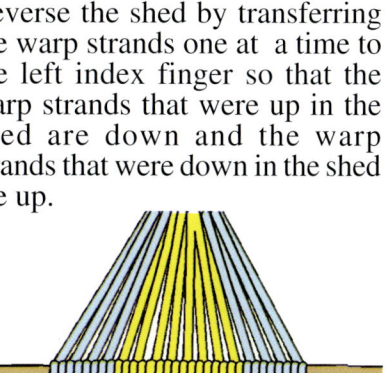

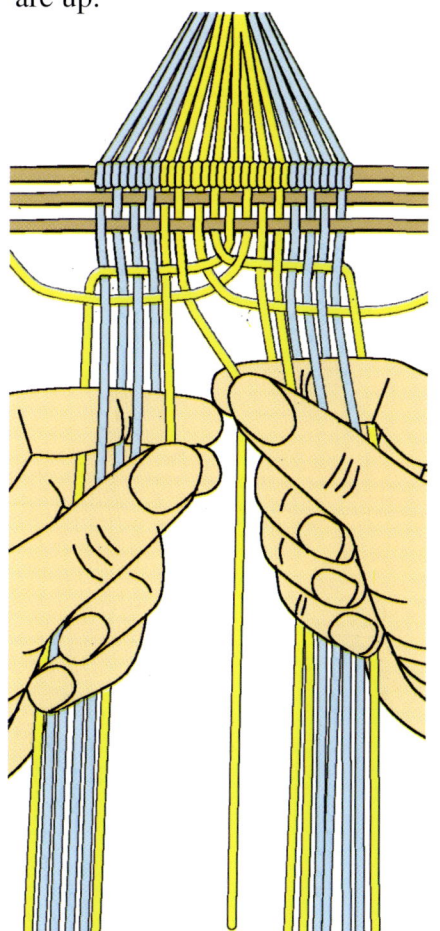

[NOTE]
As each warp strand is transferred to the other hand, check that the proper strand has been selected by observing its position as it crosses the weft strand.

[STEP 14]
Set the weft strand in place by pulling the two layers of the shed in opposite directions.

[NOTE]
Check to see if all strands are properly tightened.

[STEP 15]
Continue to weave in this manner until the desired length is reached.

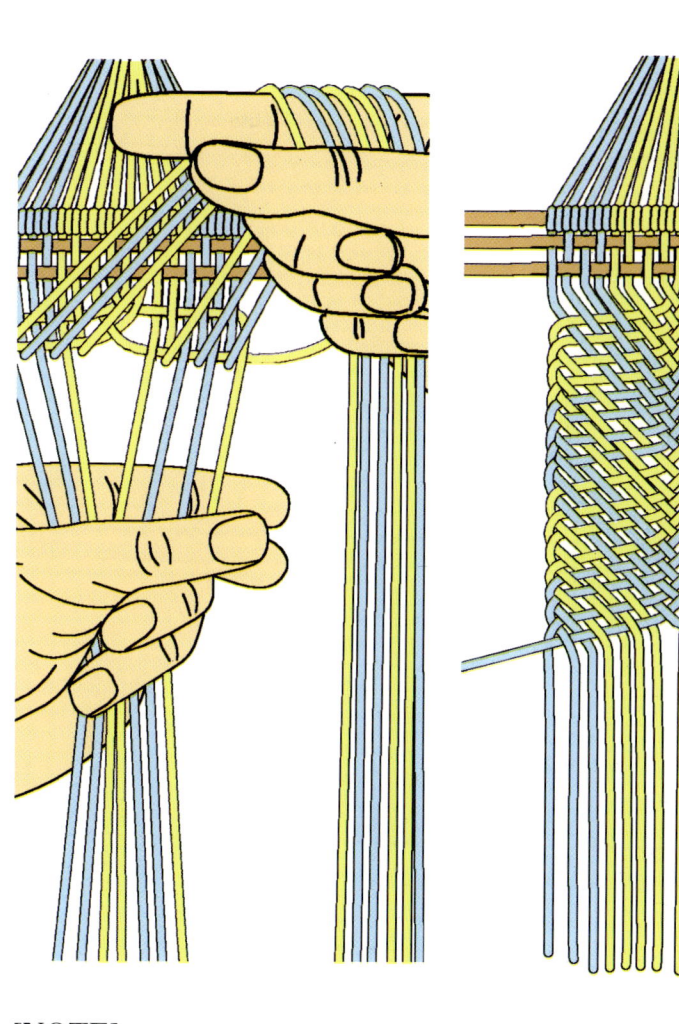

[17]

[STEP 16]
Turn the work around and reattach it to your anchor.

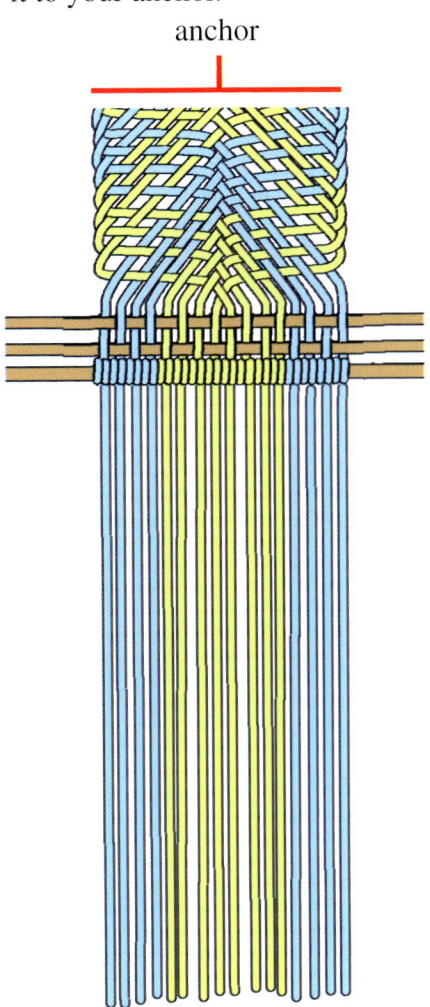

anchor

[STEP 17]
Remove the headsticks and pick up the shed.

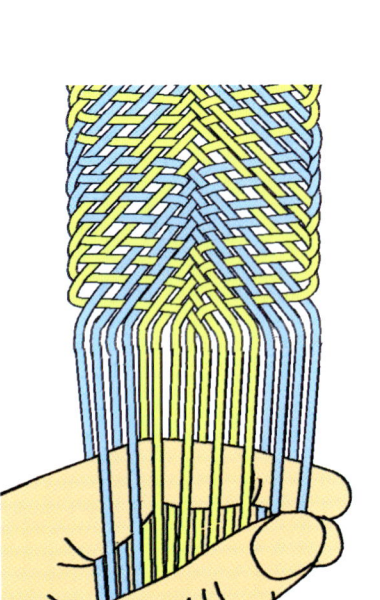

[STEP 18]
Set the weft strands in place by pulling the two layers of the shed in opposite directions.

[STEP 19]
The first warp strand to the left of the middle becomes the first weft strand as it is pulled through the open shed and placed up over the work to hold it in place.

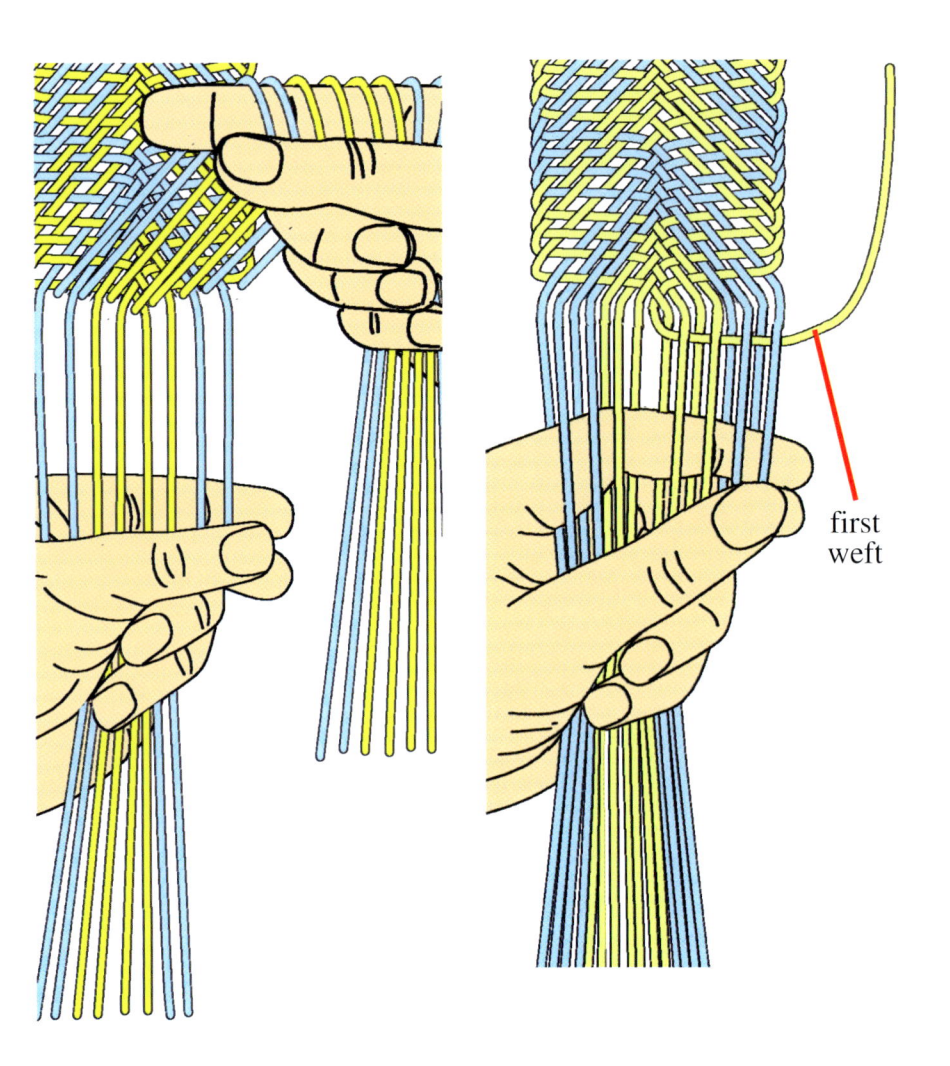

first weft

[STEP 20]
Again the first warp strand to the right of the middle becomes the second weft strand as it is pulled through the open shed and placed over the head stick to hold it in place.

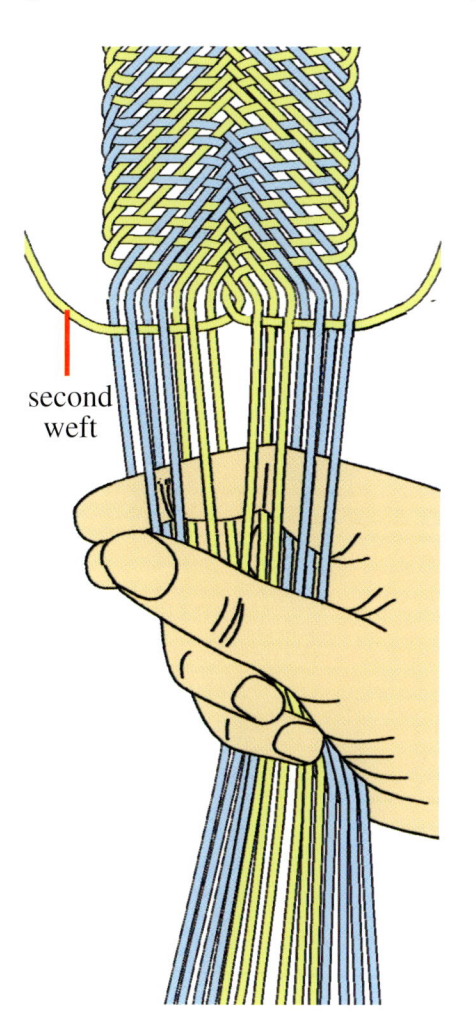

[STEP 21]
Continue weaving until the second half of the work is completed.

[NOTE]
Notice the diamond pattern that forms between the two halves.

Chevron Pattern Point Down Example:

Chevron Pattern Point Down (Center) Example:

second weft

[19]

Chevron Pattern Point Down Variation 1

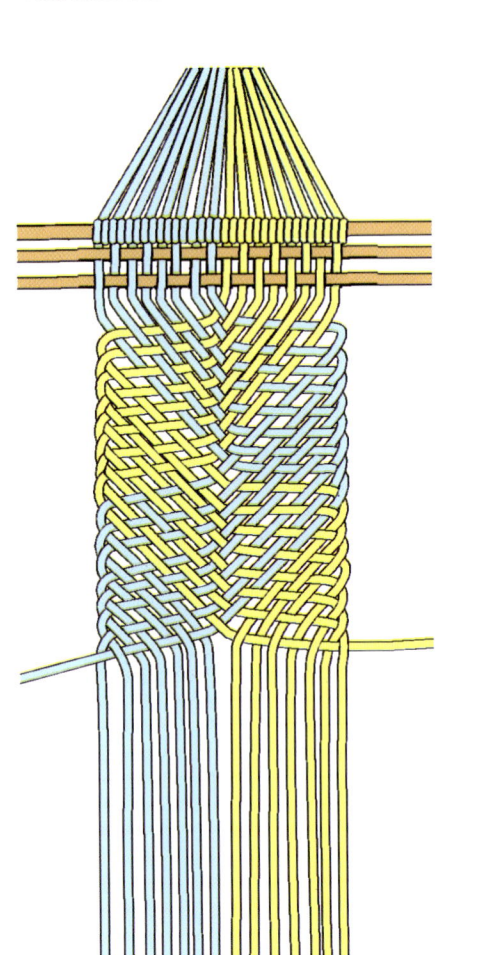

Chevron Pattern Point Down Variation 1 Example:

Chevron Pattern Point Down Variation 2

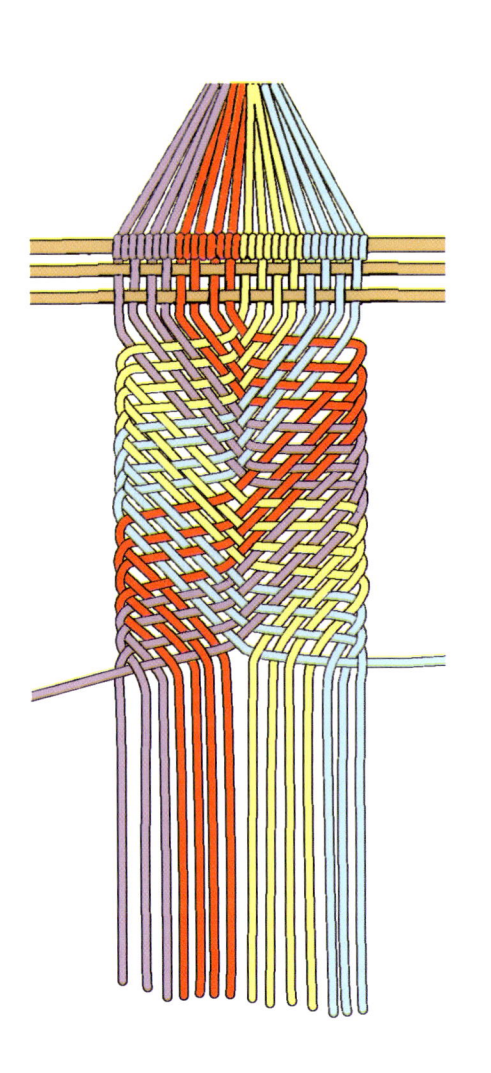

Chevron Pattern Point Down Variation 2 Example:

[20]

Reversed Chevron Pattern Over/under Weave

The name reverse chevron is used to indicate that the point of the "V" is toward the headstick instead of away from the head stick.

When the chevron pattern is worked from the edge to the middle the points of the chevrons are toward the headstick.

To have all the chevron points in the same direction, a piece can be worked from one end to the other or the second half of the chevron pattern can be worked in the reverse direction allowing a sash to be woven from the middle toward both ends. One advantage of working from the middle toward the ends is the shorter length of the strands; it takes less time to pull them through.

Being able to work the chevron pattern in both directions also makes it possible to combine the two variations to achieve several new patterns; double chevron and diamond patterns.

This setup is the same as the first chevron pattern.
The setup for the chevron pattern uses two or more colors. There must be an even number of strands of each color. The strands are arranged so that the two sides are mirror images of each other.

[STEP 1]
Cast the required number of strands of yarn on to the headstick. Use clove hitches to tie the yarn in place. See (Part 1: Getting Started).

- anchor
- clove hitches
- headstick
- equal number of strands on both sides of the middle.
- the two side are mirror images of each other

[STEP 2]
Set up the over/under weaving pattern of the shed with two smaller sticks. Pick up the shed on the index finger of the left hand.

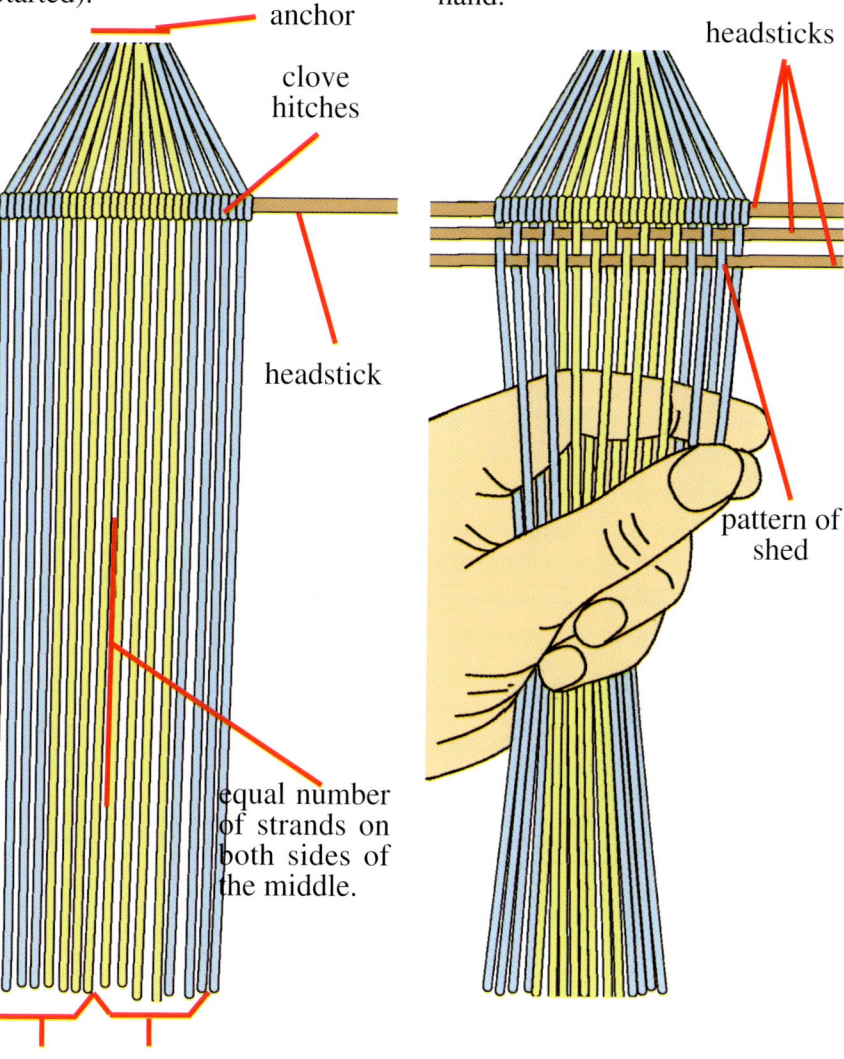

- headsticks
- pattern of shed

[21]

[STEP 3]

The first warp strand on the left becomes a weft strand when it is pulled to the right through the open shed to the middle and hooked over the headstick to hold it in place.

middle
first weft strand

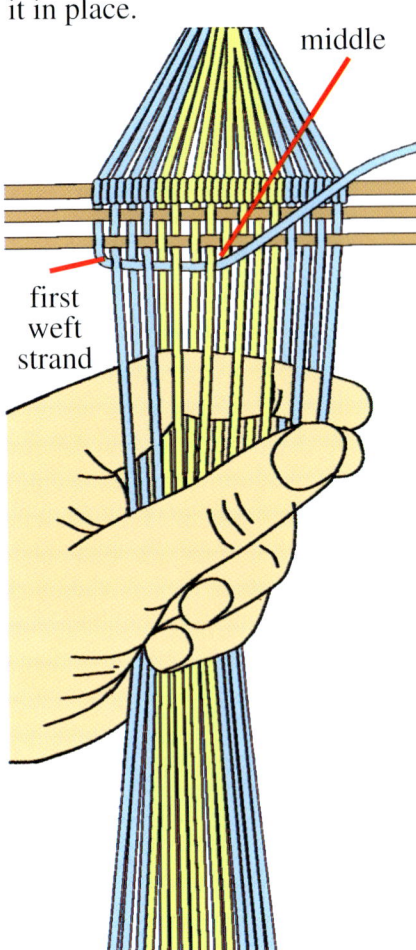

[STEP 4]

The first warp strand on the right becomes a weft strand when it is pulled to the left through the open shed to the middle and hooked over the headstick to hold it in place.

second weft strand
first weft
middle

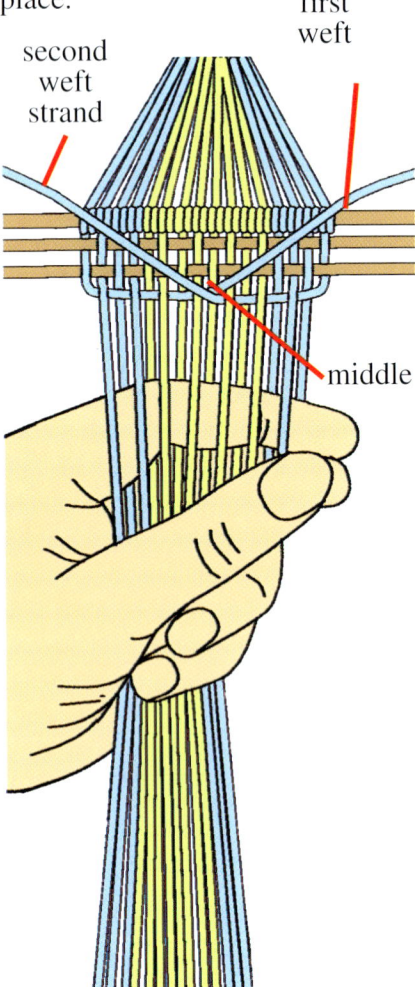

[STEP 5]

Turn the first weft strand down so that it becomes a warp strand again.

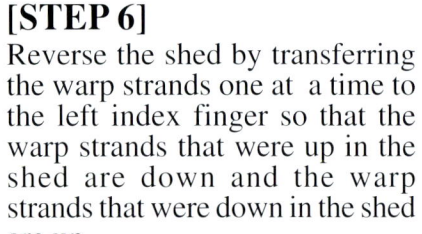

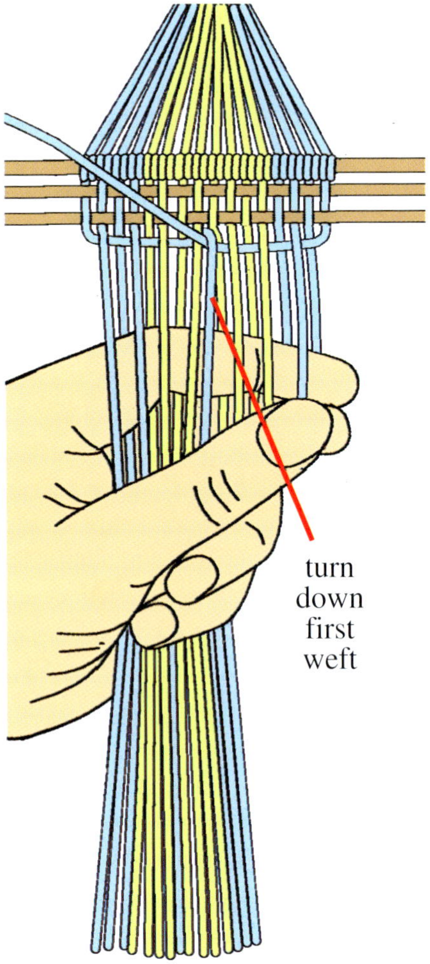

turn down first weft

[STEP 6]

Reverse the shed by transferring the warp strands one at a time to the left index finger so that the warp strands that were up in the shed are down and the warp strands that were down in the shed are up.

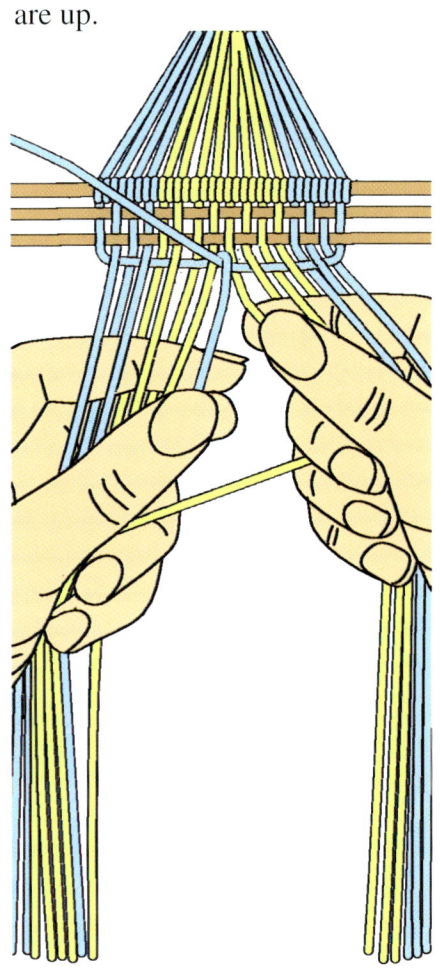

[NOTE]

As each warp strand is transferred to the other hand, check that the proper strand has been selected by observing its position as it crosses the weft strand.

[22]

[STEP 7]
Set the weft strand in place by pulling the two layers of the shed in opposite directions.

[STEP 8]
Transfer the open shed to the left hand.

[STEP 9]
Again the first warp strand on the left becomes a weft strand when it is pulled to the right through the open shed to the middle and hooked over the headstick to hold it in place.

[STEP 10]
Turn the second weft strand of the previous row down so that it becomes a warp strand again.

first weft strand

turn down second weft

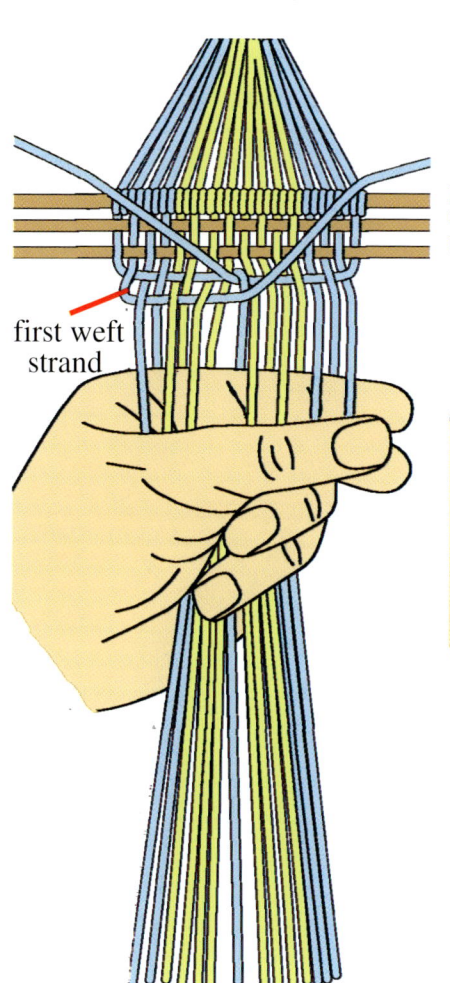

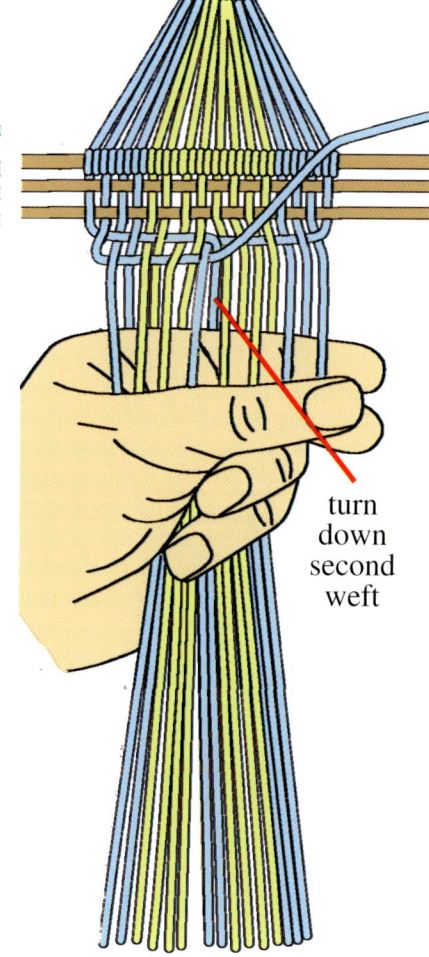

[NOTE]
Check to see if all strands are properly tightened.

[23]

[STEP 11]

Again the first warp strand on the right becomes a weft strand when it is pulled to the middle through the open shed and hooked over the headstick to hold it in place.

second weft strand

[STEP 12]

Turn the first weft strand down so that it becomes a warp strand again.

turn down first weft

[STEP 13]

Reverse the shed by transferring the warp strands one at a time to the left index finger so that the warp strands that were up in the shed are down and the warp strands that were down in the shed are up.

[NOTE]

As each warp strand is transferred to the other hand, check that the proper strand has been selected by observing its position as it crosses the weft strand.

[STEP 14]

Set the weft strand in place by pulling the two layers of the shed in opposite directions.

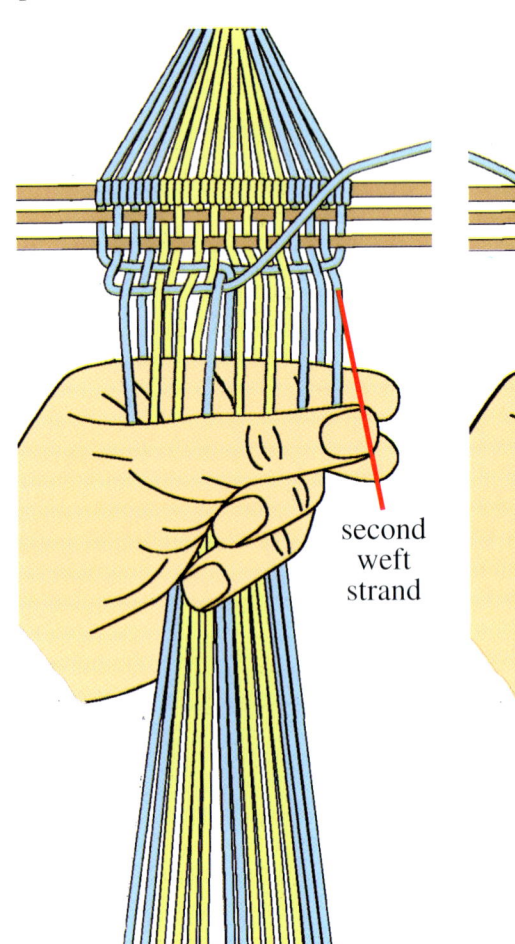

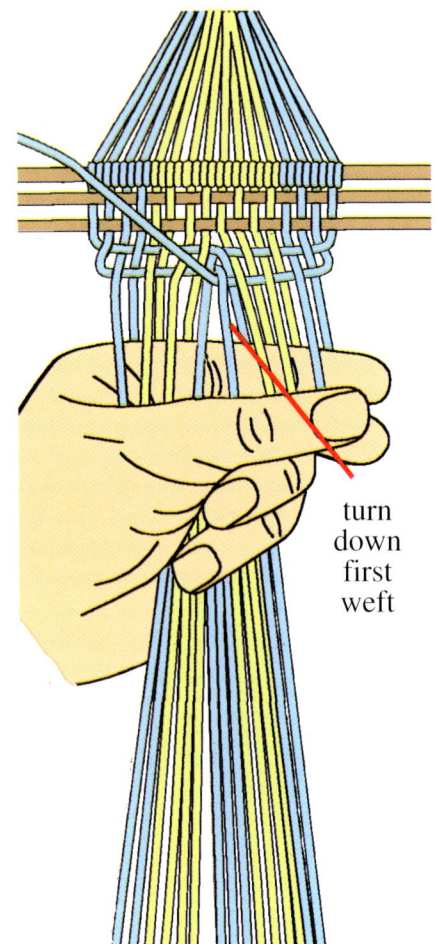

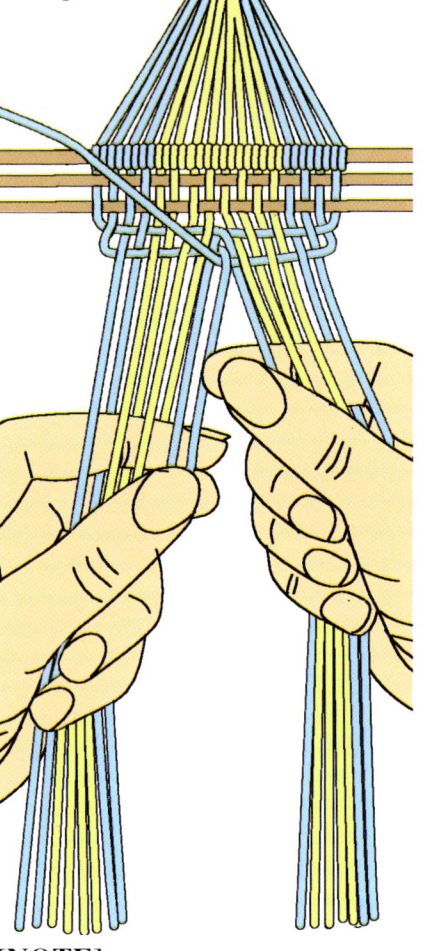

[NOTE]

Check to see if all strands are properly tightened.

[24]

[STEP 15]
When the desired length is reached, turn the work around and reattach it to your anchor.

[STEP 16]
Remove the headsticks and pick up the shed.

[STEP 17]
Set the weft strands in place by pulling the two layers of the shed in opposite directions.

[STEP 18]
Weave the first set of weft strands: The first warp strand on the left becomes a weft strand when it is pulled to the right through the open shed to the middle and hooked up over the work to hold it in place.

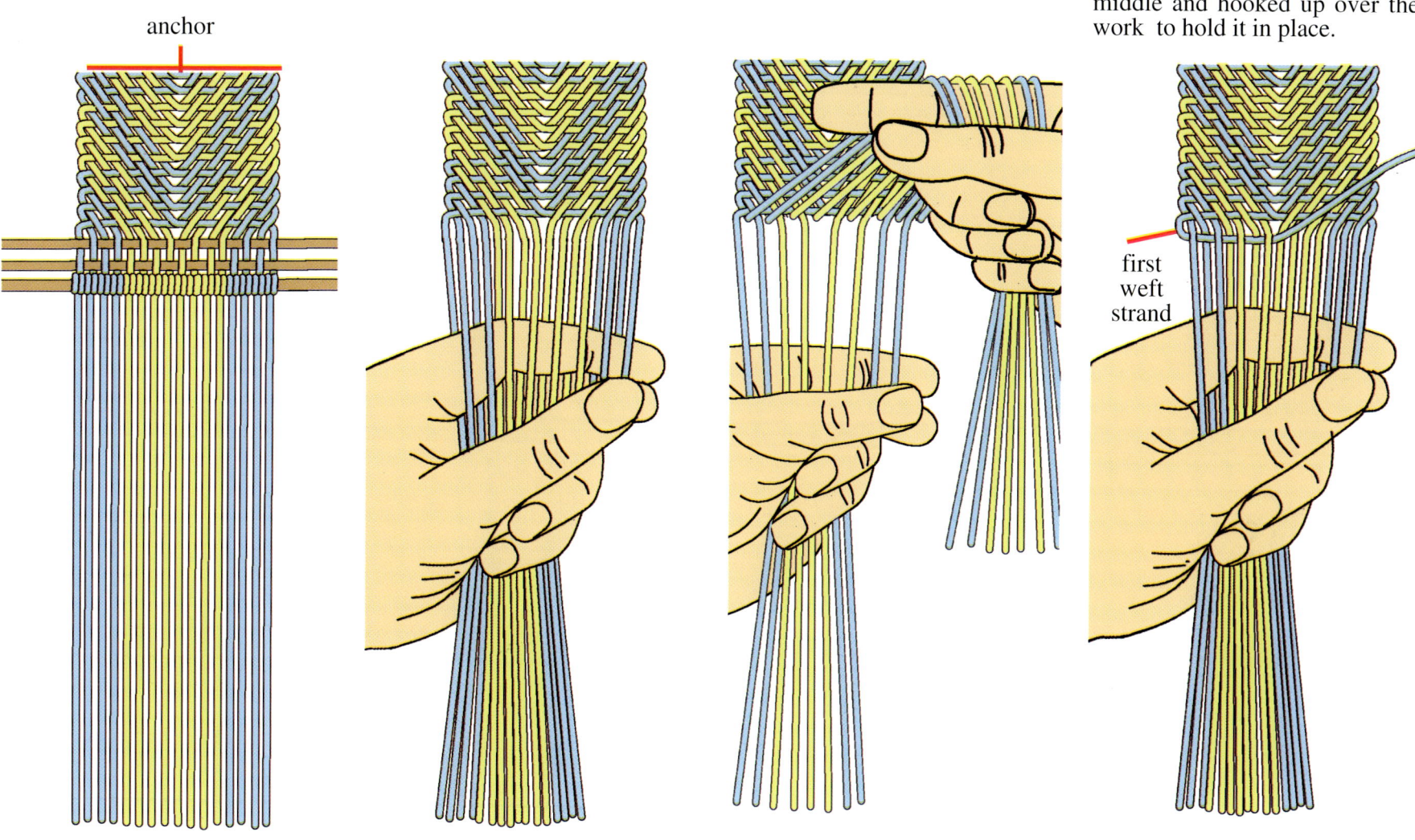

anchor

first weft strand

[25]

[STEP 19]

The first warp strand on the right becomes a weft strand when it is pulled to the left through the open shed to the middle and hooked over the work to hold it in place.

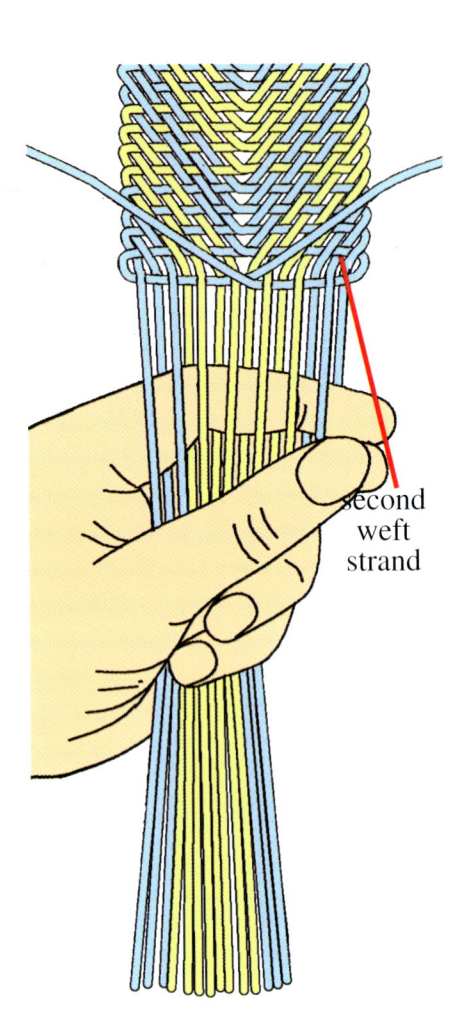

second weft strand

[STEP 20]

Continue weaving, until the second half of the work is completed.

[NOTE]

Notice the point to point pattern that forms between the two halves.

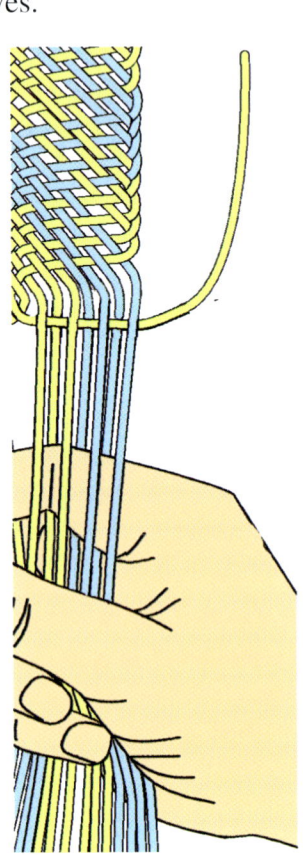

Reversed Chevron Pattern Point Up Example:

Reversed Chevron Pattern Point Up (Center) Example:

[26]

Double Chevron

The double chevron is achieved by combining the two forms of the chevron pattern, point down and point up. The sequence of the combinations allows the double chevron to take two different forms, [W] and [M].

The [W] form combines two point down chevron patterns joined by one point up chevron pattern.

The [M] form combines two point up chevron patterns joined by one point down chevron pattern.

Double Chevron W Pattern

[STEP 1]
Set up the headstick as shown. The two sides must be mirror images of each other.

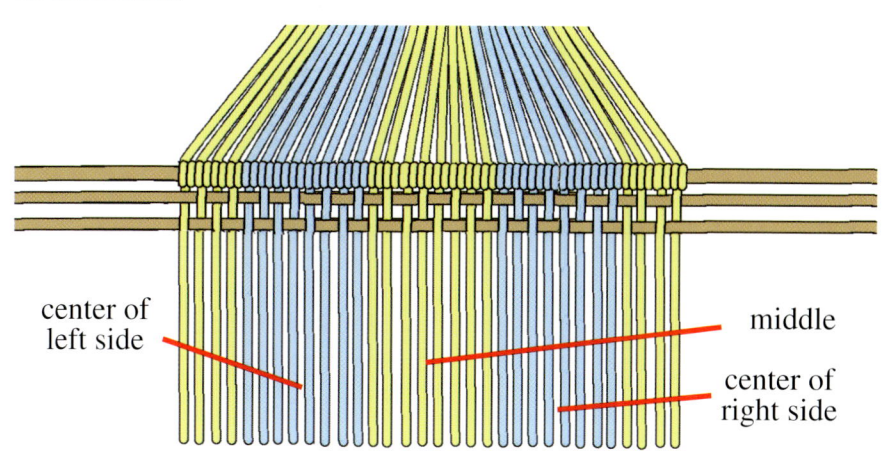

[STEP 2]
The first warp strand to the right of the center of the left side, becomes the first weft strand as it is pulled to the left through the open shed and hooked up over the headstick.

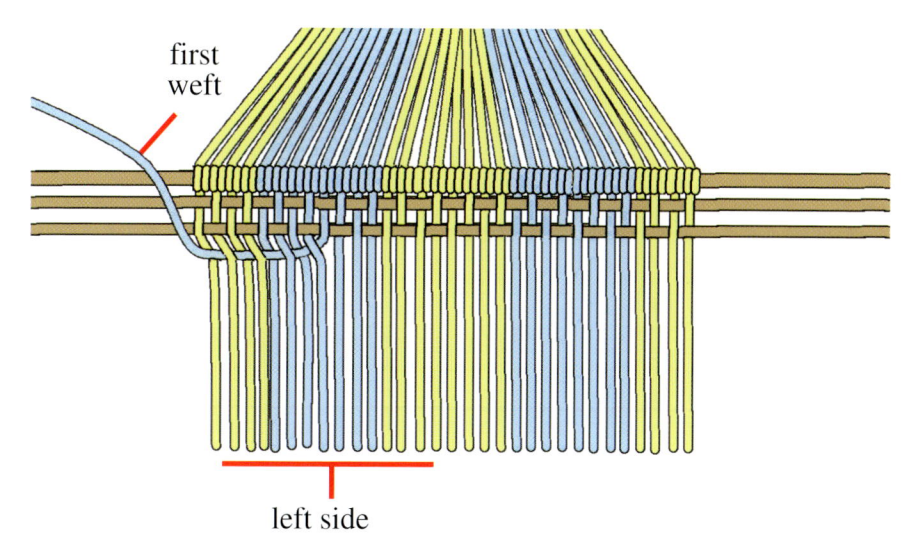

[27]

[STEP 3]

The warp strand to the left of the center of the left side becomes the second weft strand. It makes a transition from the chevron pattern (point down) to the chevron pattern (point up) when it is pulled to the right through the open shed to the middle and hooked up over the headstick.

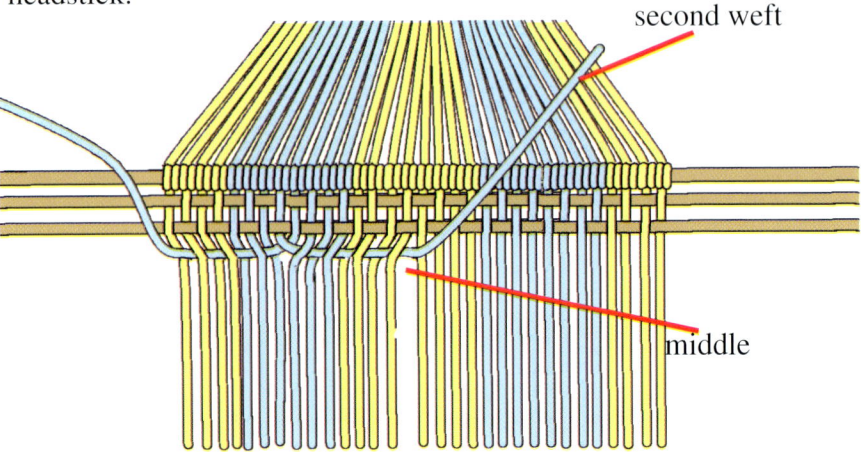

[STEP 4]

The warp strand to the right of the center of the right side becomes the third weft strand. It makes a transition from the chevron pattern (point down) to the chevron pattern (point up) when it is pulled to the left through the open shed to the center and hooked up over the headstick.

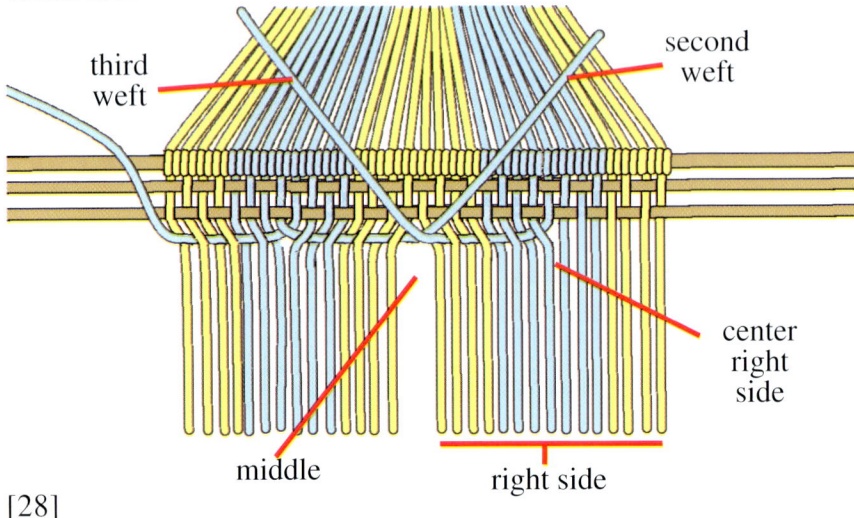

[STEP 5]

Following the instructions for the chevron pattern (point up), return the second weft strand to the bundle of warp strands by turning it down over the third weft strand.

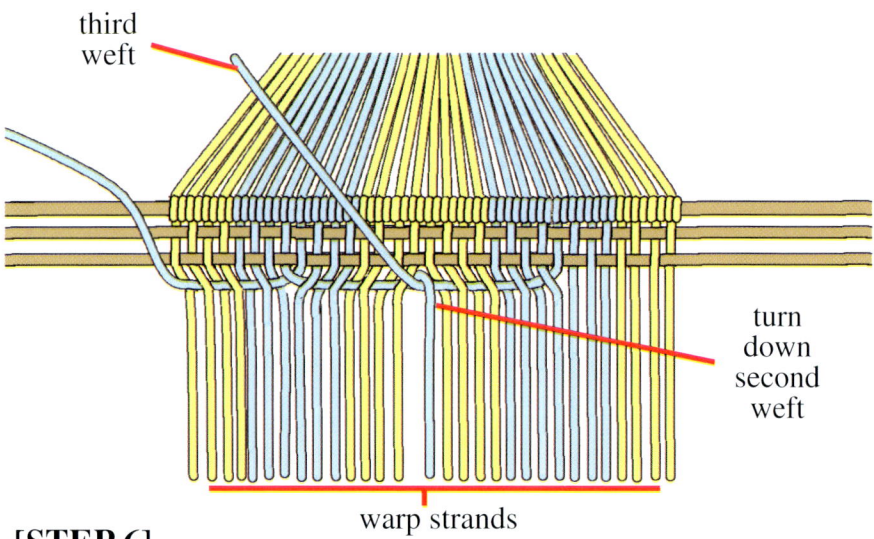

[STEP 6]

The warp strand that is to the left of the center of the right side becomes the fourth weft strand when it is pulled to the right through the open shed.

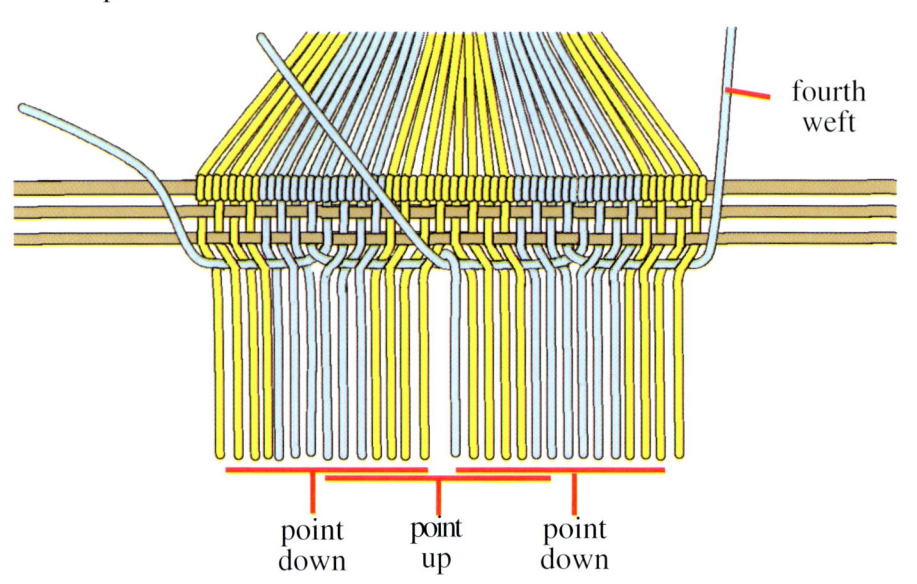

[STEP 7]
Continue weaving by following the combined instructions for chevron pattern (point down) and chevron pattern (point up) until the desired length is reached.

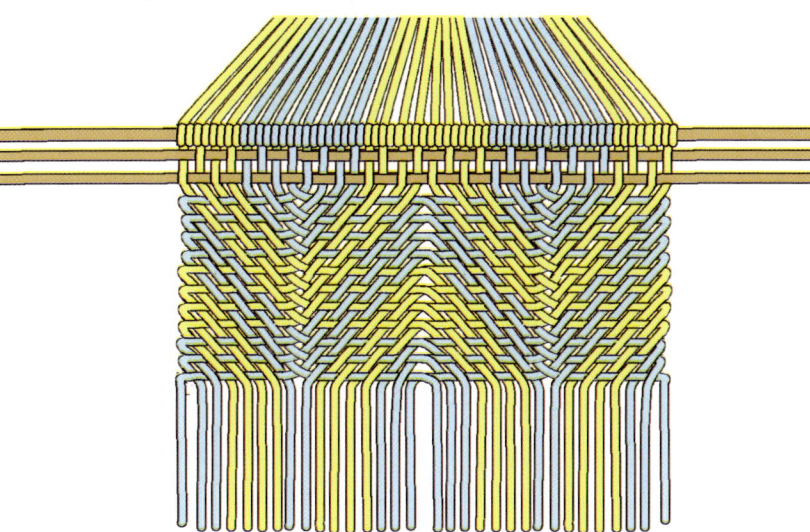

Double Chevron W Pattern Example:

Double Chevron M Pattern

[STEP 1]
Set up the headstick as shown. The two sides must be mirror images of each other.

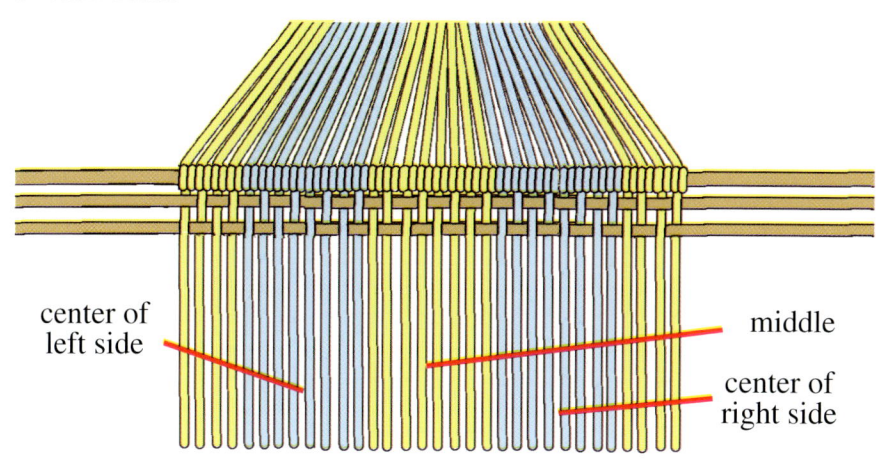

center of left side

middle

center of right side

[STEP 2]
Start at the left side, follow instructions for chevron pattern (point up). Pull the left warp strand through the open shed to the center of the left side.

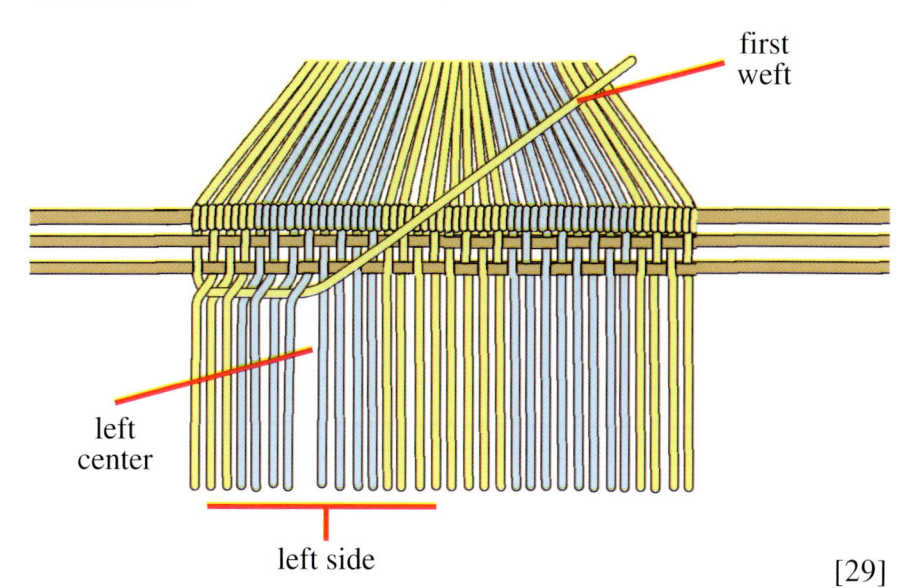

first weft

left center

left side

[29]

[STEP 3]

The warp strand to the right of the middle becomes the second weft strand. It makes a transition from the chevron pattern (point up) to the chevron pattern (point down) when it is pulled through the open shed to the center of the left side and hooked up over the headstick.

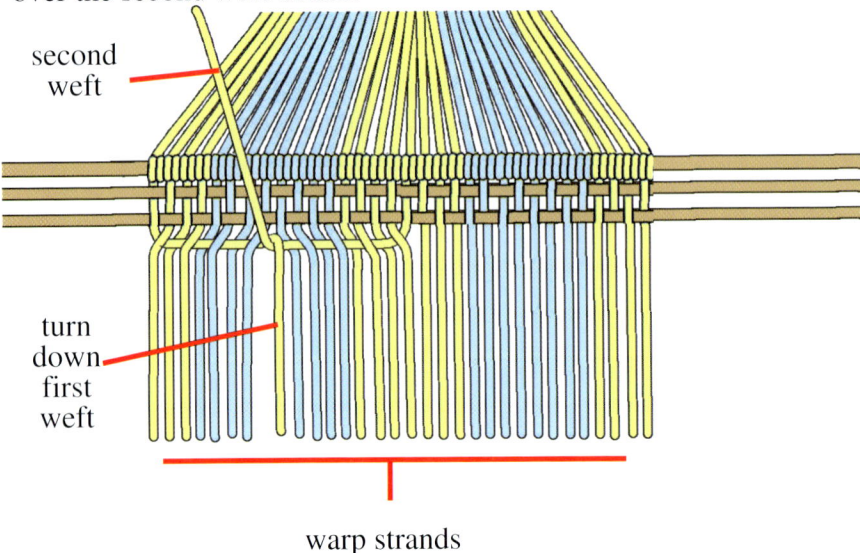

[STEP 5]

The Warp strand to the left of the middle becomes the third weft strand. It makes a transition from the chevron pattern (point down) to the chevron pattern (point up) when it is pulled to the right through the open shed to the center of the right side and hooked up over the headstick.

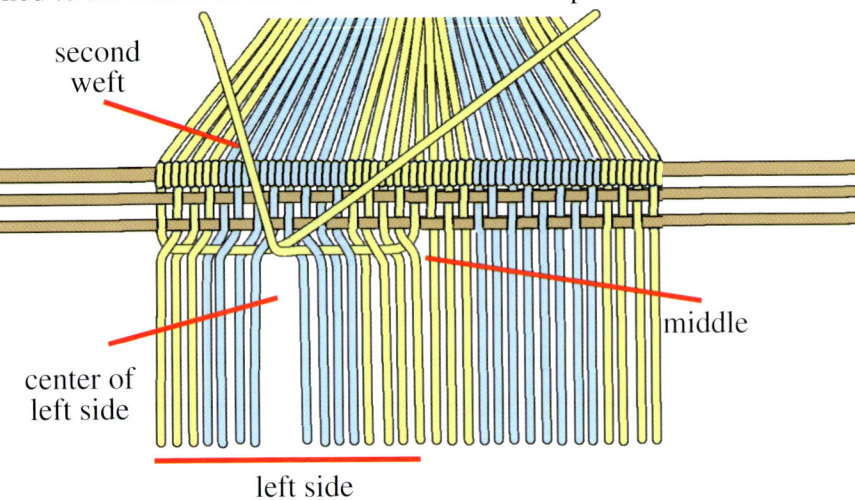

[STEP 4]

Following the instruction for the chevron pattern (point up), return the first weft strand to the bundle of warp strands by turning it down over the second weft strand.

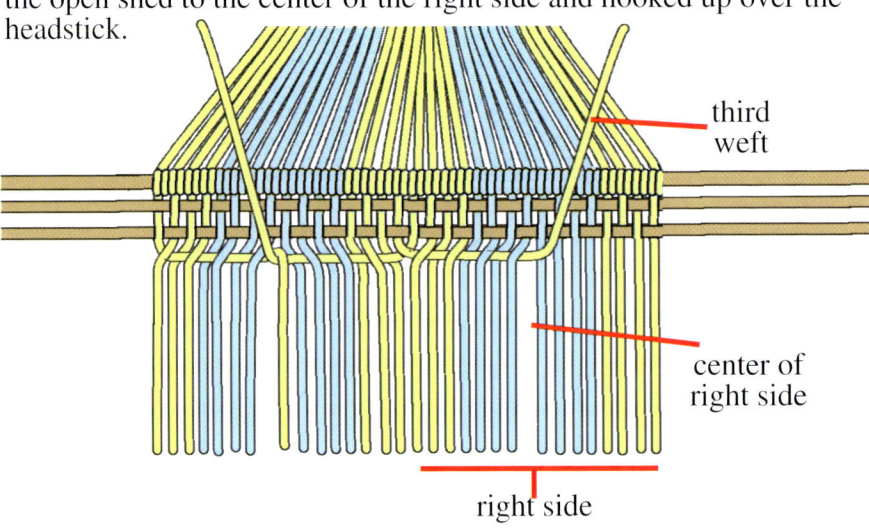

[STEP 6]

The right warp strand becomes the fourth weft strand when it is pulled to the left through the open shed to the center of the right side and hooked up over the headstick.

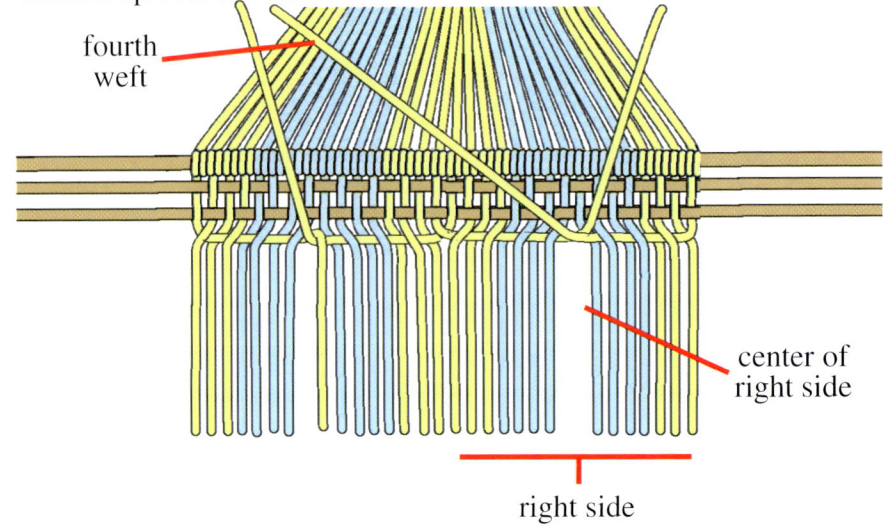

[STEP 7]
Following the instructions for the chevron pattern (point up), return the third weft strand to the bundle of warp strands by turning it down over the fourth weft strand.

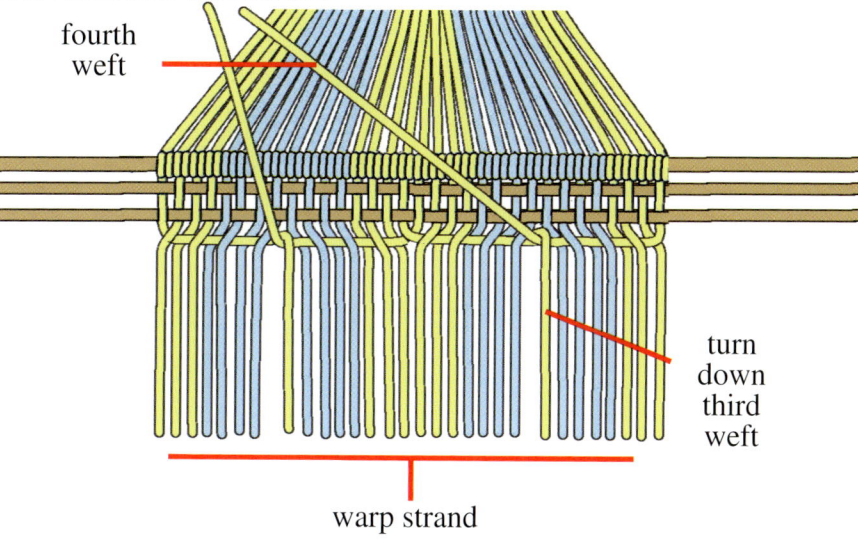

fourth weft

turn down third weft

warp strand

[STEP 8]
Continue weaving by following the combined instructions for chevron pattern (point down) and chevron pattern (point up) until the desired length is reached.

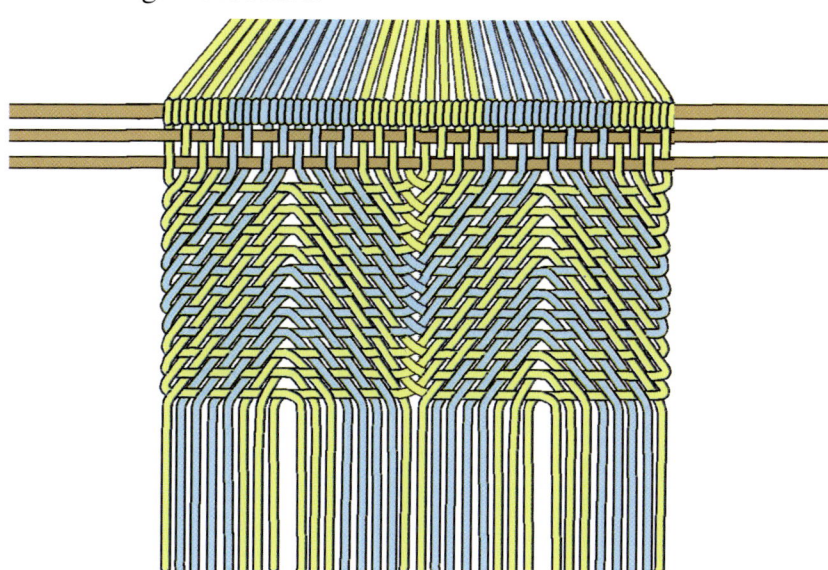

Double Chevron M Pattern Example:

[31]

Chevron Pattern
Over Two/Under Two

The chevron pattern is named for the "V" shaped pattern that develops when two or more colors are used. Over two/under two variation is used to make the two halves of the pattern mirror images of each other. This causes the strands at the edges of the pattern to turn the same direction. Turning the edge strands in the same direction facilitates combining of patterns especially when adding borders to the work.

The setup for the chevron pattern uses two or more colors. There must be an even number of strands of each color. The strands are arranged so that the two sides are mirror images of each other.

[STEP 1]
Cast the required number of strands of yarn on to the headstick. Use clove hitches to tie the yarn in place. See (Part 1: Getting Started).

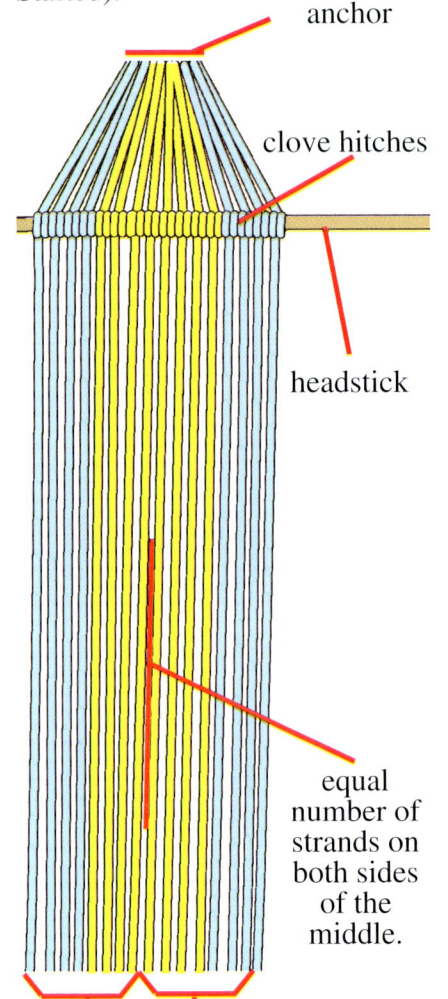

- anchor
- clove hitches
- headstick
- equal number of strands on both sides of the middle.
- the two side are mirror images of each other

[STEP 2]
Use two smaller sticks to set up the weaving pattern. The two center strands are both over the head stick. Starting with these center strands, the remainder of the strands follow an over/under pattern as you move toward the edges.

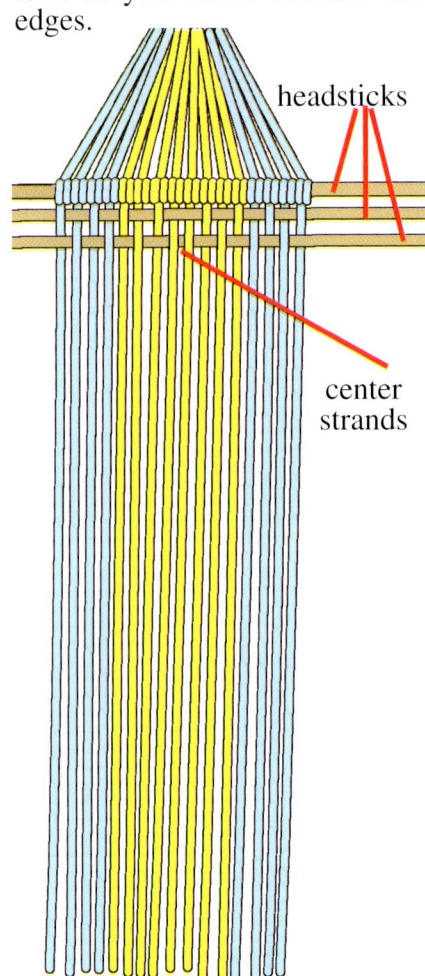

- headsticks
- center strands

[32]

[STEP 3]
Pick up the shed. Use the index finger of the left hand to hold the shed open.

[STEP 4]
The first warp strand to the left of the middle becomes a weft strand when it is pulled to the right through the open shed and hooked over the headstick to hold it in place.

first weft strand

middle

[STEP 5]
The first warp strand to the right of the middle becomes a weft strand when it is pulled to the left through the open shed and hooked over the headstick to hold it in place.

second weft strand

[NOTE] under two

[STEP 6]
Reverse the shed by transferring the warp strands one at a time to the left index finger so that the warp strands that were up in the shed are down and the warp strands that were down in the shed are up.

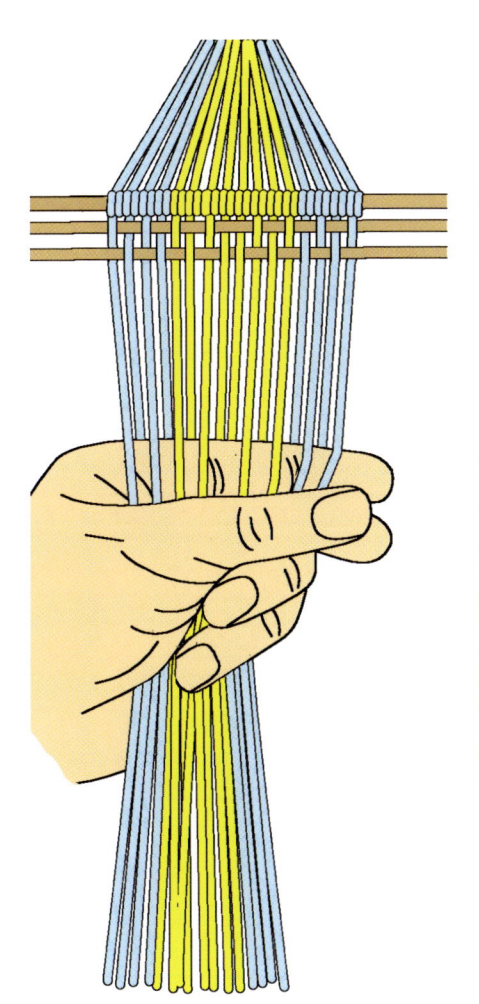

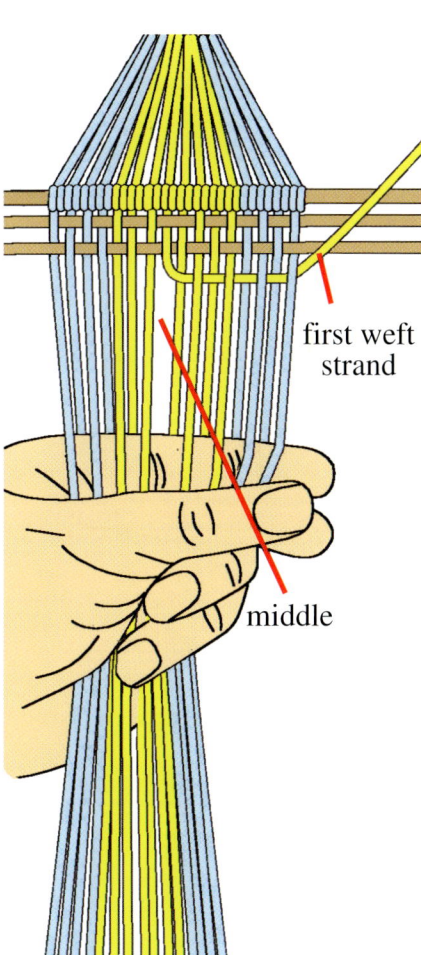

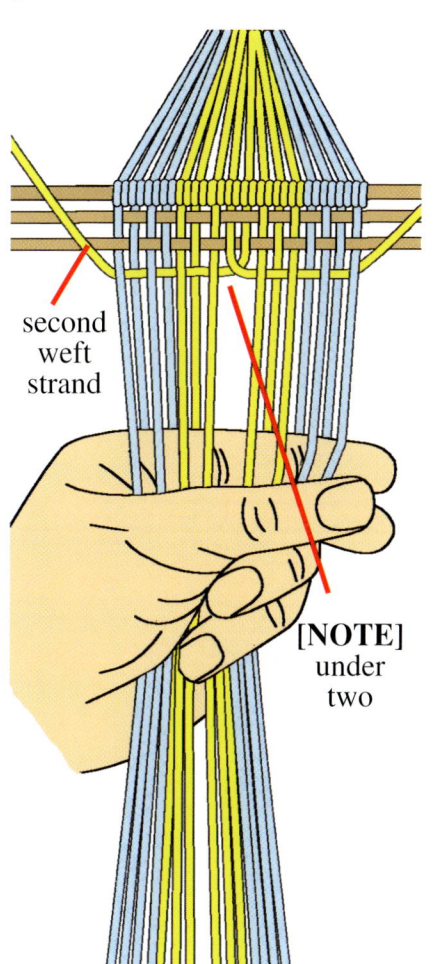

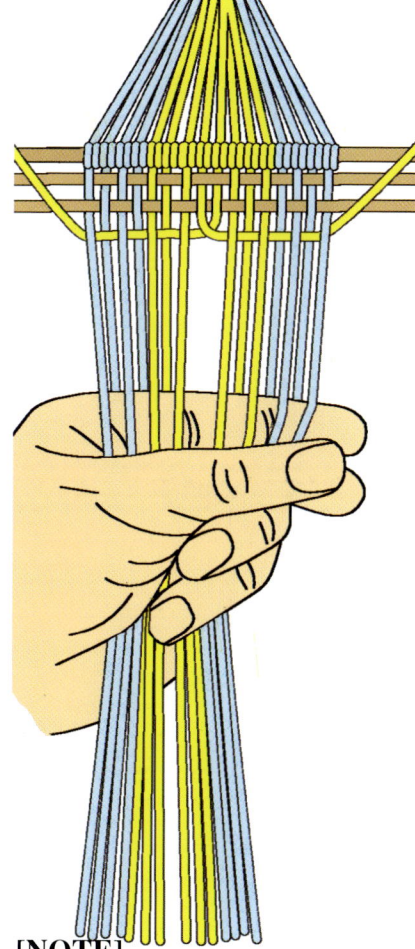

[NOTE]
As each warp strand is transferred to the other hand, check that the proper strand has been selected by observing its position as it crosses the weft strand.

[33]

[STEP 7]
Set the weft strands in place by pulling the two layers of the shed in opposite directions.

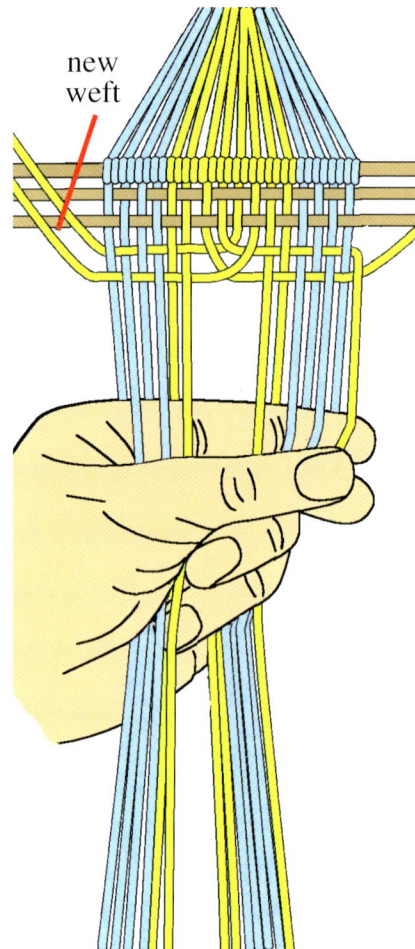

[NOTE]
Check to see if all strands are properly tightened.

[STEP 8]
Again the first warp strand to the left of the middle becomes a weft strand when it is pulled to the right through the open shed and placed over the headstick to hold it in place.

first weft

[NOTE] over two

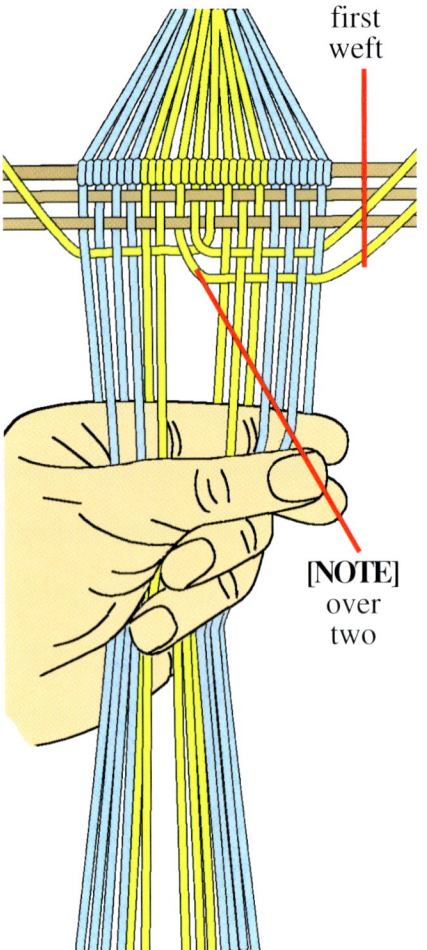

[STEP 9]
Turn the first weft strand of the previous row down. The first weft strand on the right is now a warp strand again.

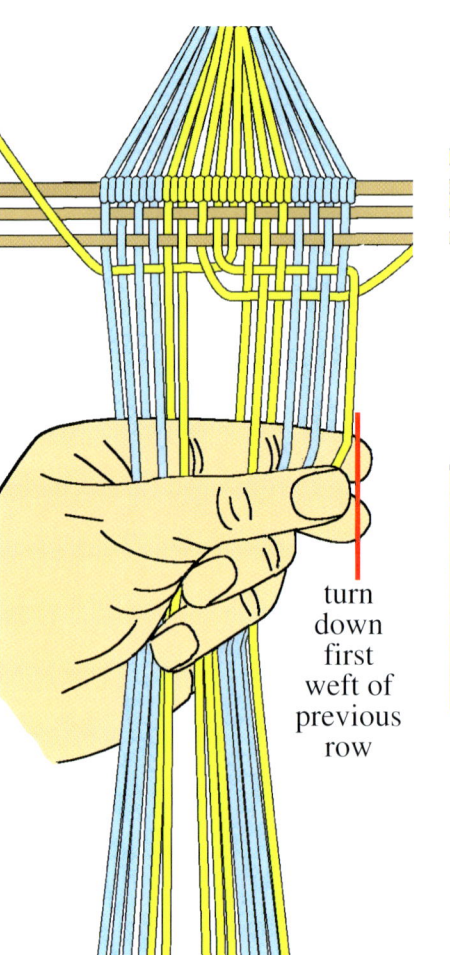

turn down first weft of previous row

[STEP 10]
Again the first warp strand to the right of the middle becomes a weft strand when it is pulled to the left through the open shed and hooked over the headstick to hold it in place.

new weft

[STEP 11]
Turn the second weft strand of the previous row down. This weft strand is now a warp strand again.

turn down second weft strand of previous row

[STEP 12]
Reverse the shed and set the weft.

[STEP 13]
Continue to weave in this manner until the desired length is reached.

[NOTE]
See page 78 for information about changing the direction of the weave.

Chevron Pattern Over Two/Under Two Example:

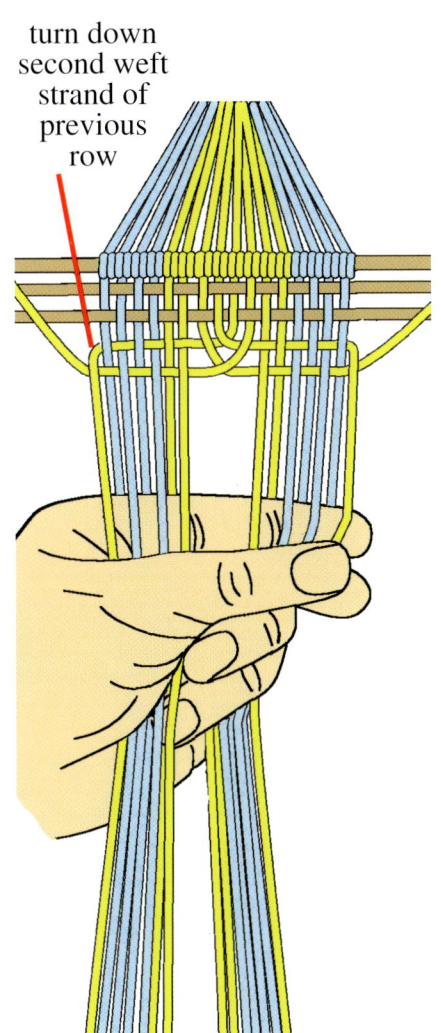

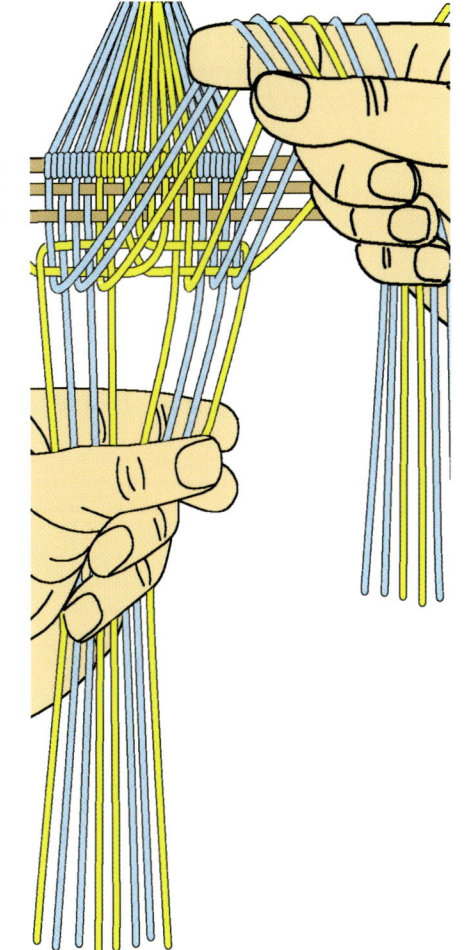

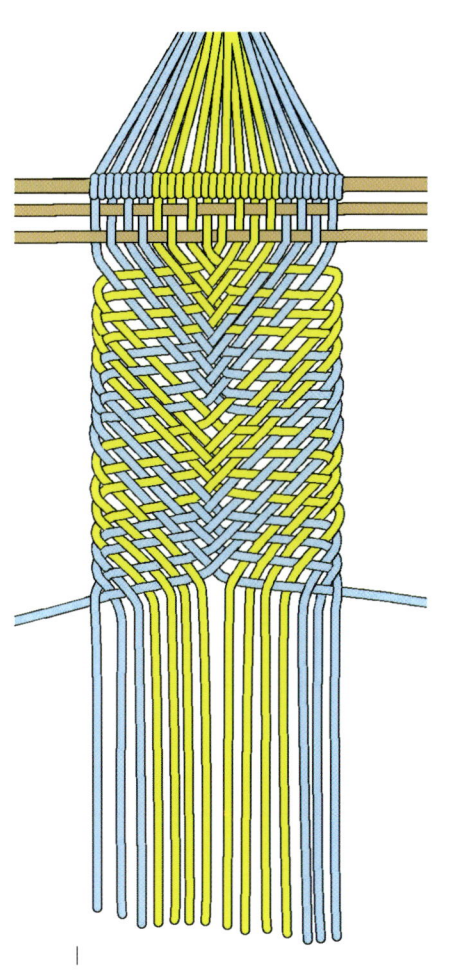

[35]

Reversed Chevron Over Two/Under Two

The reverse chevron pattern is named for the upside down "V" shaped pattern that develops when two or more colors are used. Over two/under two variation is used to make the two halves of the pattern mirror images of each other. This causes the strands at the edges of the pattern to turn in the same direction. Turning the edge strands in the same direction facilitates combining of patterns, especially when adding borders to the work..

The setup for the chevron pattern uses two or more colors. There must be an even number of strands of each color. The strands are arranged so that the two sides are mirror images of each other.

[STEP 1]

Cast the required number of strands of yarn on to the headstick. Use clove hitches to tie the yarn in place. See (part 1: Getting Started).

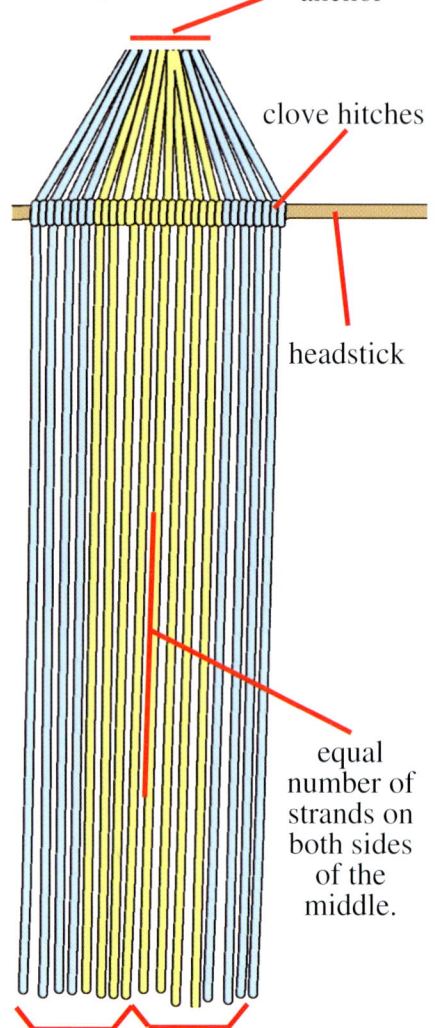

- anchor
- clove hitches
- headstick
- equal number of strands on both sides of the middle.
- the two side are mirror images of each other

[STEP 2]

Use two smaller sticks to set up the weaving pattern. The two center strands are both under the headstick. Starting with these center strands, the remainder of the strands follow an over/under pattern as you move toward the edges.

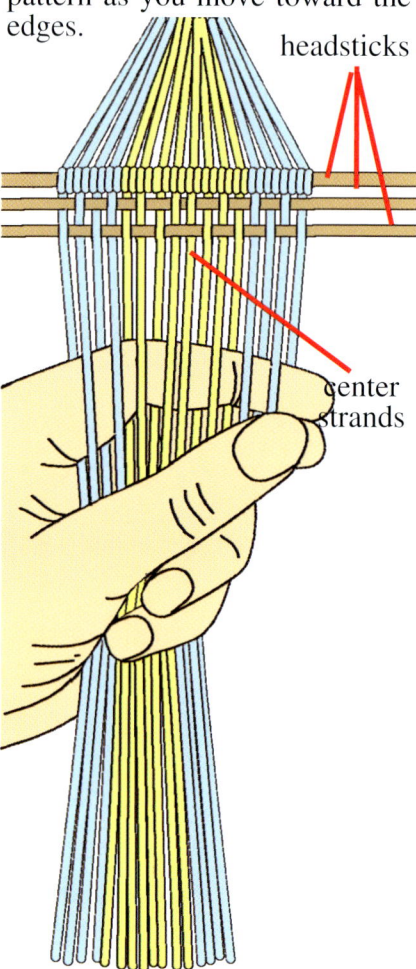

- headsticks
- center strands

Pick up the shed. Use the index finger of the left hand to hold the shed open.

[STEP 3]

The first warp strand on the right becomes a weft strand when it is pulled to the left through the open shed to the middle and hooked over the headstick to hold it in place.

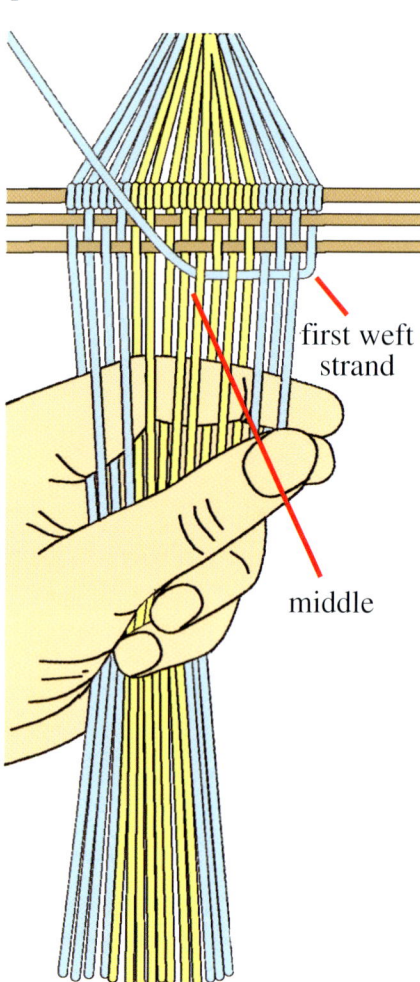

- first weft strand
- middle

[36]

[STEP 4]
The first warp strand to the left becomes the second weft strand when it is pulled to the right through the open shed to the middle and hooked over the headstick to hold it in place.

[STEP 5]
Turn the first weft strand down over the second weft strand so that it becomes a warp strand again.

[STEP 6]
Reverse the shed by transferring the warp strands one at a time to the left index finger so that the warp strands that were up in the shed are down and the warp strands that were down in the shed are up.

STEP 7
Set the weft strands in place by pulling the two layers of the shed in opposite directions.

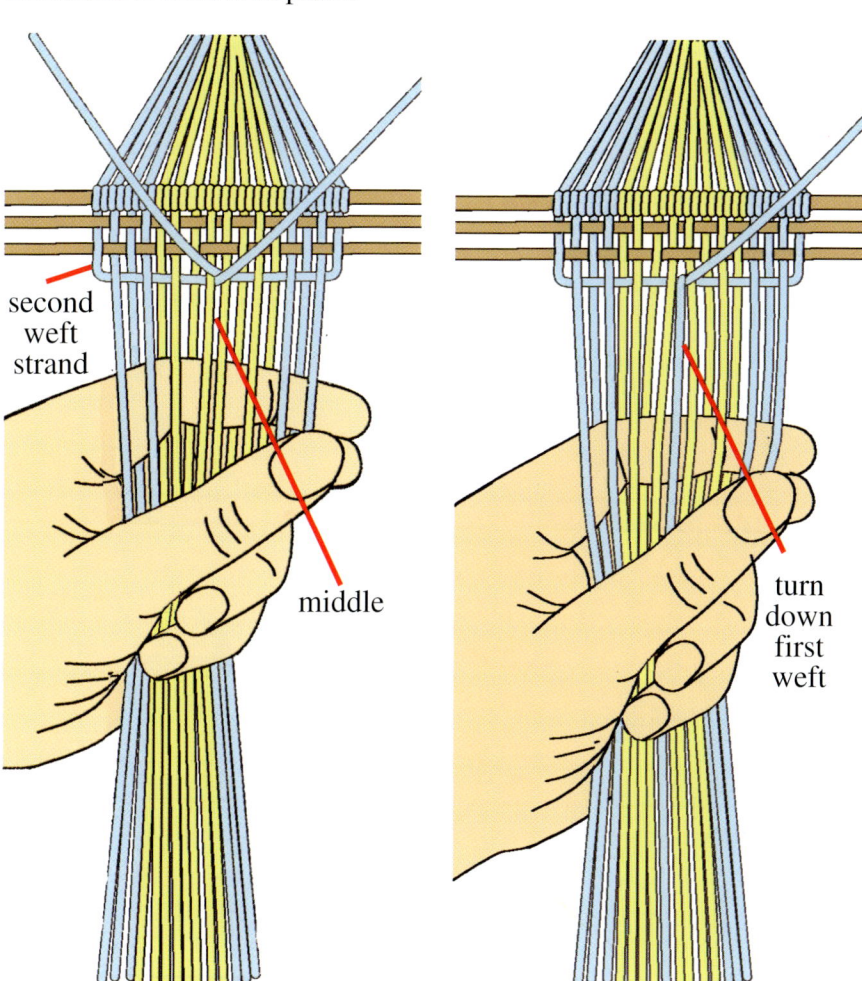

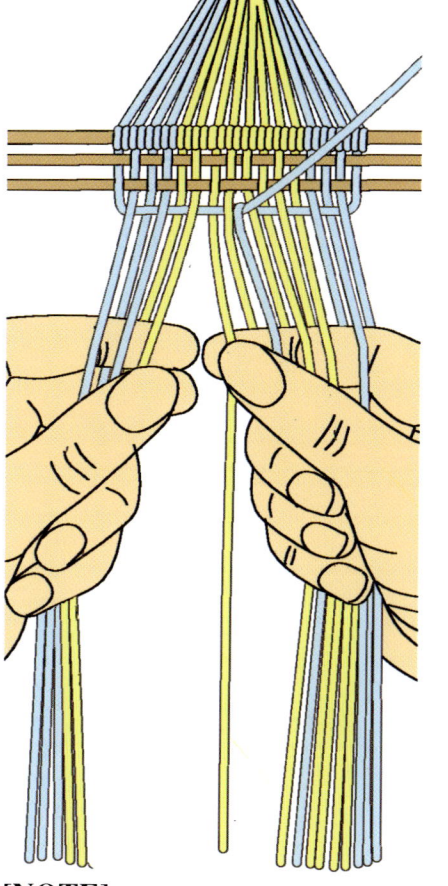

[NOTE]
As each warp strand is transferred to the other hand, check that the proper strand has been selected by observing its position as it crosses the weft strand.

[NOTE]
Check to see if all strands are properly tightened.

[37]

[STEP 8]

Again the first warp strand on the right becomes a weft strand when it is pulled to the left through the open shed to the middle and placed over the headstick to hold it in place.

first weft

[STEP 9]

Turn the second weft strand of the previous row down over the first weft strand of the present row so that it becomes a warp strand again.

turn down second weft

[STEP 10]

Again the first warp strand on the left becomes the second weft strand when it is pulled through the open shed to the middle and hooked over the headstick to hold it in place.

second weft

[STEP 11]

Turn the first weft strand down over the second weft strand so that it becomes a warp strand again.

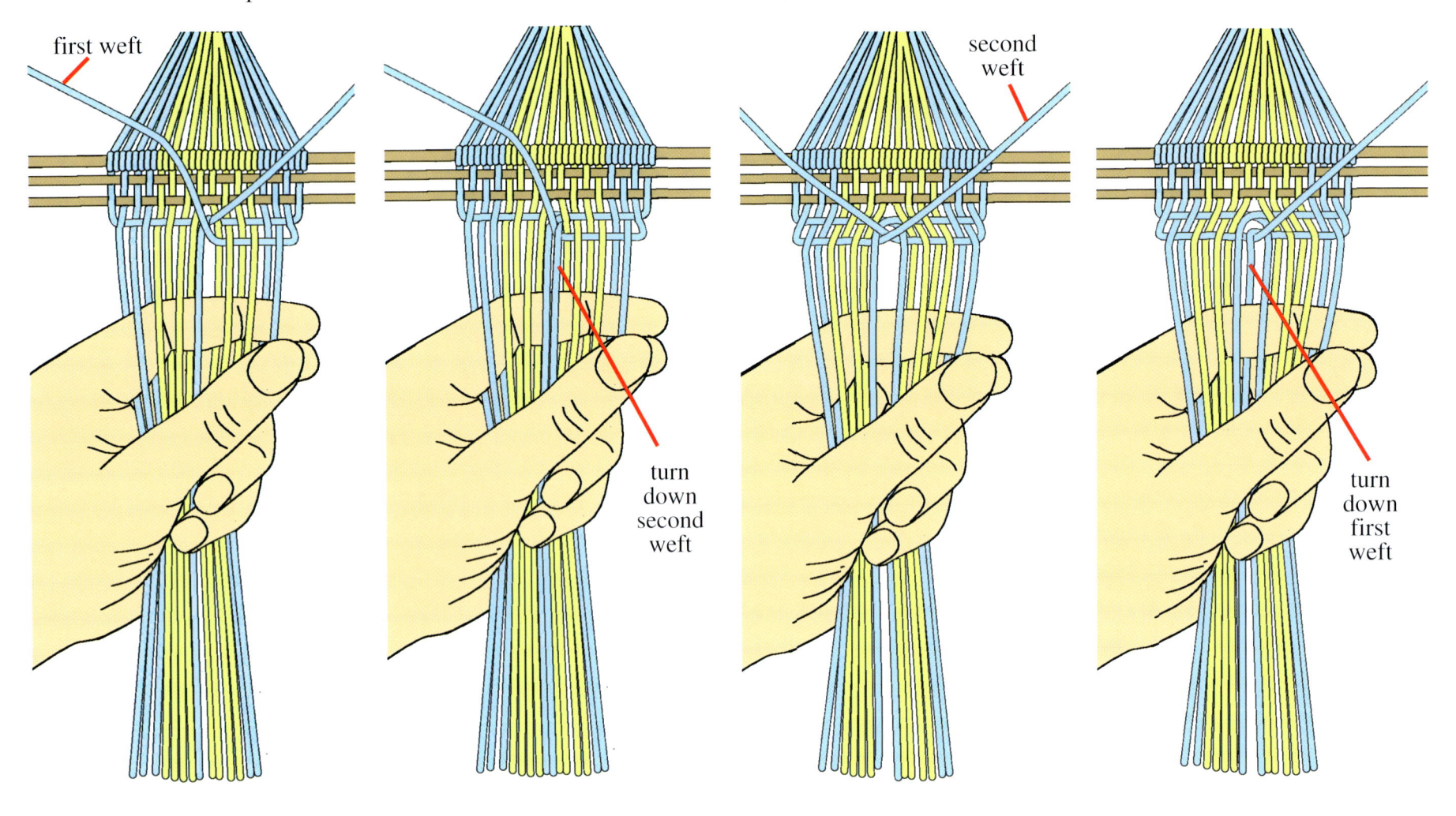

turn down first weft

[38]

[STEP 12]
Reverse the shed by transferring the warp strands one at a time to the left index finger so that the warp strands that were up in the shed are down and the warp strands that were down in the shed are up.

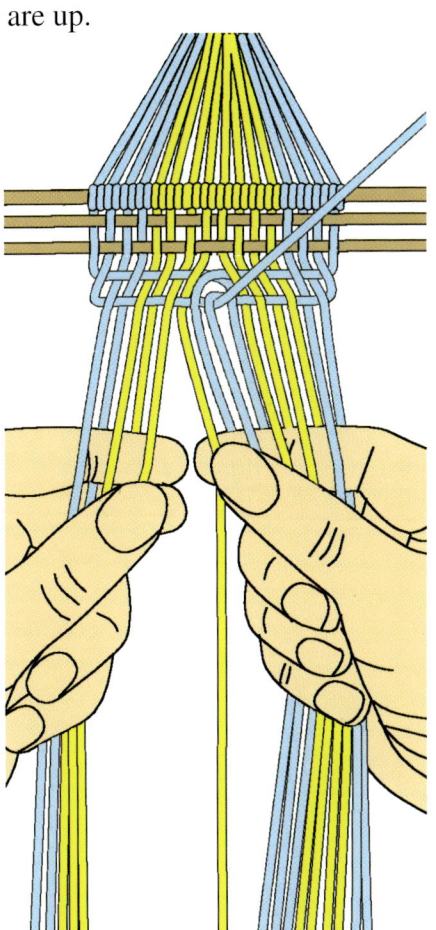

[NOTE]
As each warp strand is transferred to the other hand, check that the proper strand has been selected by observing its position as it crosses the weft strand.

[STEP 13]
Set the weft strands in place by pulling the two layers of the shed in opposite directions.

[NOTE]
Check to see if all strands are properly tightened.

[STEP 14]
Continue to weave in this manner until the desired length is reached.

[NOTE]
See page 78 for information about changing the direction of the weave.

Reversed Chevron Pattern Over Two/Under Two Example:

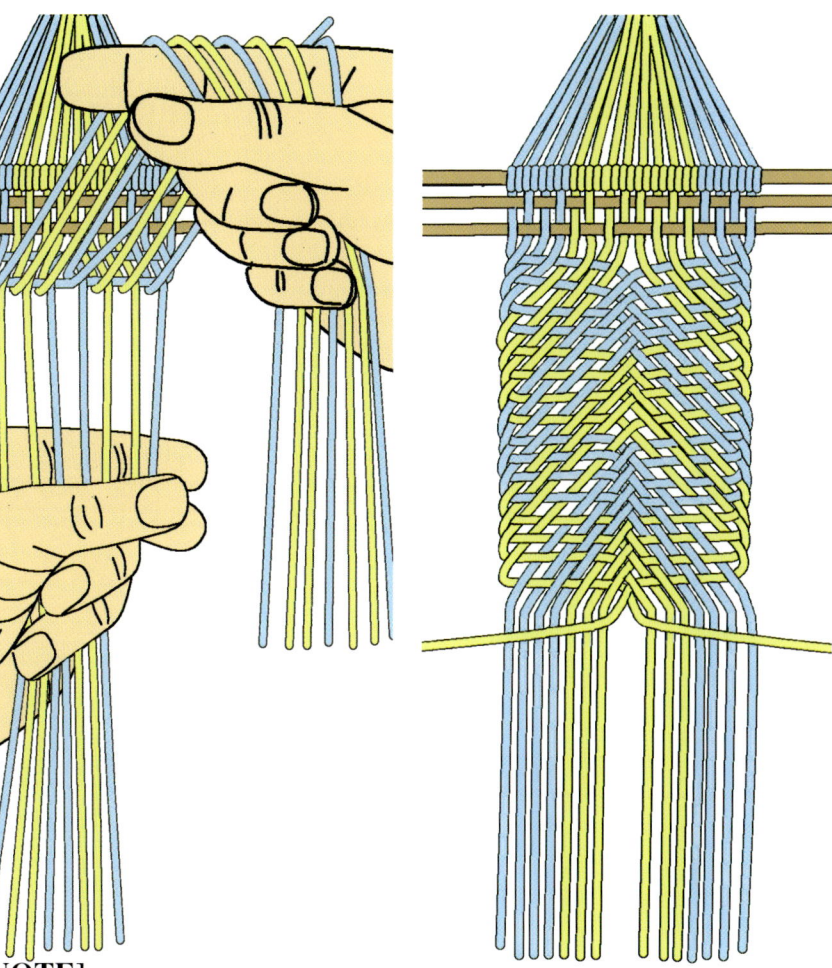

[39]

Lightning Pattern

The lightning pattern is worked in a similar manner to the diagonal pattern. To obtain the lightning pattern, the weft strand changes color as it is pulled through the open shed. The color change is accomplished by interlocking a weft strand with a warp strand. When the interlocking takes place, the original weft strand becomes a warp strand and the warp strand that is interlocked with it becomes the weft strand.

The setup for the lightning pattern requires the number of strands used for the center color (the lightning) to be divisible by 2. The number of strands in each edge color must be equal to or greater than one half the number of the center strands.

In the example shown here there are eight strands used for the center color and eight for each of the edge colors.

[40]

[STEP 1]
Cast the required number of strands of yarn on to the headstick. Use clove hitches to tie the yarn in place. See (Part 1: Getting Started).

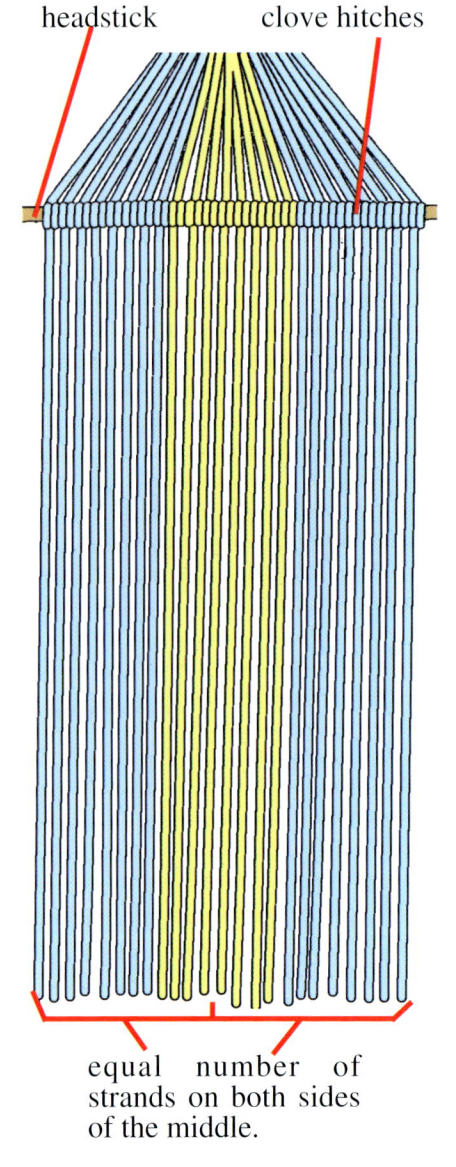

headstick clove hitches

equal number of strands on both sides of the middle.

[STEP 2]
Set up the over/under weaving pattern of the shed with two smaller sticks.

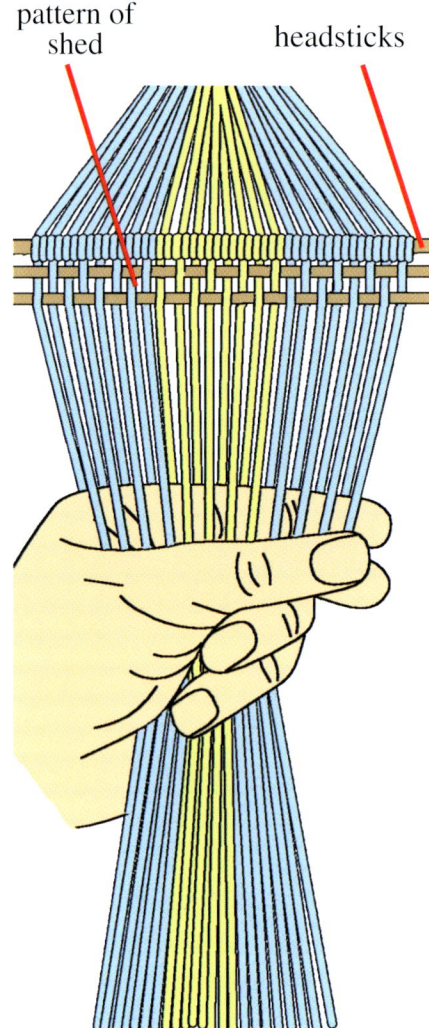

pattern of shed headsticks

Pick up the shed. Use the index finger of the left hand to hold the shed open.

[STEP 3]
The first warp strand on the left becomes a weft strand when it is pulled to the right through the open shed to the middle of the center color and hooked up over the headstick.

first weft

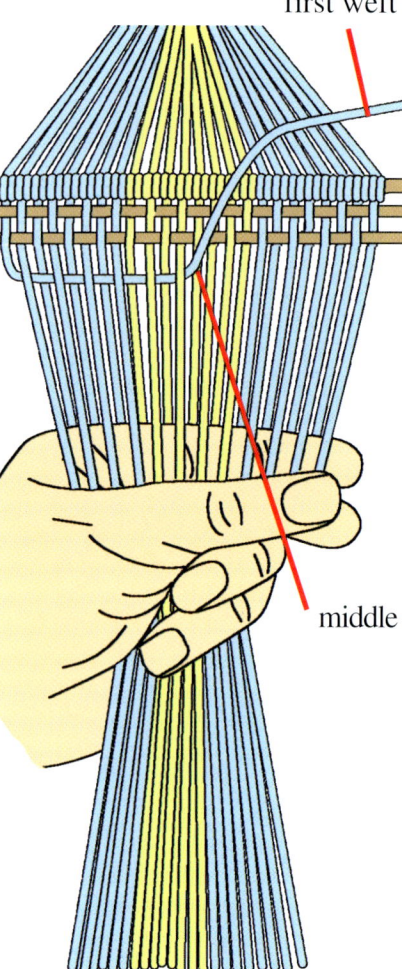

middle

[STEP 4]
Start the first interlocking of the weft strands by pulling the first warp strand to the left of the middle through the open shed so that it has been pulled through the open shed of the right hand color the number of strands equal to one half the number of strands of the center color. This warp strand is now the second weft strand.

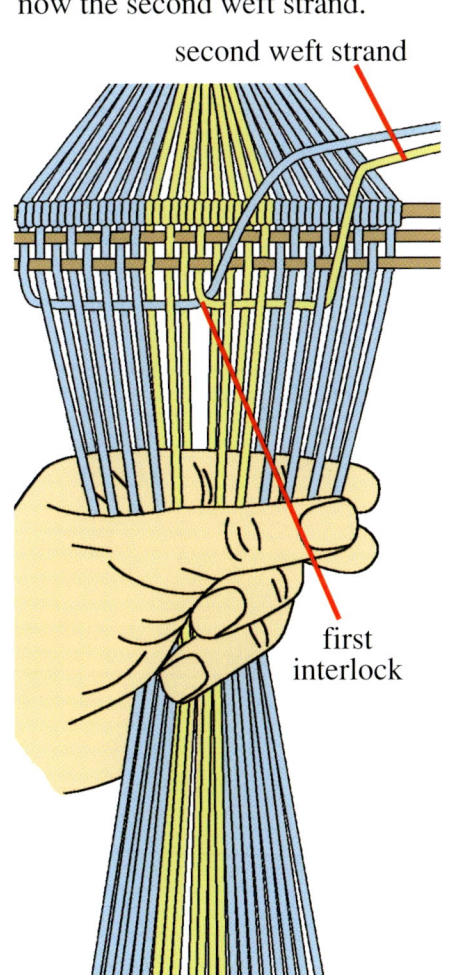

[STEP 5]
Start second interlocking of the weft strands by pulling the warp strand that is to the left of the second weft strand through the open shed to the right edge and hooking it over the headstick.

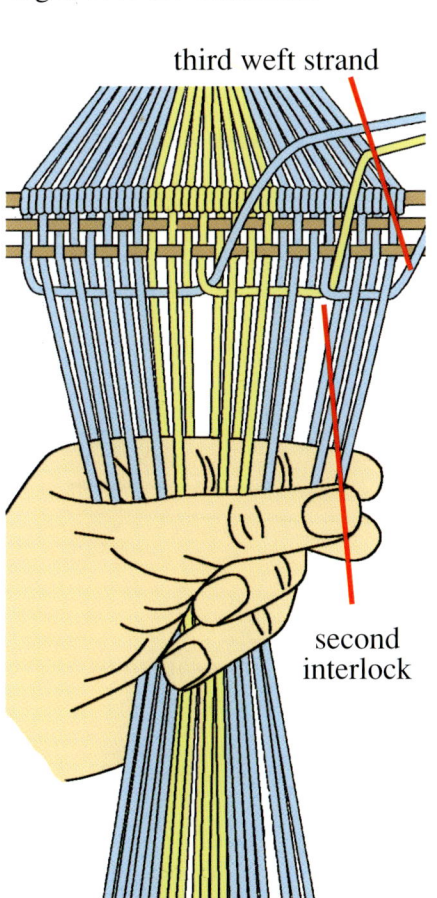

[STEP 6]
Complete the interlocking by placing the first two weft strands back into the bundle of the warp strands.

[STEP 7]
Reverse the shed by transferring the warp strands one at a time to the right index finger so that the warp strands that were up in the shed are down and the warp strands that were down in the shed are up.

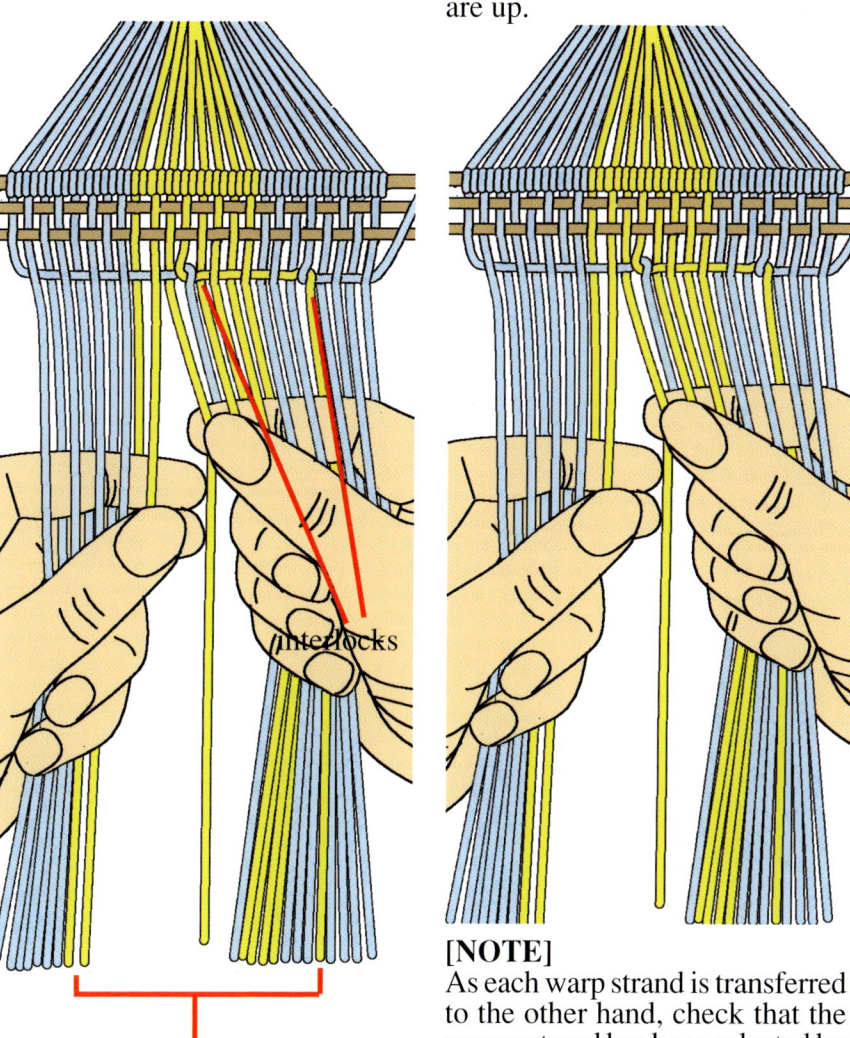

[NOTE]
As each warp strand is transferred to the other hand, check that the proper strand has been selected by observing its position as it crosses the weft strand.

[41]

[STEP 8]
Set the weft strands in place by pulling the two layers of the shed in opposite directions.

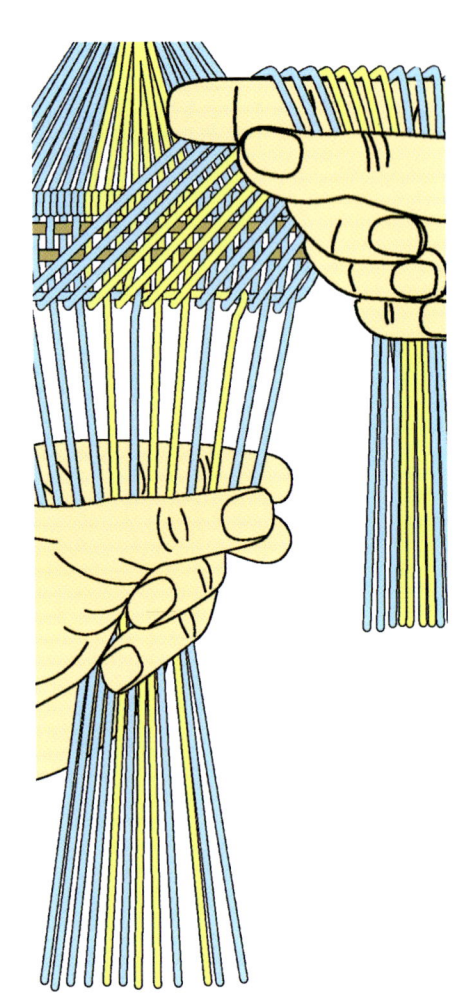

[NOTE]
Check to see if all strands are properly tightened.

[STEP 9]
The first warp strand on the left becomes a weft strand when it is pulled to the right through the open shed to the left of the first interlock in the previous row and hooked up over the headstick.

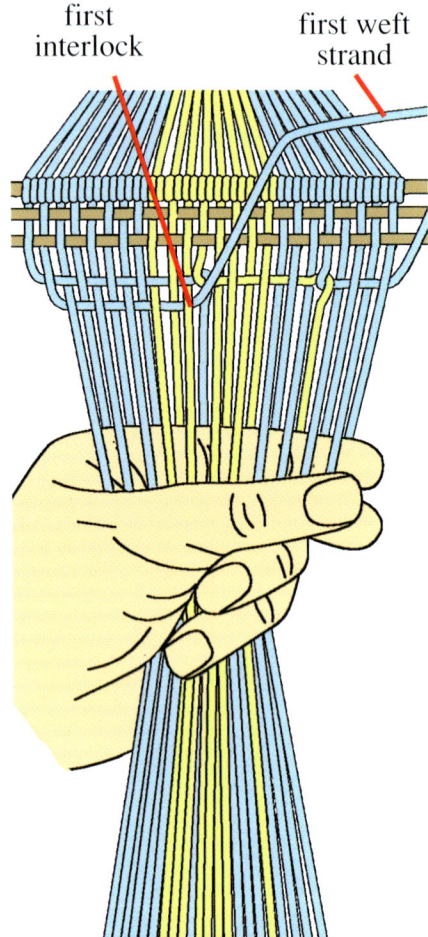

[STEP 10]
Start the first interlocking in this row of the weft strand by pulling the warp strand that is to the left of the first interlock in the previous row to the right through the shed to the left of the second interlock and hooking it over the headstick.

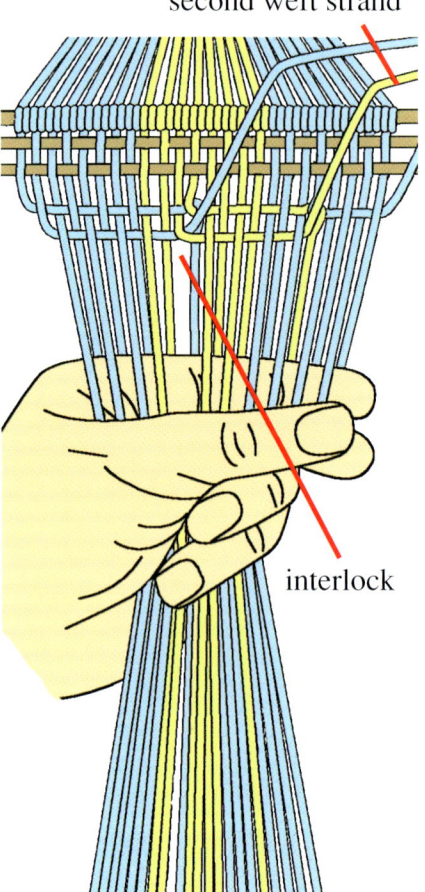

[STEP 11]
Start the second interlocking of the weft strand by pulling the warp strand that is to the left of the second interlock in the previous row through the open shed to the right edge and hooking it over the headstick.

[42]

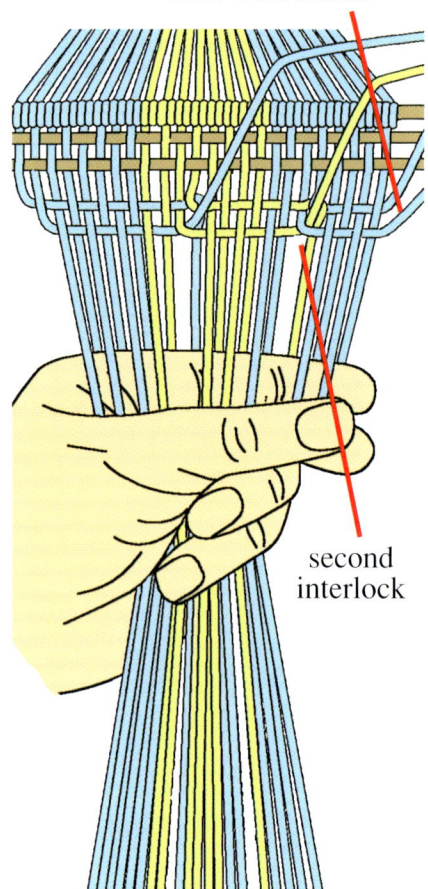

[STEP 12]

Turn down the last weft strand of the previous row. This weft strand is now a warp strand again.

turn down last weft strand previous row

[STEP 13]

Complete the interlocking by placing the first two weft strands of the present row back into the bundle of the warp strands.

interlocks

warp strands

[STEP 14]

Reverse the shed by transferring the warp strands one at a time to the right index finger so that the warp strands that were up in the shed are down and the warp strands that were down in the shed are up.

[NOTE]

As each warp strand is transferred to the other hand, check that the proper strand has been selected by observing its position as it crosses the weft strand.

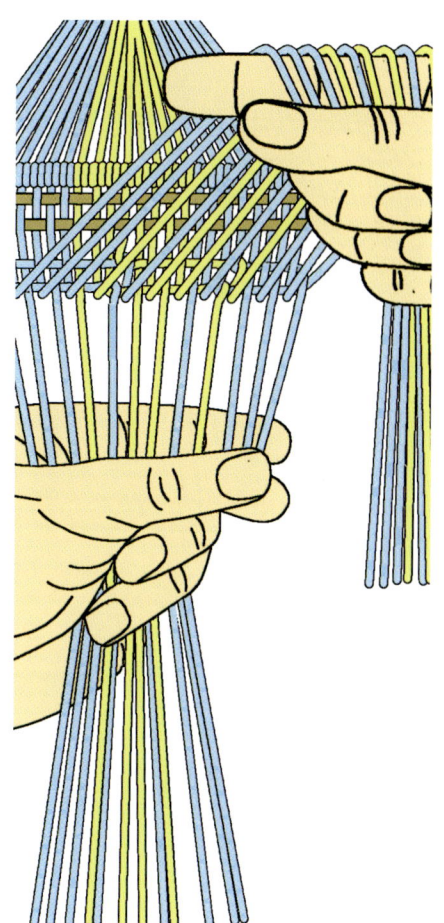

[STEP 15]

Set the weft strands in place by pulling the two layers of the shed in opposite directions.

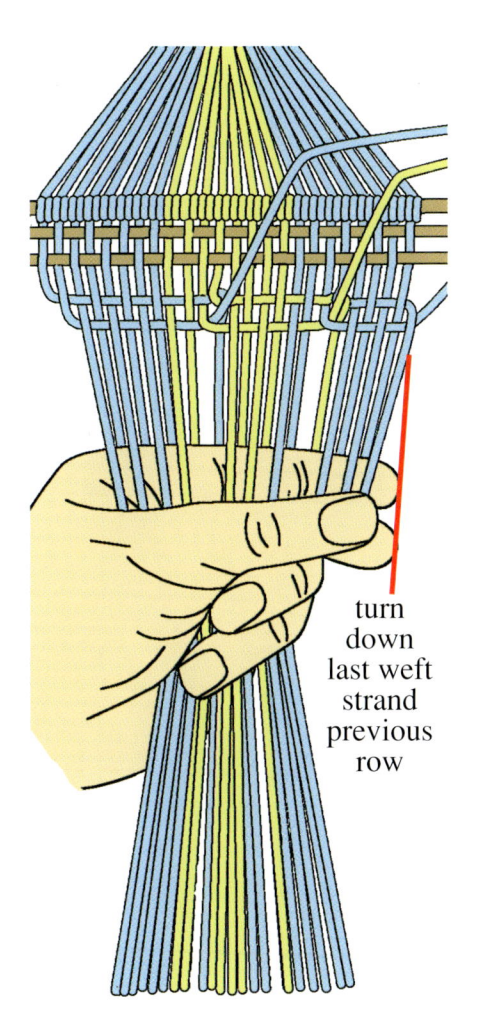

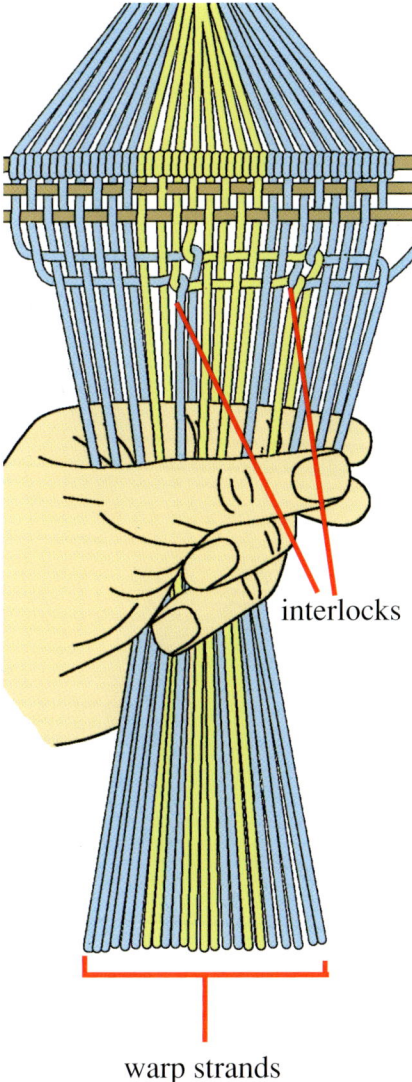

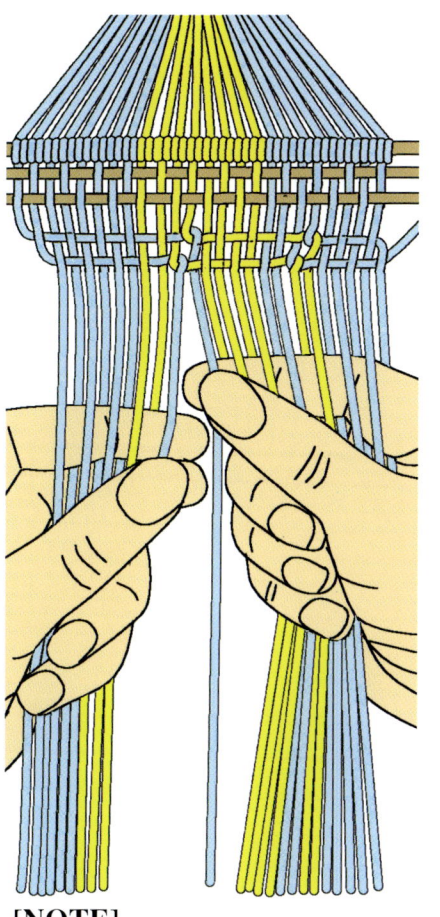

[NOTE]

Check to see if all strands are properly tightened.

[43]

[STEP 16]
Continue to weave additional rows until the warp strands are back to their original sequence.

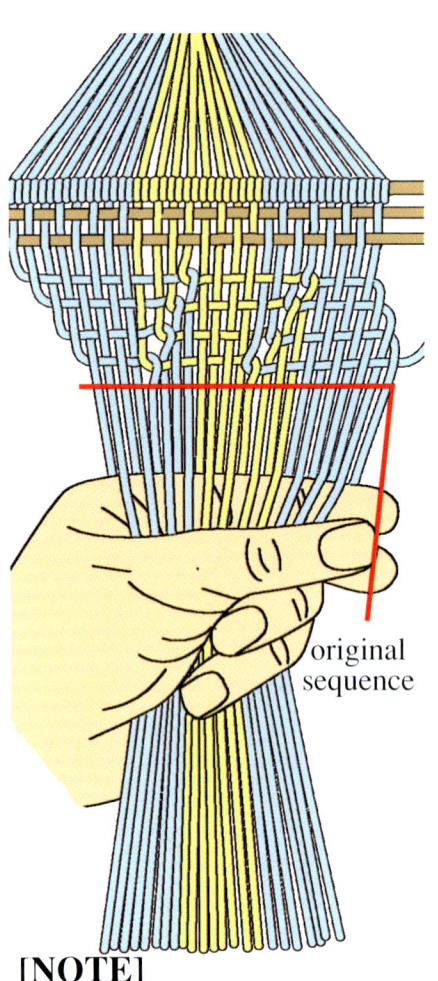

[STEP 17]
The next row of weaving in this pattern is the same as the first row of weaving. See **[STEP 4]**.

[STEP 18]
Continue to weave in this manner until the desired length is reached.

Lightning Pattern Example:

[NOTE]
The number of rows of weaving is equal to one half the number of strands in the center color.

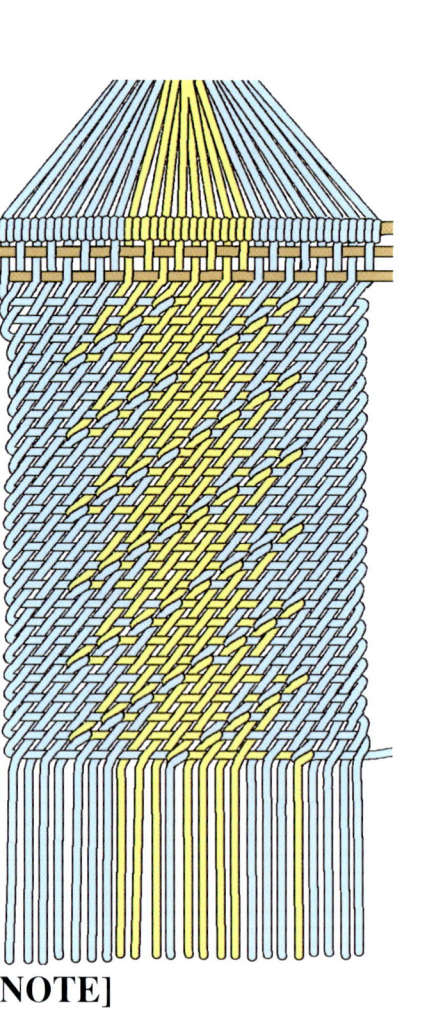

[NOTE]
The second half of the work piece is woven by turning the work piece around, removing the head stick, and continuing to weave until the desired length is reached.

[44]

**Lightning Pattern
Three Colors
Variation 1**

**Lightning Pattern
Three Colors
Variation 1 Example:**

**Lightning Pattern
Added Strands
Variation 2**

added strands

**Lightning Pattern
Added Strands
Variation 2 Example:**

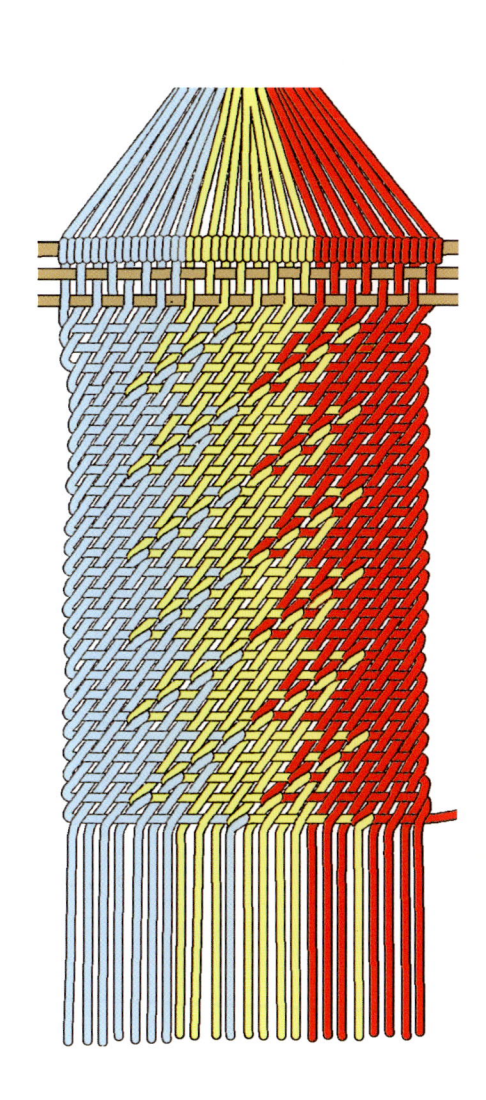

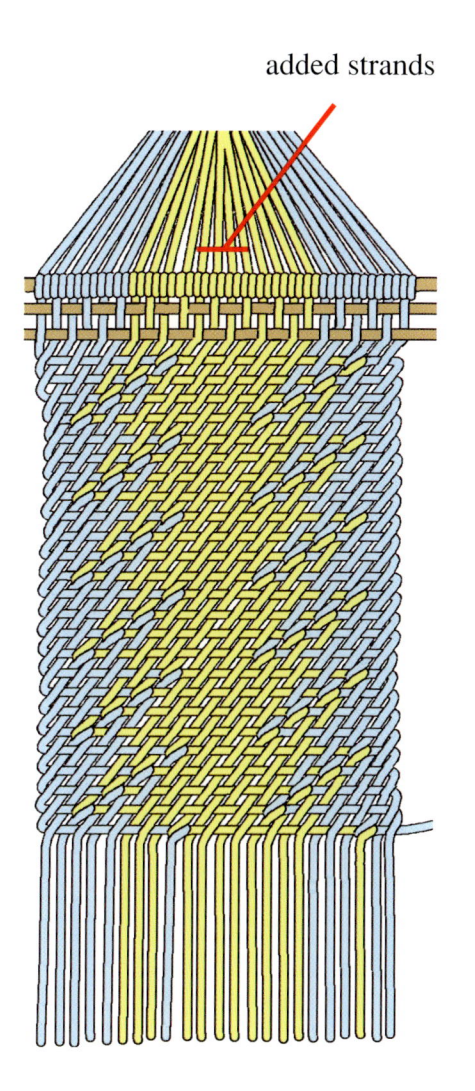

Increase the number of strands of the middle color, but interlock at the same number of strands in the edge color.

[45]

**Lightning Pattern
Added Color Bands
Variation 3**

**Lightning Pattern
Added Color Bands
Variation 3 Example:**

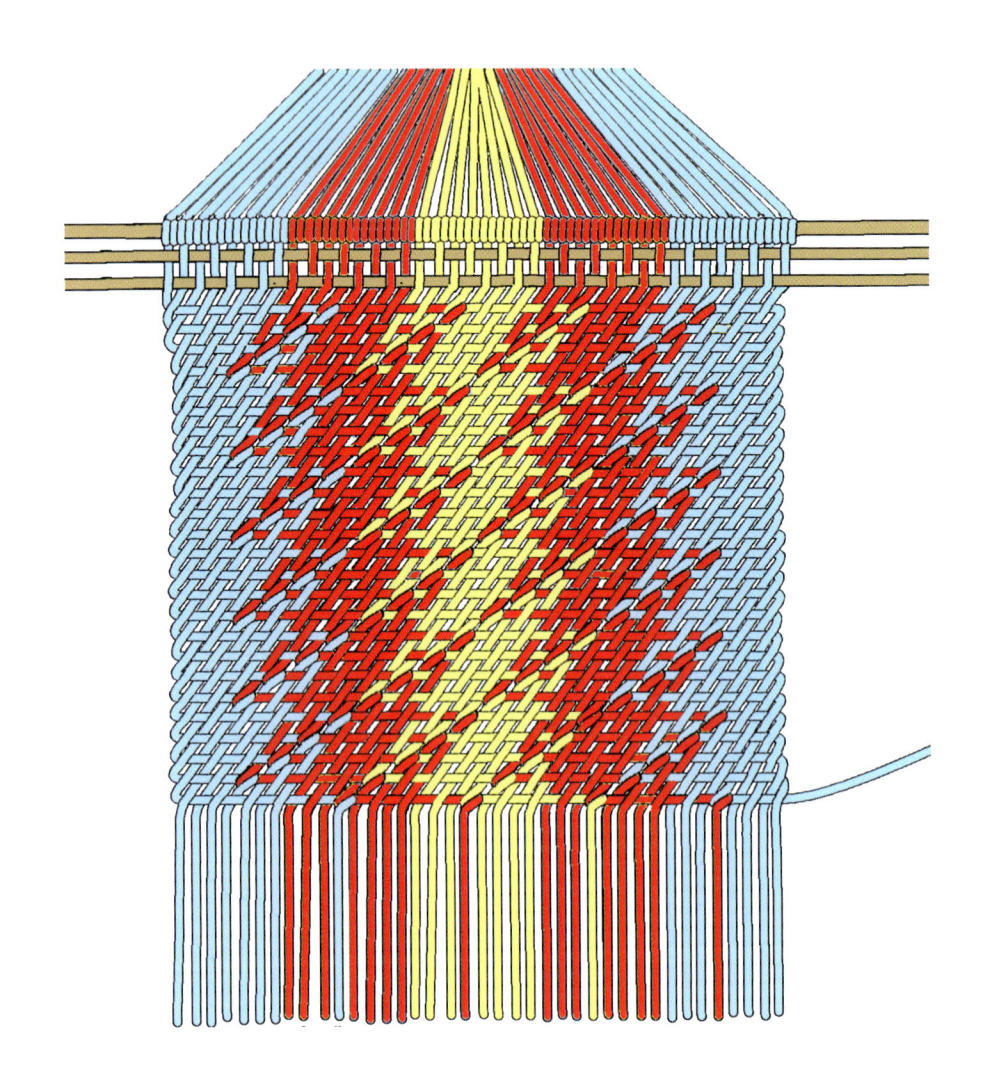

[46]

Double Lightning Pattern

The double lightning pattern is produced by combining two lightning patterns that are mirror images of each other.

The double lightning pattern is worked in a similar manner to the chevron pattern. To obtain the double lightning pattern, the weft strand changes color as it is pulled through the open shed. The color change is accomplished by interlocking a weft strand with a warp strand. When the interlocking takes place, the original weft strand becomes a warp strand and the warp strand that it is interlocked with it becomes the weft strand.

The setup for the double lightning pattern requires that the number of strands used for each lightning pattern be divisible by 2. The number of strands in each edge color is equal to or greater than one half the number of strands for each lightning pattern. The number of strands for the center color must be an even number greater than the number of strands used for the lightning pattern.

In the example shown here there are six strands used for each lightning pattern, five for each of the edge colors and twelve for the center color.

[STEP 1]
Set up the headstick as shown and pick up the shed. The two sides must be mirror images of each other.

[STEP 2]
The first weft strand is the strand that is to the left of the middle. Pull the first weft strand to the right through the open shed to the center of the right lightning color. Hook weft strand over headstick.

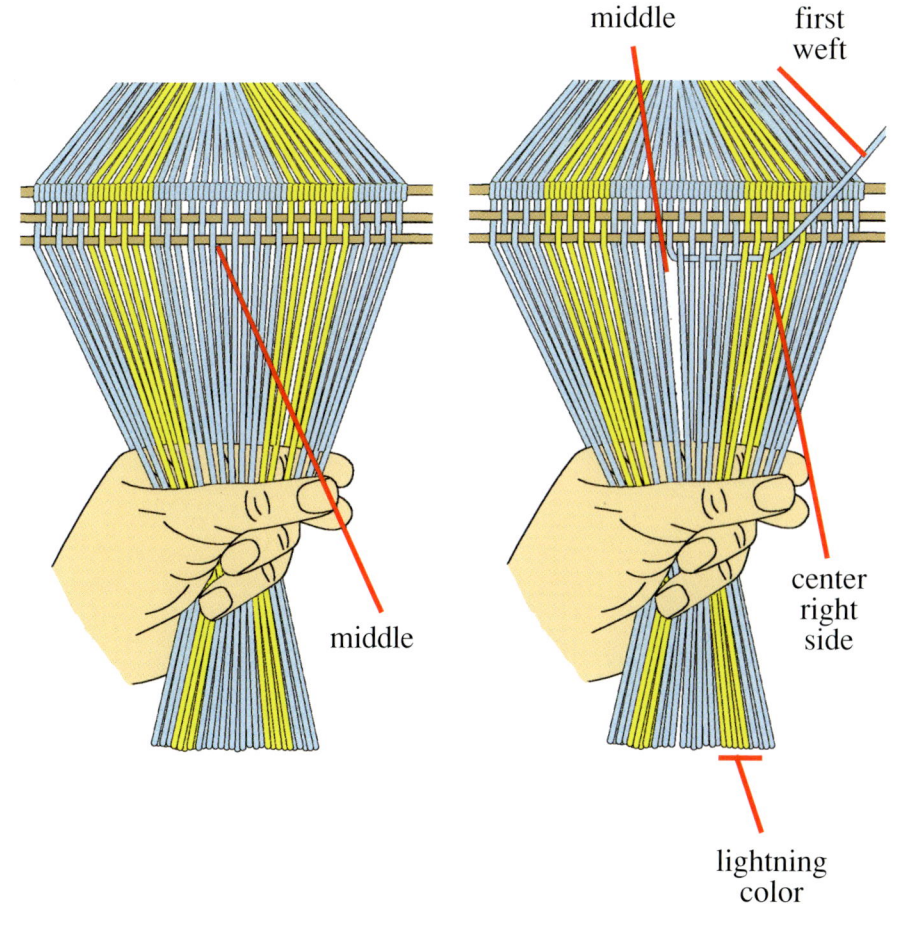

middle

first weft

middle

center right side

lightning color

[47]

[STEP 3]

Interlock the first weft strand and the warp strand that is to the left of the center of the lightning color. The warp strand that was to the left of the center of the lightning color is now the second weft strand. Pull the second weft strand to the right through the open shed to the edge color warp strand that is one half the number of lightning color strands. Hook weft strand over headstick.

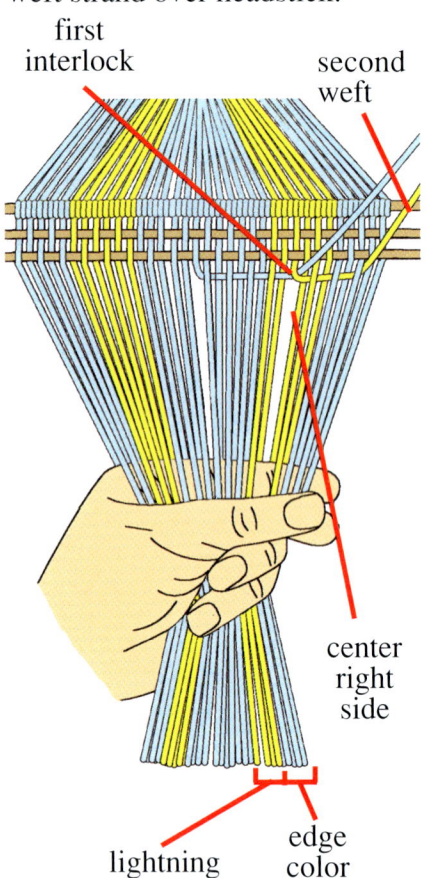

[STEP 4]

Interlock the second weft strand and the edge color warp strand that is to the left of the second weft strand. The interlocked edge warp strand becomes the third weft strand. Pull the third weft strand through the rest of the open shed and hook it over the headstick.

[STEP 5]

Turn the first and second weft strands down so that they return to the warp bundle.

[STEP 6]

The fourth weft strand is the strand that is to the right of the middle. Pull the fourth weft strand to the left through the open shed to the center of the left lightning color.

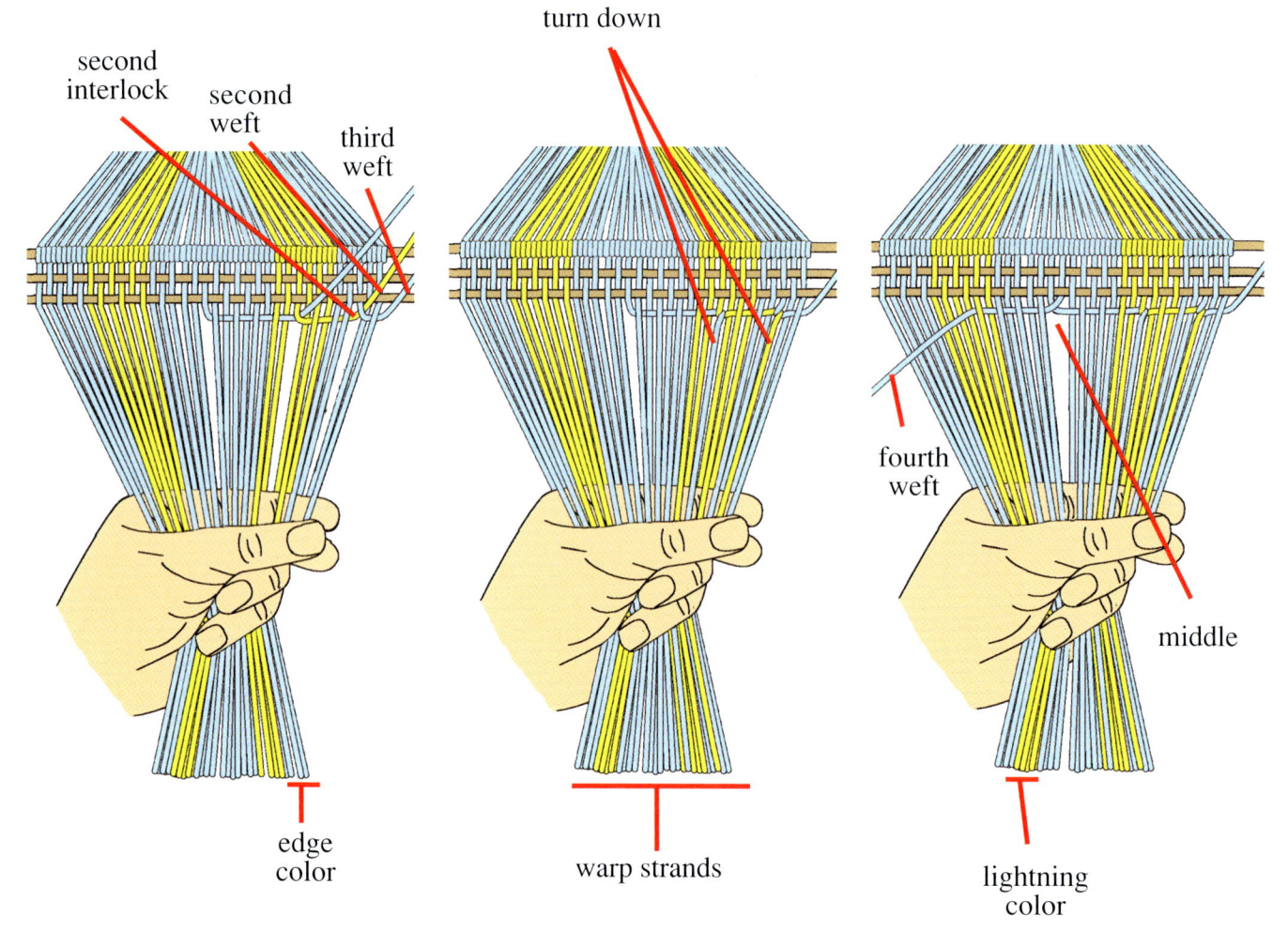

[48]

[STEP 7]
Interlock the fourth weft strand and the warp strand that is to the right of the center of the lightning color. The warp strand that was to the right of the center of the lightning color is now the fifth weft strand. Pull the fifth weft strand to the left through the open shed to left edge color warp strand that is one half the number of lightning color strands.

[STEP 8]
Interlock the fifth weft strand and the edge color warp strand that is one half the number of lightning color strands. The interlocked edge warp strand becomes the sixth weft strand. Pull the sixth weft strand through the rest of the open shed and hook it over the headstick.

[STEP 9]
Return the fourth and fifth weft strands to the warp bundle.

[STEP 10]
Reverse the shed by transferring the warp strands one at a time to the right index finger so that the warp strands that were up in the shed are down and the warp strands that were down in the shed are up.

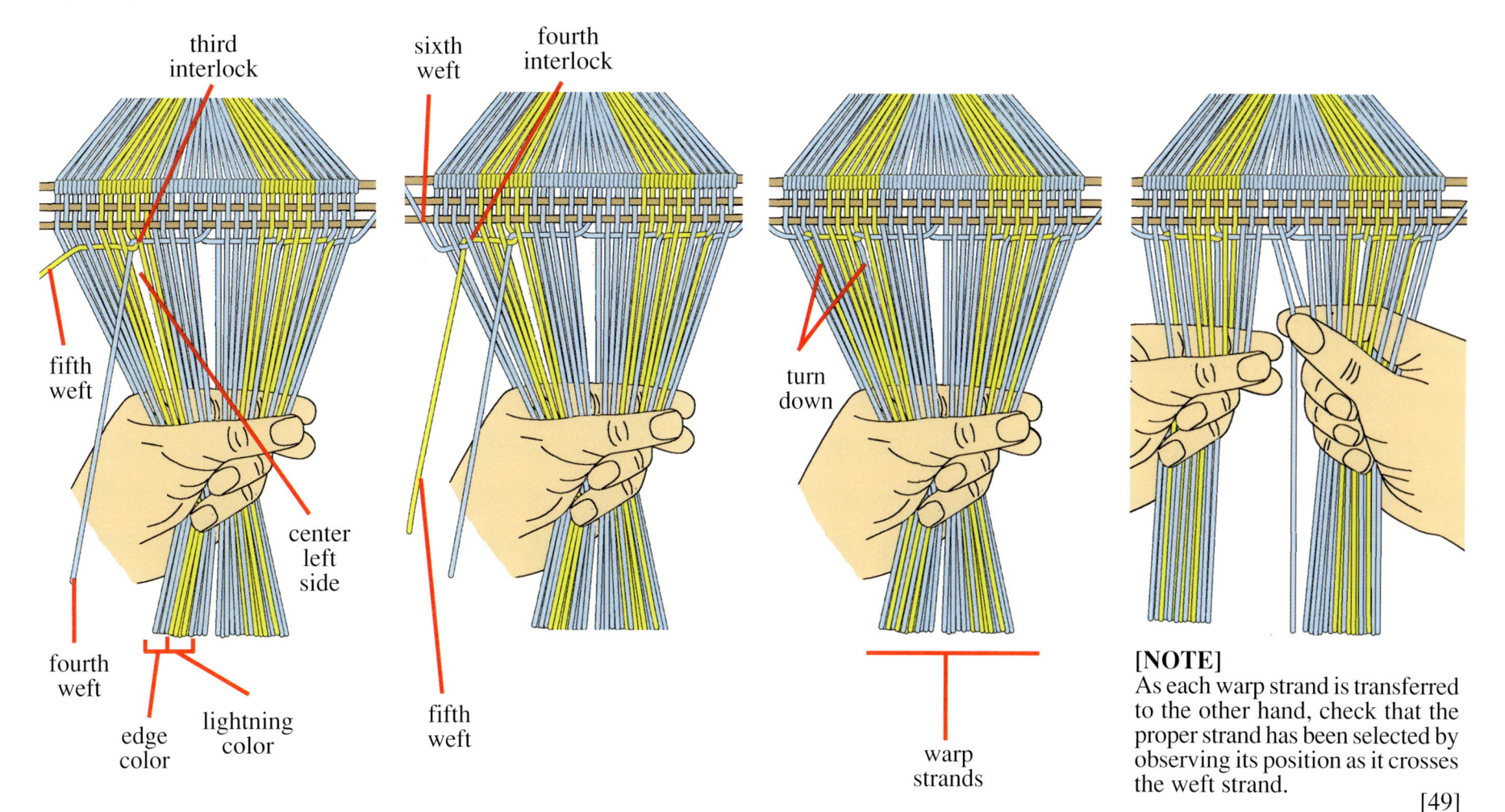

[NOTE]
As each warp strand is transferred to the other hand, check that the proper strand has been selected by observing its position as it crosses the weft strand.

[49]

[STEP 11]

Set the weft strands in place by pulling the two layers of the shed in opposite directions.

[STEP 12]

The first weft strand of the next row is the strand that is to the left of the middle. Pull the first weft strand to the right through the open shed to the left of the first interlock of the previous row. Hook this weft strand over the headstick.

[STEP 13]

Interlock the first weft strand and the warp strand that is to the left of the first interlock in the previous row. This strand is now the second weft strand. Pull the second weft strand to the right through the open shed to the warp strand that is to the left of the second interlock in the previous row. Hook this weft strand over the headstick.

[STEP 14]

Interlock the second weft strand and the edge color warp strand that is to the left of the second interlock in the previous row. The interlocked edge warp strand becomes the third warp strand. Pull the third weft strand through the rest of the open shed and hook it over the headstick.

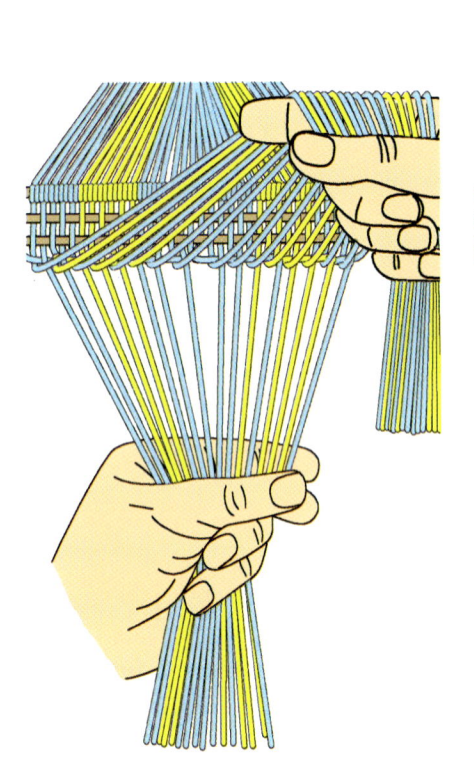

[NOTE]

Check to see if all strands are properly tightened.

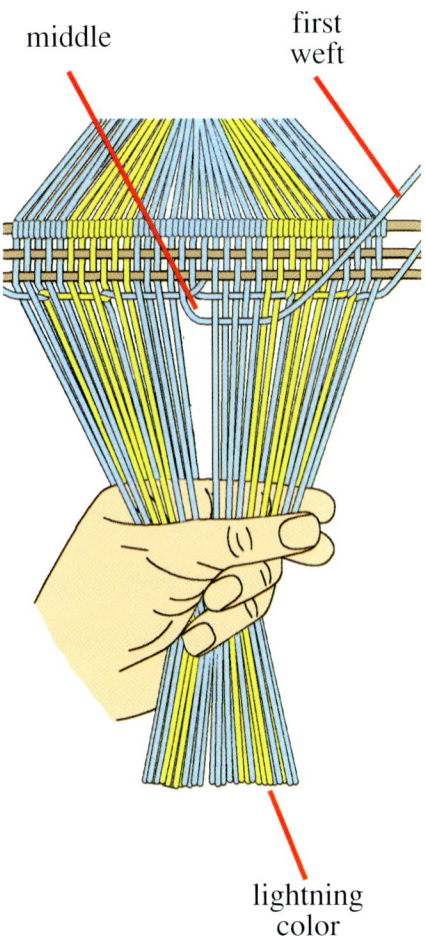

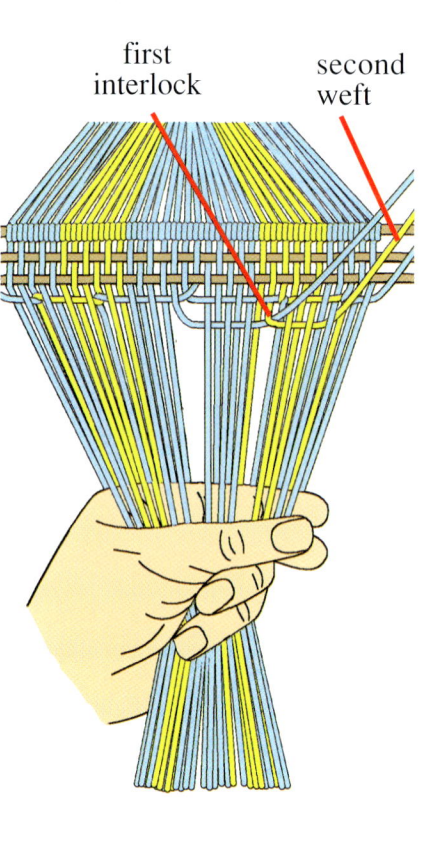

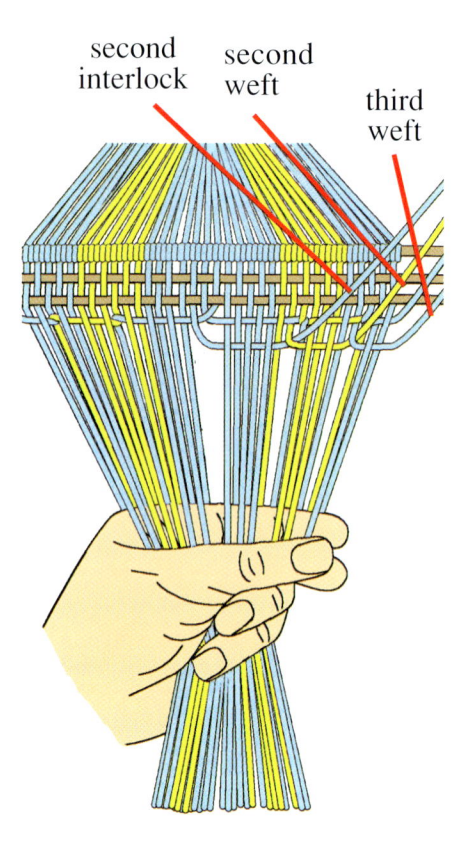

[50]

[STEP 15]
Turn the first and second weft strands of the present row and the third weft strand from the previous row down so that they are returned to the warp bundle.

[STEP 16]
The fourth weft strand is the strand that is to the right of the middle. Pull the fourth weft strand to the left through the open shed to the right of the third interlock in the previous row.

[STEP 17]
Interlock the fourth weft strand and the warp strand that is to the right of the third interlock in the previous row. This warp strand is now the fifth weft strand. Pull the fifth weft strand to the left through the open shed to the right of the fourth interlock in the previous row.

[STEP 18]
Interlock the fifth weft strand and the edge color warp strand that is to the right of the fourth interlock in the previous row. The interlocked edge warp strand becomes the sixth weft strand. Pull the sixth weft strand through the rest of the open shed and hook it over the headstick.

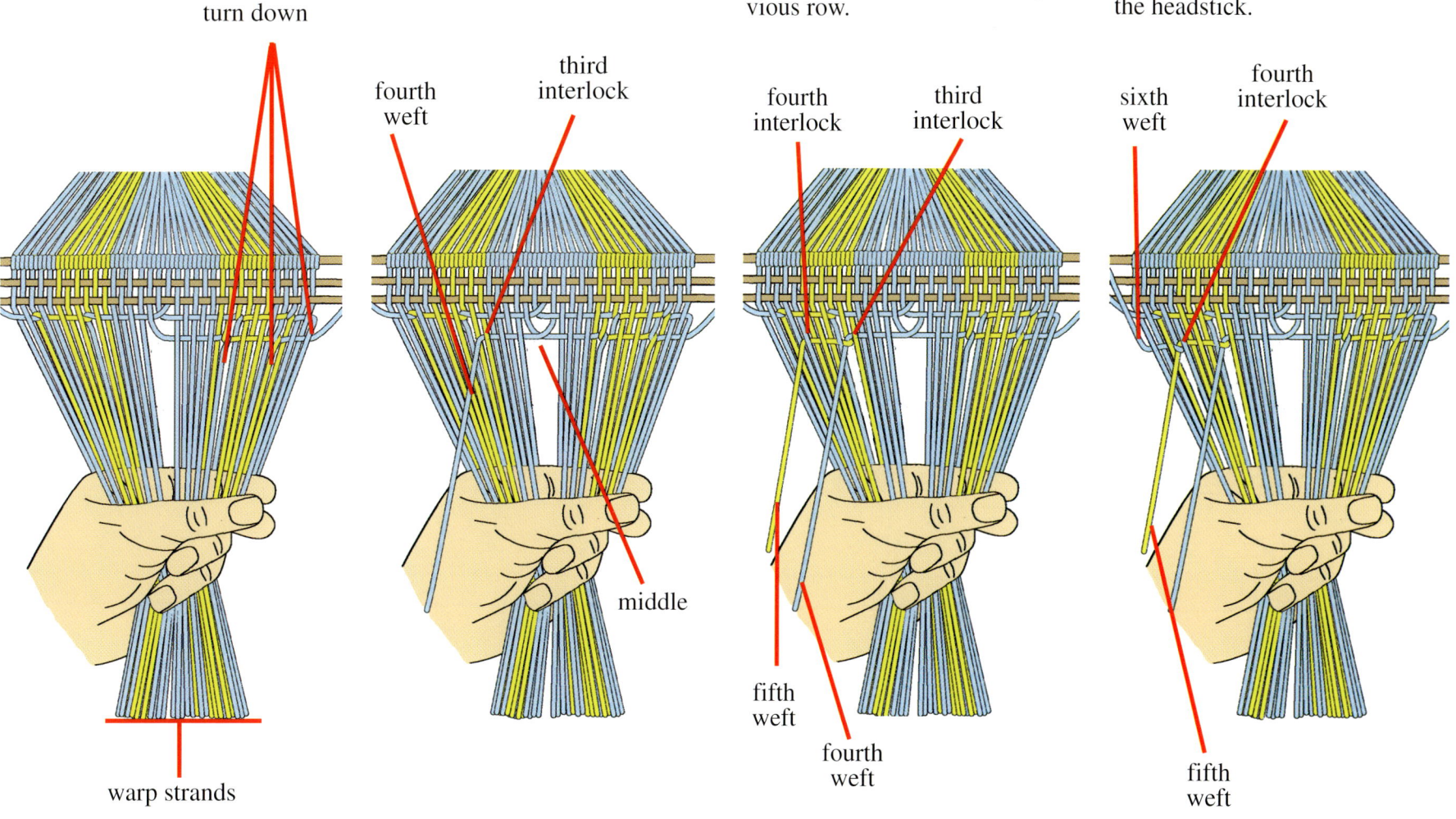

[51]

[STEP 19]

Turn the fourth and fifth weft strands of the present row and the sixth weft strand from the previous row down so that they are returned to the warp bundle.

[STEP 20]

Continue to weave in this manner. When the original strand arrangement has been reestablished, start the pattern over. Repeat the pattern until the desired length is reached.

Double Lightning Example:

Double Lightning Over Two/Under Two Example:

[NOTE]

If an over two/under two setup is used the two lightning strokes are mirror images of each other. (See Chevron Pattern, Over Two/Under Two page 32.)

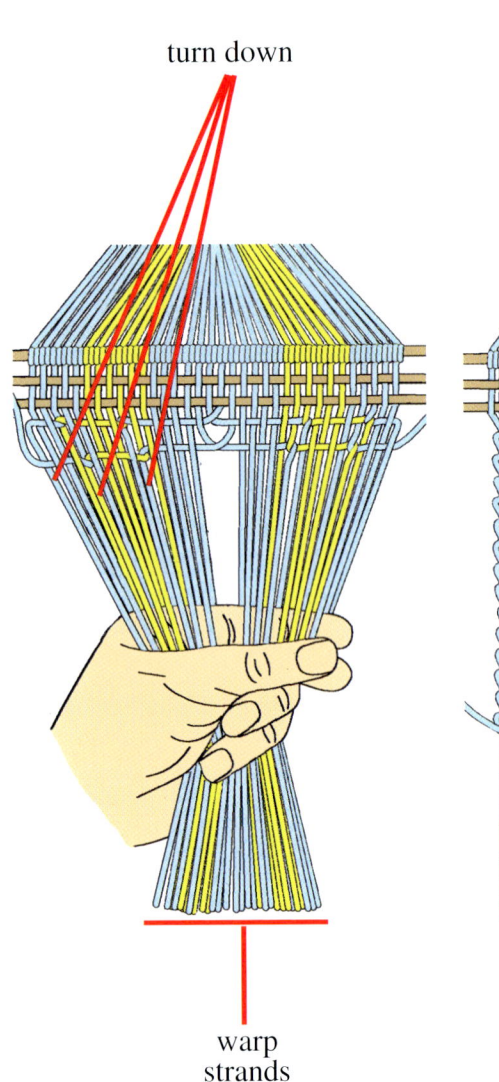

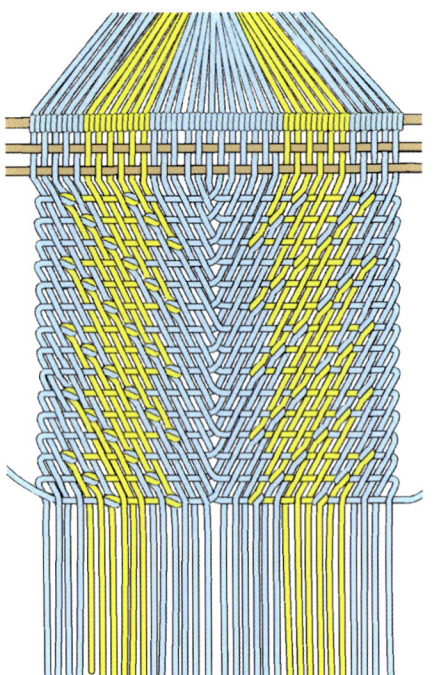

[52]

Arrowhead Pattern Over/under Weave (Point Down)

The arrowhead pattern is named for the arrowhead shaped pattern that develops when two or more colors are used.

The arrowhead pattern is a variation of the double lightning pattern. The center color band and the edge color bands meet at the center to form the point of the arrowhead.

The setup for the arrowhead pattern requires the center color band to have an even number of strands. The number of strands in each edge color band must be equal to or greater than one half the number of strands in the center color band.

[STEP 1]
Cast the required number of strands of yarn on to the headstick. Use clove hitches to tie the yarn in place. See (Part 1: Getting Started).

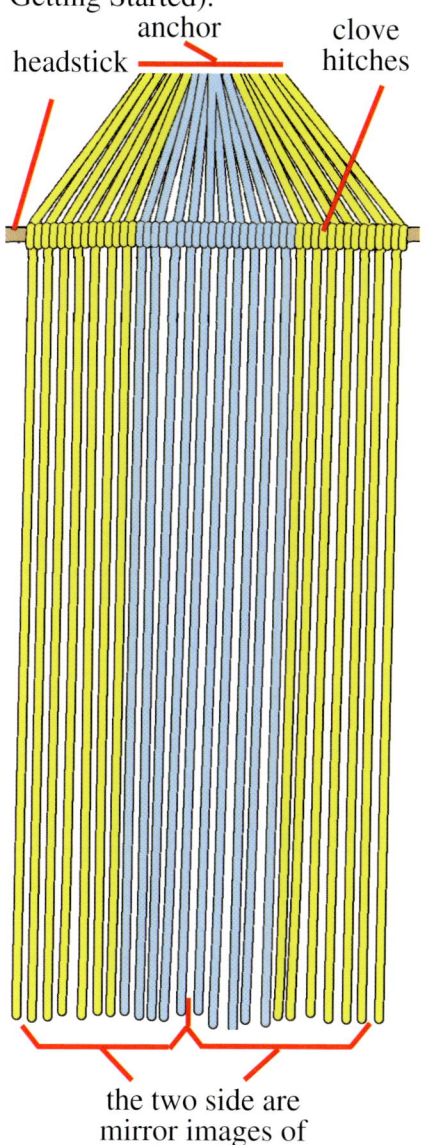

headstick — anchor — clove hitches

the two side are mirror images of each other

[STEP 2]
Set up the over/under weaving pattern of the shed with two smaller sticks.

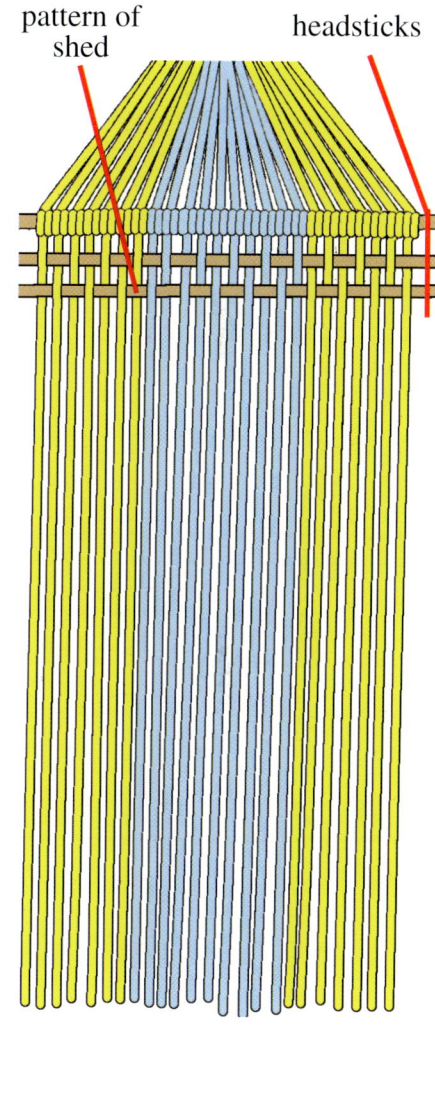

pattern of shed — headsticks

[53]

[STEP 3]
Pick up the shed. Use the index finger of the left hand to hold the shed open.

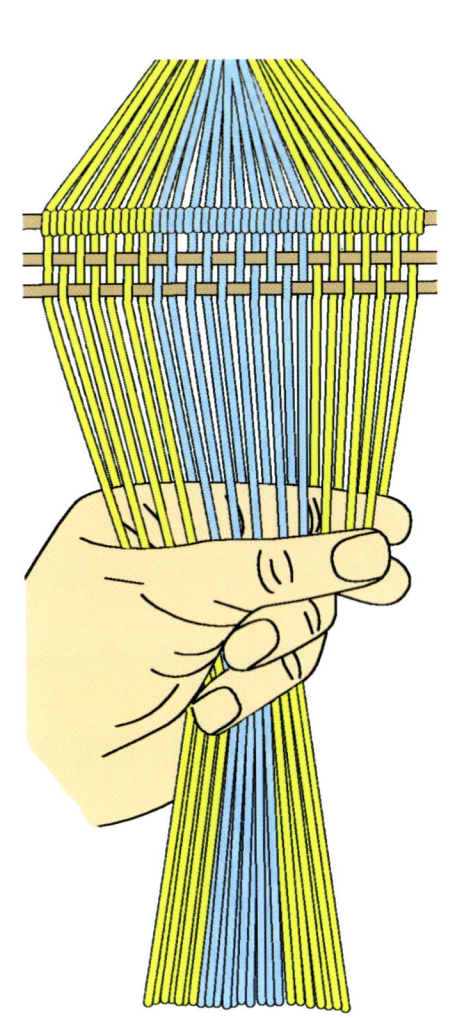

[STEP 4]
The first warp strand to the left of the middle becomes a weft strand when it is pulled to the right through the open shed. This weft strand is pulled through the open shed of the right hand color for one half the number of strands of the center color.

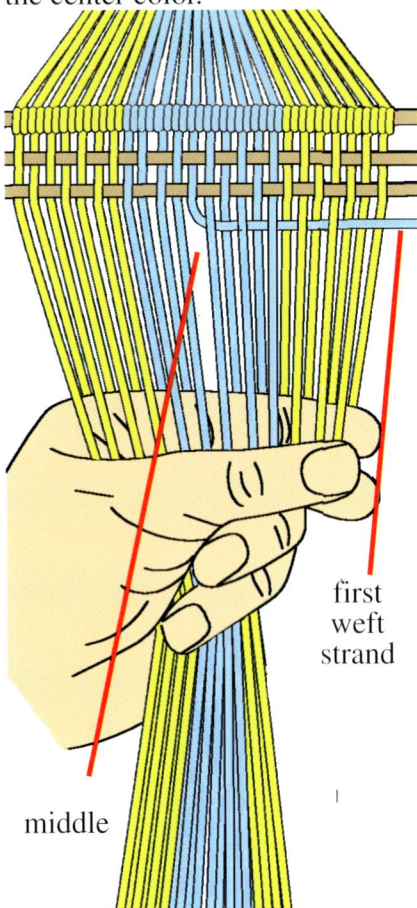

middle

first weft strand

[STEP 5]
Interlock the first weft strand and the warp strand that is 1/2 the number of center color strands into the right hand color.

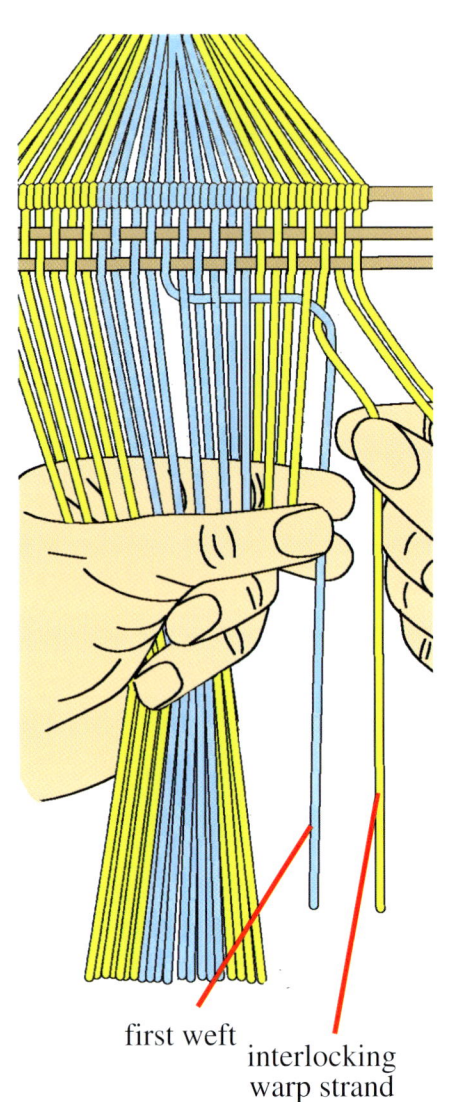

first weft

interlocking warp strand

[STEP 6]
When the interlocking warp strand is pulled through the remaining part of the open shed and hooked over headstick, it becomes the second weft strand. The first weft strand is returned to the bundle of warp strands.

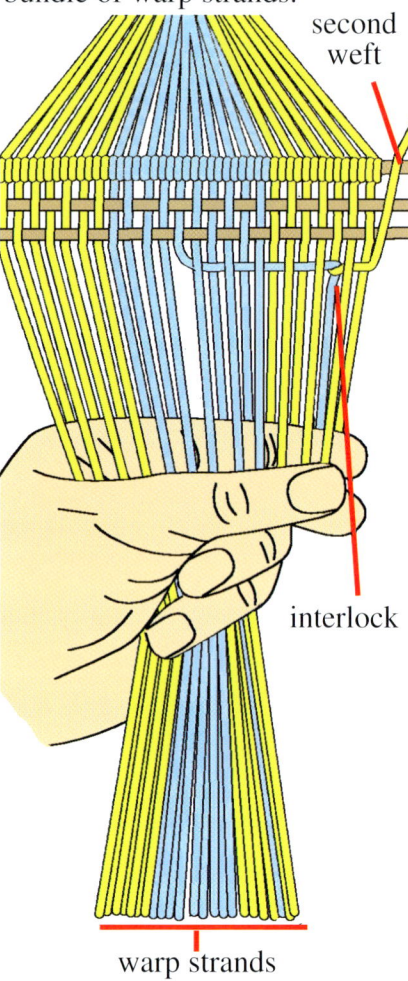

second weft

interlock

warp strands

[NOTE]
On this side of the pattern the interlocking warp strand is picked up from the bottom layer of the shed.

[54]

[STEP 7]

The first warp strand to the right of the middle becomes a weft strand when it is pulled to the left through the open shed. This weft strand is pulled through the open shed of the left hand color for one half the number of strands of the center color.

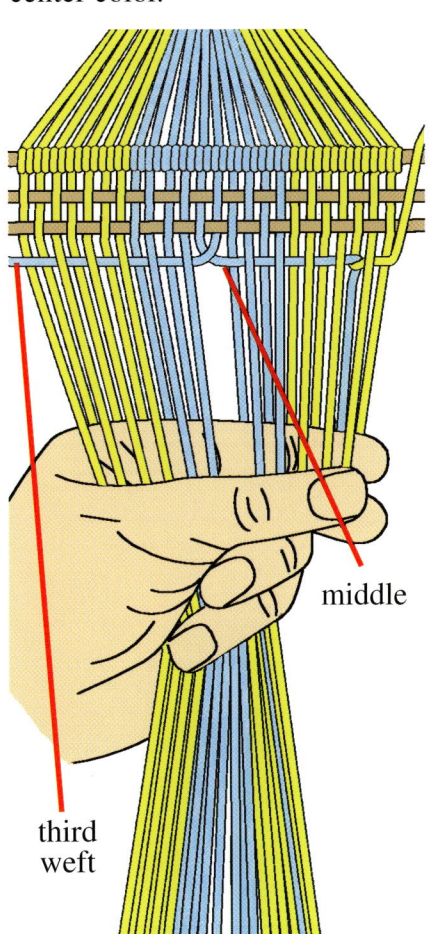

middle

third weft

[STEP 8]

Interlock the third weft strand and the warp strand that is 1/2 the number of center color strands into the left color.

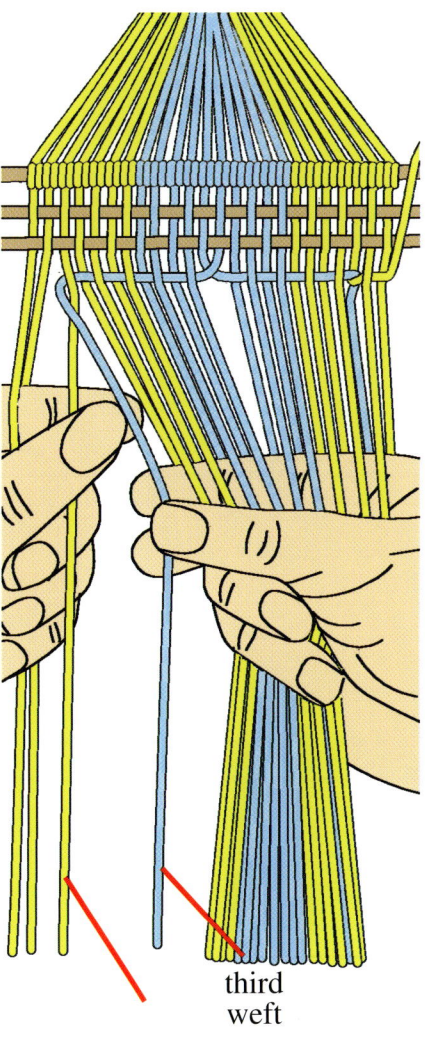

third weft

interlocking warp strand

[STEP 9]

When the interlocked warp strand is pulled through the remaining part of the open shed and hooked over headstick it becomes the fourth weft strand. The third weft strand is returned to the bundle of warp strands.

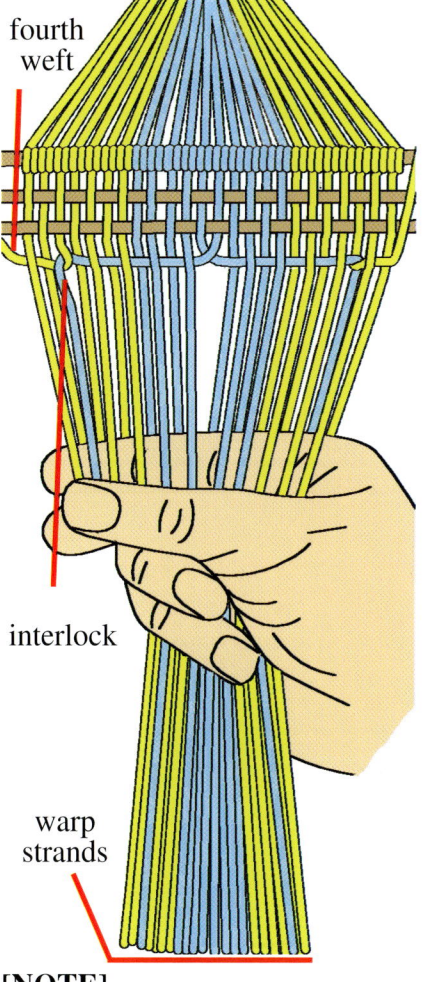

fourth weft

interlock

warp strands

[NOTE]
On this side of the pattern the interlocking warp strand is picked up from the top layer of the shed.

[STEP 10]

Reverse the shed by transferring the warp strands one at a time to the right index finger so that the warp strands that were up in the shed are down and the warp strands that were down in the shed are up.

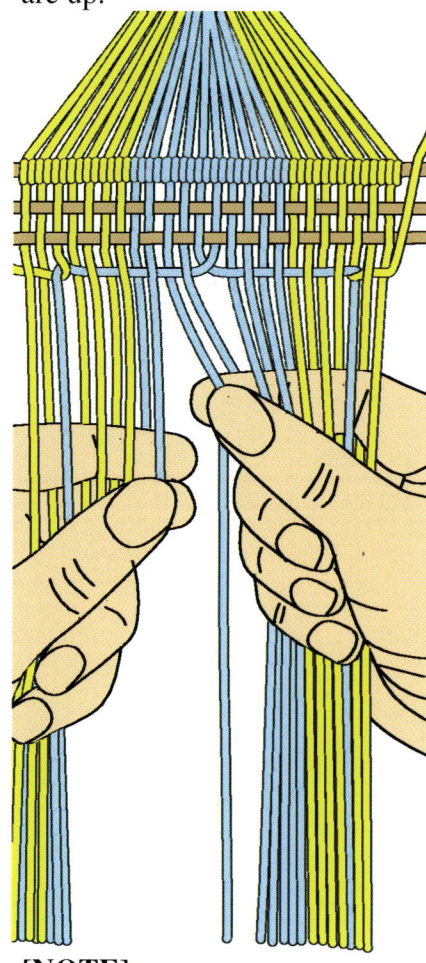

[NOTE]
As each warp strand is transferred to the other hand, check that the proper strand has been selected by observing its position as it crosses the weft strand.

[55]

[STEP 11]
Set the weft strands in place by pulling the two layers of the shed in opposite directions.

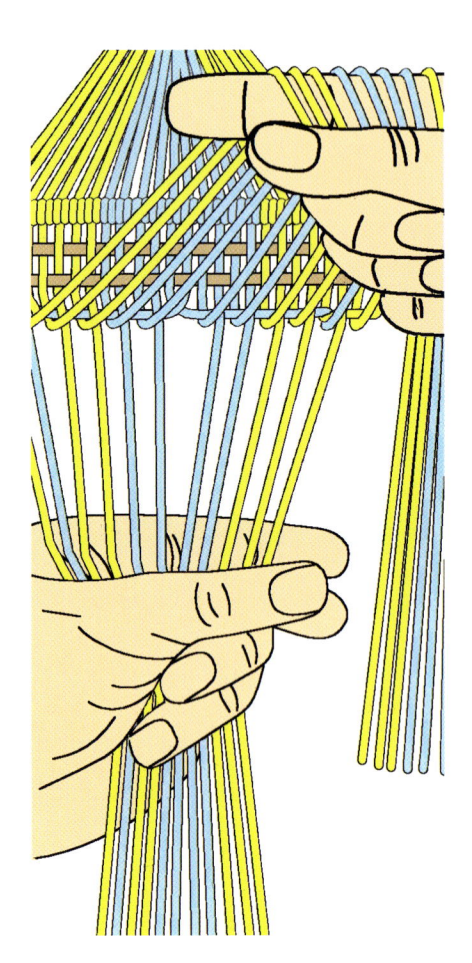

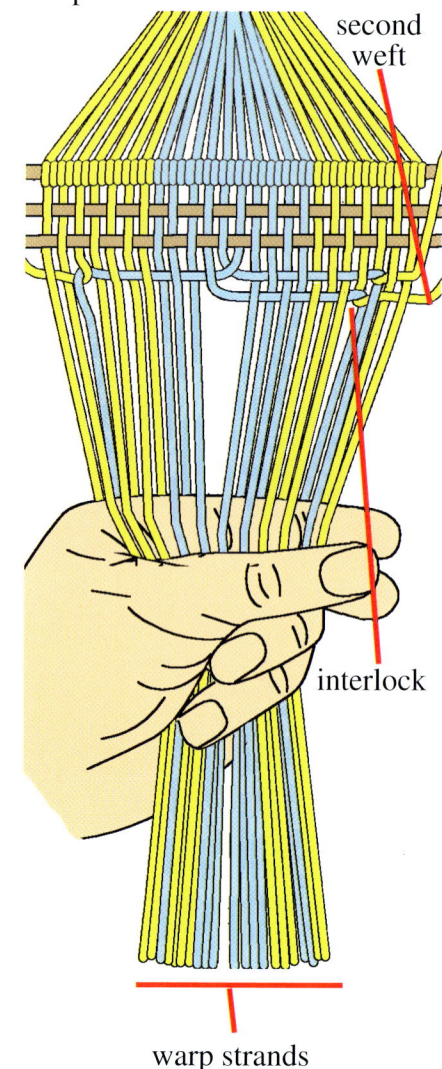

[NOTE]
Check to see if all strands are properly tightened.
[56]

[STEP 12]
Again the first warp strand to the left of the middle becomes a weft strand when it is pulled to the right through the open shed. This weft strand is pulled through the open shed to the left of the first interlock in the previous row.

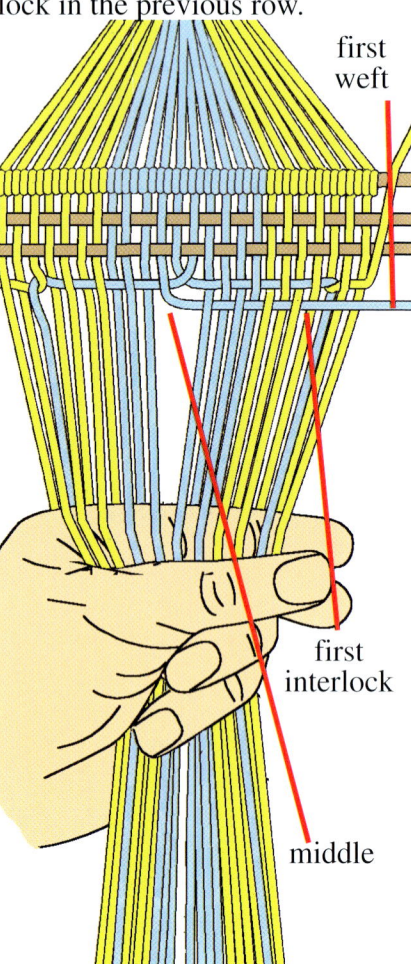

first weft

first interlock

middle

[STEP 13]
Interlock the first weft strand and the warp strand that is to the left of the first interlock.

first interlock

first weft

interlocking warp strand

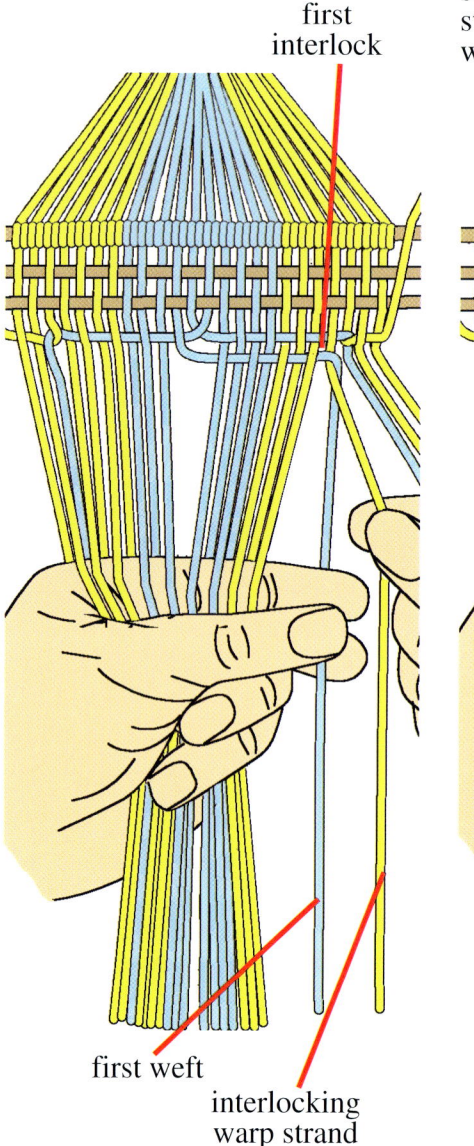

[STEP 14]
When the interlocked warp strand is pulled through the remaining part of the open shed and hooked over the headstick it becomes the second weft strand. The first weft strand is returned to the bundle of warp strands.

second weft

interlock

warp strands

[STEP 15]
Turn the last weft strand of the previous row down. This weft strand is now a warp strand again.

[STEP 16]
The first warp strand to the right of the middle becomes the third weft strand of this row when it is pulled to the left through the open shed of the left hand color to the strand that is to the right of the second interlock in the previous row.

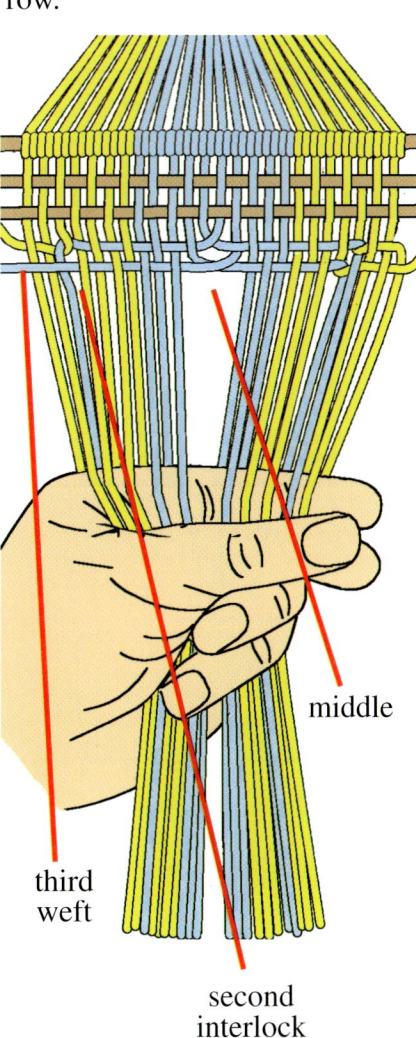

[STEP 17]
Interlock the third weft strand and the warp strand that is to the right of the second interlock in the previous row.

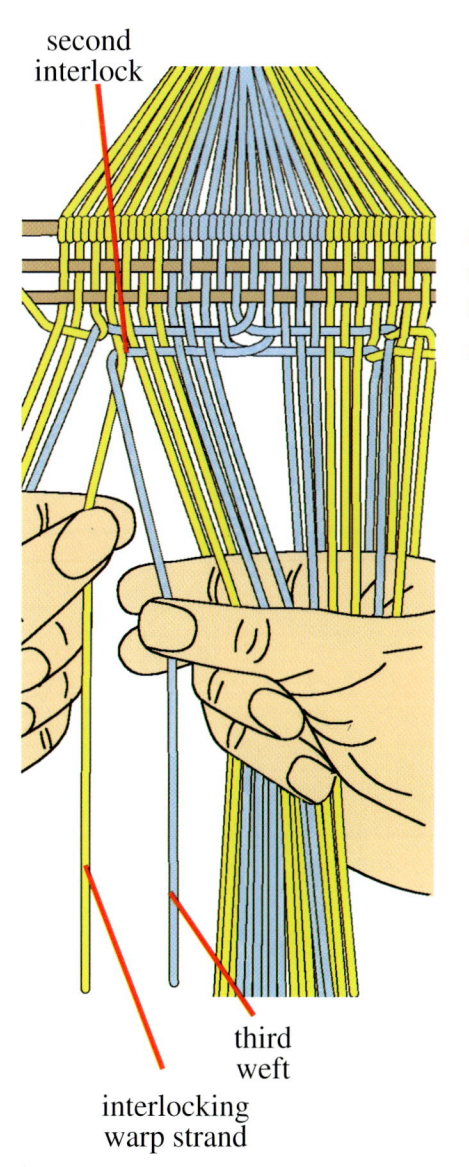

[STEP 18]
When the interlocked warp strand is pulled through the remaining part of the open shed and hooked over the headstick, it becomes the fourth weft strand of this row. The third weft strand is returned to the bundle of warp strands.

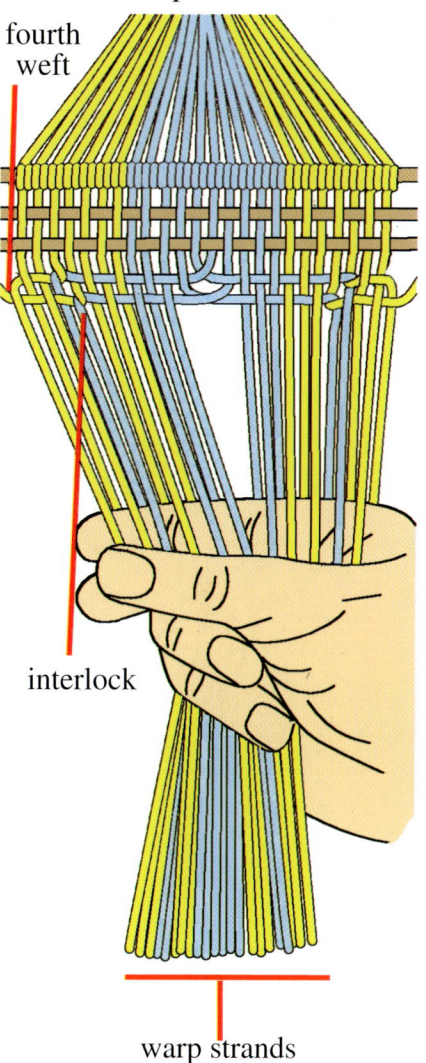

[57]

[STEP 19]
Turn the last weft strand of the previous row down. This weft strand is now a warp strand again.

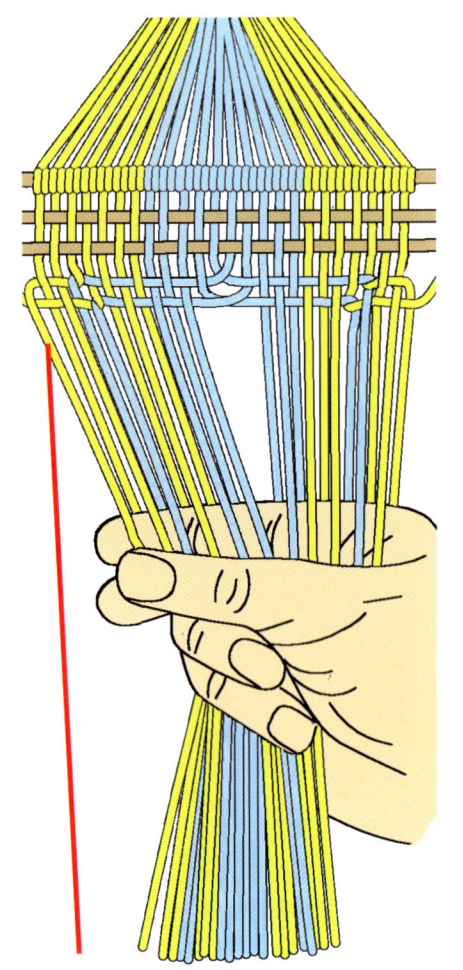

turn down last weft strand previous row

[STEP 20]
Reverse the shed by transferring the warp strands one at a time to the right index finger so that the warp strands that were up in the shed are down and the warp strands that were down in the shed are up.

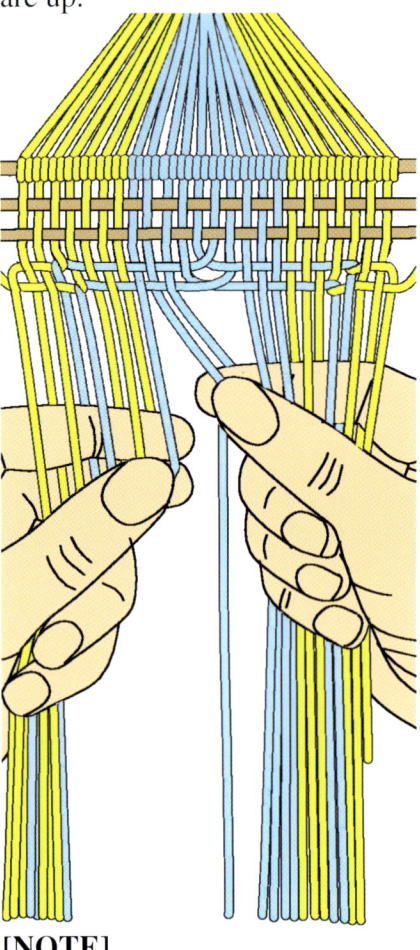

[NOTE]
As each warp strand is transferred to the other hand, check that the proper strand has been selected by observing its position as it crosses the weft strand.

[STEP 21]
Set the weft strands in place by pulling the two layers of the shed in opposite directions.

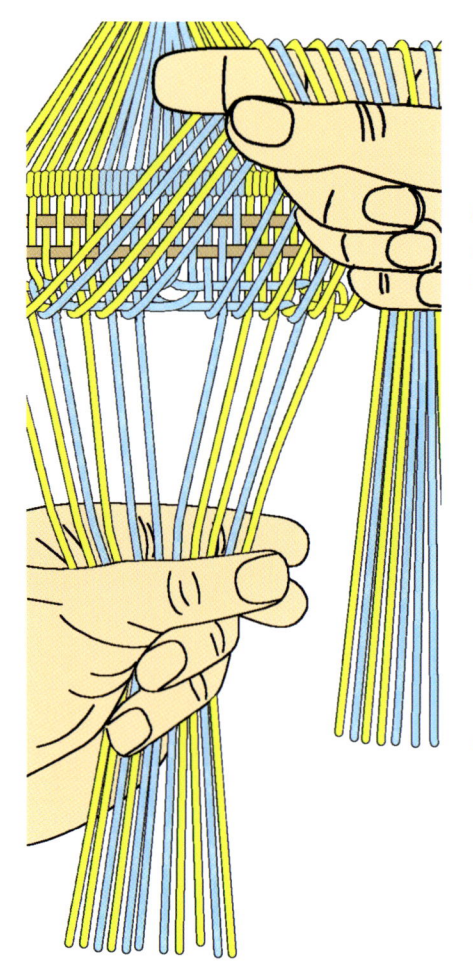

[NOTE]
Check to see if all strands are properly tightened.

[STEP 22]
Continue to weave in this manner. When the original strand arrangement has been reestablished, start the pattern over. Repeat the pattern until the desired length is reached.

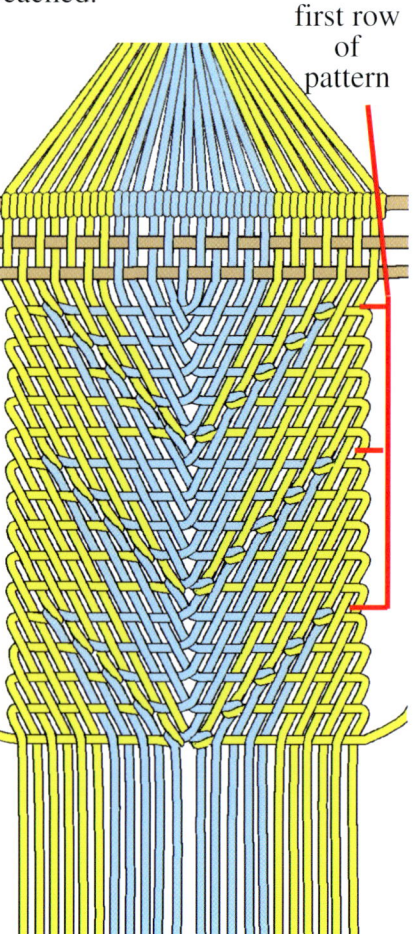

first row of pattern

[NOTE]
The center color band and the edge color bands meet to form the point of the arrowhead. When the point is formed the original strand arrangement is reestablished.

[58]

[STEP 23]
Turn the work around and reattach it to your anchor.

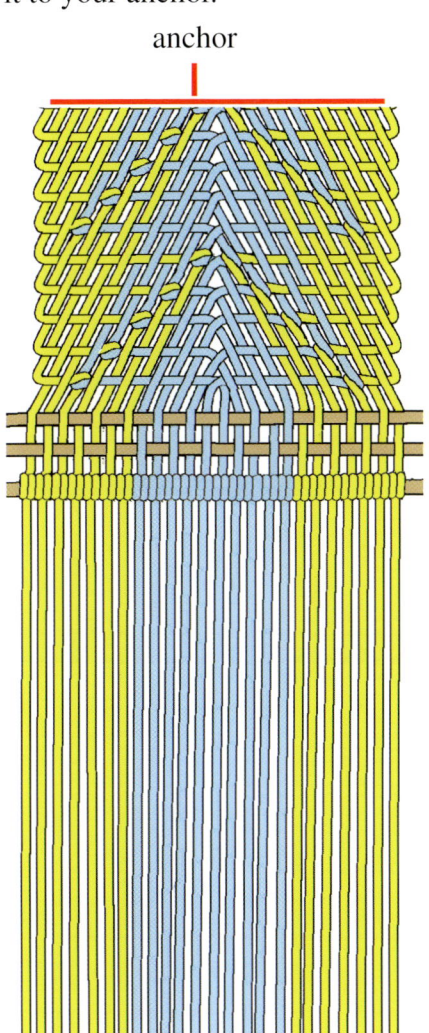

anchor

[STEP 24]
Remove the headsticks and pick up the shed.

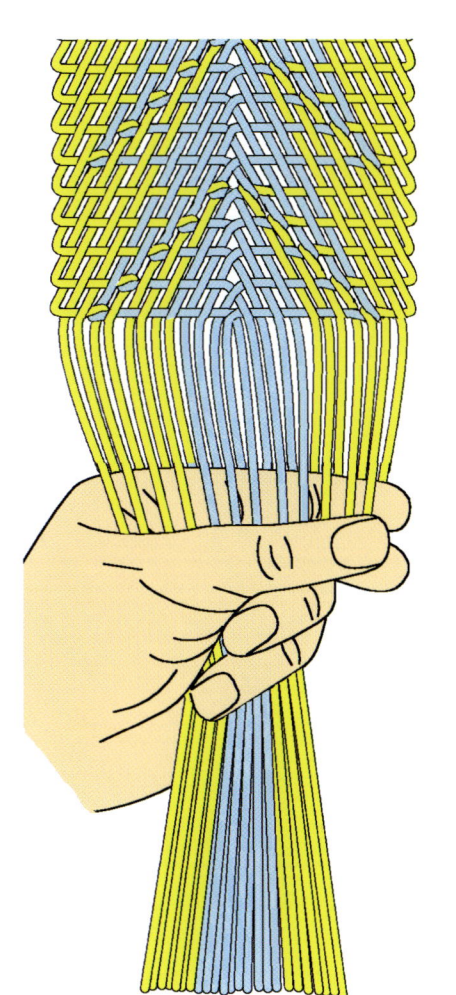

[STEP 25]
Set the weft strands in place by pulling the two layers of the shed in opposite directions.

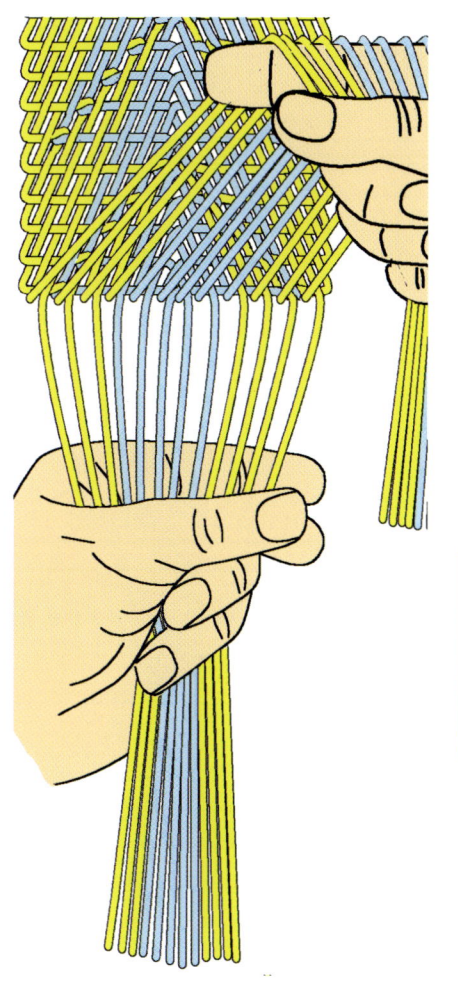

[STEP 26]
The first warp strand to the left of the middle becomes a weft strand when it is pulled to the right through the open shed. This weft strand is pulled through the open shed of the right hand color for one half the number of strands of the center color.

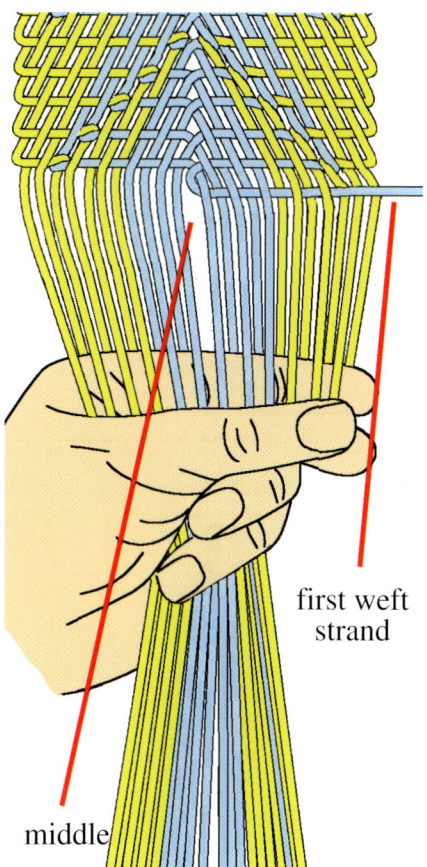

first weft strand

middle

[NOTE]
Check to see if all strands are properly tightened.

[59]

[STEP 27]
Interlock the first weft strand and the warp strand that is 1/2 the number of center color strands into the right color.

[STEP 28]
When the interlocked warp strand is pulled through the remaining part of the open shed and hooked over headstick, it becomes the second weft strand. The first weft strand is returned to the bundle of warp strands.

[STEP 29]
The first warp strand to the right of the middle becomes the third weft strand when it is pulled to the left through the open shed. This weft strand is pulled through the open shed of the left hand color for one half the number of strands of the center color.

[STEP 30]
Interlock the third weft strand and the warp strand that is 1/2 the number of the center color strands into the left color.

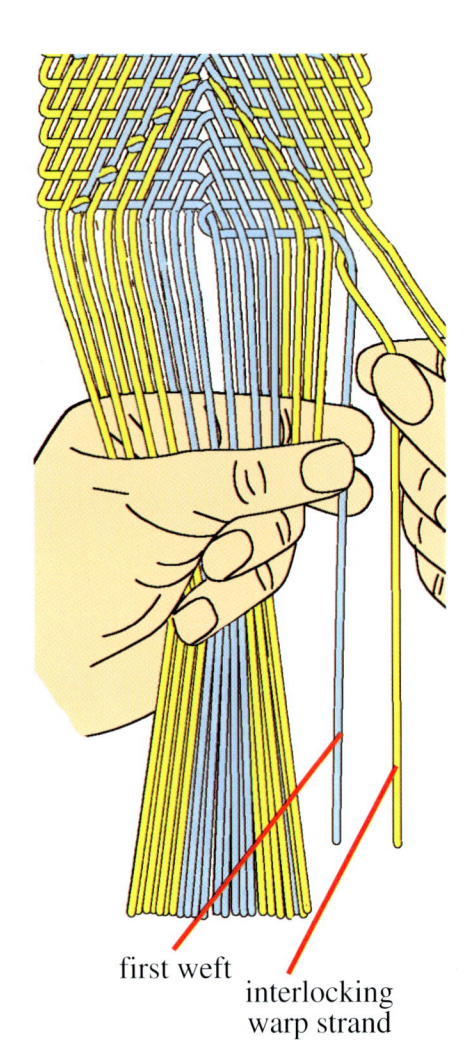

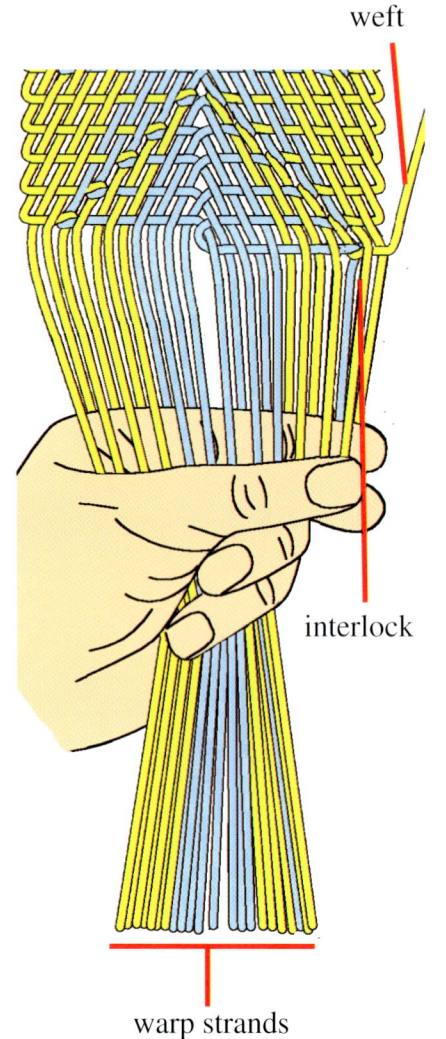

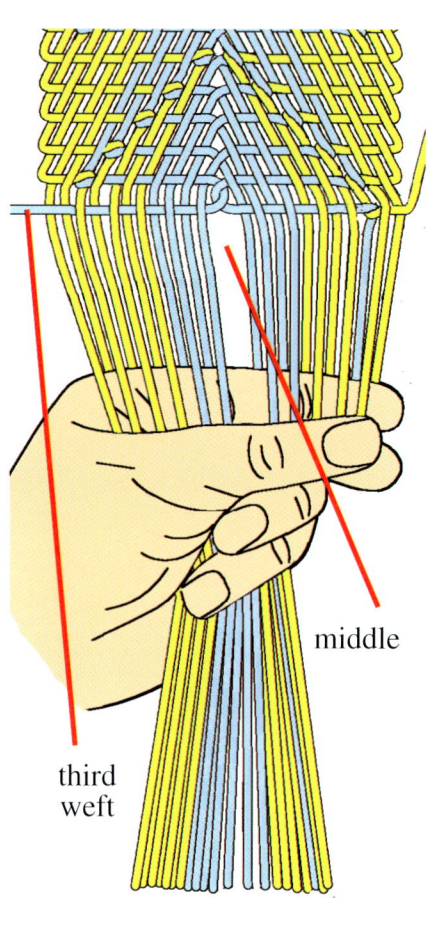

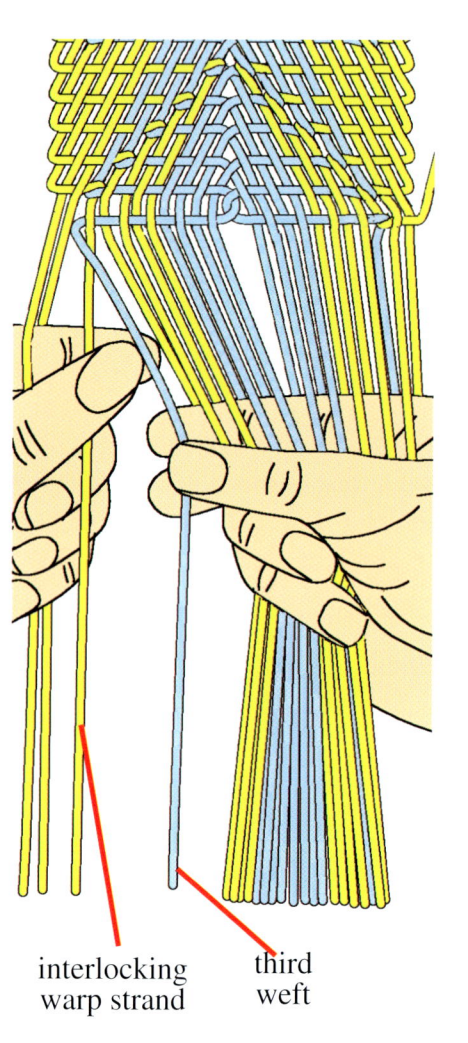

[60]

[STEP 31]

When the interlocking warp strand is pulled through the remaining part of the open shed and hooked over headstick it becomes the fourth weft strand. The third weft strand is returned to the bundle of warp strands.

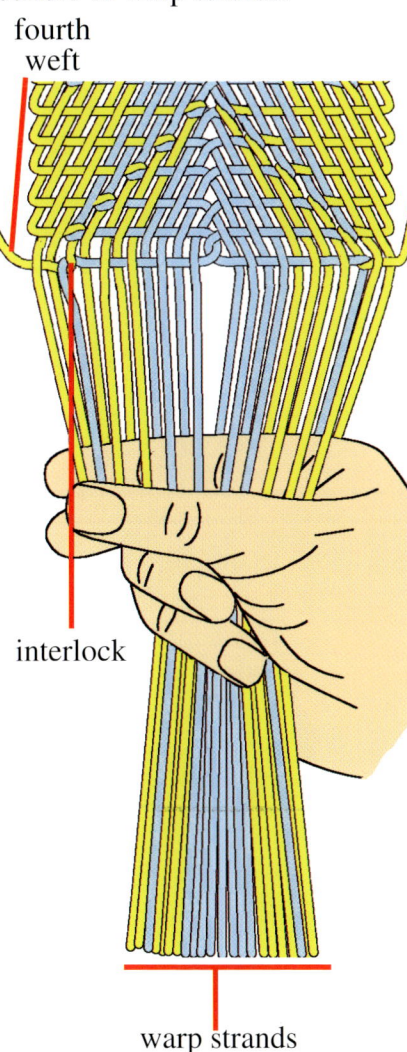

fourth weft

interlock

warp strands

[STEP 32]

Continue to weave until the desired length is reached.

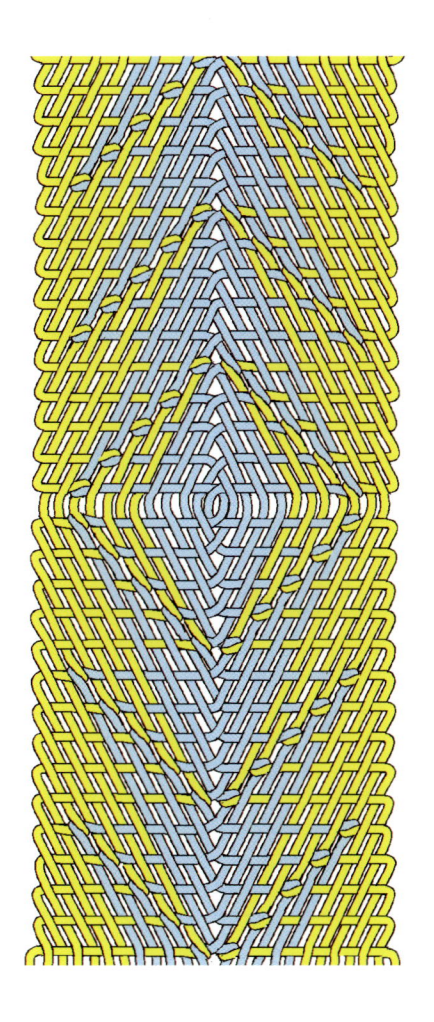

[NOTE]

Notice the diamond pattern formed by the base to base arrangement of the center arrowheads.

Arrowhead Pattern Over/under Weave (Point Down) Example:

Arrowhead Pattern Over/under Weave (Point Down) Center Example:

[61]

Arrowhead Pattern Over/under Weave (Point Down) Variation 1

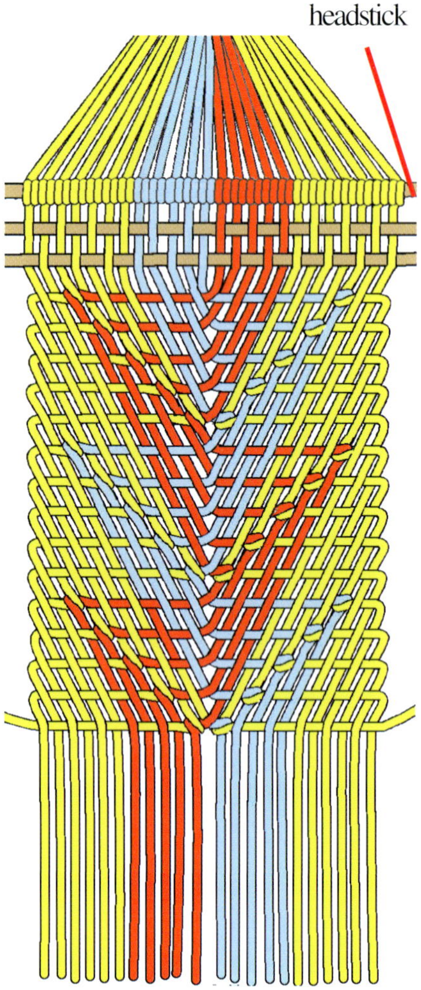

headstick

[NOTE]
Arrange the colored strands on the headstick as shown above. Then follow the weaving instructions shown in STEP 3 through STEP 22.

[62]

Arrowhead Pattern Over/under Weave (Point Down) Variation 1 Example:

Arrowhead Pattern Over/under Weave (Point Down) Variation 2

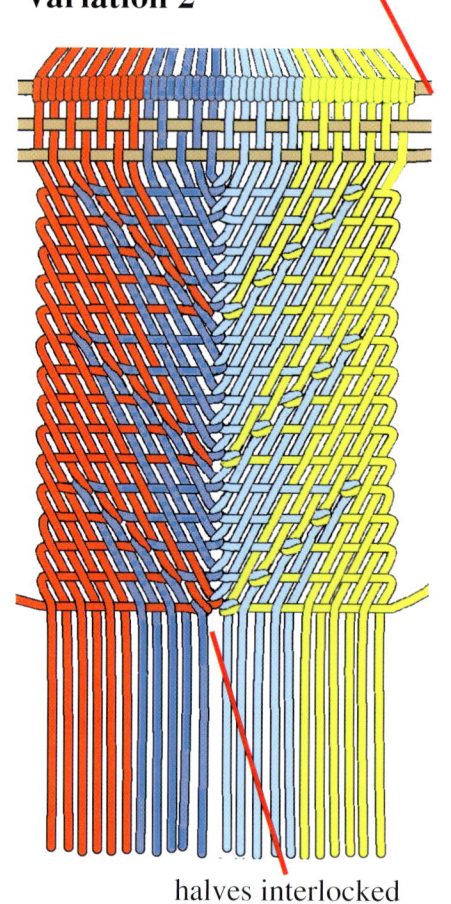

headstick

halves interlocked at center

[NOTE]
Arrange the colored strands on the headstick as shown above. Then follow the weaving instructions shown in **[STEP 3]** through **[STEP 22]**, except the two halves of the pattern are formed by interlocking them at the center of the work.

Arrowhead Pattern Over/under Weave (Point Down) Variation 2 Example:

Arrowhead Pattern Over/under Weave (Point Down) Bead Accent Example:

Procedure
Follow the directions [STEP 1] and [STEP 2] for Arrowhead (point down). Then add beads to the center two strands and the two outside strands of the arrow point color.

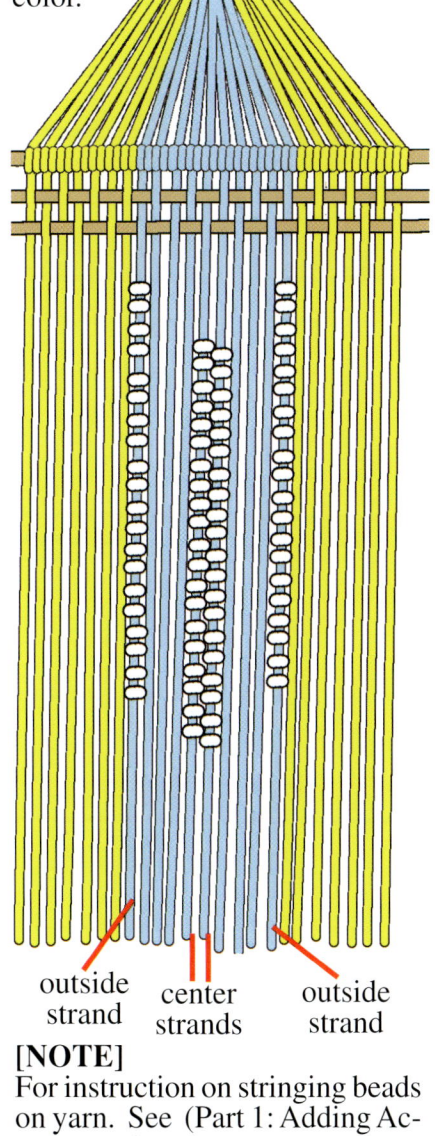

outside strand   center strands   outside strand

[NOTE]
For instruction on stringing beads on yarn. See (Part 1: Adding Accent Beads).

[NOTE]
The red strands show the path of the strands that have the beads on them.

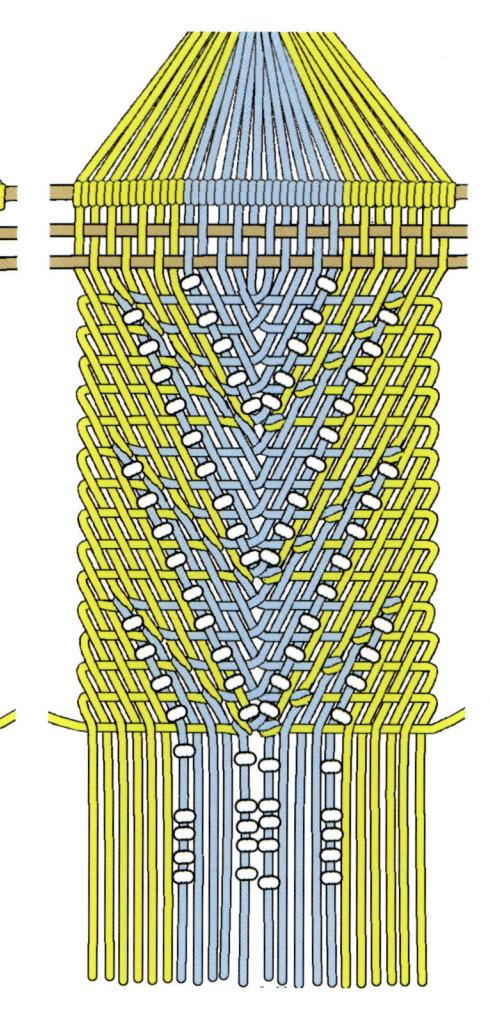

[NOTE]
Follow the directions for weaving the arrowhead pattern but place the beads as shown.

[63]

Arrowhead Pattern Over/under Weave (Point Up)

The arrowhead pattern is named for the arrowhead shaped pattern that develops when two or more colors are used.

In this set of instructions the pattern is worked from the edge toward the center. The result is a series of arrowheads pointing up (toward the center of the work piece).

The setup for the arrowhead pattern requires the center color band to have an even number of strands. The number of strands in the edge color bands must be equal to or greater than one half the number of strands in the center color band.

[64]

[STEP 1]
Cast the required number of strands of yarn on to the headstick. Use clove hitches to tie the yarn in place. See (Part 1: Getting Started).

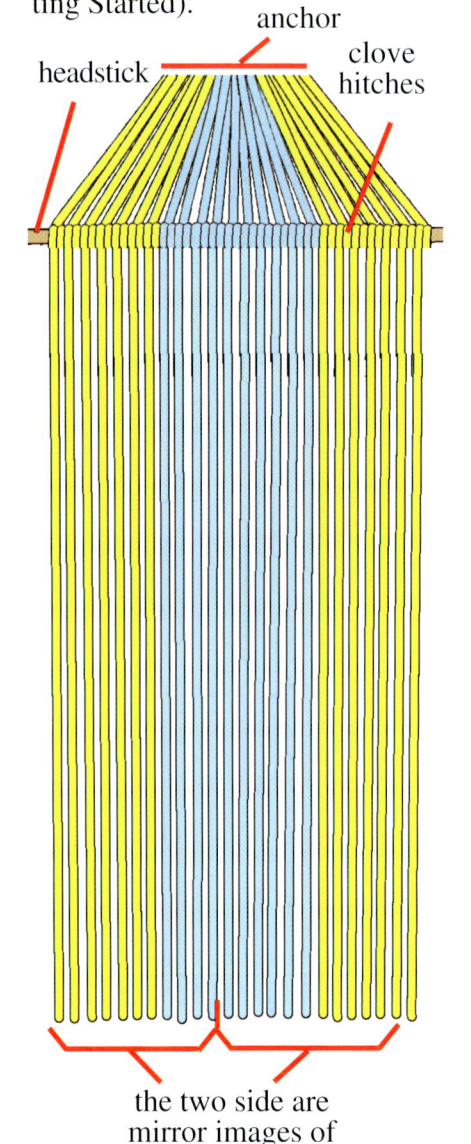

headstick — anchor — clove hitches

the two side are mirror images of each other

[STEP 2]
Use two smaller sticks to set up the weaving pattern.

pattern of shed — headsticks

[STEP 3]
Pick up the shed. Use the index finger of the left hand to hold the shed open.

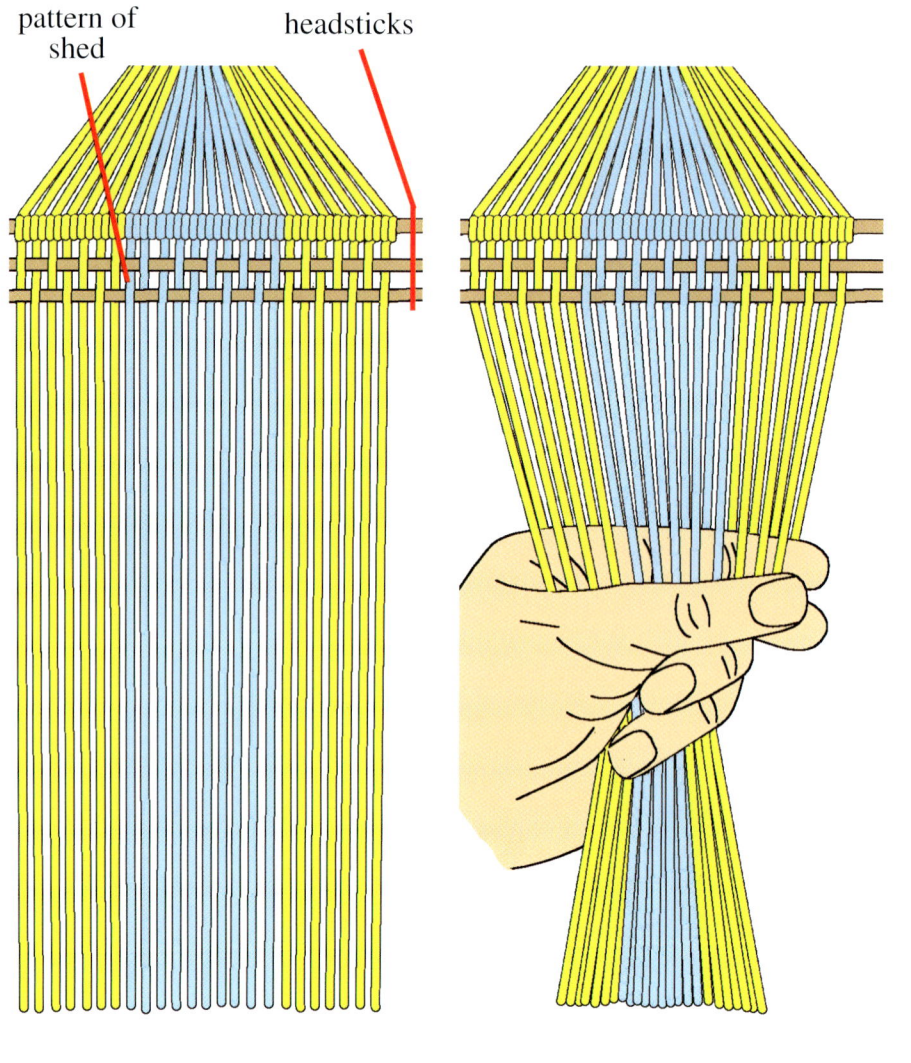

[STEP 4]
The first warp strand on the right side becomes a weft strand when it is pulled to the left through the open shed to the center.

center

first weft

[STEP 5]
Interlock the first weft strand and the warp strand that is to the right of the center.

center

interlocking warp strand

first weft

[NOTE]
On this side of the pattern the interlocking warp strand is picked up from the top layer of the shed.

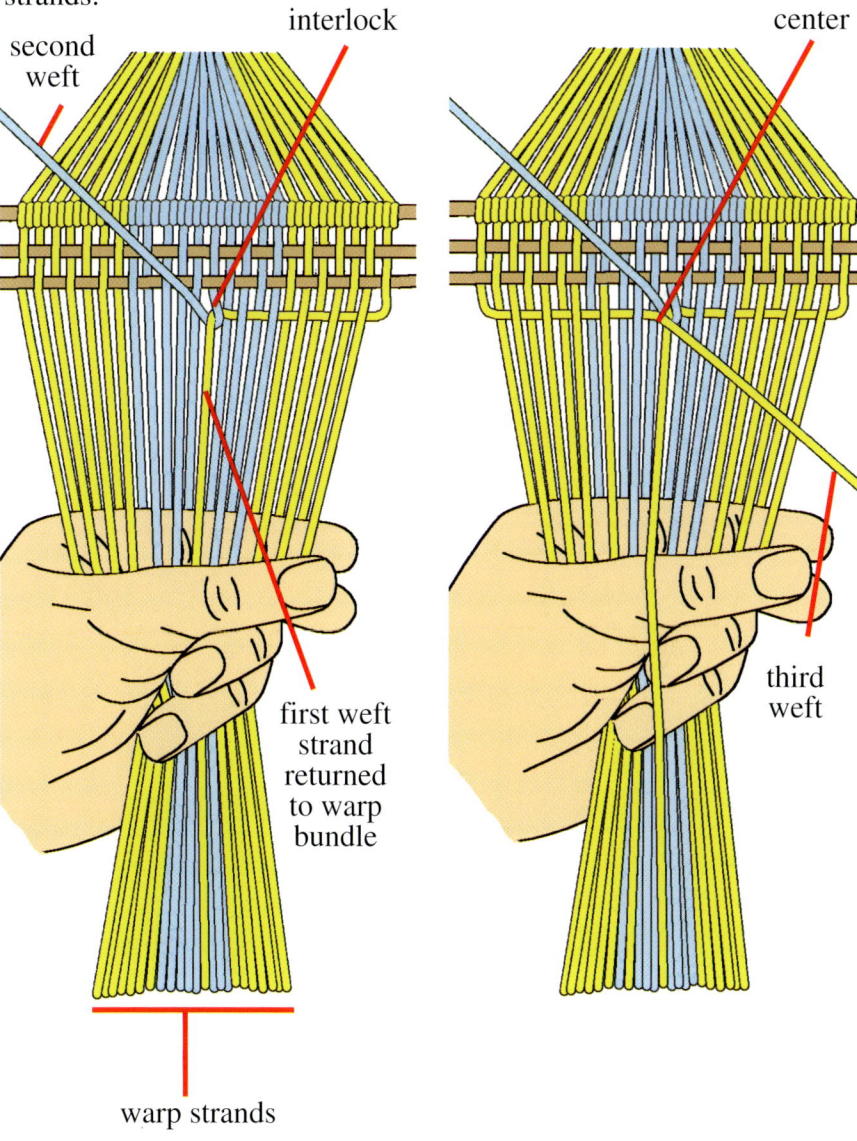

[STEP 6]
When the interlocking warp strand is hooked over the headstick, it becomes the second weft strand. The first weft strand is returned to the bundle of warp strands.

second weft

interlock

first weft strand returned to warp bundle

warp strands

[STEP 7]
The first warp strand on the left becomes the third weft strand when it is pulled to the right through the open shed to the center.

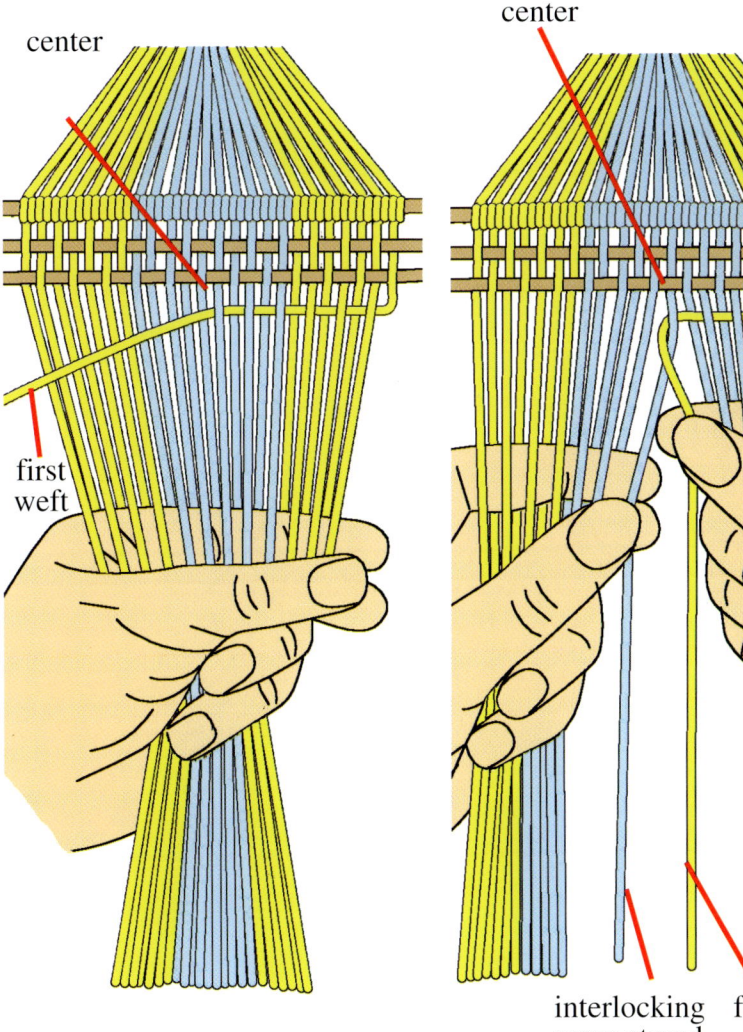

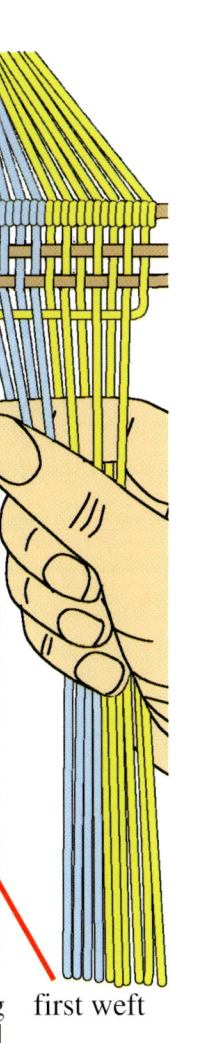

center

third weft

[65]

[STEP 8]
Interlock the third weft strand and the warp strand that is to the left of center. The warp strand becomes the fourth weft strand.

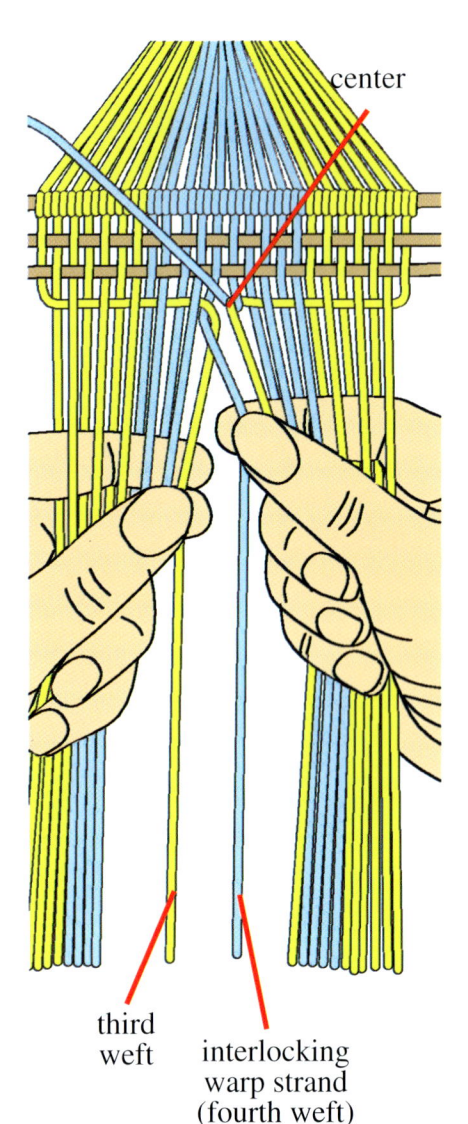

center

third weft

interlocking warp strand (fourth weft)

[STEP 9]
Return the second weft strand to the bundle of warp strands by turning it down over the fourth weft strand. Hook the fourth weft strand over the headstick.

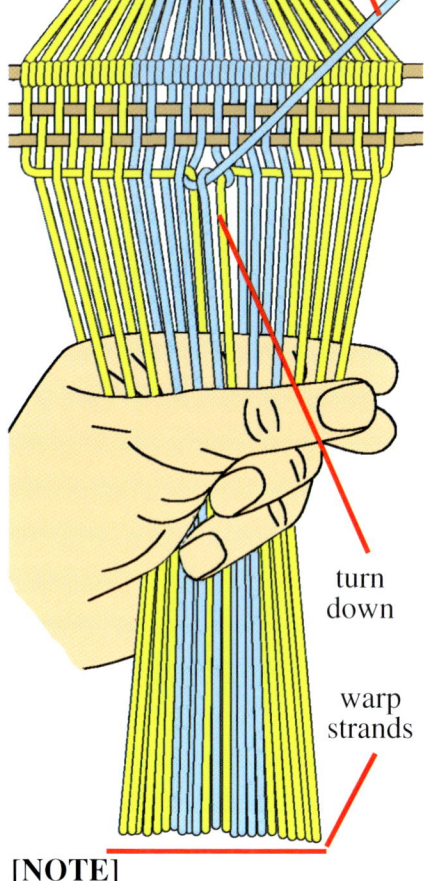

fourth weft

turn down

warp strands

[NOTE]
On this side of the pattern the interlocking warp strand is picked up from the bottom layer of the shed.

[STEP 10]
Reverse the shed by transferring the warp strands one at a time to the right index finger so that the warp strands that were up in the shed are down and the warp strands that were down in the shed are up.

[NOTE]
As each warp strand is transferred to the other hand, check that the proper strand has been selected by observing its position as it crosses the weft strand.

[STEP 11]
Set the weft strands in place by pulling the two layers of the shed in opposite directions.

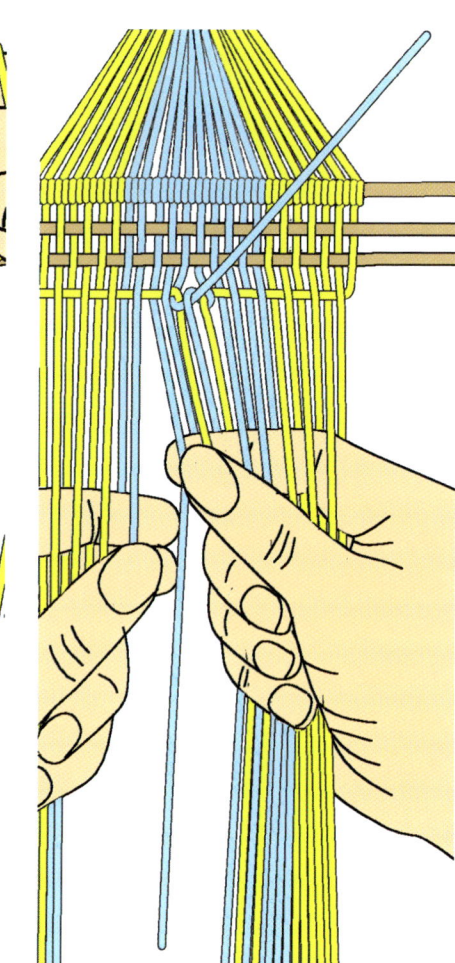

[NOTE]
Check to see if all strands are properly tightened.

[66]

[STEP 12]
The first warp strand on the right side becomes a weft strand when it is pulled to the left through the open shed to the strand that is to the right of the first interlock in the previous row.

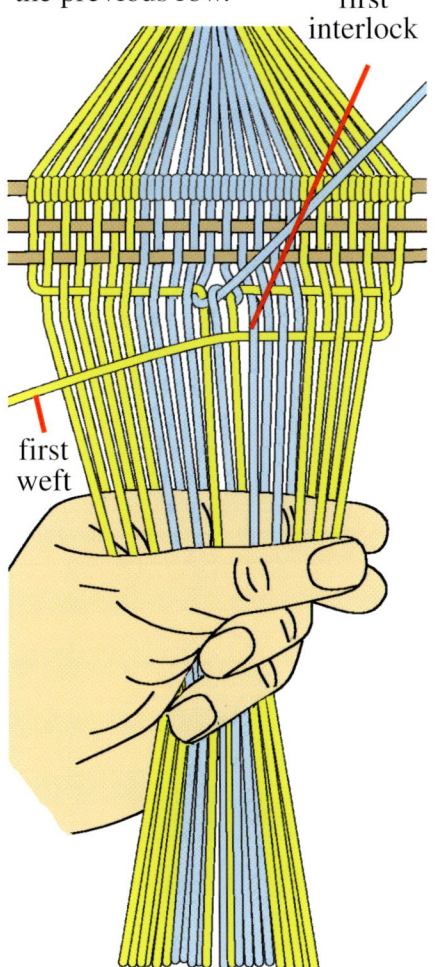

[STEP 13]
Interlock the first weft strand and the warp strand that is to the right of the first interlock in the previous row.

[STEP 14]
Pull the second weft strand through the shed to the center and hook it over the headstick.

[STEP 15]
Return the fourth weft strand of the previous row to the bundle of warp strands by turning it down over the second weft strand in this row.

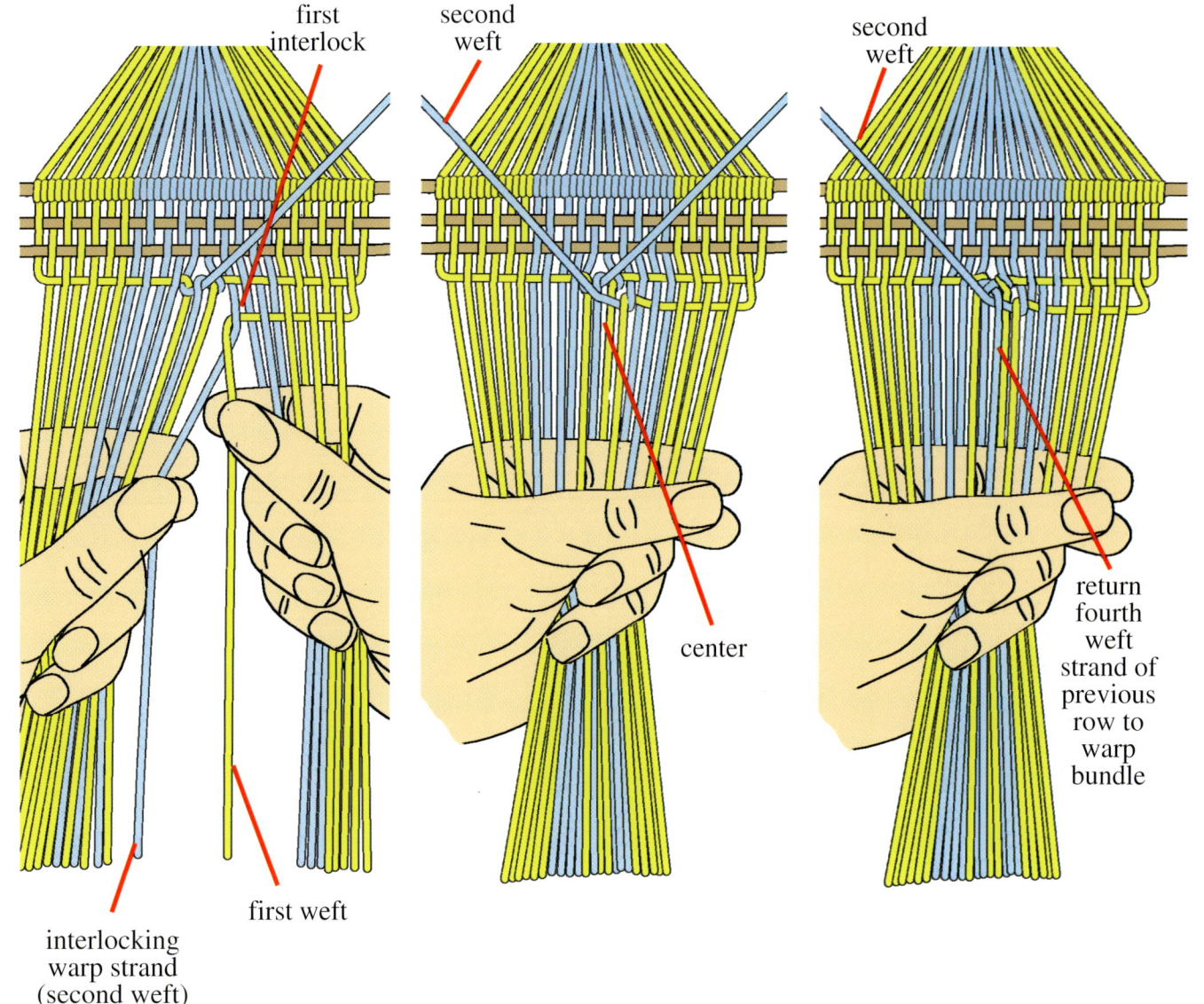

[67]

[STEP 16]
Again the first warp strand on the left becomes the third weft strand when it is pulled to the right through the open shed to the warp strand that is to the left of the second interlock of the previous row.

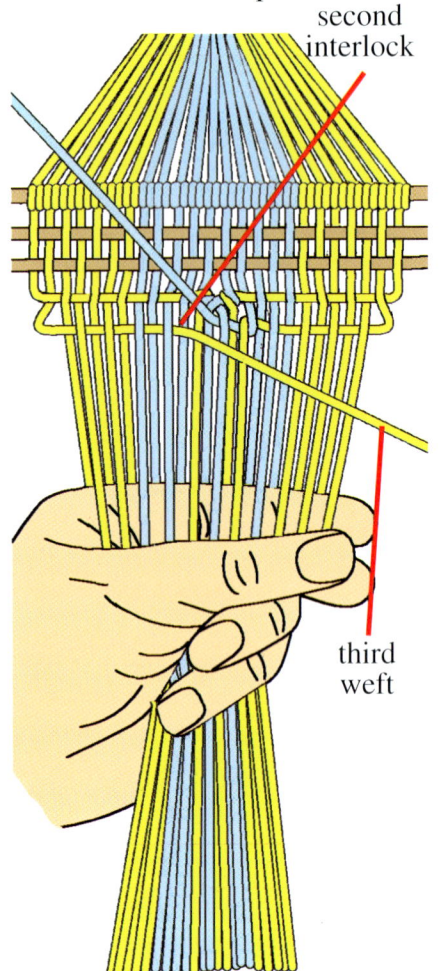

second interlock

third weft

[STEP 17]
Interlock the third weft strand and the warp strand that is to the left of the second interlock of the previous row.

second interlock

third weft

interlocking warp strand (fourth weft)

[STEP 18]
Pull the third weft strand through the shed to the center and hook it over the headstick.

third weft

center

[STEP 19]
Return the second weft to the bundle of warp strands by turning it down over the fourth weft.

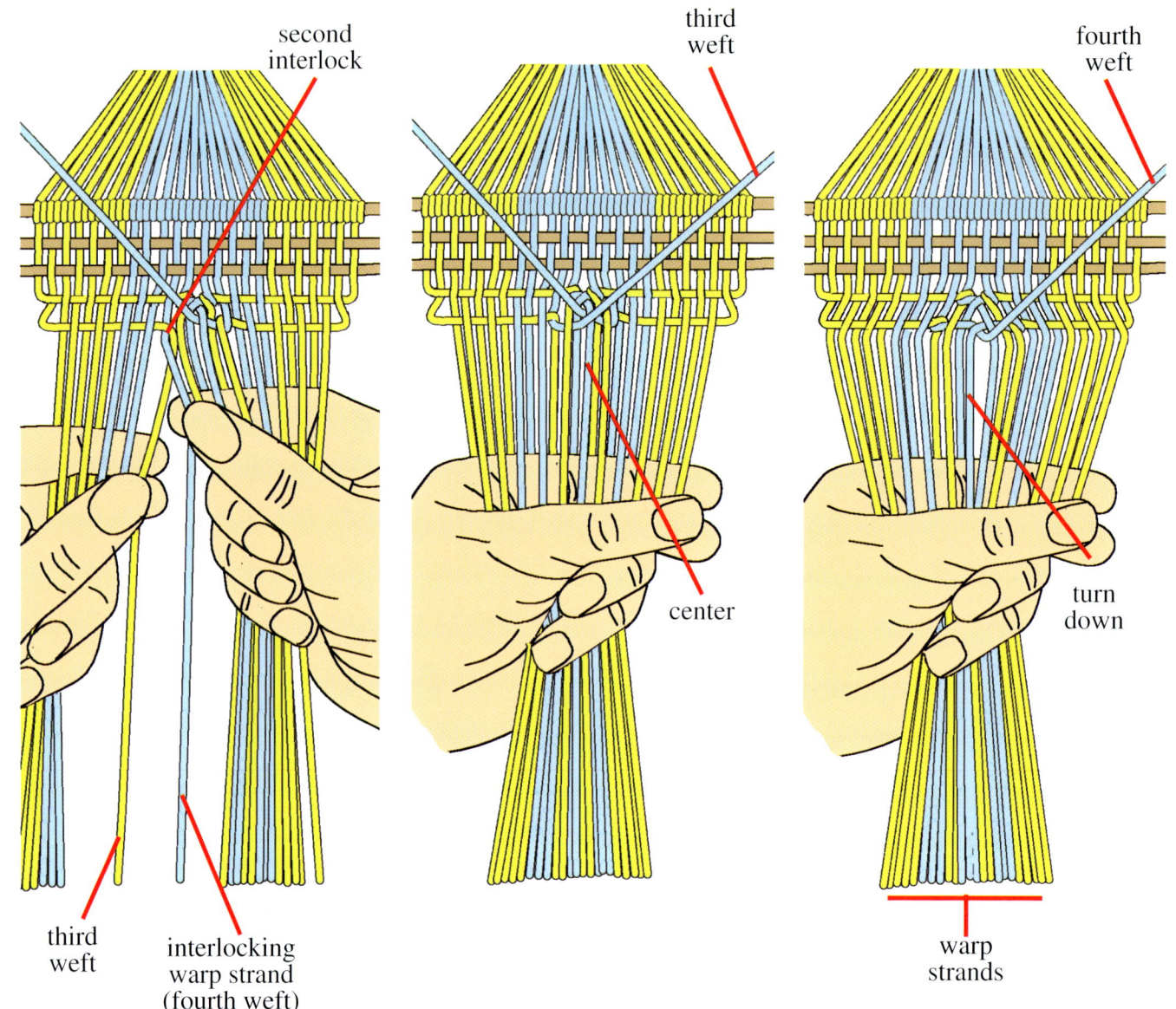

fourth weft

turn down

warp strands

[68]

[STEP 20]
Set the weft strands in place by pulling the two layers of the shed in opposite directions.

[STEP 21]
Continue weaving following the directions for STEP 12 through STEP 20 until the strands return to their original sequence.

original sequence

[STEP 22]
Start the pattern over again. The first warp strand on the right side becomes a weft strand when it is pulled to the left through the open shed to the center.

fourth weft of previous row

first weft

center

[STEP 23]
Interlock the first weft strand and the fourth weft strand from the previous row.

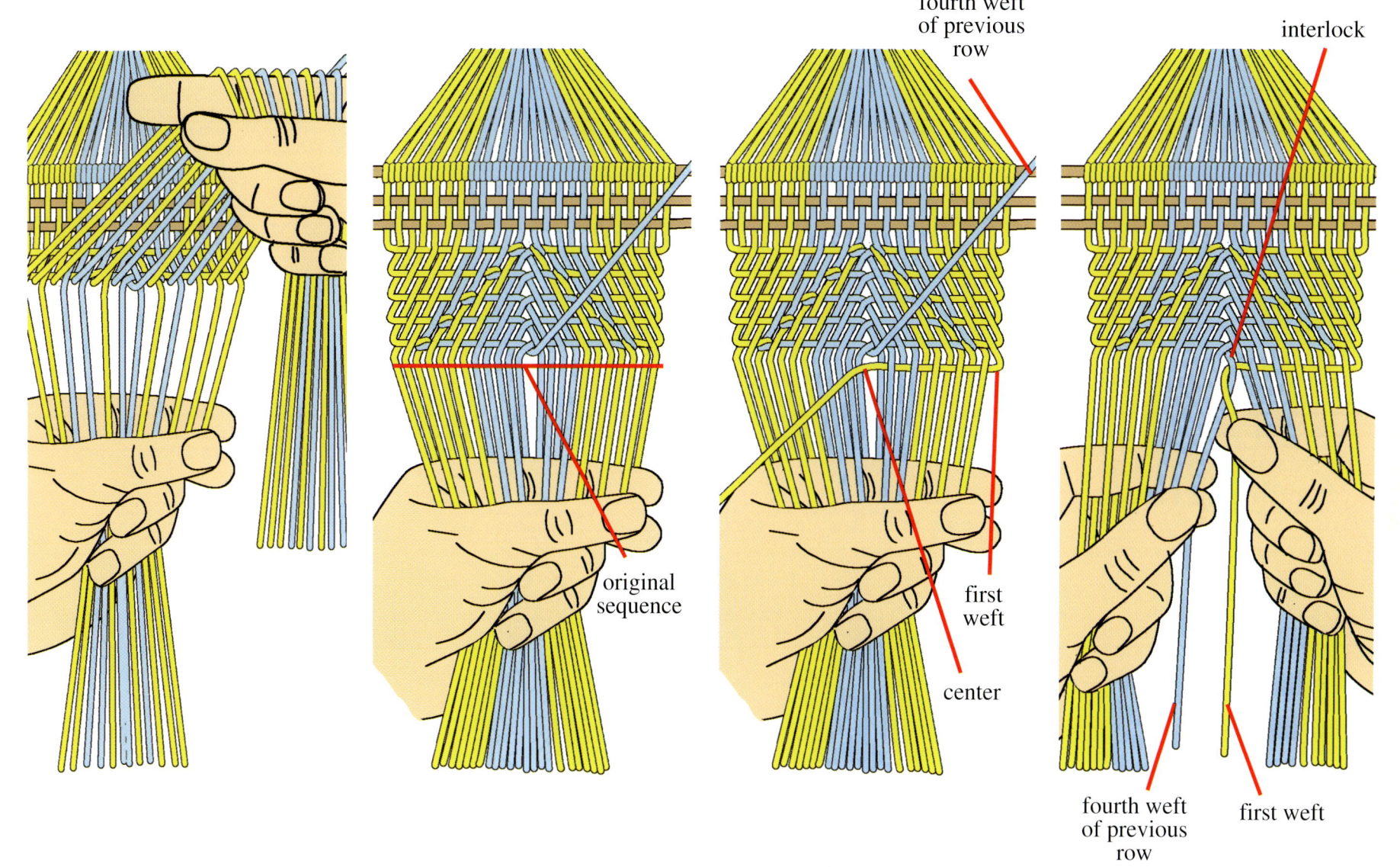

interlock

fourth weft of previous row

first weft

[69]

[STEP 24]
The fourth weft strand of the previous row becomes the second weft of this row when it is hooked over the headstick.

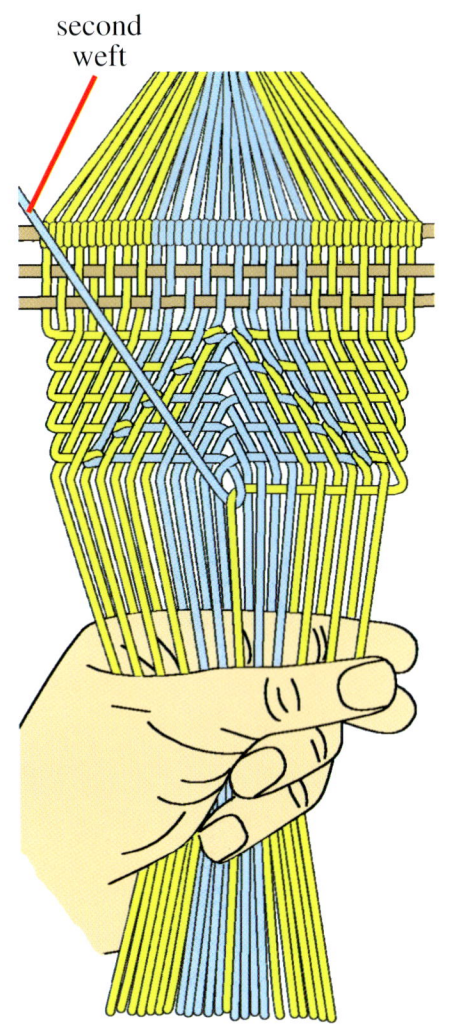

second weft

[NOTE] Follow the directions for [STEP 7] through [STEP 22] to complete the pattern.

[70]

[STEP 25]
Continue to weave in this manner. When the original strand arrangement has been reestablished, start the pattern over. Repeat the pattern following the directions for STEP 5 through STEP 24 until the desired length is reached.

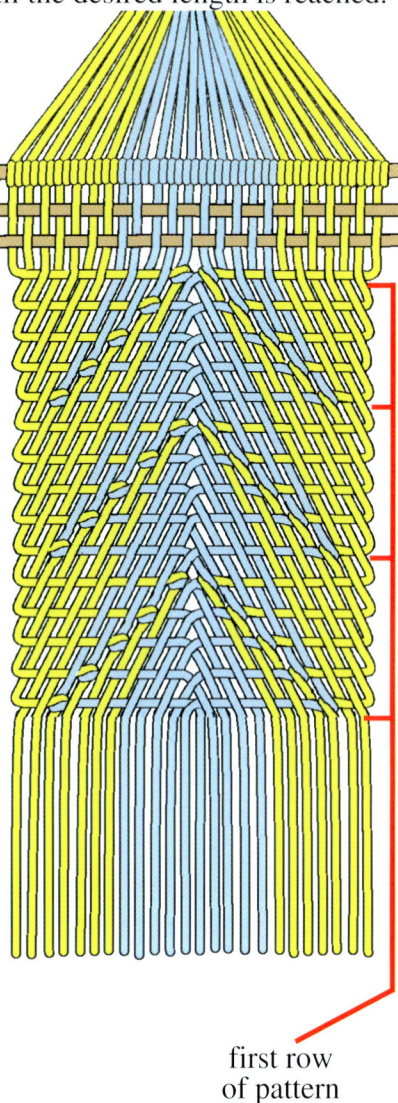

first row of pattern

[STEP 26]
Turn the work around and reattach it to your anchor. Remove the headsticks and pick up the shed.

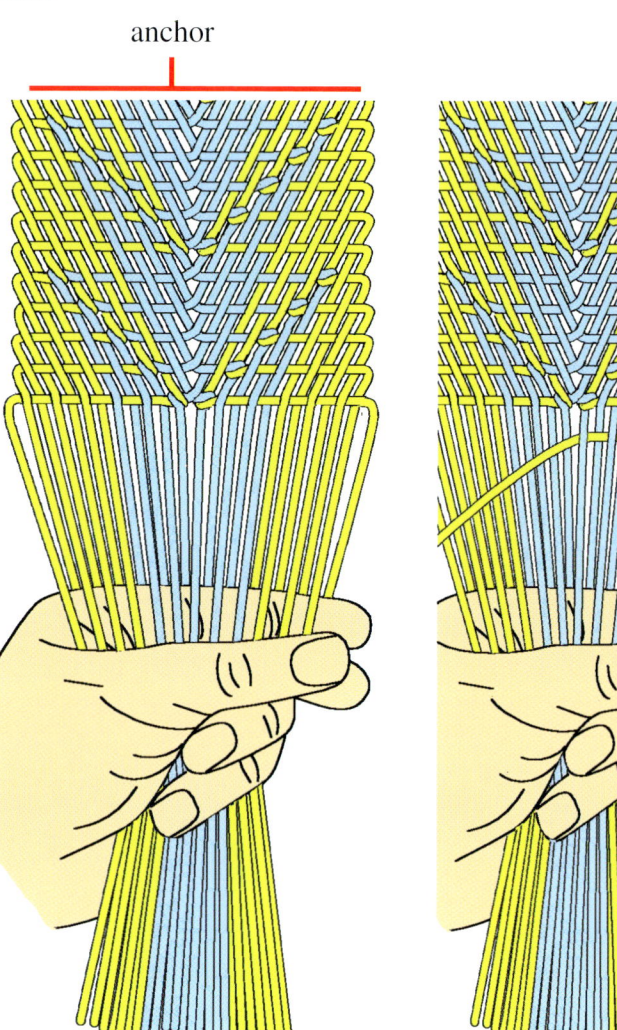

anchor

[STEP 27]
Set the weft strands in place by pulling the two layers of the shed in opposite directions.

[STEP 28]
Start the second half of the piece. The first warp strand on the right side becomes a weft strand when it is pulled to the left through the open shed to the center.

[STEP 29]
Following STEP 5 through STEP 25 continue weaving until the desired length is reached.

Arrowhead Pattern Over/under Weave (Point Up) Example:

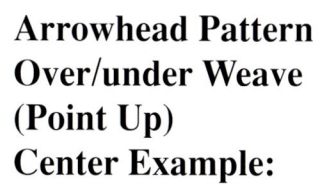

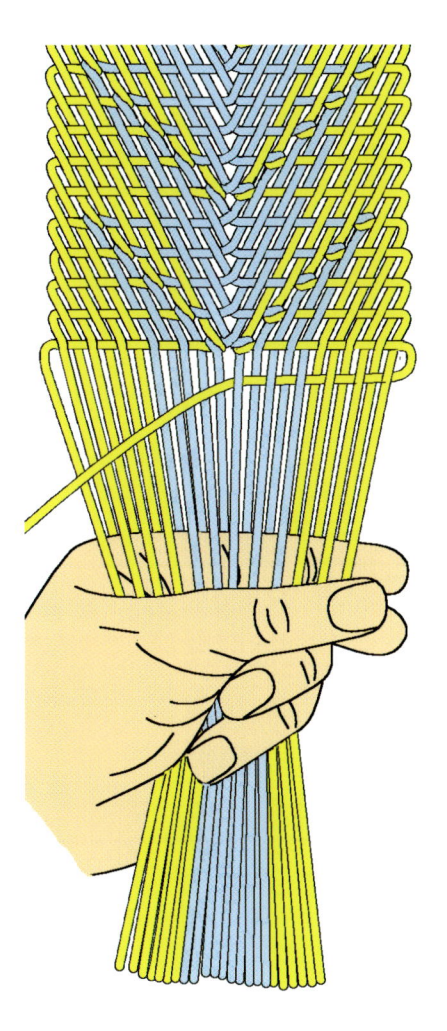

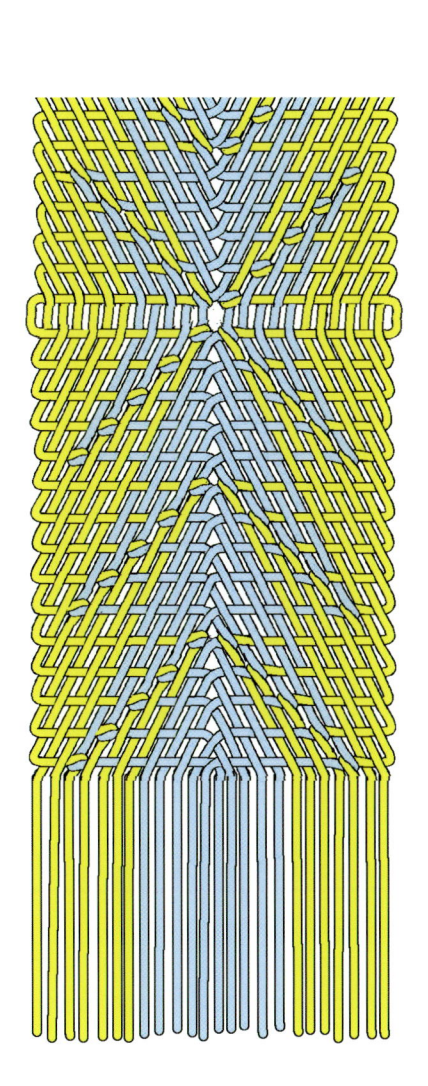

Arrowhead Pattern Over/under Weave (Point Up) Center Example:

[71]

Arrowhead Pattern Over Two/Under Two (Point Down)

The arrowhead pattern is named for the arrowhead shaped pattern that develops when two or more colors are used. Over two/under two variation is used to make the two halves of the pattern mirror images of each other. This causes the strands at the edges of the pattern to turn in the same direction. Turning the edge strands in the same direction facilitates combining of patterns, especially when adding borders to the work.

The setup for the arrowhead pattern requires an even number of strands of each color. The strands are arranged so that the two sides are mirror images of each other.

[STEP 1]
Cast the required number of strands of yarn on to the headstick. Use clove hitches to tie the yarn in place. See (Part 1: Getting Started).

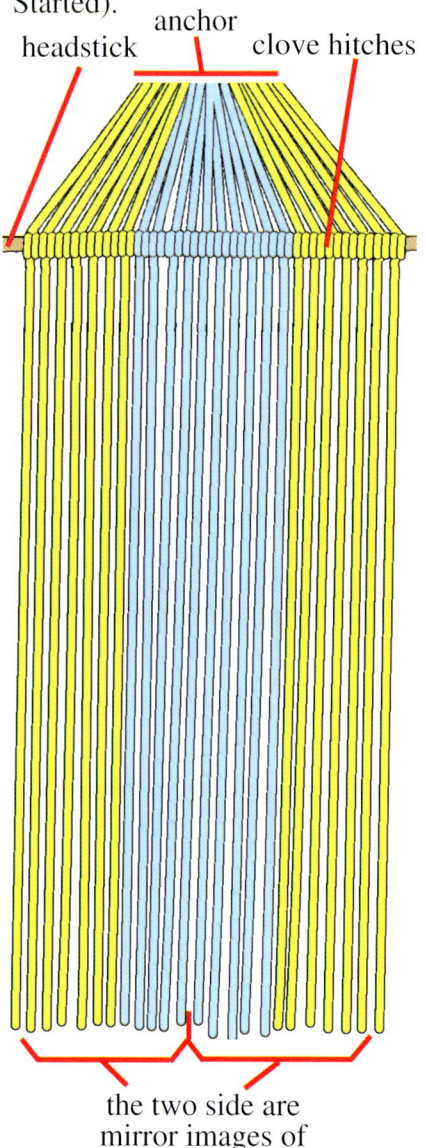

- headstick
- anchor
- clove hitches
- the two side are mirror images of each other

[STEP 2]
Use two smaller sticks to set up the weaving pattern. The two center strands are both over the head stick. Starting with these center strands, the remainder of the strands follow an over under pattern as you move toward the edges.

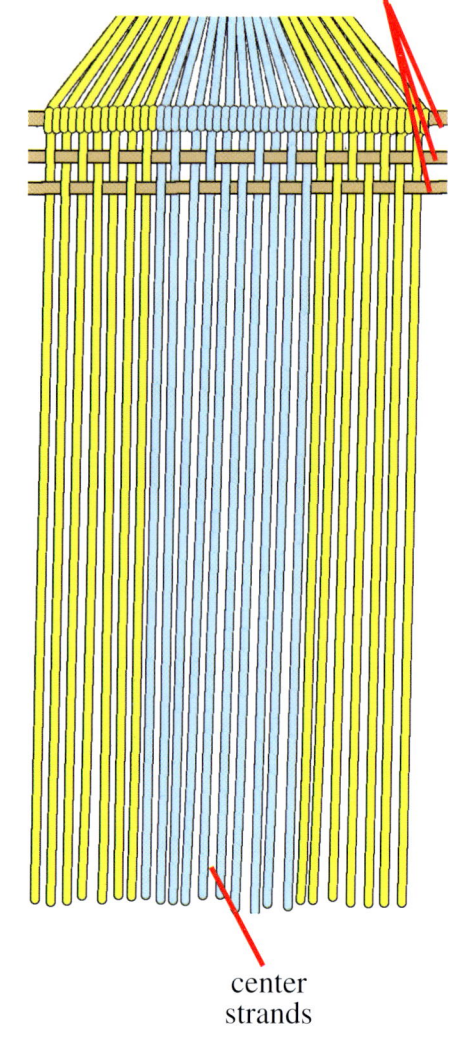

- headsticks
- center strands

[72]

[STEP 3]
Pick up the shed. Use the index finger of the left hand to hold the shed open.

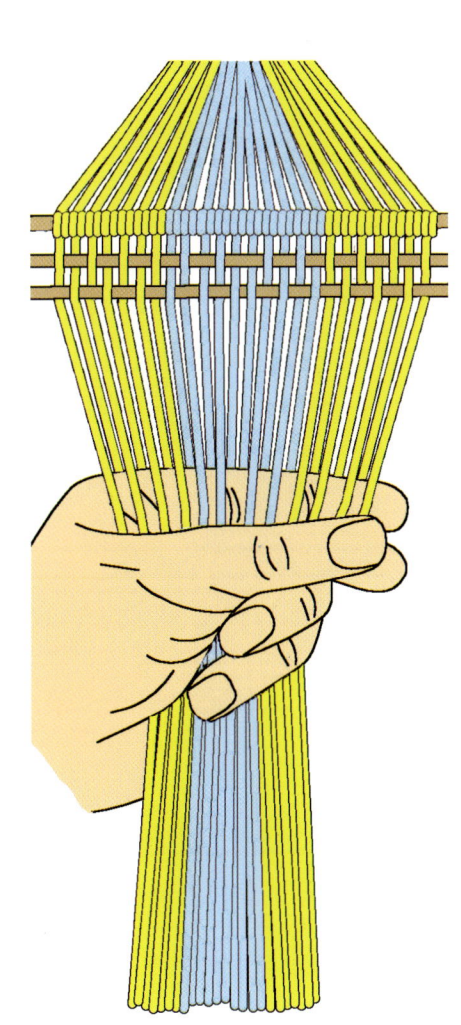

[STEP 4]
The first warp strand to the left of the middle becomes a weft strand when it is pulled to the right through the open shed. This weft strand is pulled through the open shed of the right hand color for one half the number of strands of the center color.

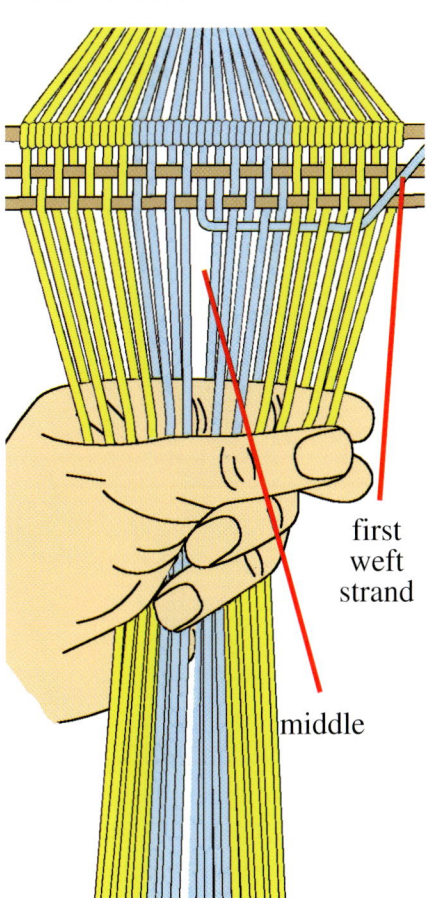

first weft strand

middle

[STEP 5]
Interlock the first weft strand and the warp strand that is 1/2 the number of strands in the center color band into the right hand color band.

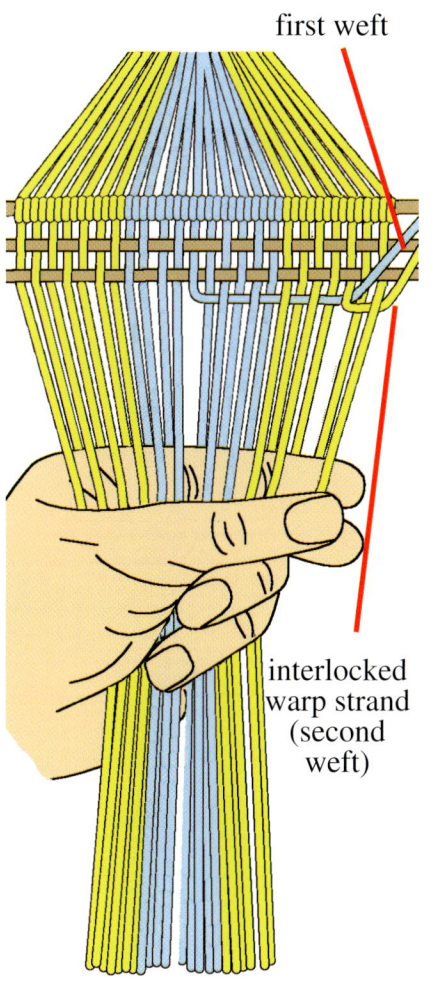

first weft

interlocked warp strand (second weft)

When the interlocked warp strand is pulled through the remaining part of the open shed and hooked over the headstick, it becomes the second weft strand.

[STEP 6]
Complete the interlock by turning the first weft strand down over the second weft strand. The first weft strand becomes a warp strand again.

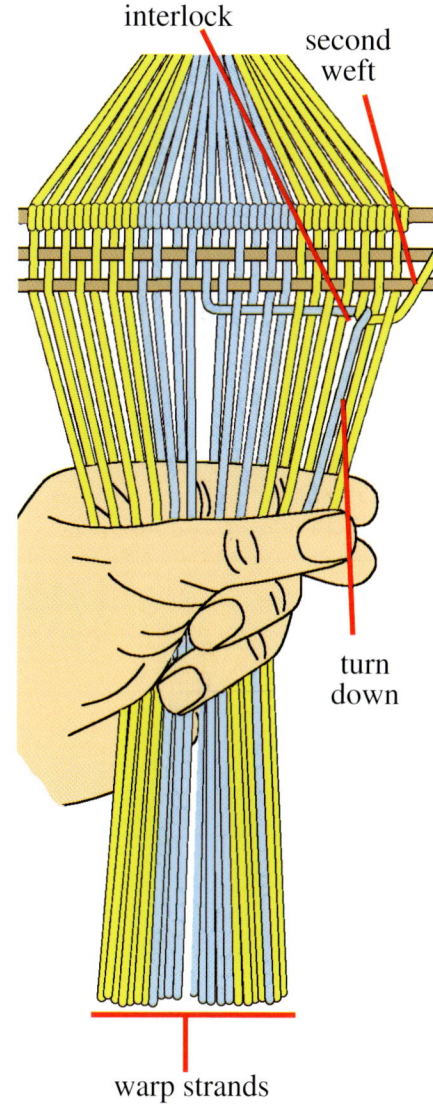

interlock

second weft

turn down

warp strands

[73]

[STEP 7]

The first warp strand to the right of the middle becomes a weft strand when it is pulled to the left through the open shed. This weft strand is pulled through the open shed of the left hand color for one half the number of strands of the center color.

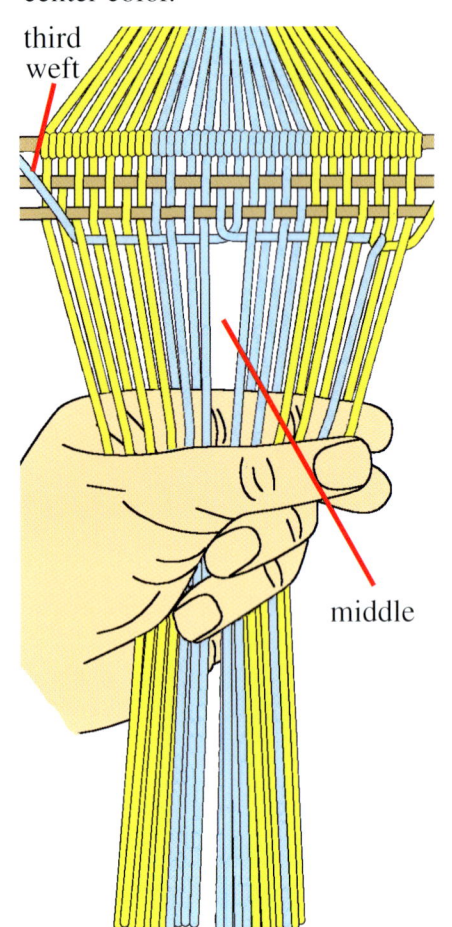

[STEP 8]

Begin the interlock of the third weft strand and the warp strand that is 1/2 the number of the of center color strands into the left color.

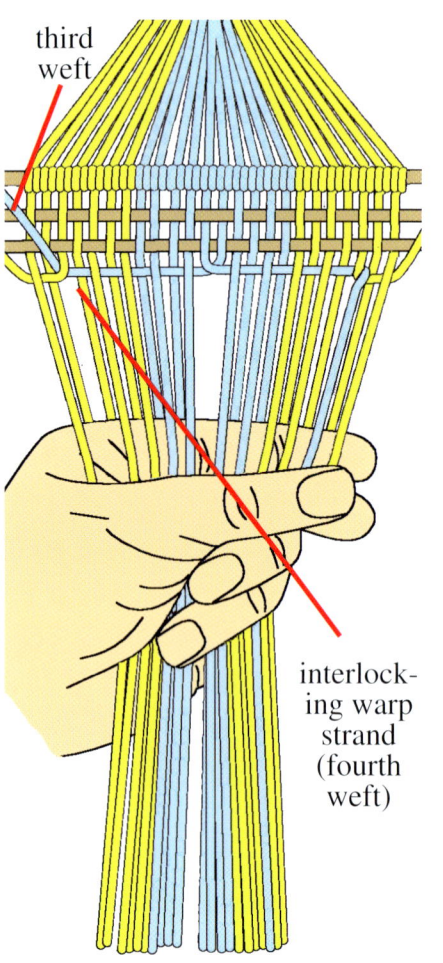

When the interlocking warp strand is pulled through the remaining part of the open shed and hooked over the headstick, it becomes the fourth weft strand.

[STEP 9]

Complete the interlock by turning the third weft strand down over the fourth weft strand. The third weft strand becomes a warp strand again.

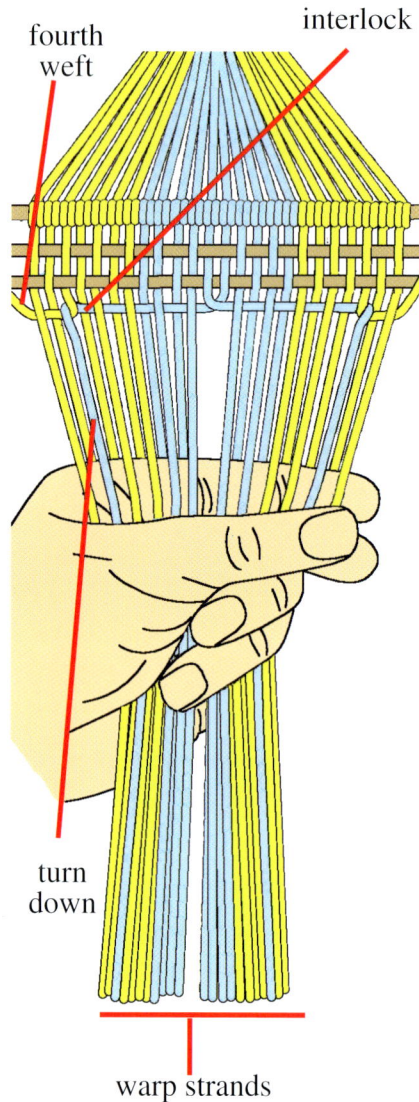

[STEP 10]

Reverse the shed by transferring the warp strands one at a time to the right index finger so that the warp strands that were up in the shed are down and the warp strands that were down in the shed are up.

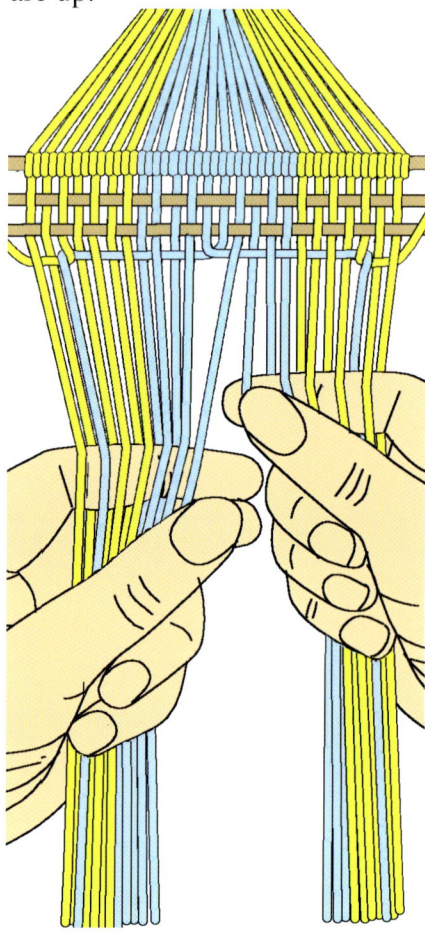

[NOTE]

As each warp strand is transferred to the other hand, check that the proper strand has been selected by observing its position as it crosses the weft strand.

[74]

[STEP 11]
Set the weft strands in place by pulling the two layers of the shed in opposite directions.

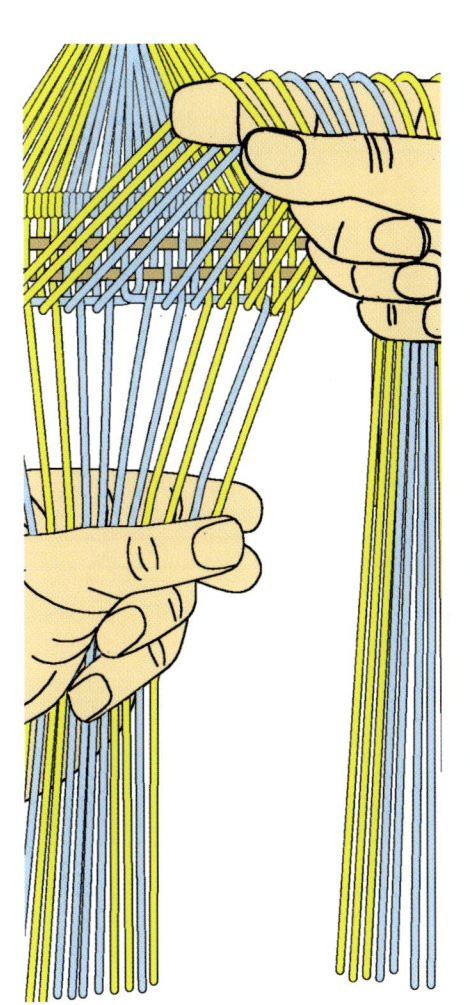

[NOTE]
Check to see if all strands are properly tightened.

[STEP 12]
Again the first warp strand to the left of the middle becomes a weft strand when it is pulled to the right through the open shed past the strand that is to the left of the first interlock in the previous row.

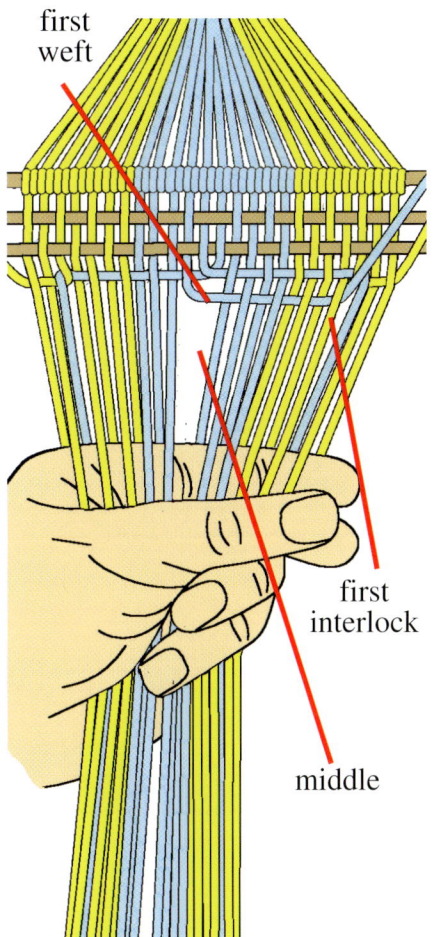

first weft

first interlock

middle

[STEP 13]
Begin the interlock of the first weft strand and the warp strand that is to the left of the first interlock in the previous row by pulling the warp strand to the right through the open shed.

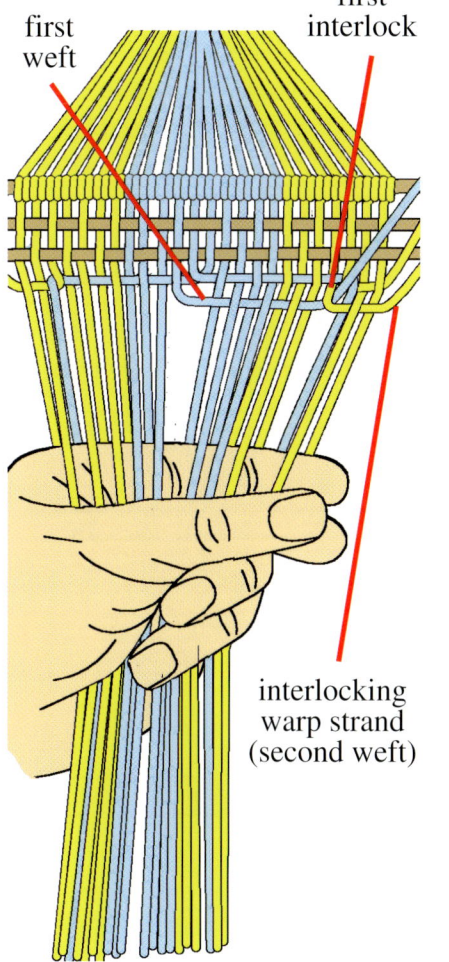

first weft

first interlock

interlocking warp strand (second weft)

When the interlocking warp strand is pulled through the remaining part of the open shed and hooked over the headstick it becomes the second weft strand.

[STEP 14]
Complete the interlock by turning the first weft strand down over the second weft strand. The first weft strand becomes a warp strand again.

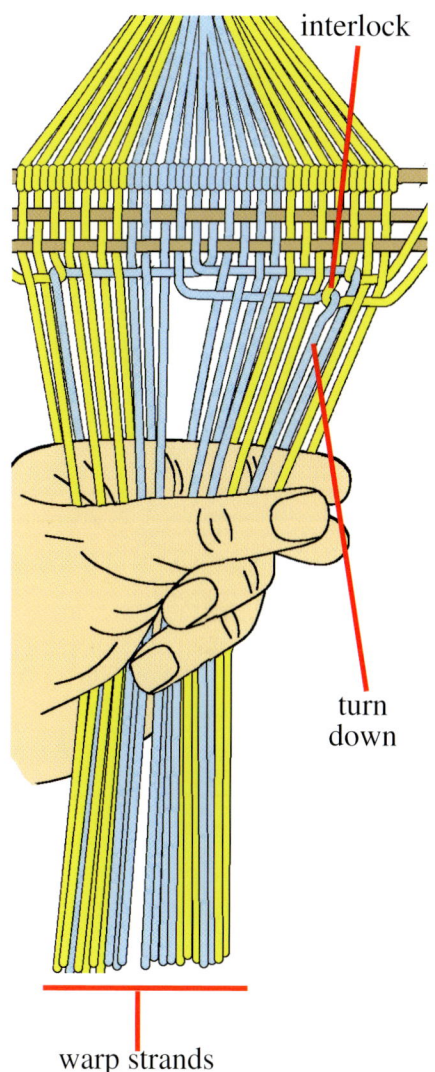

interlock

turn down

warp strands

[75]

[STEP 15]
Turn the last weft strand of the previous row down. This weft strand is now a warp strand again.

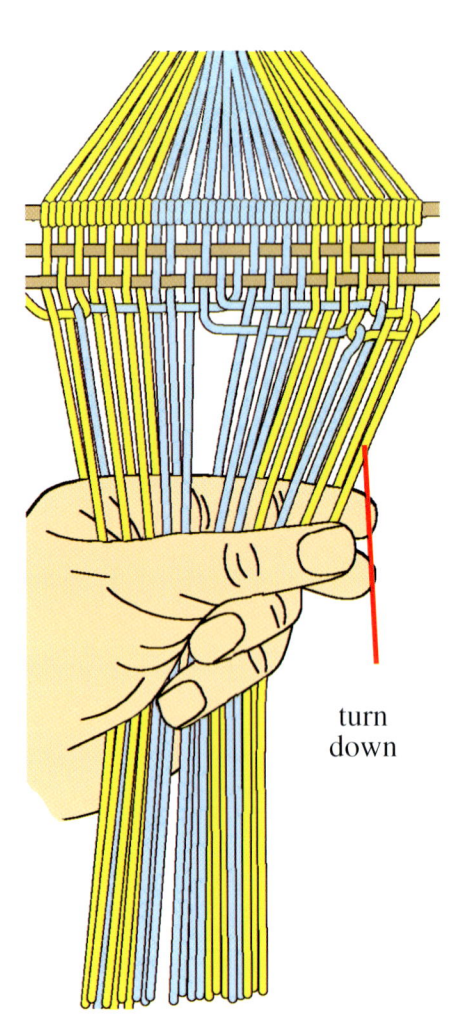

[STEP 16]
The first warp strand to the right of the middle becomes the third weft strand of the second row when it is pulled to the left through the open shed of the left hand color to the strand that is to the right of the second interlock in the previous row.

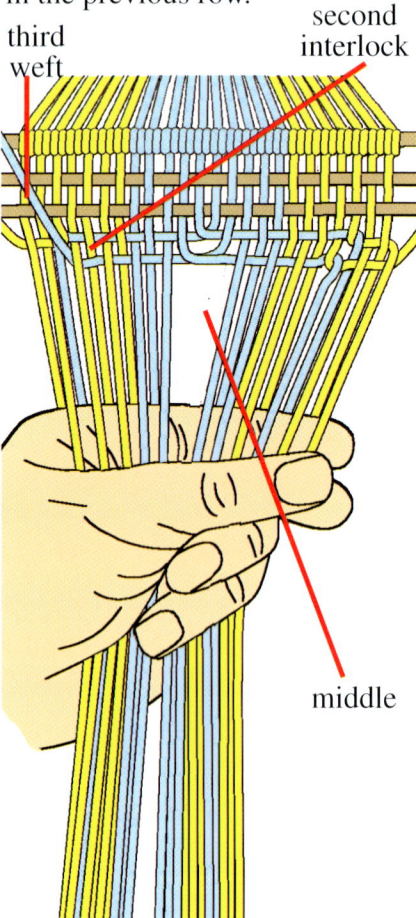

[STEP 17]
Interlock the third weft strand and the warp strand that is to the right of the second interlock in the previous row.

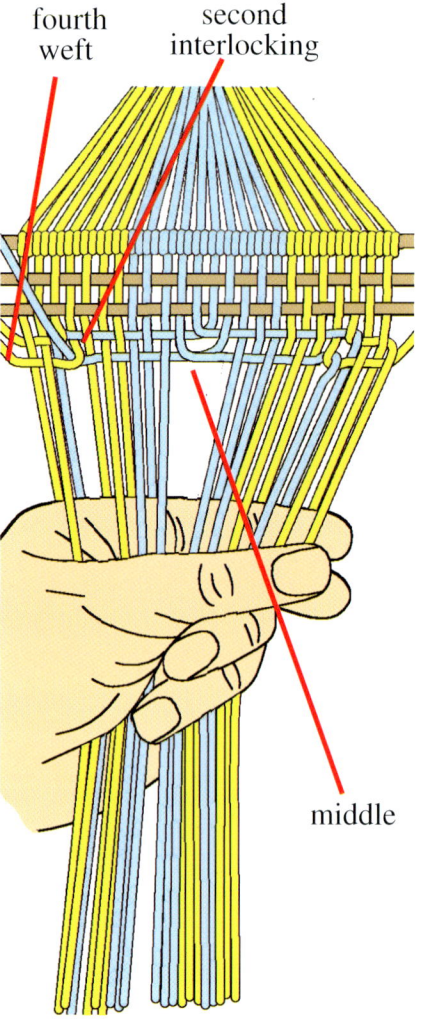

When the interlocked warp strand is pulled through the remaining part of the open shed and hooked over the headstick, it becomes the fourth weft strand.

[STEP 18]
Complete the interlock by turning the third weft strand down over the fourth weft strand. The third weft strand becomes a warp strand again.

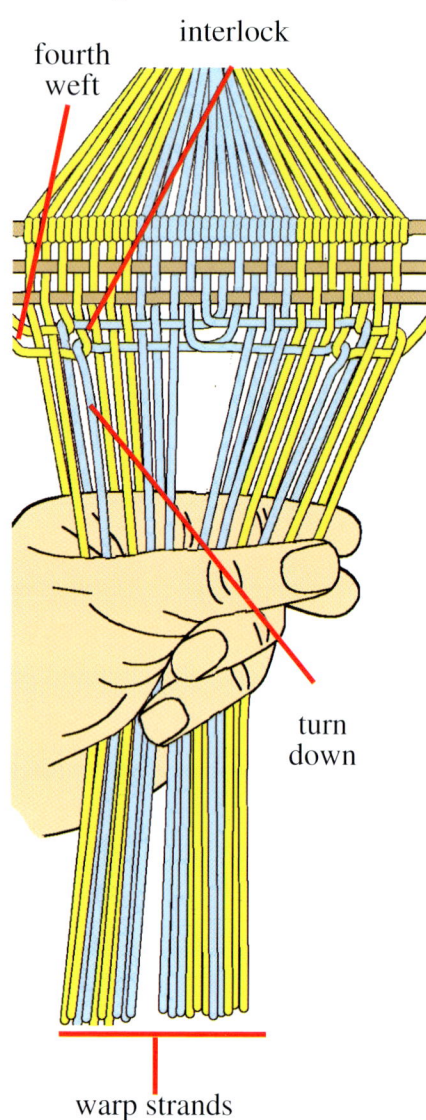

[76]

[STEP 19]
Turn the last weft strand of the previous row down. This weft strand is now a warp strand again.

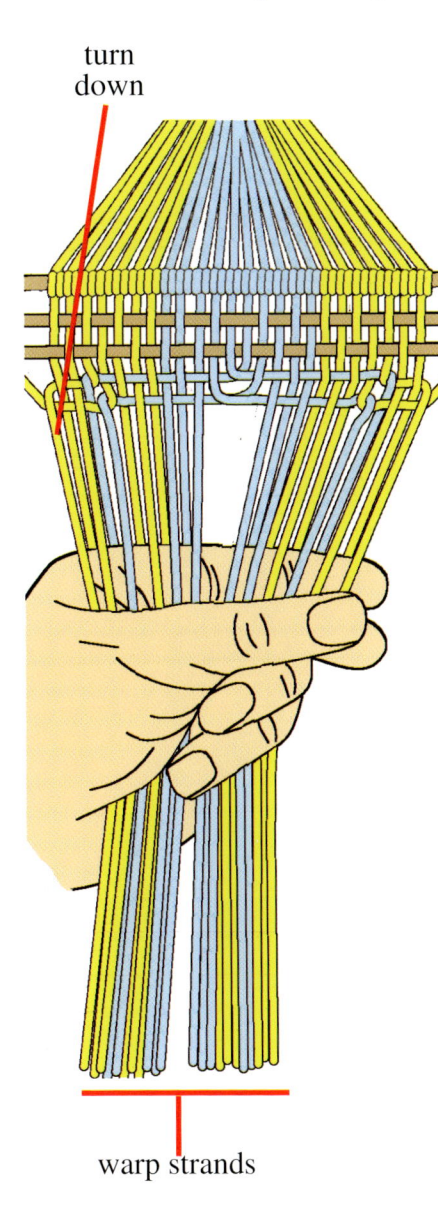

turn down

warp strands

[STEP 20]
Continue to weave in this manner. When the original strand arrangement has been reestablished, start the pattern over. Repeat the pattern until the desired length is reached.

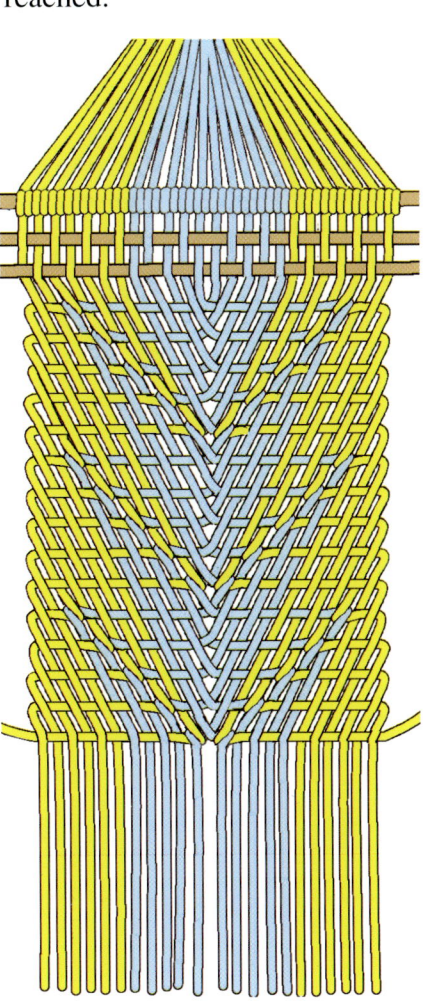

Arrowhead Pattern Over Two/Under Two (Point Down) Example:

Arrowhead Pattern Over Two/Under Two (Point Down) Center Example:

[77]

Changing Direction of Weave
Over Two/Under Two

In "Over Two/Under Two" work the front and back patterns of the work are different. If the direction of the weave is changed, the front and back patterns of the work also change . This is OK if the work is folded in half when it is displayed but if the work is dislayed flat the difference is unacceptable. To keep the front and back patterns the same when the direction of the weave is changed, the strand at the point of change must be doubled. [See diagram Arrowhead Pattern, Over Two/Under Two, (Point Up) Center]

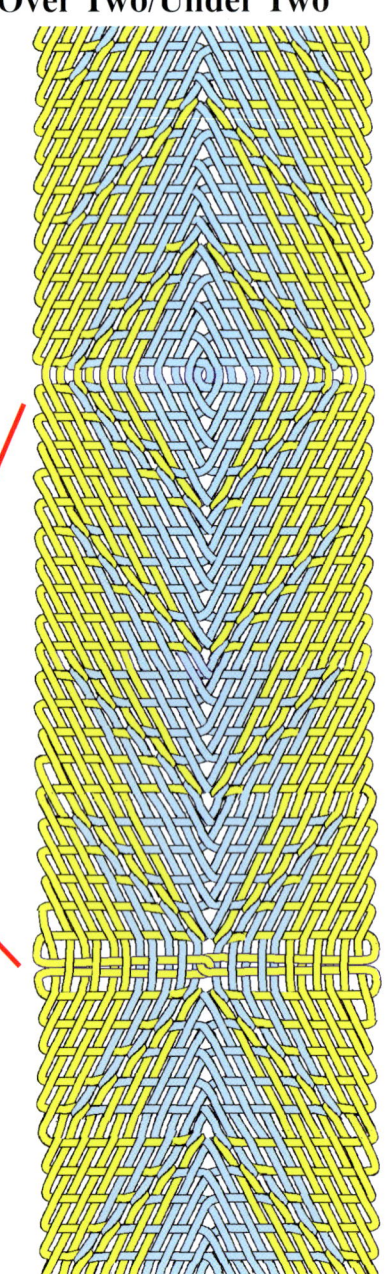

doubled strand at change of weave direction

[NOTE]
In all "Over Two/Under Two" work the doubled strand can be used whenever the direction of weave is changed.

Arrowhead Pattern Over Two/Under Two

Arrowhead Pattern Over Two/Under Two (Point Up)

The arrowhead pattern is named for the arrowhead shaped pattern that develops when two or more colors are used. Over two/under two variation is used to make the two halves of the pattern mirror images of each other. This causes the strands at the edges of the pattern to turn in the same direction. Turning the edge strands in the same direction facilitates combining of patterns, especially when adding borders to the work.

The setup for the arrowhead pattern requires an even number of strands of each color. The strands are arranged so that the two sides are mirror images of each other.

[78]

[STEP 1]
Cast the required number of strands of yarn on to the headstick. Use clove hitches to tie the yarn in place. See (Part 1: Getting Started).

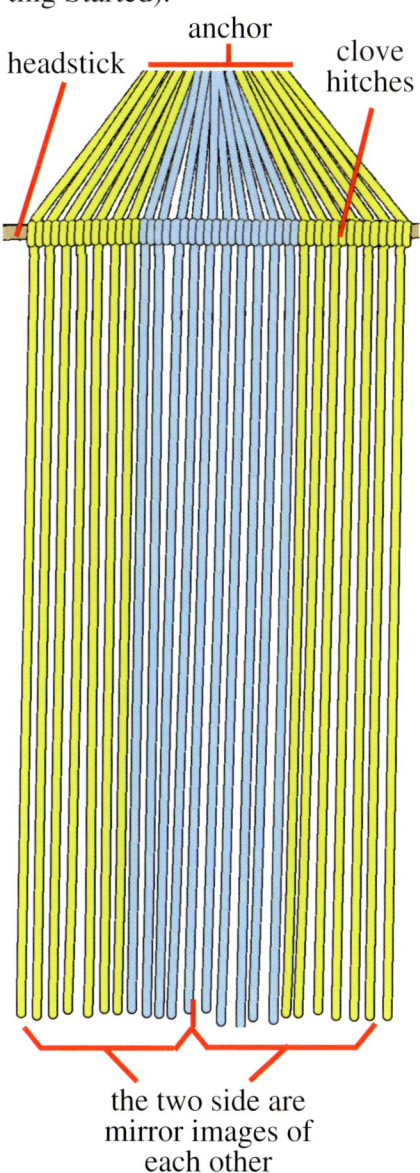

headstick — anchor — clove hitches

the two side are mirror images of each other

[STEP 2]
Use two smaller sticks to set up the weaving pattern. The two center strands are both under the head stick. Starting with these center strands, the remainder of the strands follow an over/under pattern as you move toward the edges.

headsticks

center strands

[STEP 3]
Pick up the shed. Use the index finger of the left hand to hold the shed open.

[STEP 4]
The first warp strand on the left becomes the first weft strand when it is pulled to the right through the open shed to the center.

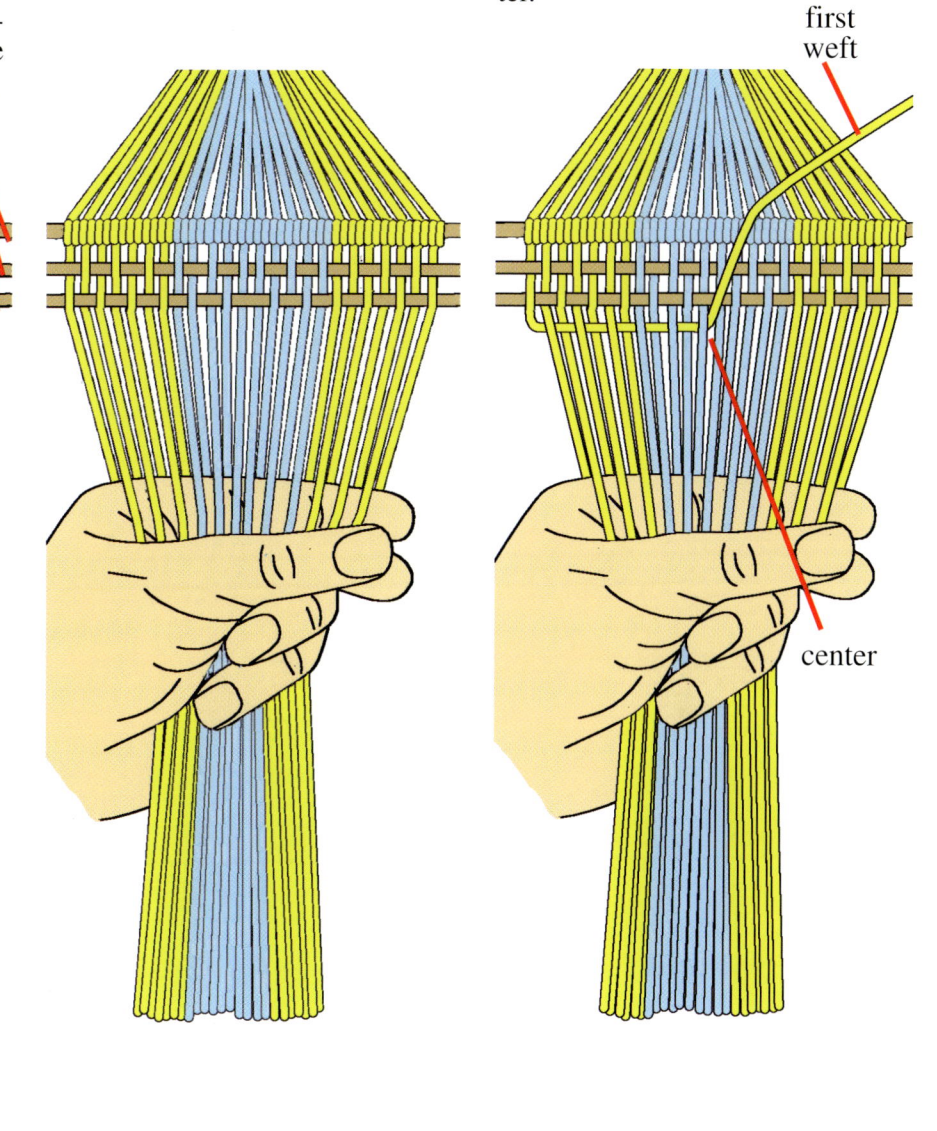

first weft

center

[79]

[STEP 5]
Interlock the first weft strand and the warp strand that is to the left of the center. This warp strand becomes the second weft strand when it is hooked up over the headstick.

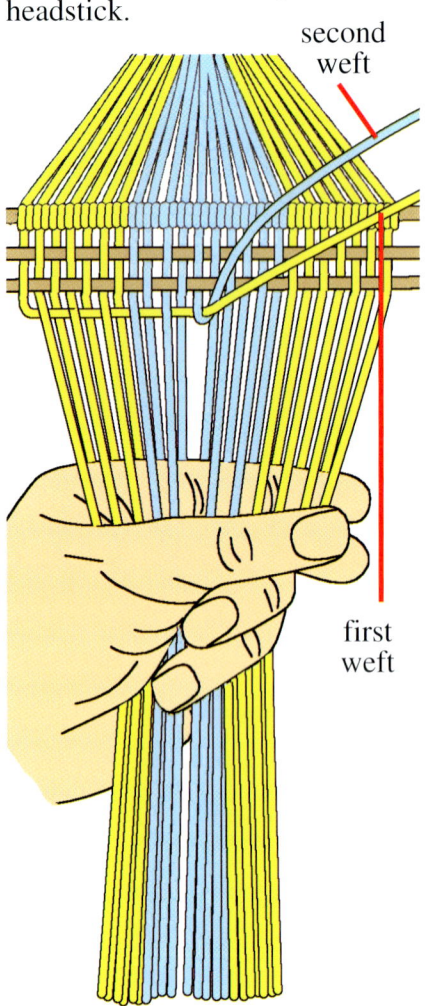

[STEP 6]
Complete the interlock by turning the first weft strand down over the second weft strand. The first weft strand becomes a warp strand again.

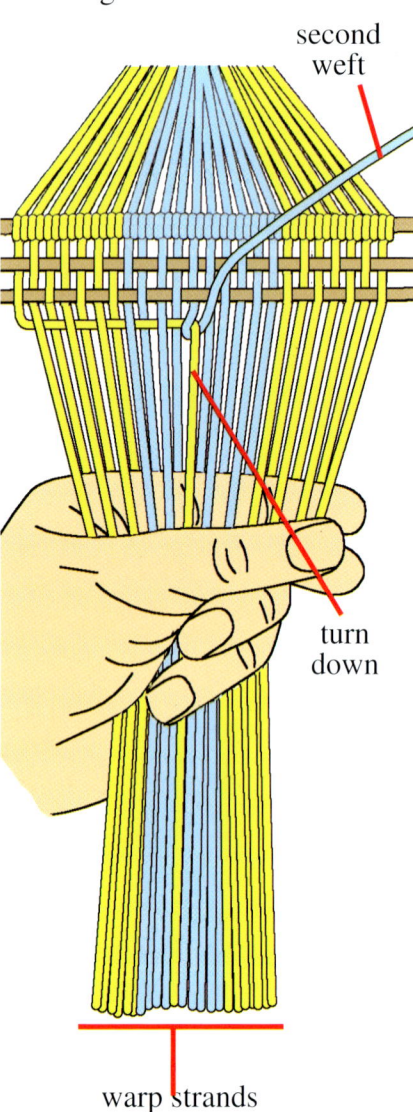

[STEP 7]
The first warp strand on the right becomes the third weft strand when it is pulled to the left through the open shed to the center.

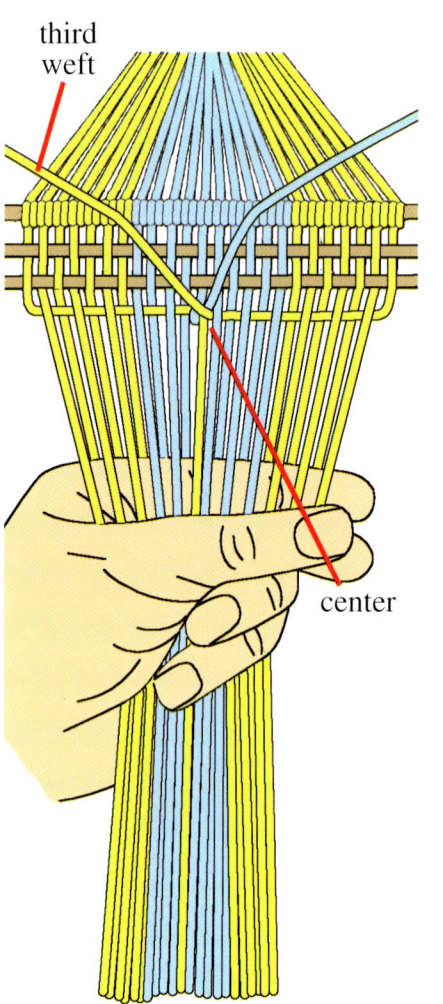

[STEP 8]
Begin the interlock of the third weft strand and the warp strand that is to the right of the center. This warp strand becomes the fourth weft strand when it is hooked up over the headstick.

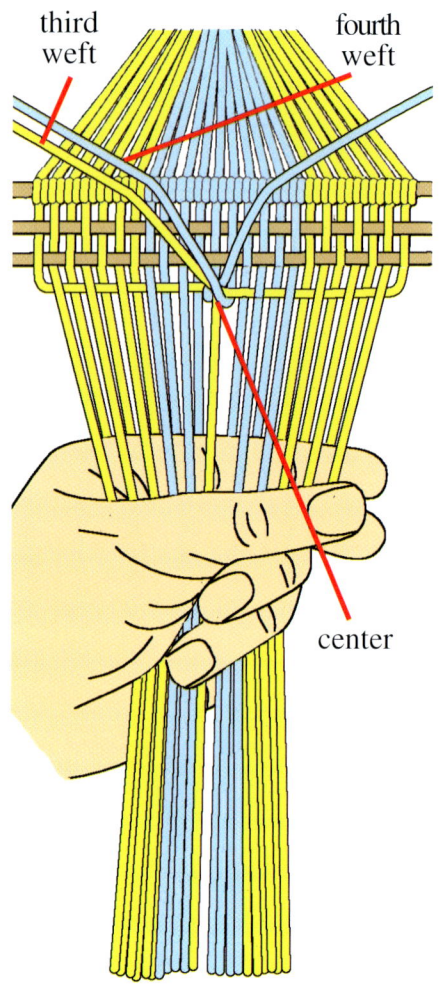

[80]

[STEP 9]
Complete the interlock by turning the third weft strand down over the fourth weft strand. The third weft strand becomes a warp strand again.

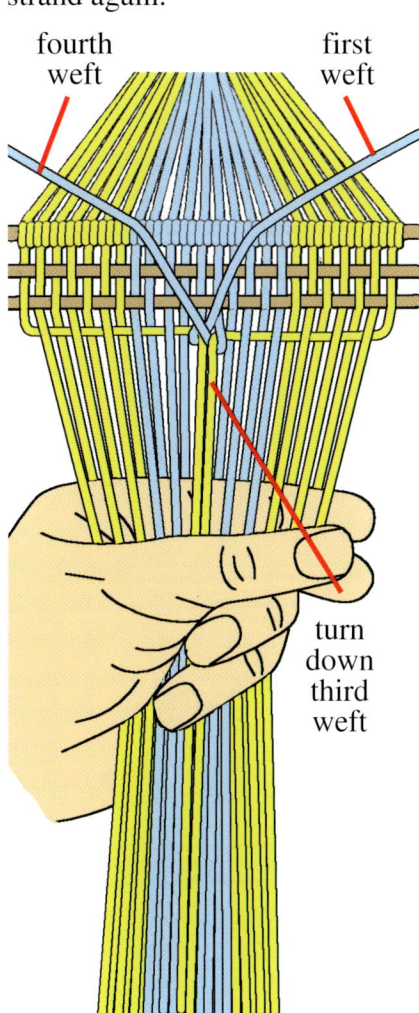

fourth weft

first weft

turn down third weft

[STEP 10]
Finish the row by turning the first weft strand down over the fourth weft strand. The first weft strand becomes a warp strand again.

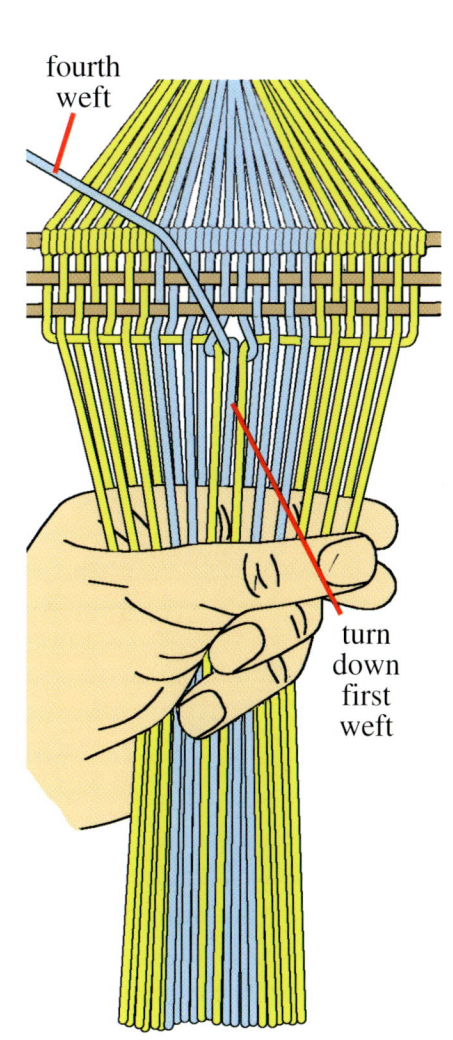

fourth weft

turn down first weft

[STEP 11]
Reverse the shed by transferring the warp strands one at a time to the right index finger so that the warp strands that were up in the shed are down and the warp strands that were down in the shed are up.

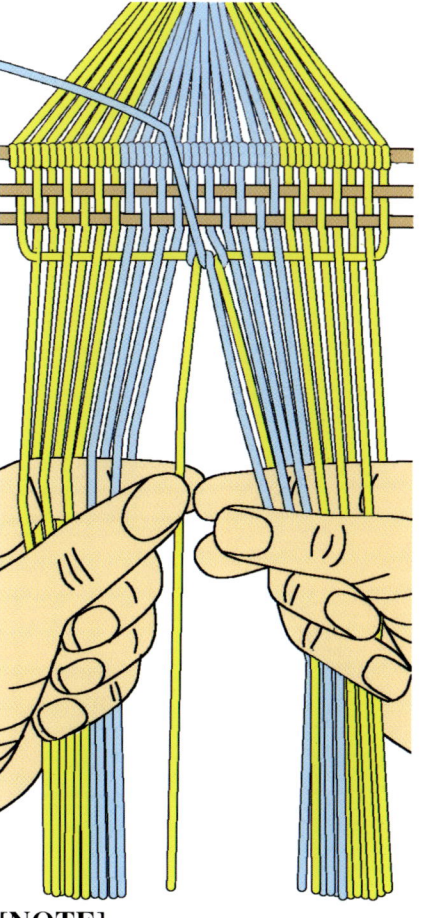

[NOTE]
As each warp strand is transferred to the other hand, check that the proper strand has been selected by observing its position as it crosses the weft strand.

[STEP 12]
Set the weft strands in place by pulling the two layers of the shed in opposite directions.

[NOTE]
Check to see if all strands are properly tightened.

[81]

[STEP 13]
Pull the first warp strand on the left through the open shed to the left of the first interlock in the previous row. When this warp strand is hooked up over the headstick it becomes the first weft strand of the new row.

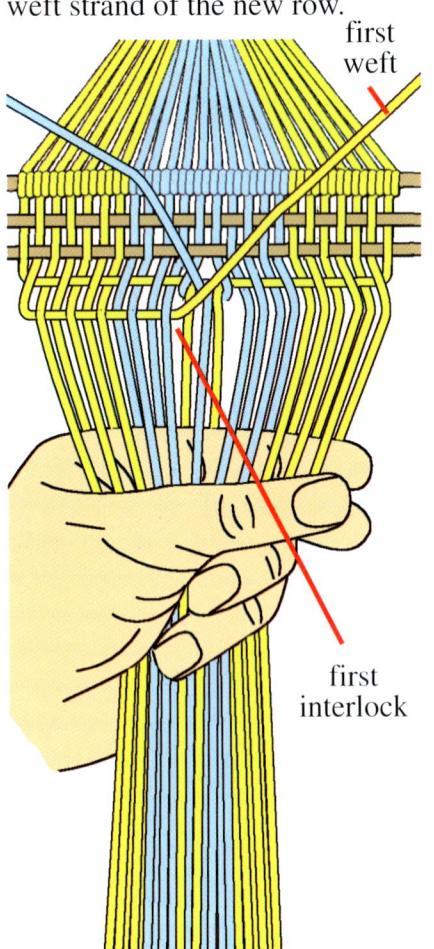

[STEP 14]
Begin the first interlock of the new row by pulling the warp strand that is to the left of the first interlock of the previous row through the open shed to the center. When this warp strand is hooked up over the headstick it becomes the second weft strand of the new row.

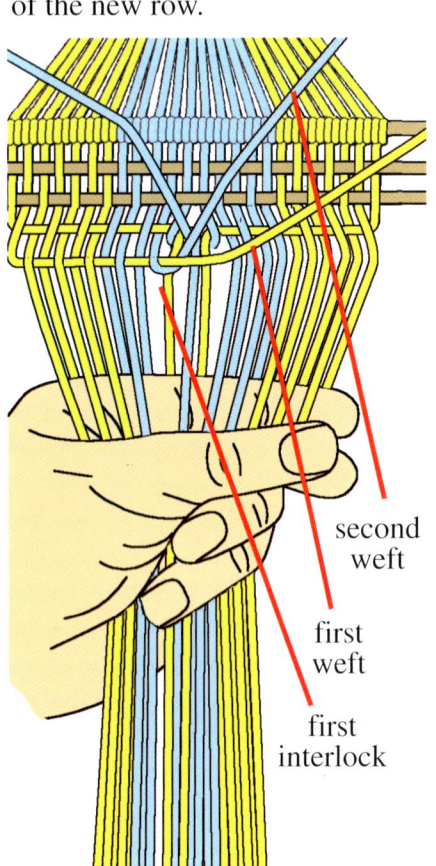

[STEP 15]
Complete the first interlock by turning the first weft strand down over the second weft strand.

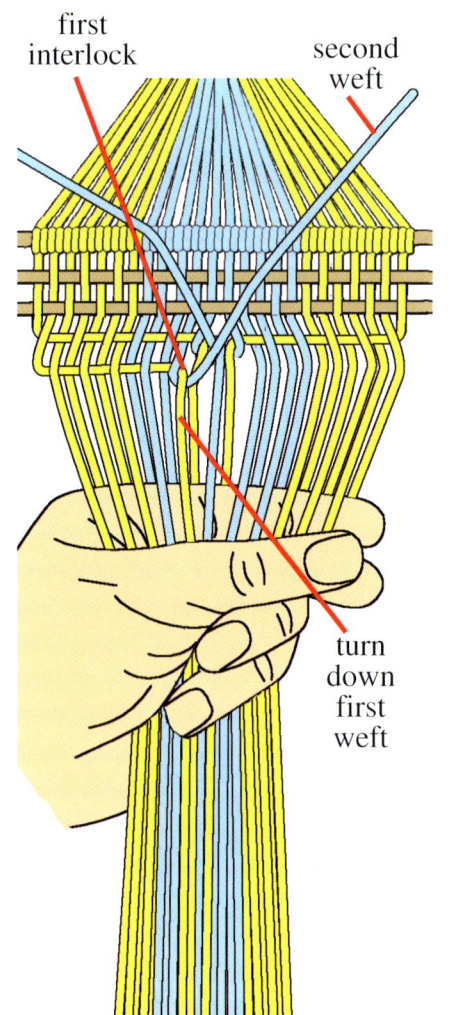

[STEP 16]
Finish the left half of the new row by turning the fourth weft strand of the previous row down over the second weft strand of the new row.

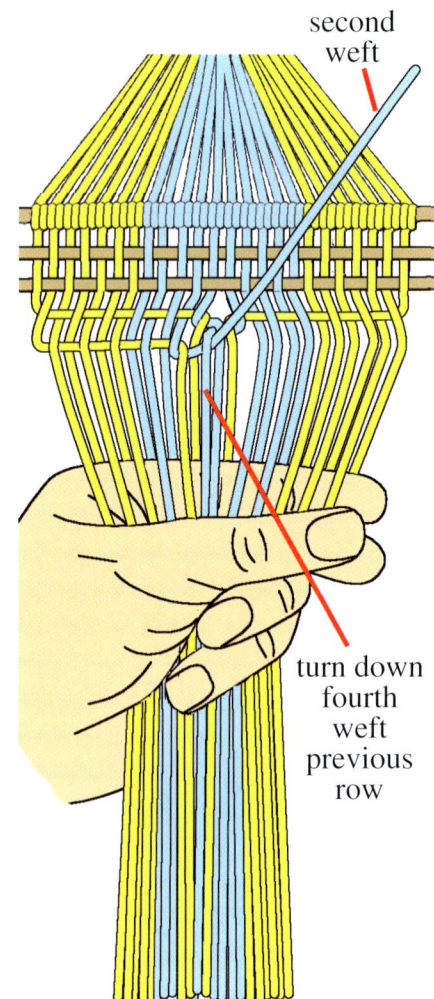

[STEP 17]

The first warp strand on the right becomes the third weft strand when it is pulled to the left through the open shed to the right of the second interlock of the previous row.

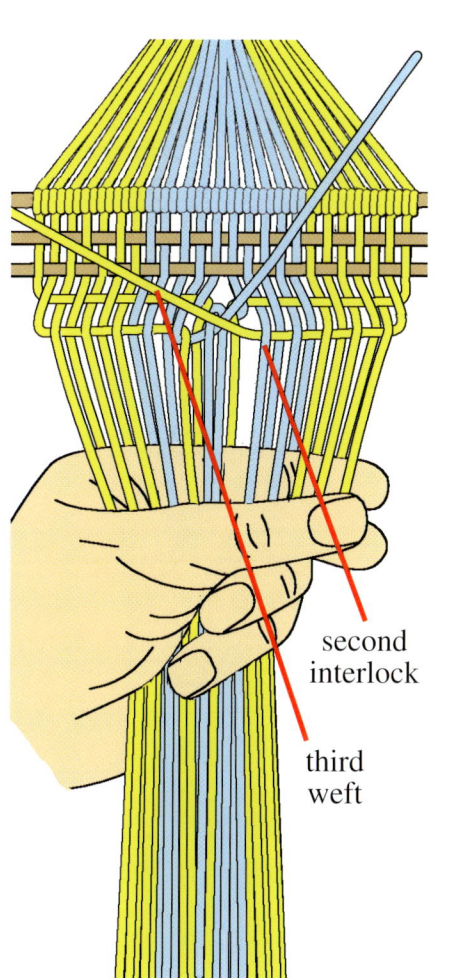

[STEP 18]

The second interlock of the new row is started when the warp strand to the right of the second interlock of the previous row is pulled through the open shed to the center. This warp strand becomes the fourth weft strand.

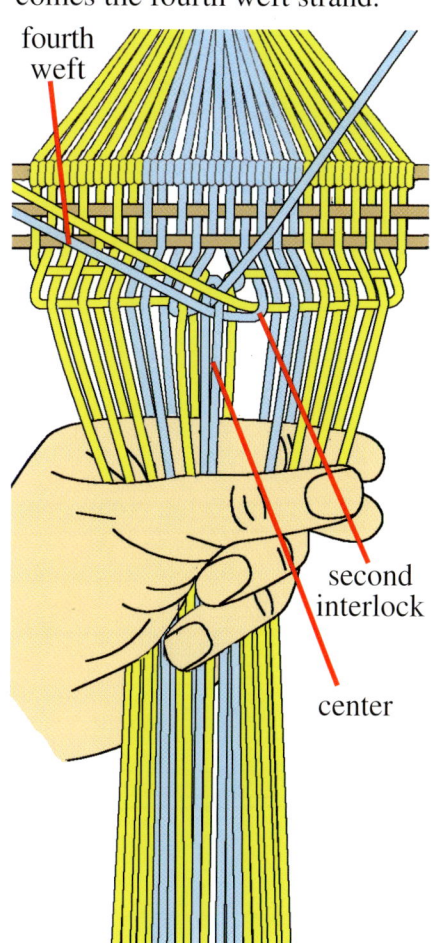

[STEP 19]

Complete the second interlock of the new row by turning the third weft strand down over the fourth weft strand.

[STEP 20]

Finish the new row by turning the second weft strand down over the fourth weft strand.

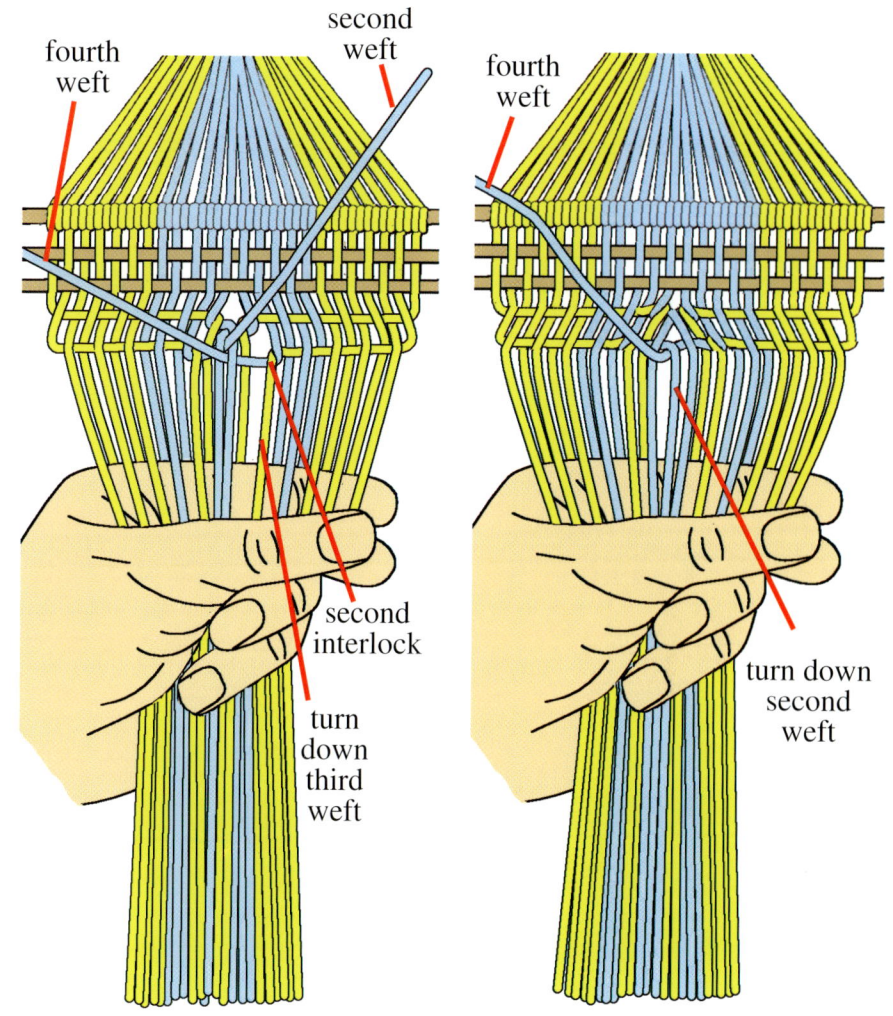

[83]

[STEP 21]
Reverse the shed by transferring the warp strands one at a time to the right index finger so that the warp strands that were up in the shed are down and the warp strands that were down in the shed are up.

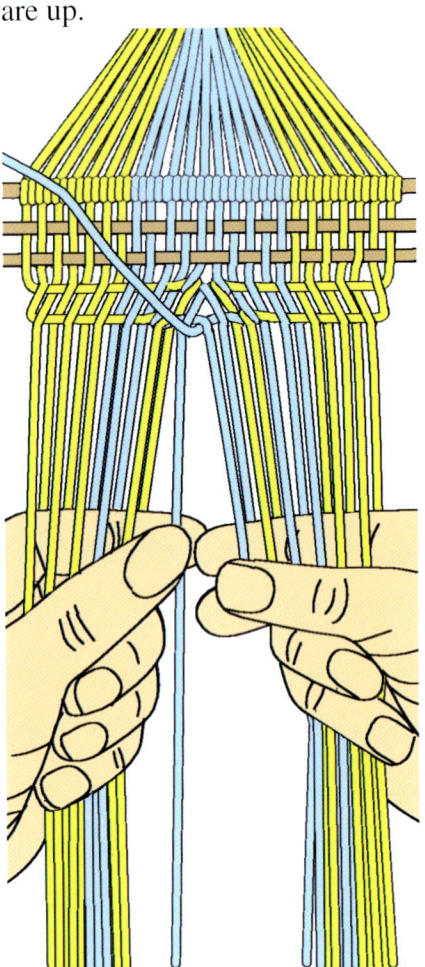

[STEP 22]
Set the weft strands in place by pulling the two layers of the shed in opposite directions.

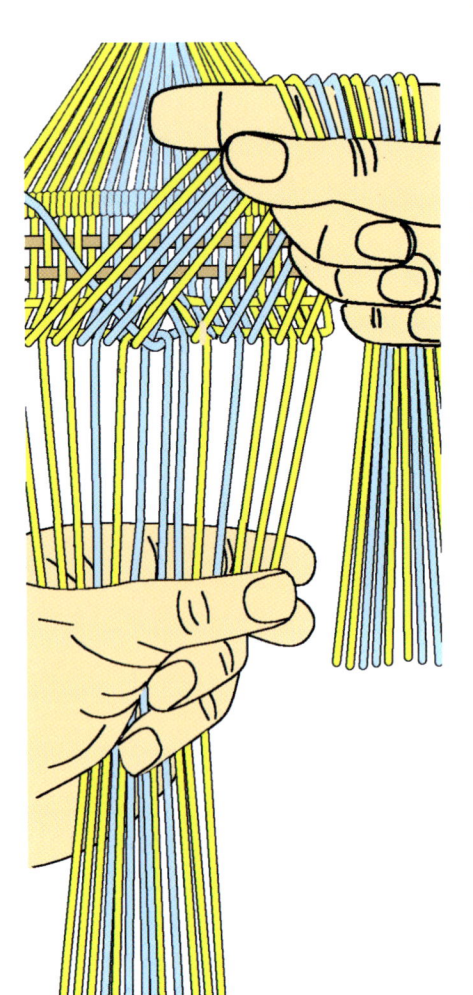

[STEP 23]
Continue to weave in this manner. When the original strand arrangement has been reestablished, start the pattern over. Repeat the pattern until the desired length is reached.

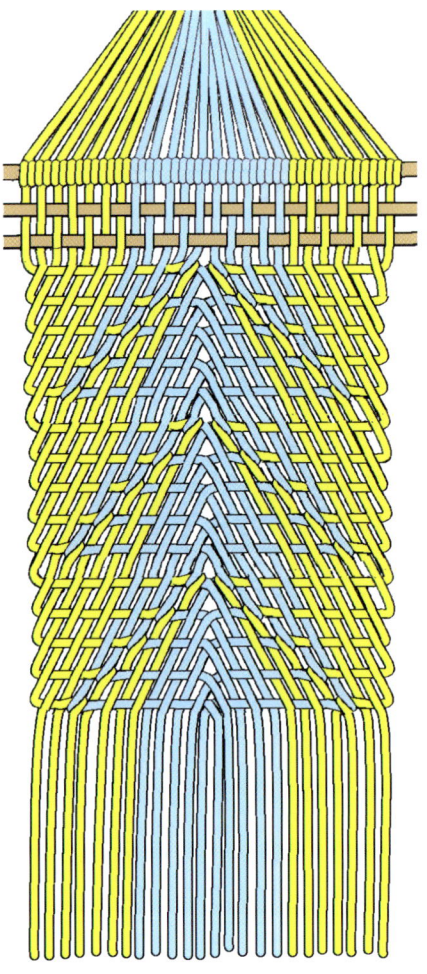

[NOTE]
See page 78 for information about changing the direction of the weave.

Arrowhead Pattern Over Two/Under Two (Point Up) Example:

[84]

PART 3: OPENFACE WEAVING

Openface weaving goes by several names. Plain face, oblique, and interface are some of the names. There are probably more names than this. The variety of names comes from the attempts to choose a name that describes this form of weaving.

In openface weaving, the weave is open so that all the strands are visible on the face of the finished work. Openface weaving is done by weaving two sets of strands together. One set of strands crosses the work on a diagonal from left to right and the other set crosses the work on a diagonal from right to left. Because there are no clear warp and weft strands as there are in warpface fingerweaving, openface weaving is more closely related to braiding than to loom weaving
The following photographs show examples of openface weaving and various ways to decorate it.

Solid Color

Twining

Diamond Weave

Colored Bands

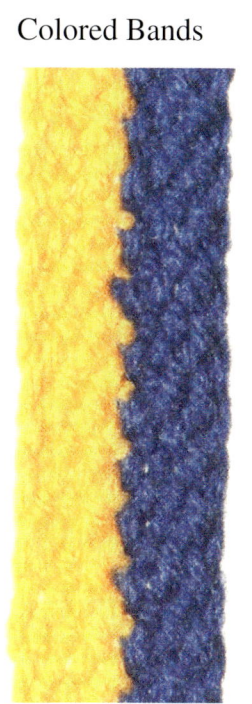

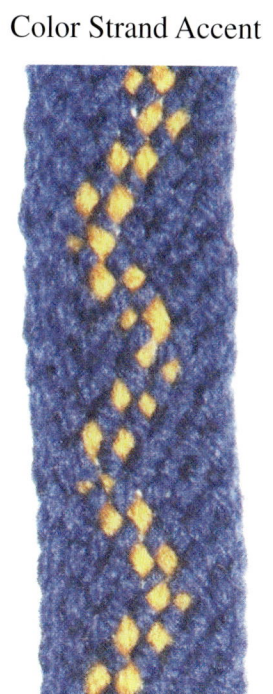

Color Strand Accent

Warp Accent

[85]

Openface Weaving
Plain Weaving

Openface fingerweaving is produced by diagonally interlacing two layers of strands. As a result of this diagonal interlacing, the strands from each layers are visible in the final work. Also, there is no clear set of warp and weft strands in open face finger weaving. When a strand reaches the edge of the work it is turned back into the work on the opposite diagonal and becomes part of the opposite layer.

Pattern options in openface weaving are limited. Most work is done in bands of solid color giving a stripe effect. Some or all of the stripes may be decorated by weaving geometric patterns of beads or strands of a contrasting colors.

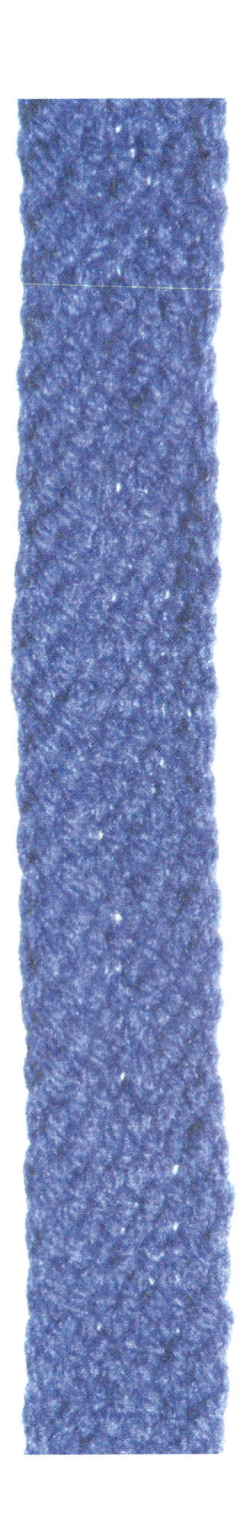

[STEP 1]
Cast the required number of strands of yarn on to the headstick. Use clove hitches to tie the yarn in place. See (Part 1: Getting Started).

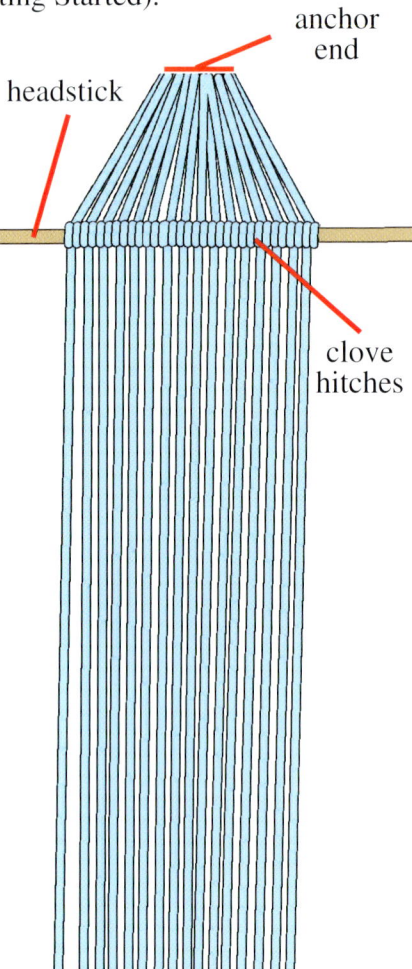

- anchor end
- headstick
- clove hitches

[STEP 2]
Set up the over/under weaving pattern of the shed with two smaller sticks.

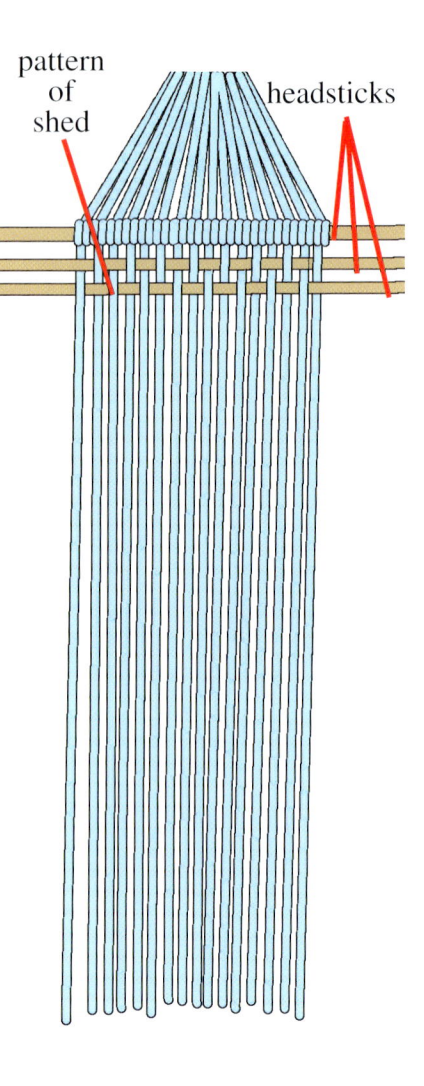

- pattern of shed
- headsticks

[NOTE] When planning a piece of work, it is best to use an even number of strands.

[86]

[STEP 3]
Pick up the shed. Use the index finger of the left hand to hold the shed open. Observe that the strands are now divided into two layers. The bottom layer is behind the index finger and the top layer is above the index finger.

— anchor

[STEP 4]
The third strand from the right is pulled to the right through the open shed.

third strand

[STEP 5]
Transfer the first and third strands to the index finger of the right hand. The third strand is still in the top layer but the first strand has been moved to the bottom layer. Observe that the next two strands are in the bottom layer.

bottom strands

[STEP 6]
Pull the next top strand down between the two bottom layer strands.

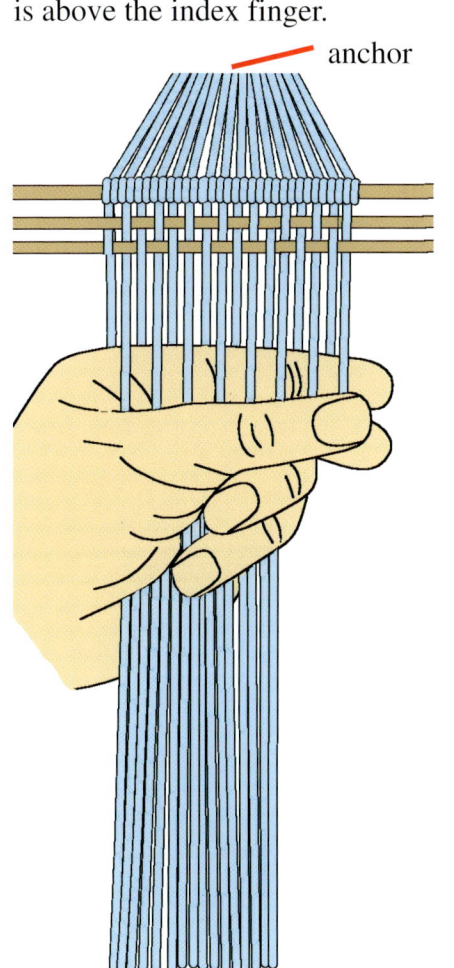

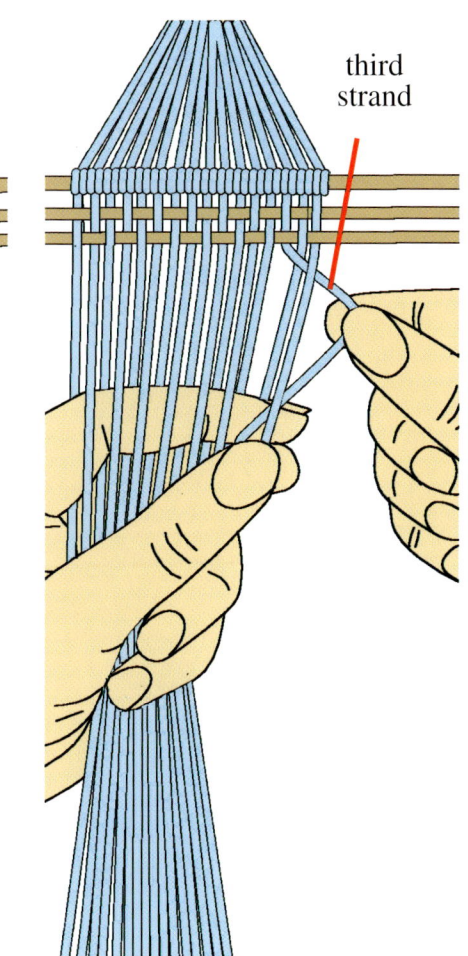

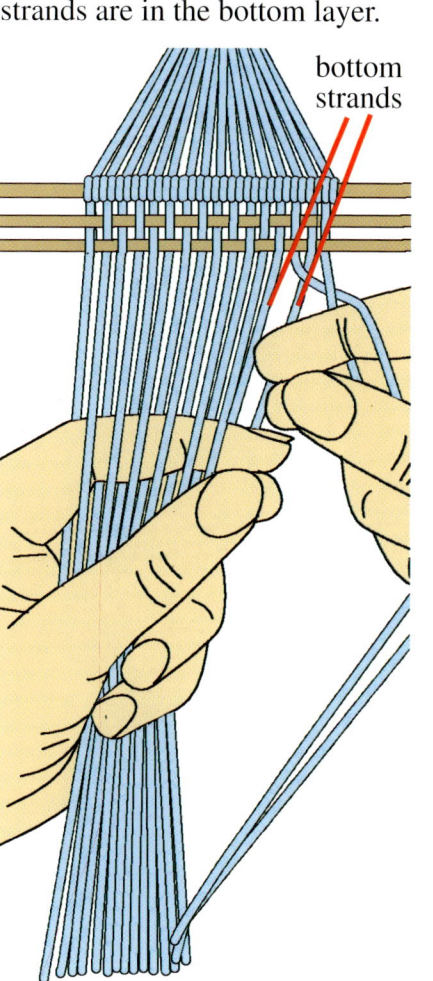

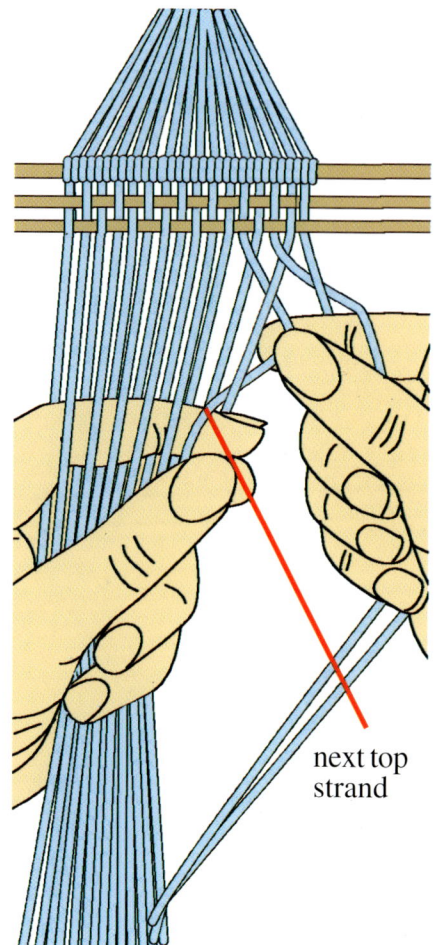

next top strand

[87]

[STEP 7]
Transfer the next pair of strands to the index finger of the right hand. Observe that the next two strands after that are again from the bottom layer.

[STEP 8]
Pull the next top strand down between the two bottom layer strands.

[STEP 9]
Transfer the next pair of strands to the index finger of the right hand. Observe that the next two strands are again from the bottom layer.

[STEP 10]
Continue to weave across the work piece in this manner. Notice that the last strand on the left has been moved from the bottom layer of strands to the top layer of strands.

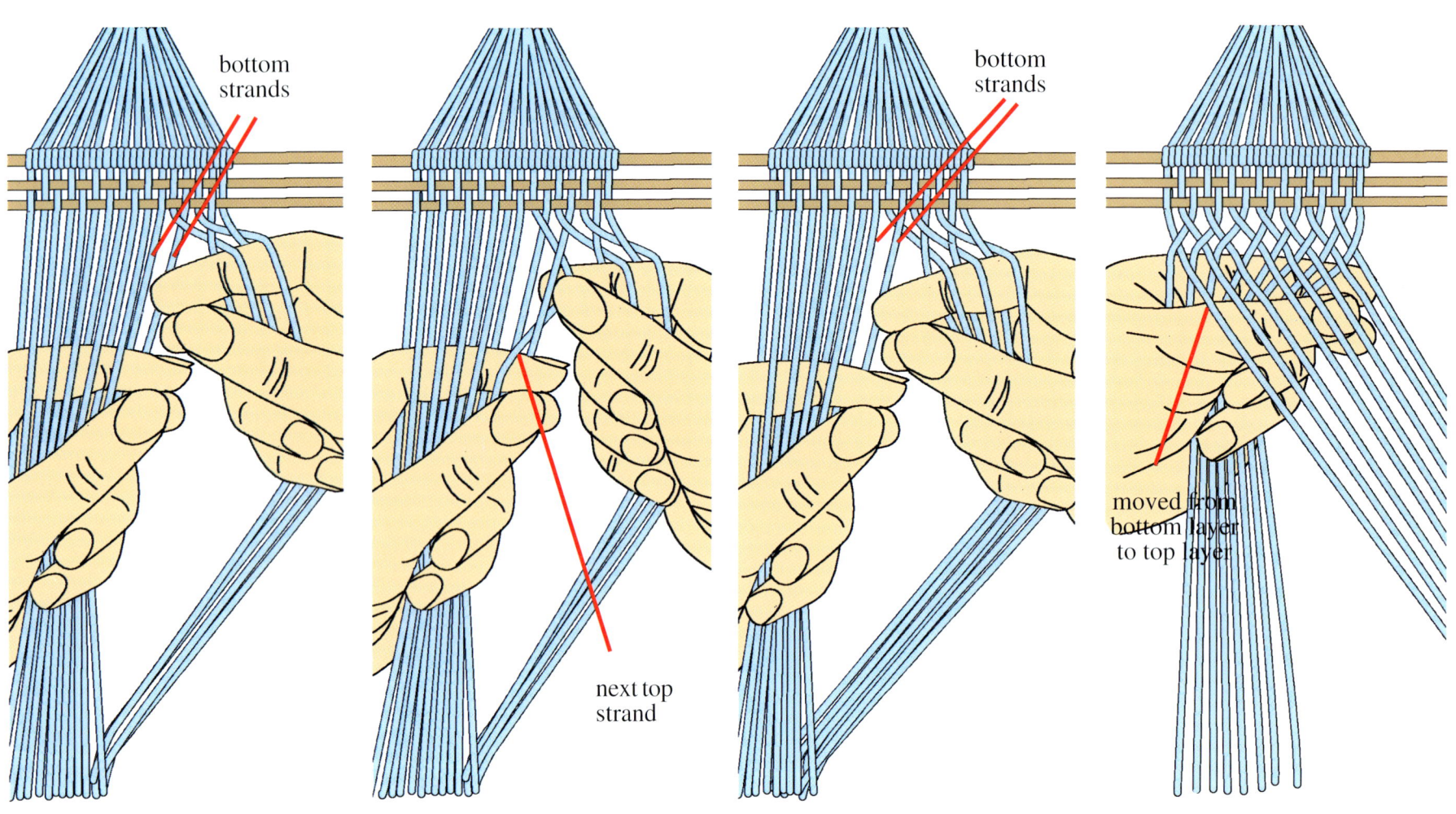

[STEP 11]
Separate the two layers of the shed. Pull 1 to 3 strands free at a time.

[STEP 12]
Set the weave by pulling the two layers of the shed in opposite directions.

[STEP 13
Transfer the open shed back to the left hand.

[STEP 14]
Start the next row of weaving by pulling the third strand from the right through the open shed to the right.

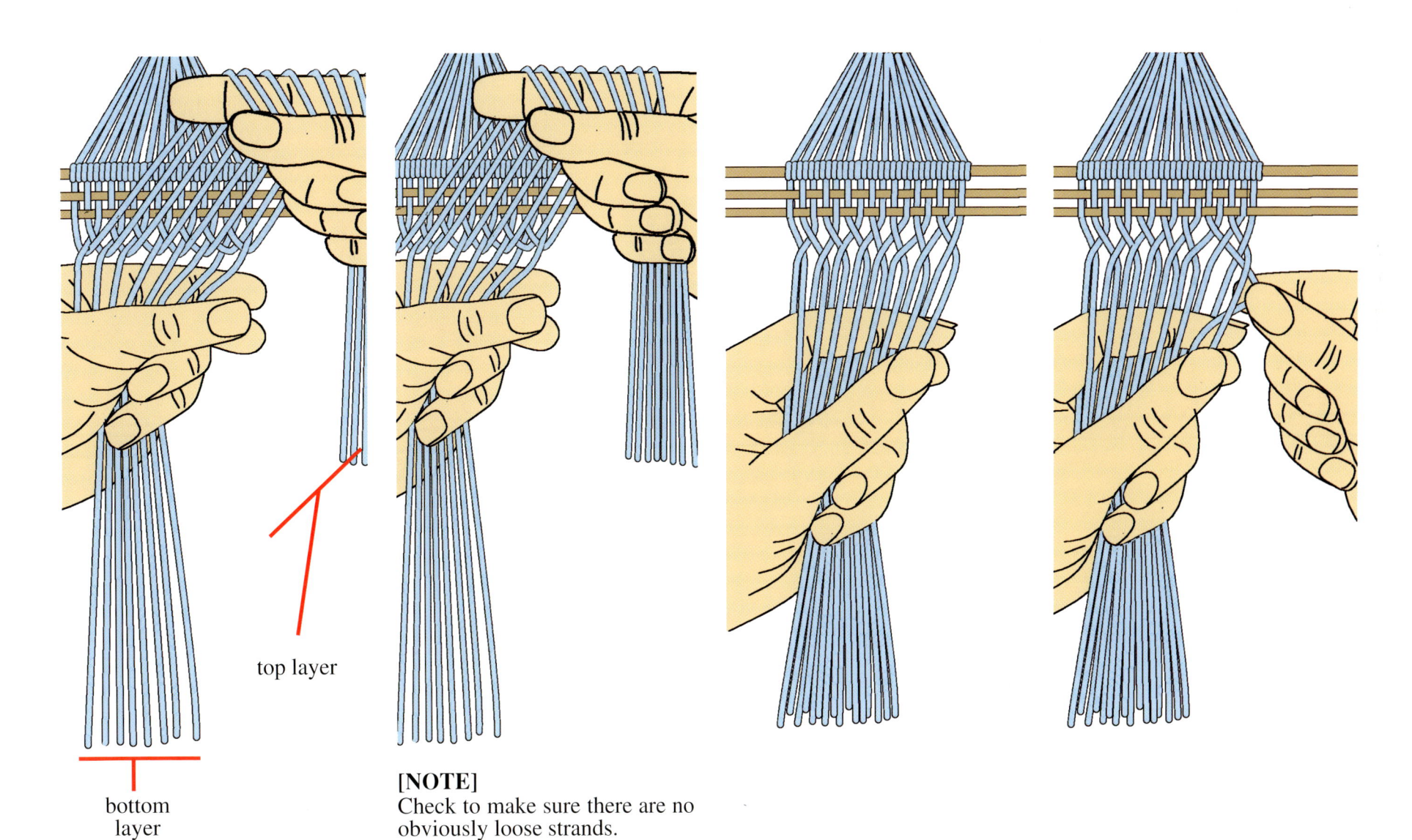

top layer

bottom layer

[NOTE]
Check to make sure there are no obviously loose strands.

[89]

[STEP 15]
Transfer the first and third strand to the index finger of the right hand. The third strand is still in the top layer but the first strand has been moved to the bottom layer. Observe that the next two strands are in the bottom layer.

[STEP 16]
Pull the next top strand down between the two bottom layer strands.

[STEP 17]
Transfer the next pair of strands to the index finger of the right hand. Observe that the next two strands in the left hand are again from the bottom layer.

[STEP 18]
Continue to weave in the manner illustrated until the desired length is reached.

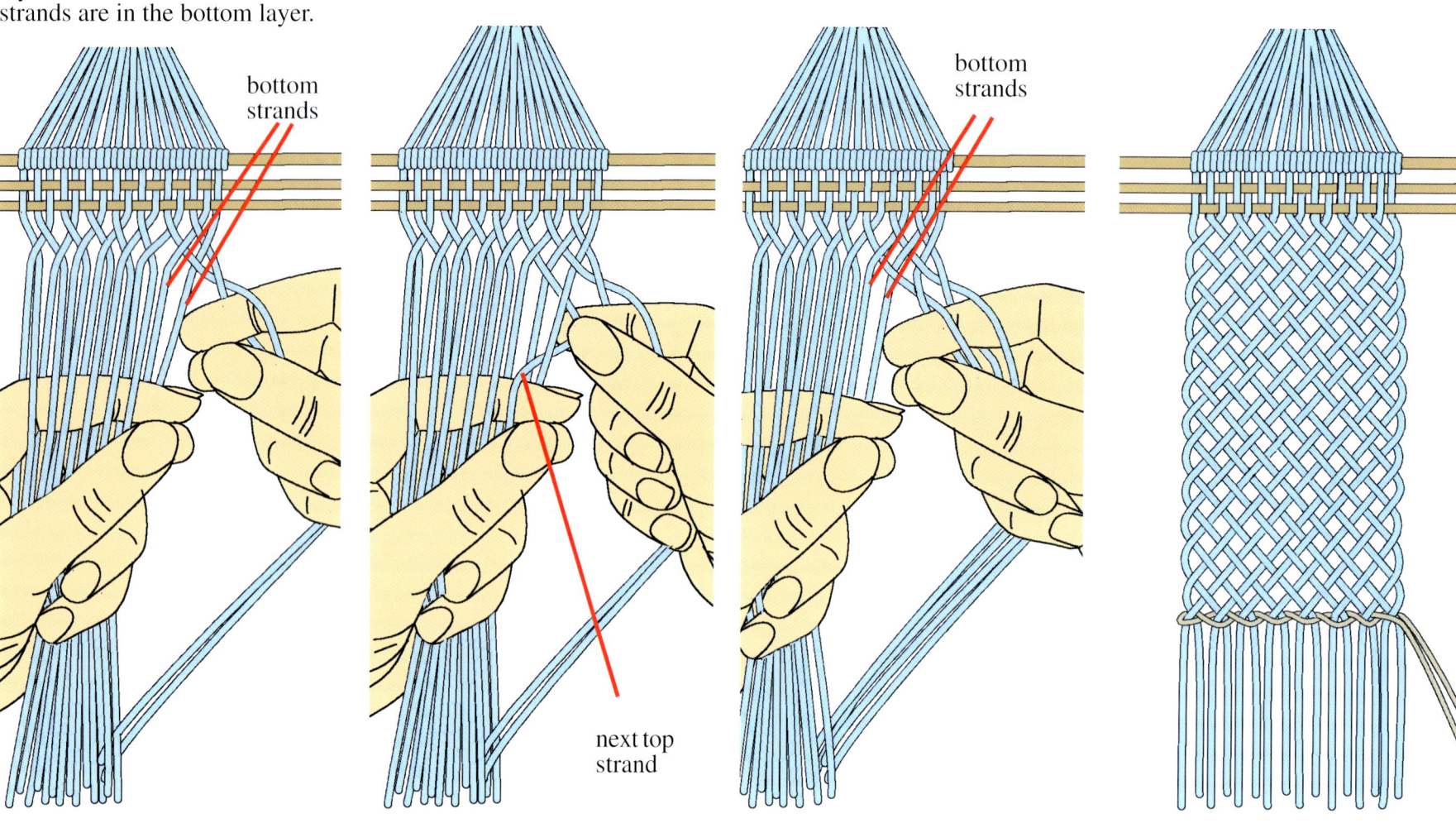

bottom strands

next top strand

bottom strands

[90]

[STEP 19 A]
End the weaving by twining a separate strand across the pairs of main strands and tie it off with a square knot.

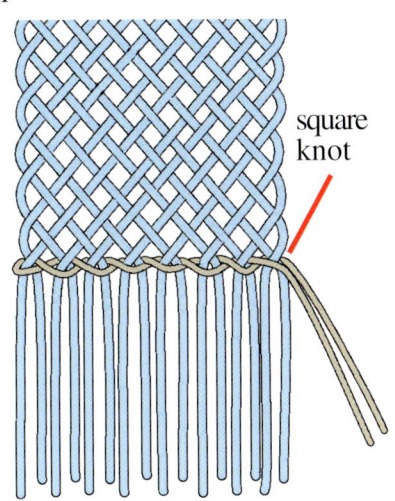

[STEP 19 B]
OR
Pull one of the edge strands through the open shed and tie it off with a square knot.

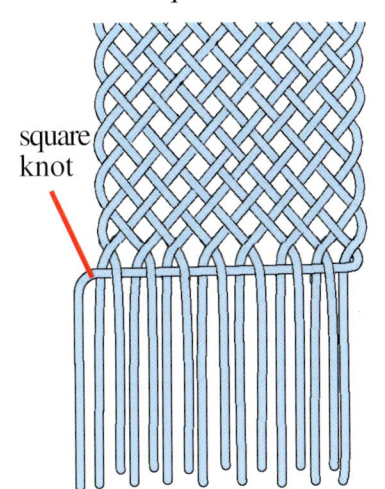

[STEP 20]
Turn the work around and reattach it to your anchor.

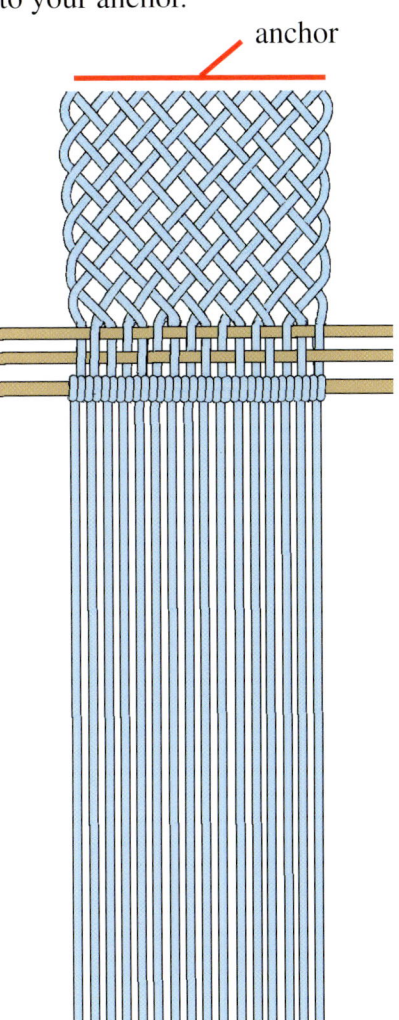

[STEP 21]
Remove the first two headsticks. Pick up the shed then remove the third headstick.

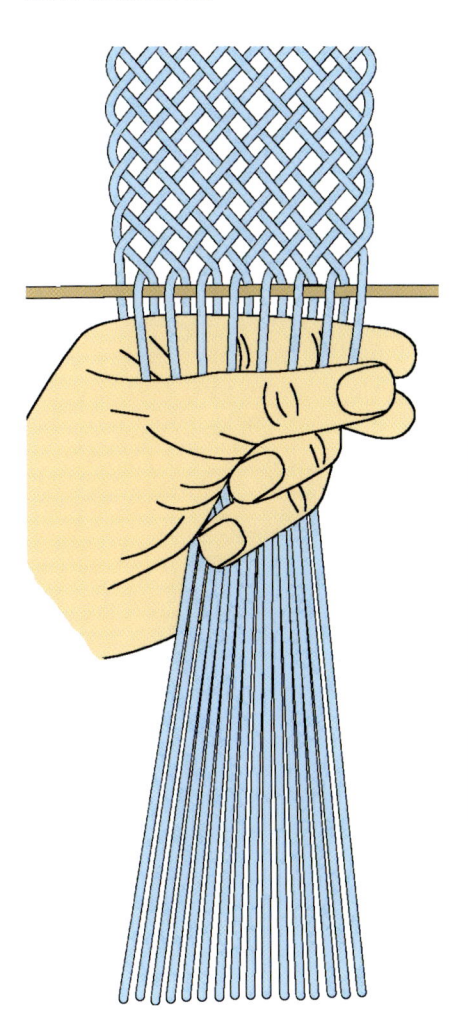

[STEP 22]
Start reversing the layers by pulling the second strand on the right under the first strand on the right.

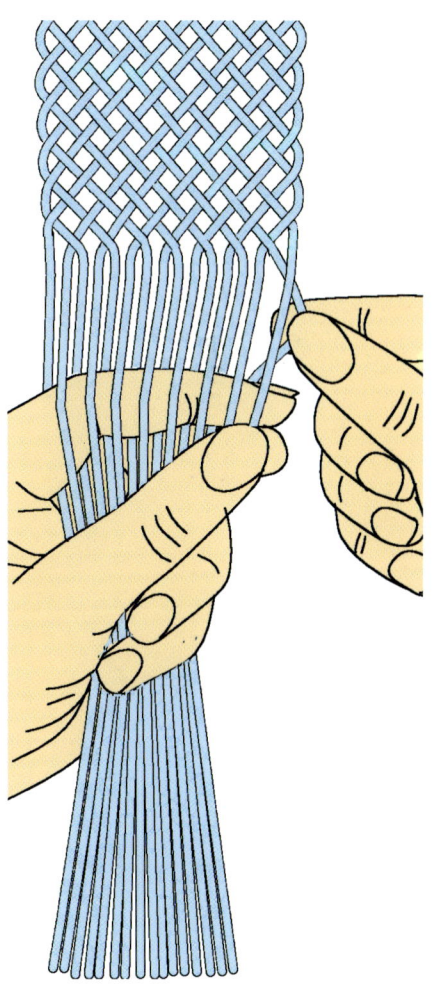

[NOTE] When the shed is picked up off the headstick, the top layer is angled to the left and the bottom layer is angled to the right. In order to continue weaving, the top layer must be angled to the right.

[91]

[STEP 23]
Transfer the first two strands to the index finger of the right hand.

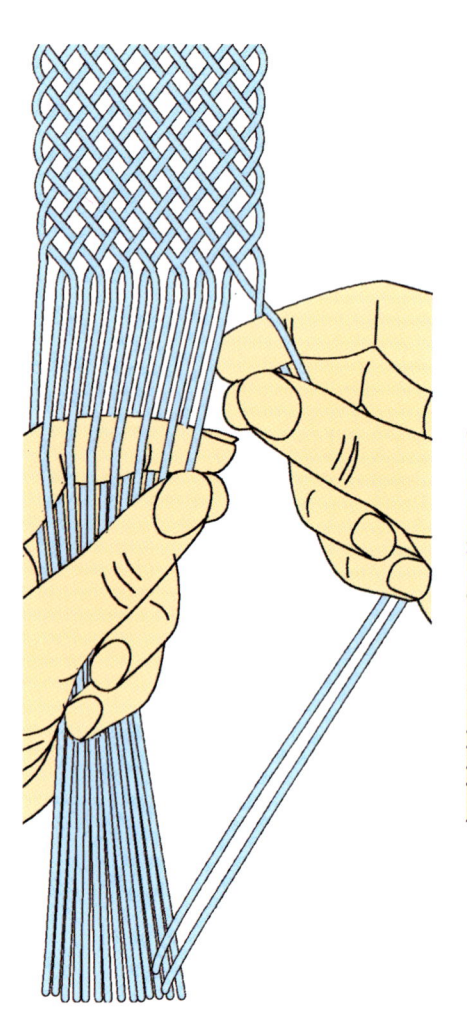

[STEP 24]
Pull the fourth strand on the right under the third strand on the right.

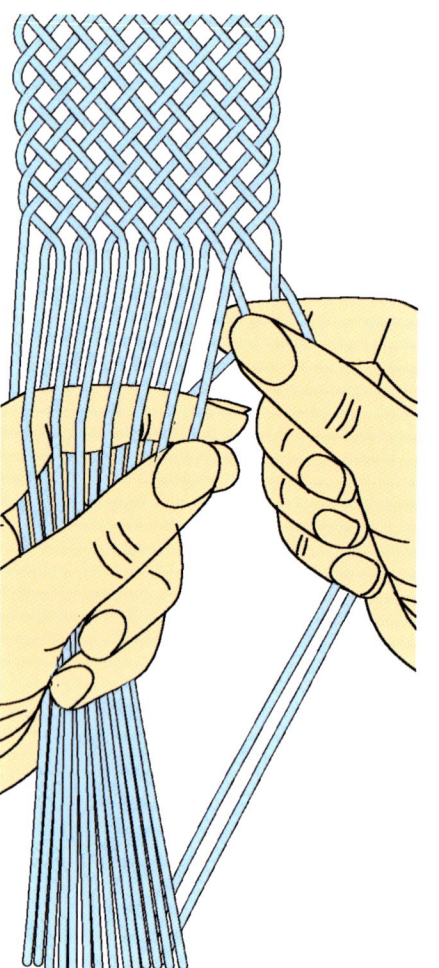

[STEP 25]
Transfer the two strands to the right hand. Continue in this manner until the layers are reversed. Then continue to weave following the directions for [STEP 4] through [STEP 16].

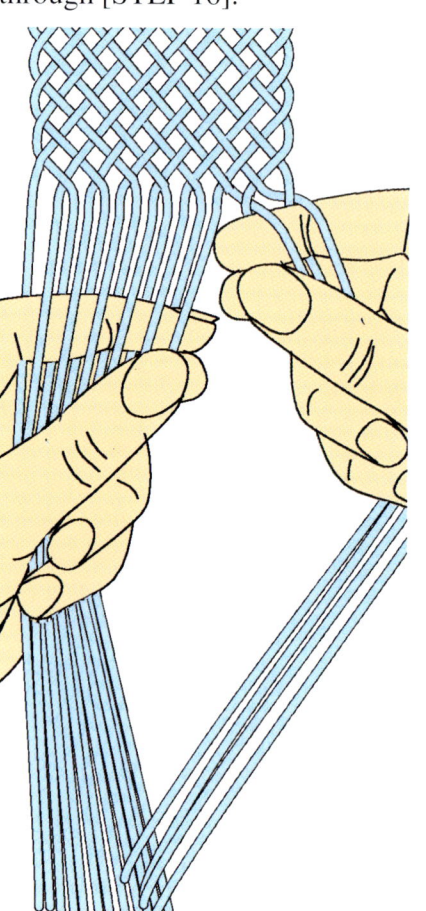

Openface Weaving Plain Weaving Example:

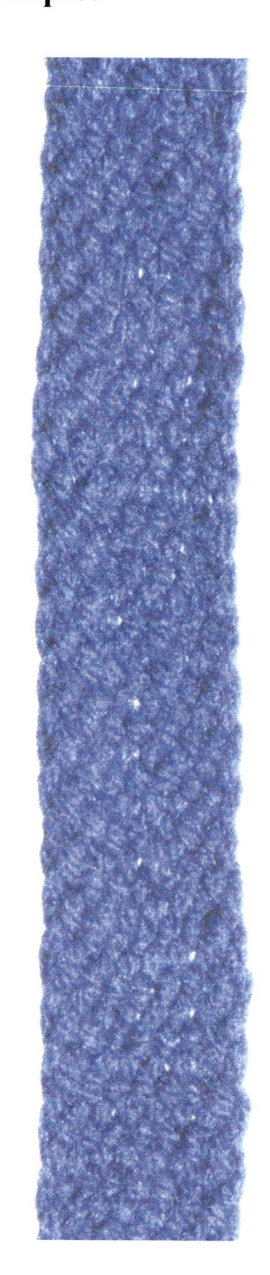

[92]

Openface Weaving Joining Bands

To create bands of different colors, the color bands are joined along their edges. As each strand is turned back into its own color band, it is interlocked with a strand from the adjoining color band.

When setting up color bands it is easier to use an even number of strands in each color band.

This technique can be used to add borders to a piece of openface weaving.

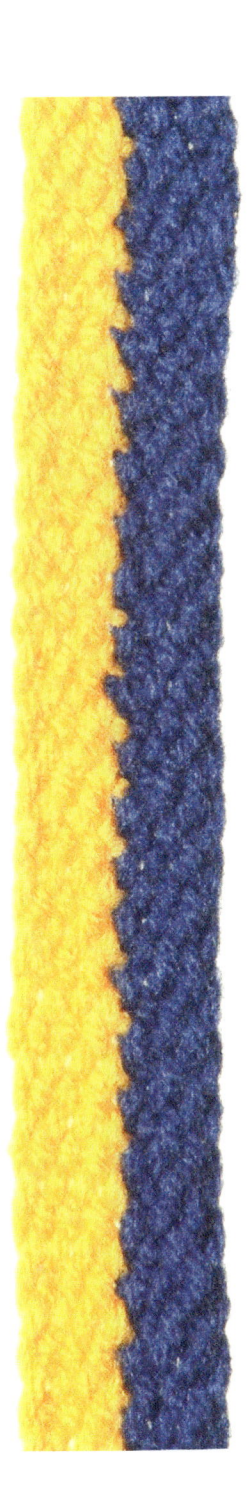

[STEP 1]
Cast on the required number of strands. Set up the shed and follow the instructions for openface weaving until there are two bottom strands left in the right hand color band.

[STEP 2]
Reach under the first of the remaining strands in the right hand band.

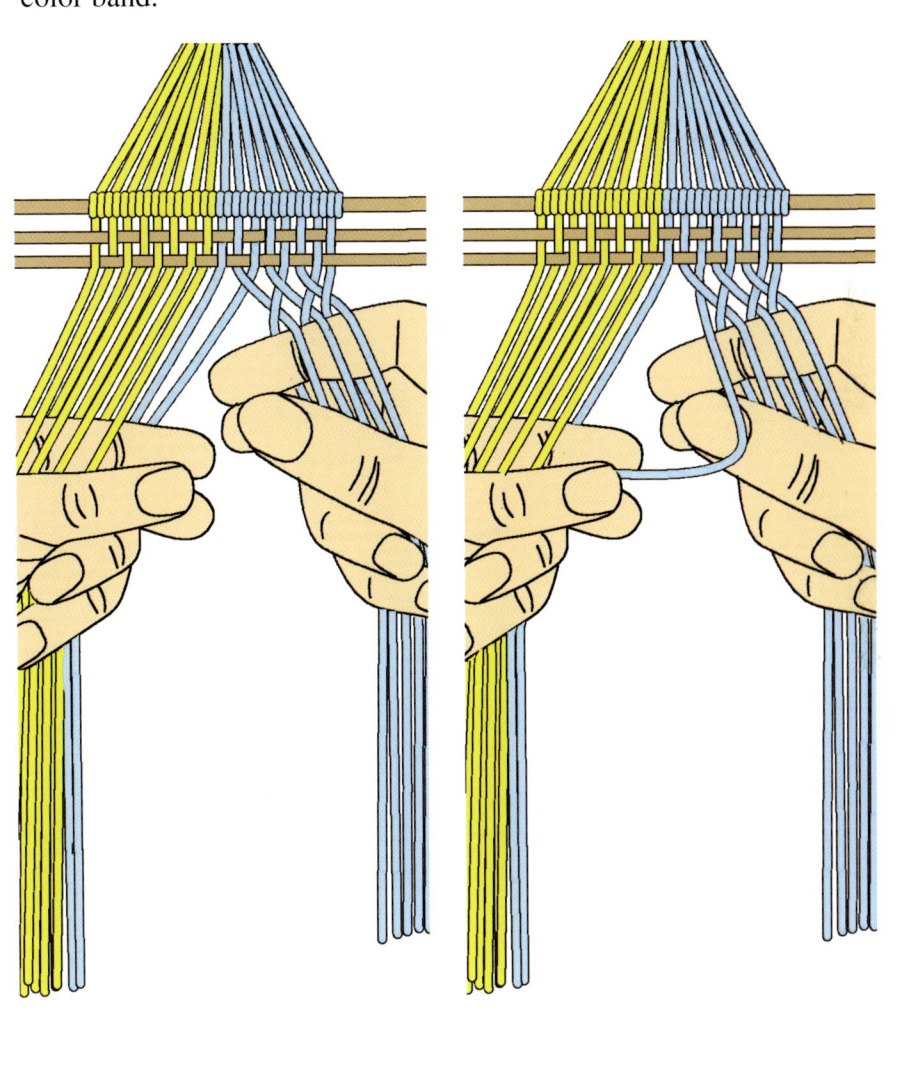

[93]

[STEP 3]
Pull the first strand of the left hand band over the last strand of the right hand band.

[STEP 4]
Interlock the last strand of the right hand band and the first strand of the left hand band.

[STEP 5]
Pull the last strand of the right hand band under the next to the last strand of the right hand band.

[STEP 6]
Transfer the last two strands of the right hand band to the right hand.

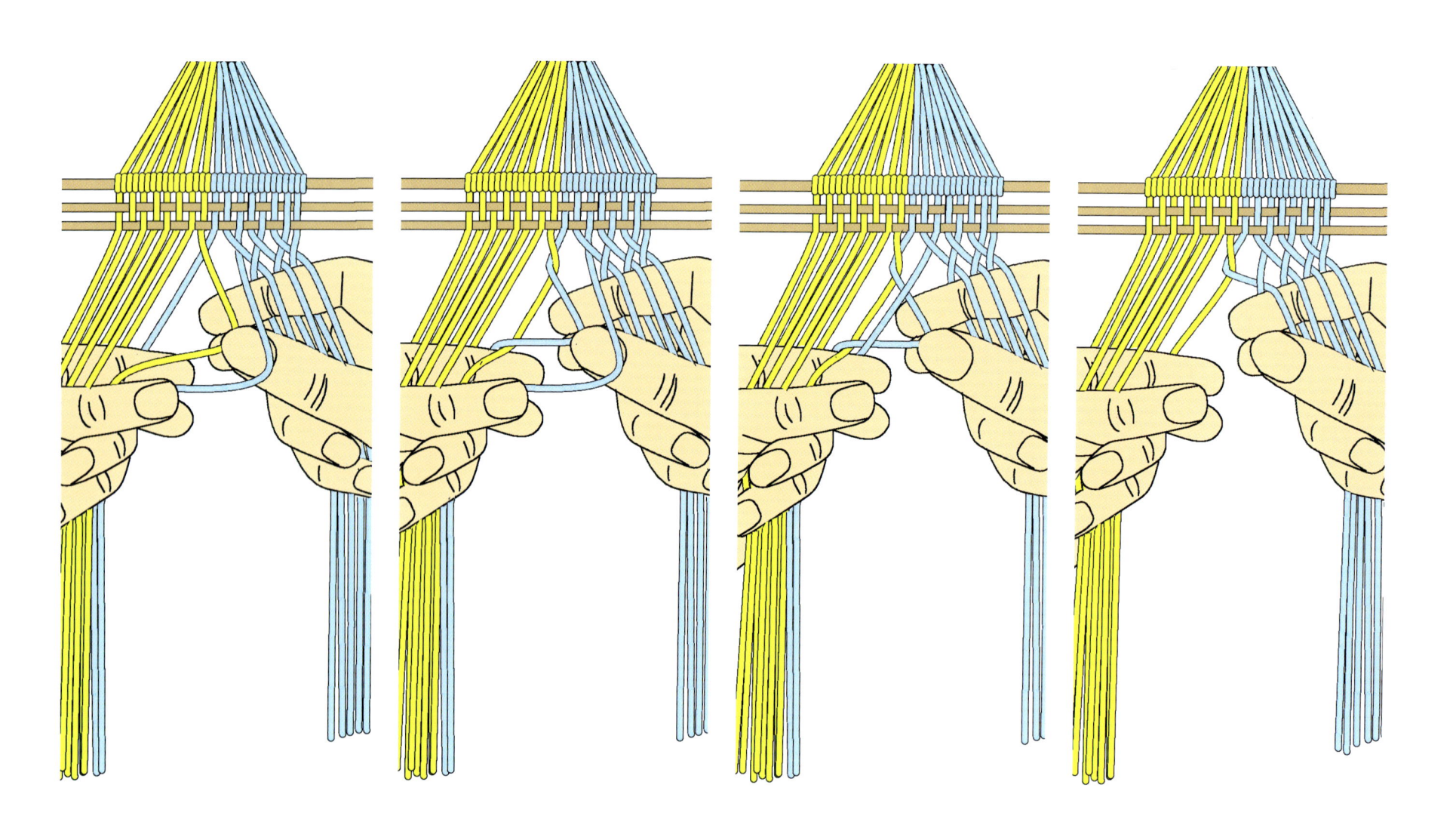

[94]

[STEP 7]
Pull the next top strand down between the two bottom layer strands.

[STEP 8]
Transfer the next pair of strands to the index finger of the right hand. Observe that the next two strands after that are again from the bottom layer.

[STEP 9]
Continue to weave across the work piece in this manner. Notice that the last strand on the left has been moved from the bottom layer of strands to the top layer of strands.

[STEP 10]
Again, follow the instructions for openface weaving until there are two bottom strands left in the right hand band.

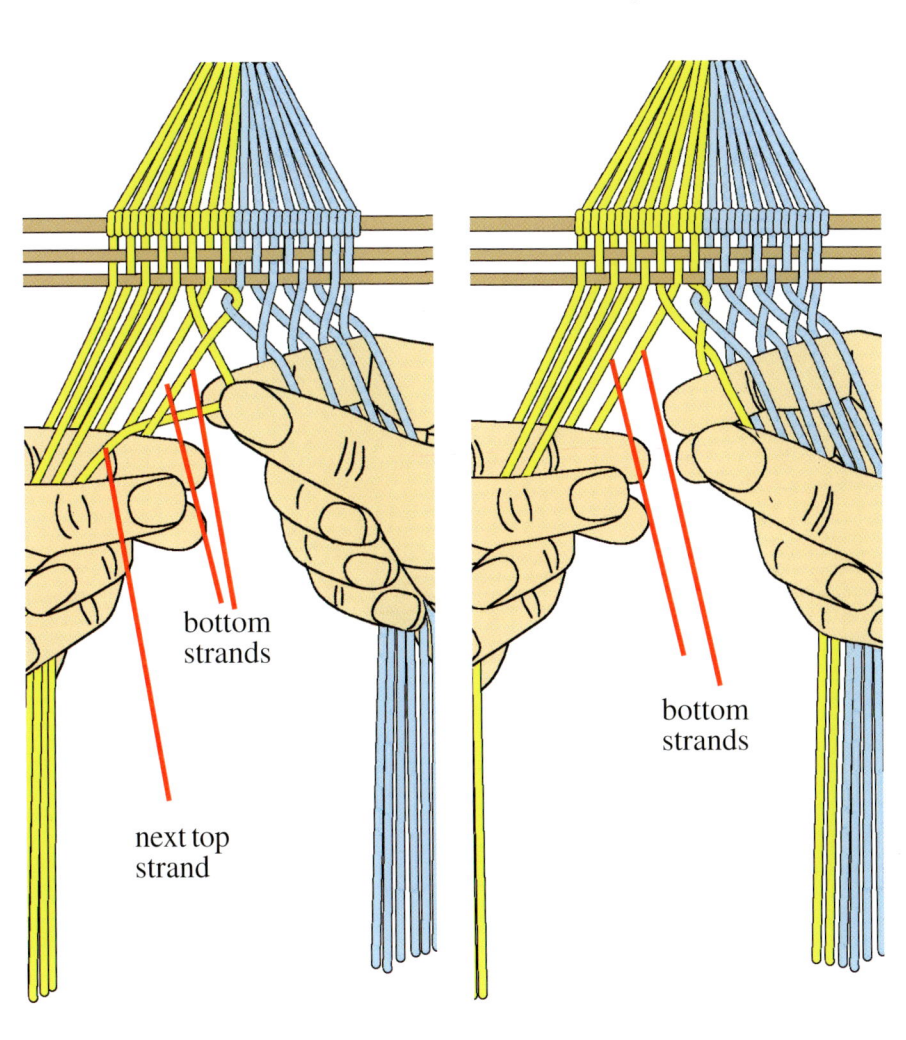

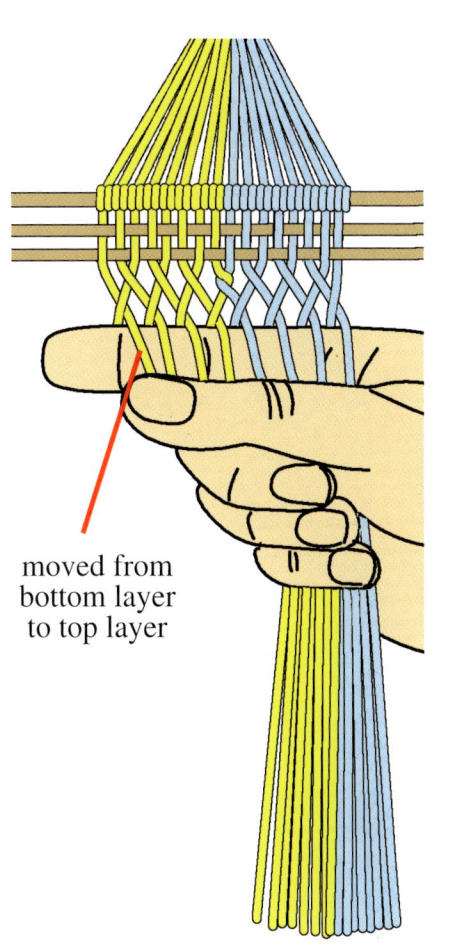

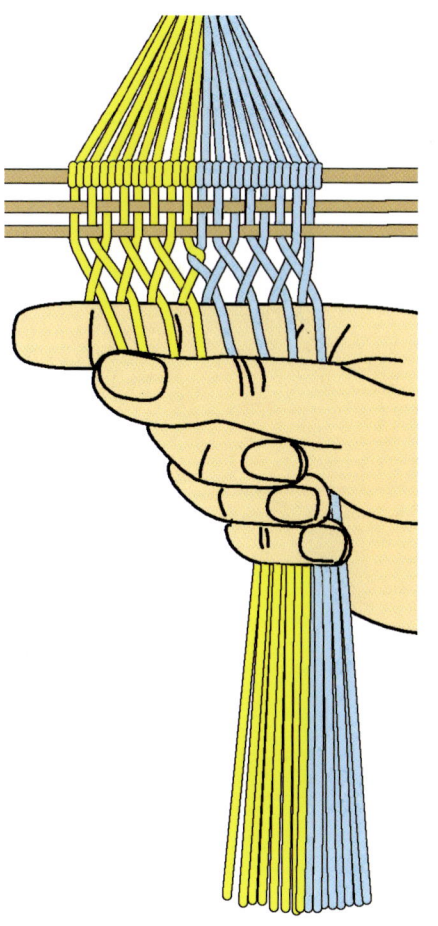

bottom strands

next top strand

bottom strands

moved from bottom layer to top layer

[NOTE] Be sure to separate the two layers. Then set the weaving by pulling the two layers in opposite directions. See [STEP 11] and [STEP 12] on page 94.

[95]

[STEP 11]
Reach under the first of the remaining strands.

[STEP 12]
Pull the first strand of the left hand band over the last strand of the right hand band.

[STEP 13]
Interlock the last strand of the right hand band and the first strand of the left hand band.

[STEP 14]
Pull the last strand of the right hand band under the next to the last strand of the right hand band.

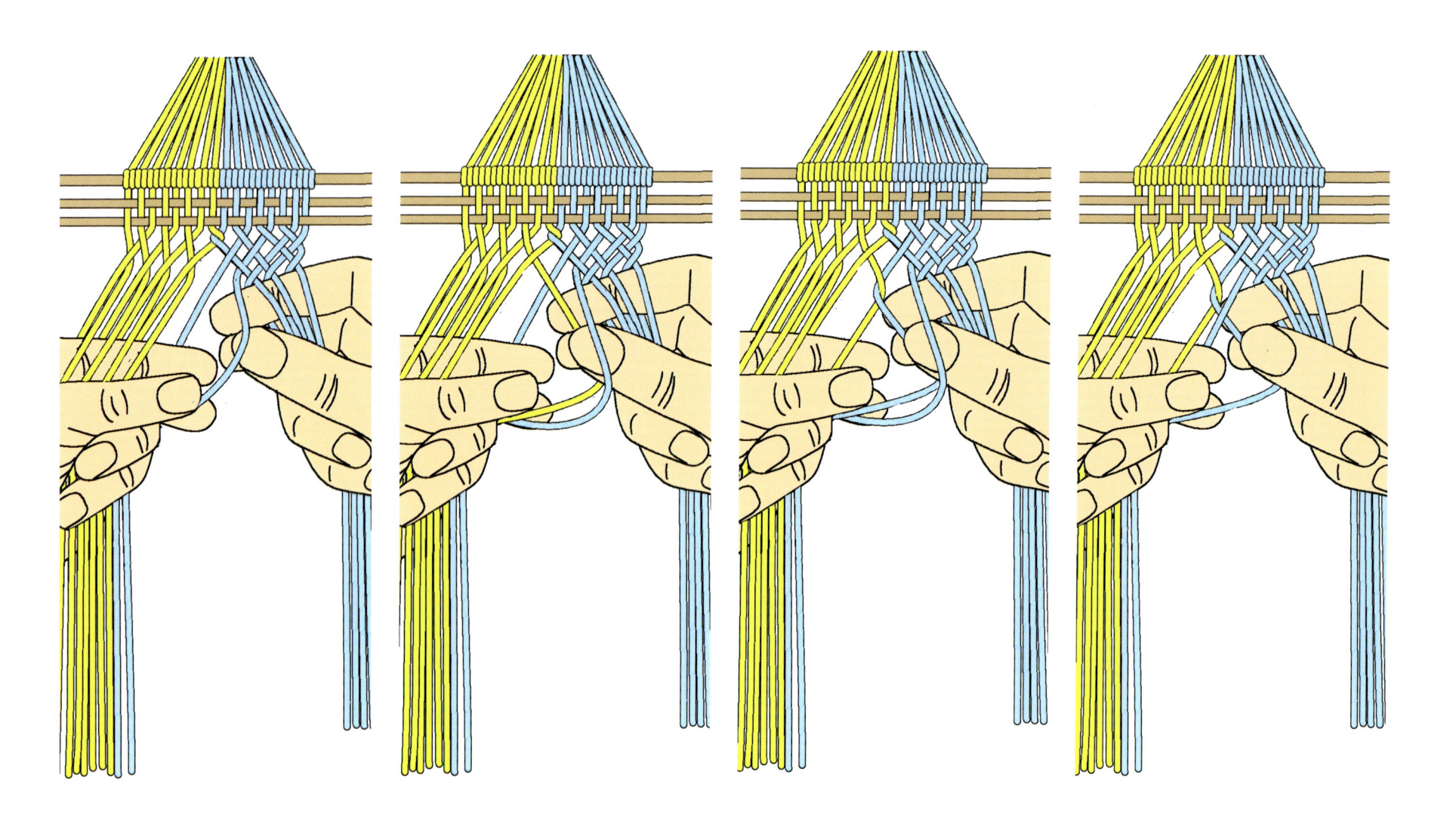

[STEP 15]
Transfer the last two strands of the right hand band to the index finger of the right hand.

[STEP 16]
Continue to weave in this manner until the desired length is reached.

Openface Weaving Joining Bands Example:

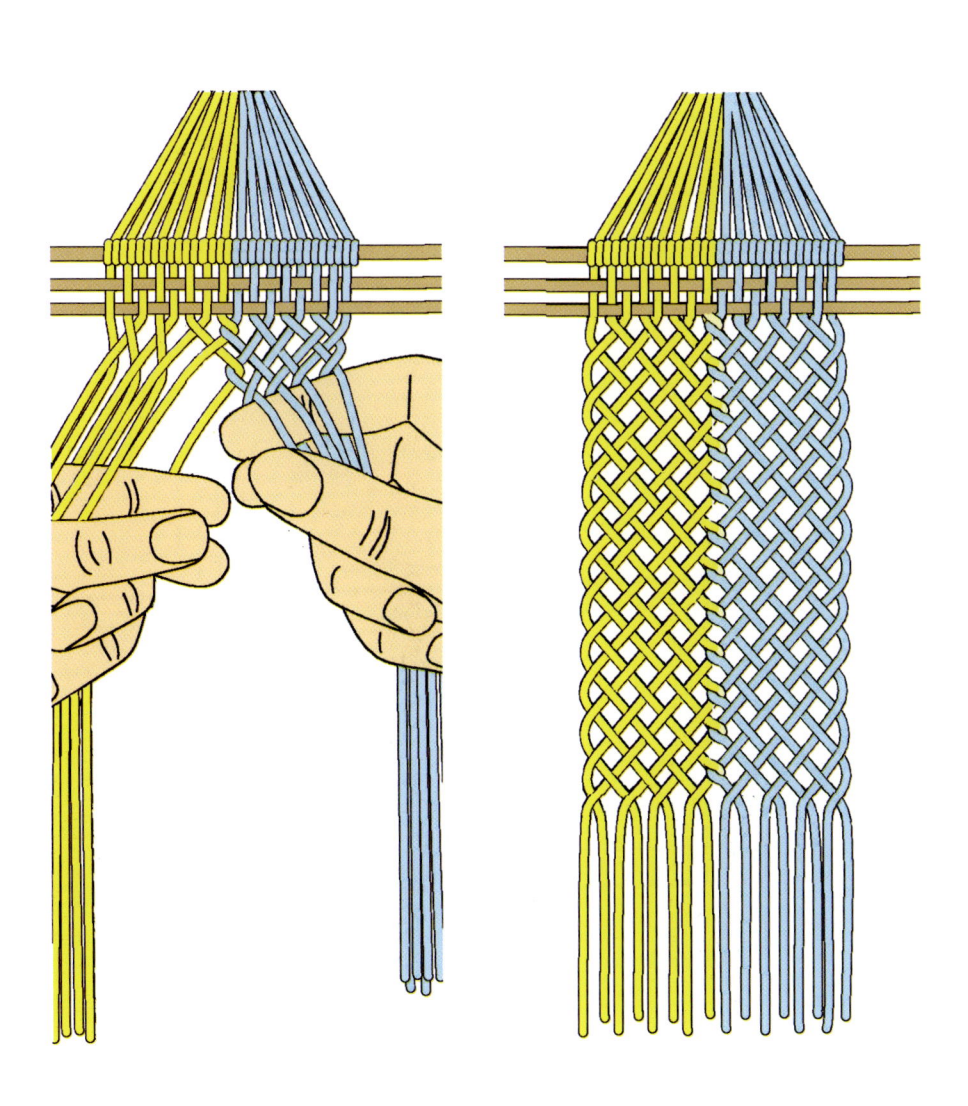

[97]

Openface Woven Borders
On Diagonal Warpface Weaving

Bands of openface weaving can be used to create borders on a piece of warpface weaving.

The example illustrated here is a piece of diagonal warpface weaving with openface woven borders.

The following steps show the weft strand moving from left to right **(L/R)**.

Diagonal warpface weaving worked from left to right.

[NOTE]
The sequence in which the various parts are worked depends on the direction that the weft strand of the warpface part of the work piece is moved.

Warpface Left to Right
[STEP 1(L/R)]
Cast the required number of strands of yarn on to the headstick. Use clove hitches to tie the yarn in place. See (Part 1: Getting Started).

Set up the over/under weaving pattern of the shed with two smaller sticks.

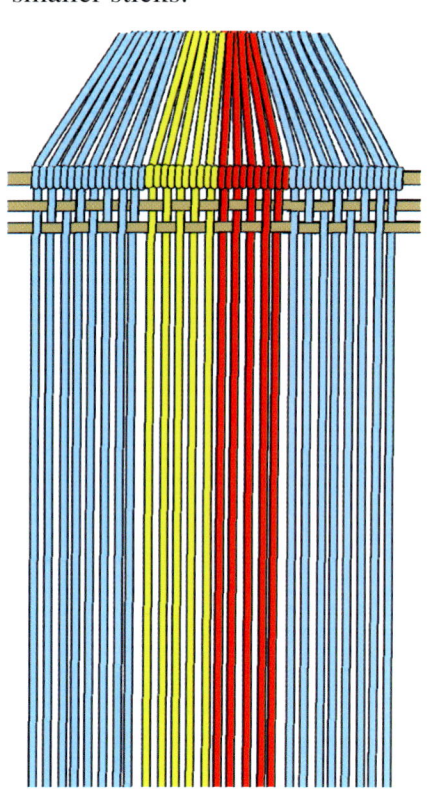

[NOTE]
When setting up a work piece it is easier to use an even number of strands in each part.

[STEP 2(L/R)]
Pick up the shed on the index finger of the left hand.

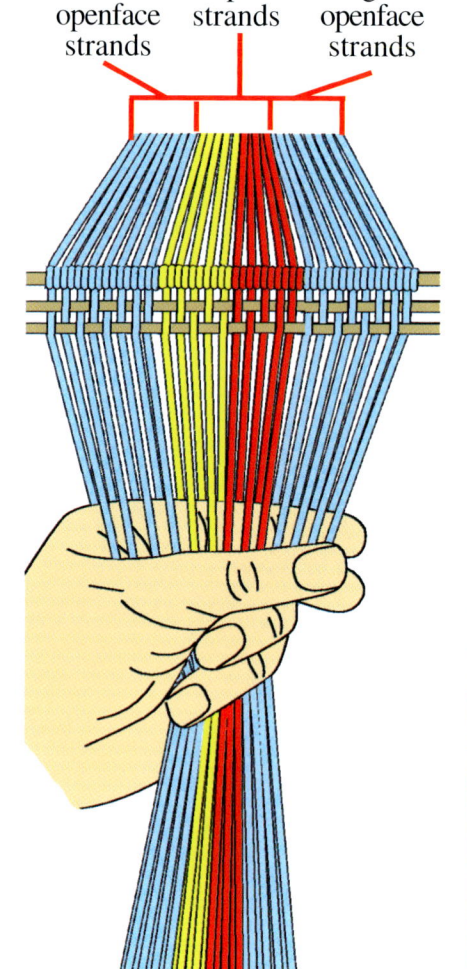

left openface strands | warpface strands | right openface strands

[STEP 3(L/R)]
Divide the open shed so that the strands of the left hand border are held by the left hand and the remaining strands are held by the right hand.

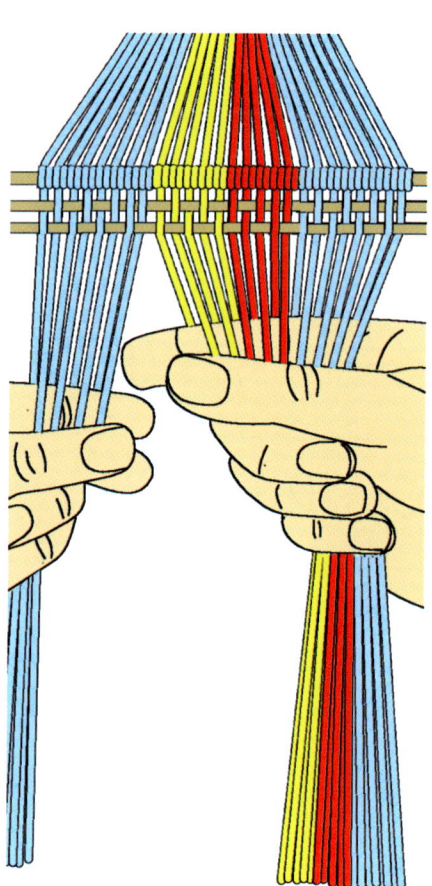

[98]

[STEP 4(L/R)]
Interlock the right hand strand of the left hand border and the left hand strand of the of the warpface weaving.

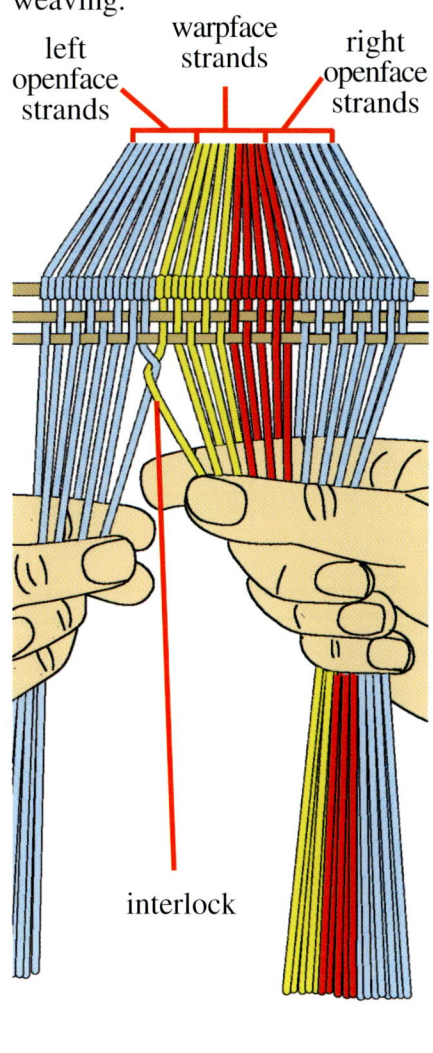

- left openface strands
- warpface strands
- right openface strands
- interlock

[STEP 5(L/R)]
After transferring all the strands back to the left hand, pull the first warp strand on the left through the open shed past the last warp strand on the right. This action changes the first warp strand into the first weft strand.

- weft
- warpface strands

[STEP 6(L/R)]
Interlock the weft strand and the first strand of the right hand border. Turn the weft strand down returning it to the warp bundle. Hook the border strand over the headstick to hold it in place.

- first border strand
- interlock
- turn down weft strand

[STEP 7(L/R)]
Reverse the shed of the warpface portion of the work piece.

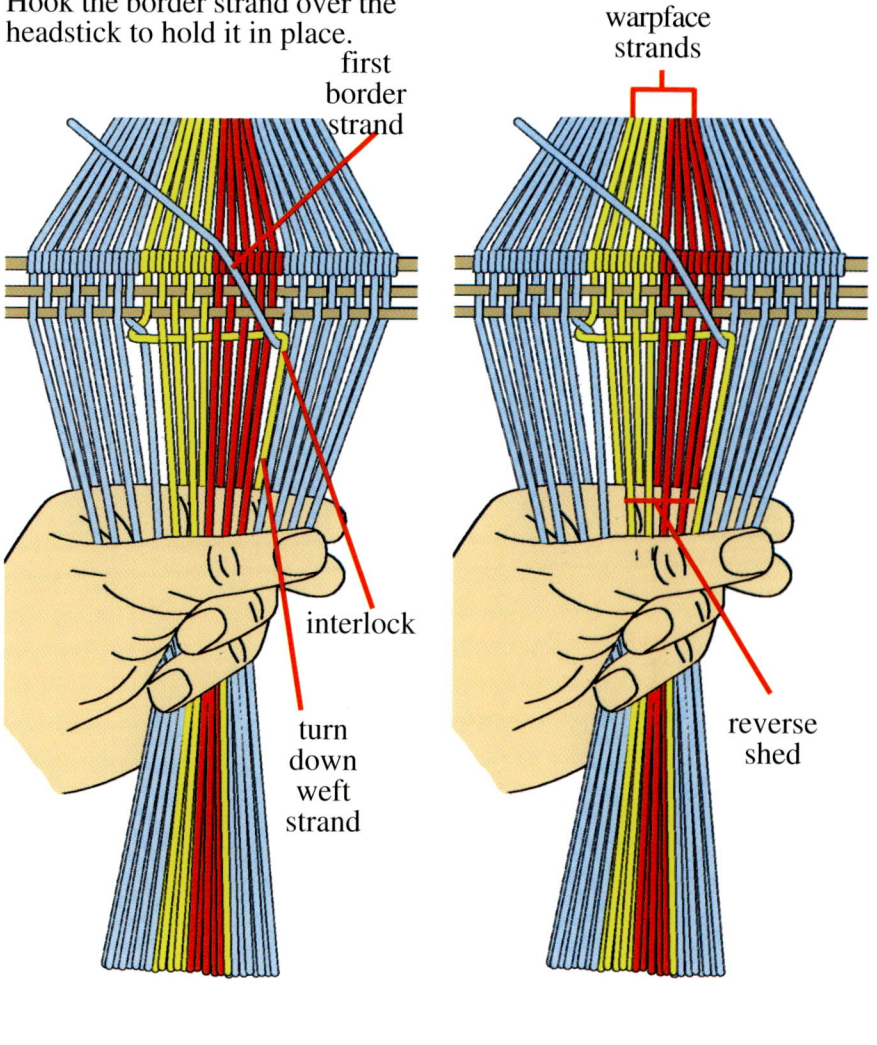

- warpface strands
- reverse shed

[99]

[STEP 8(L/R)]
Use openface weaving to weave the first row of the right hand border until there are two strands remaining.

[STEP 9(L/R)]
Complete the interlocking of the right hand border and the warpface portion of the work piece by pulling the left hand strand of the right hand border under the next to last strand of the border.

interlock

[STEP 10(L/R)]
Transfer the first two openface border strands to the right hand.

warpface strands

right hand border

interlock

[STEP 11(L/R)]
Transfer the warpface strands to the right hand.

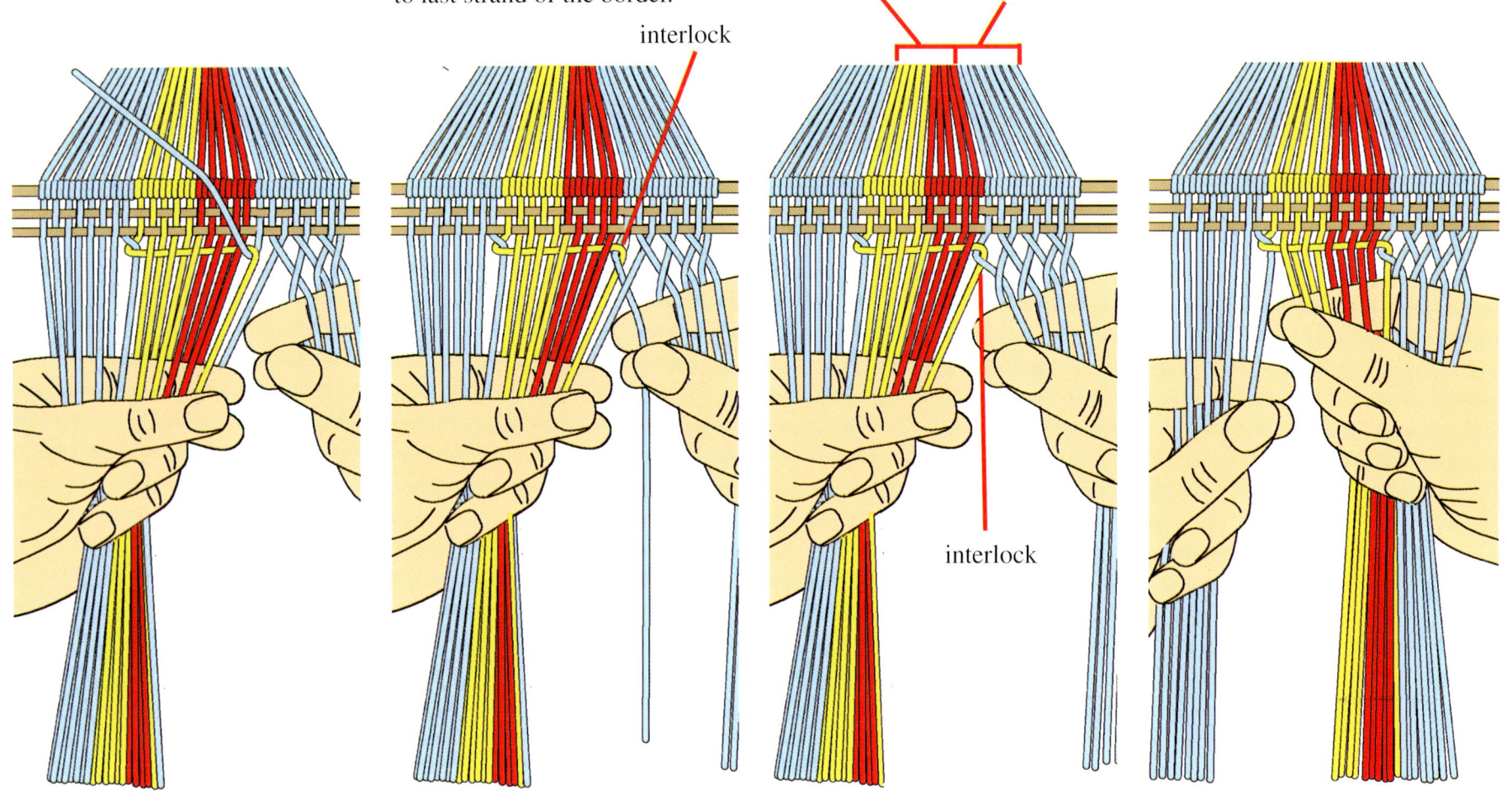

[100]

[STEP 12(L/R)]
Use openface weaving to weave the first row of the left hand border.

[STEP 13(L/R)]
Continue to weave in this manner until the desired length is reached.

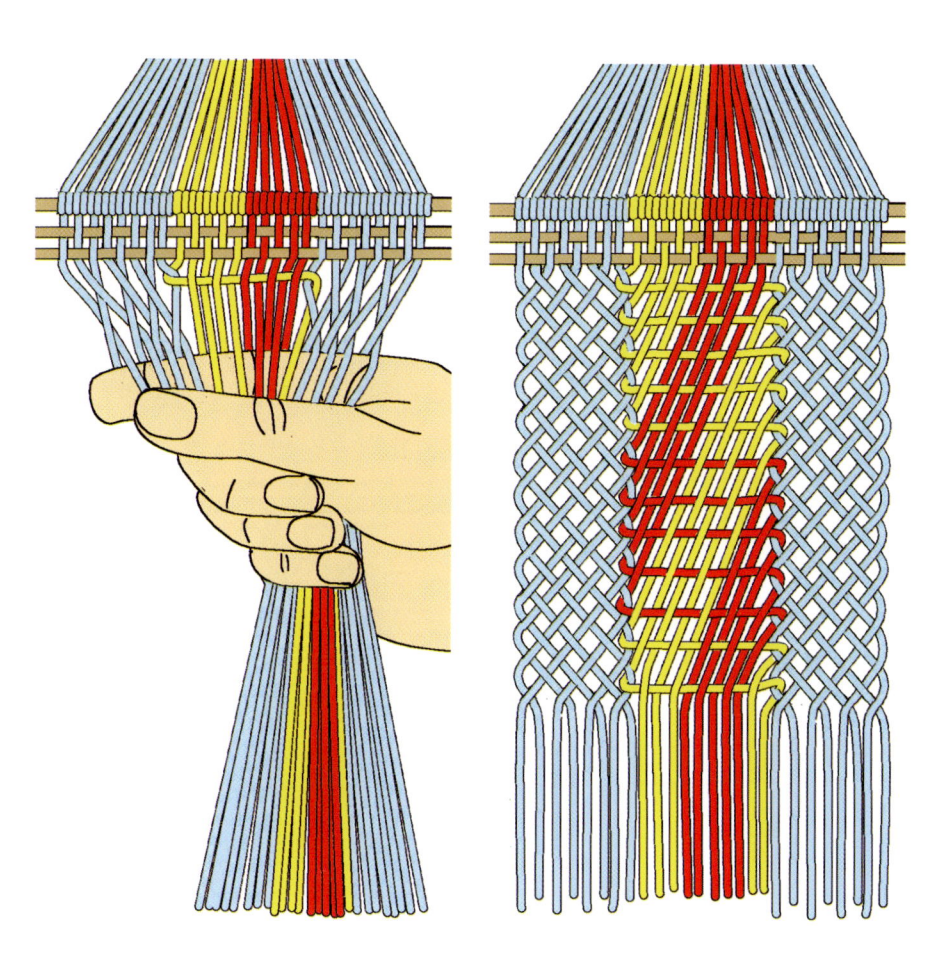

Warpface Weft Worked Right to Left

Bands of openface weaving can be used to create borders on a piece of warpface weaving.

The example illustrated here is a piece of diagonal warpface weaving with openface woven borders.

The following steps show the weft strand moving from right to left (R/L).

Diagonal warpface weaving worked from right to left.

[STEP 1(R/L)]
Cast the required number of strands of yarn on to the headstick. Use clove hitches to tie the yarn in place. See (Part 1: Getting Started).

Set up the over/under weaving pattern of the shed with two smaller sticks.

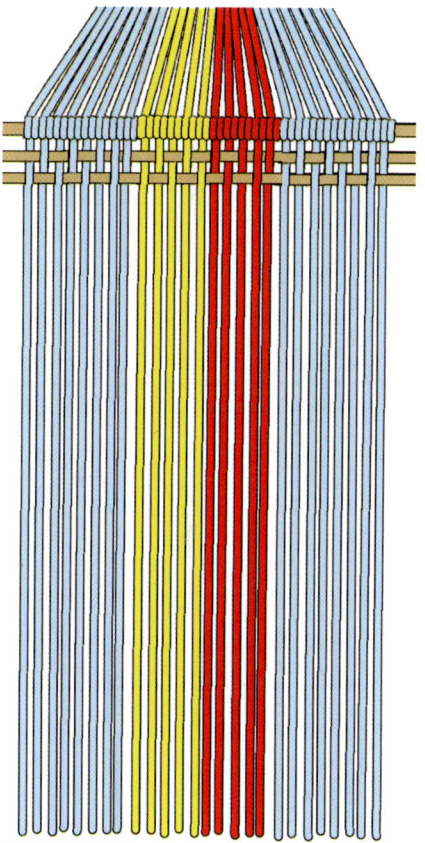

[NOTE]
The sequence in which the various parts are worked depends on the direction that the weft strand of the warpface part of the work piece is moved.

[101]

[STEP 2(R/L)]
Pick up the shed on the index finger of the left hand.

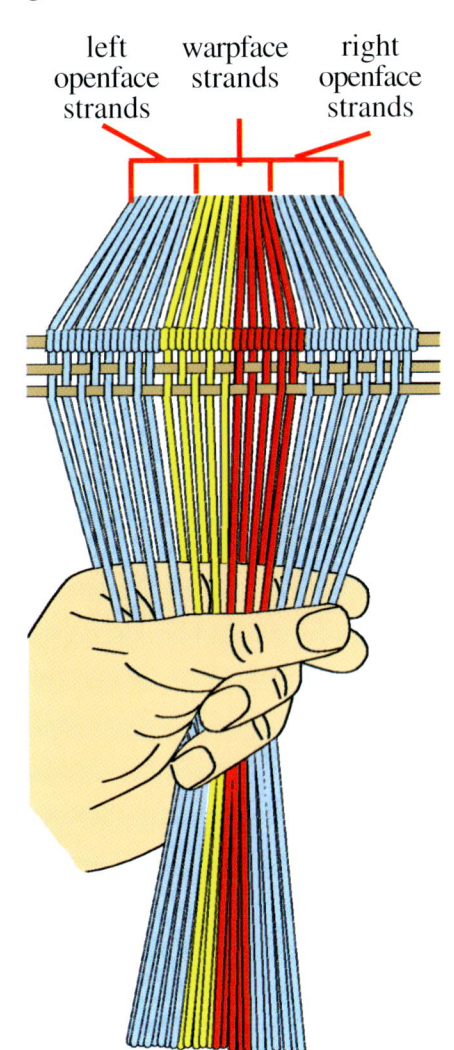

left openface strands • warpface strands • right openface strands

[STEP 3(R/L)]
Use openface weaving to weave the first row of the right hand border until there are two bottom layer strands remaining.

[STEP 4(R/L)]
Start the interlocking of the right hand border and the warpface portion of the work piece. Pull the right hand strand of the warpface strands over the last strand of the right hand border.

warpface strand

border strand

[STEP 5(R/L)]
Interlock the right hand strand of the warpface strands and the last strand of the right hand border.

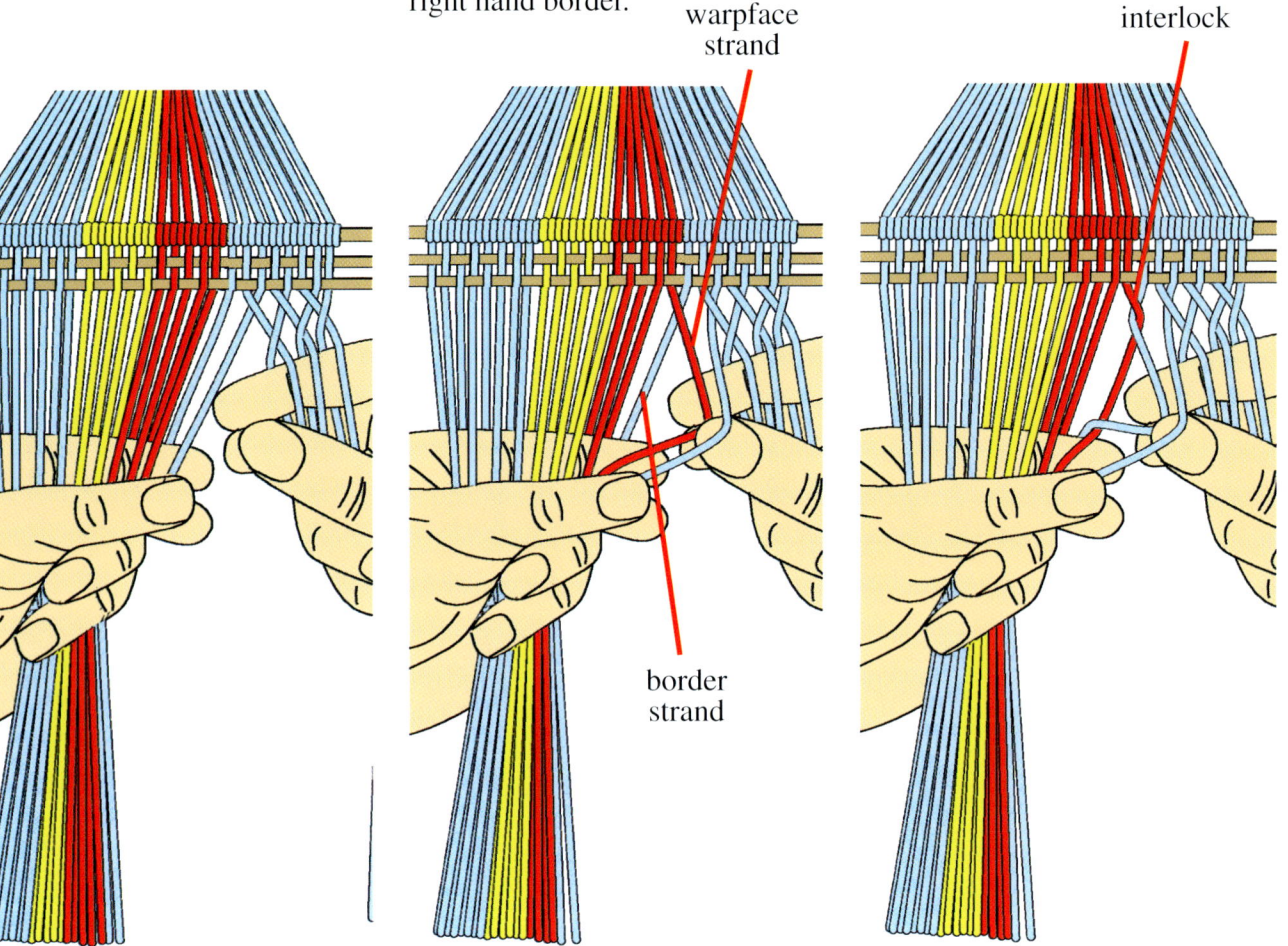

interlock

[102]

[STEP 6(R/L)]
Transfer the last two strands of the right hand border to the index finger of the right hand.

[STEP 7(R/L)]
Transfer the warp strands to the index finger of the right hand.

[STEP 8(R/L)]
Pull the first warp strand on the right through the open shed past the first strand of the left hand border. This action changes the warp strand into the first weft strand.

weft

[STEP 9(R/L)]
Interlock the weft strand and the first strand of the left hand border.

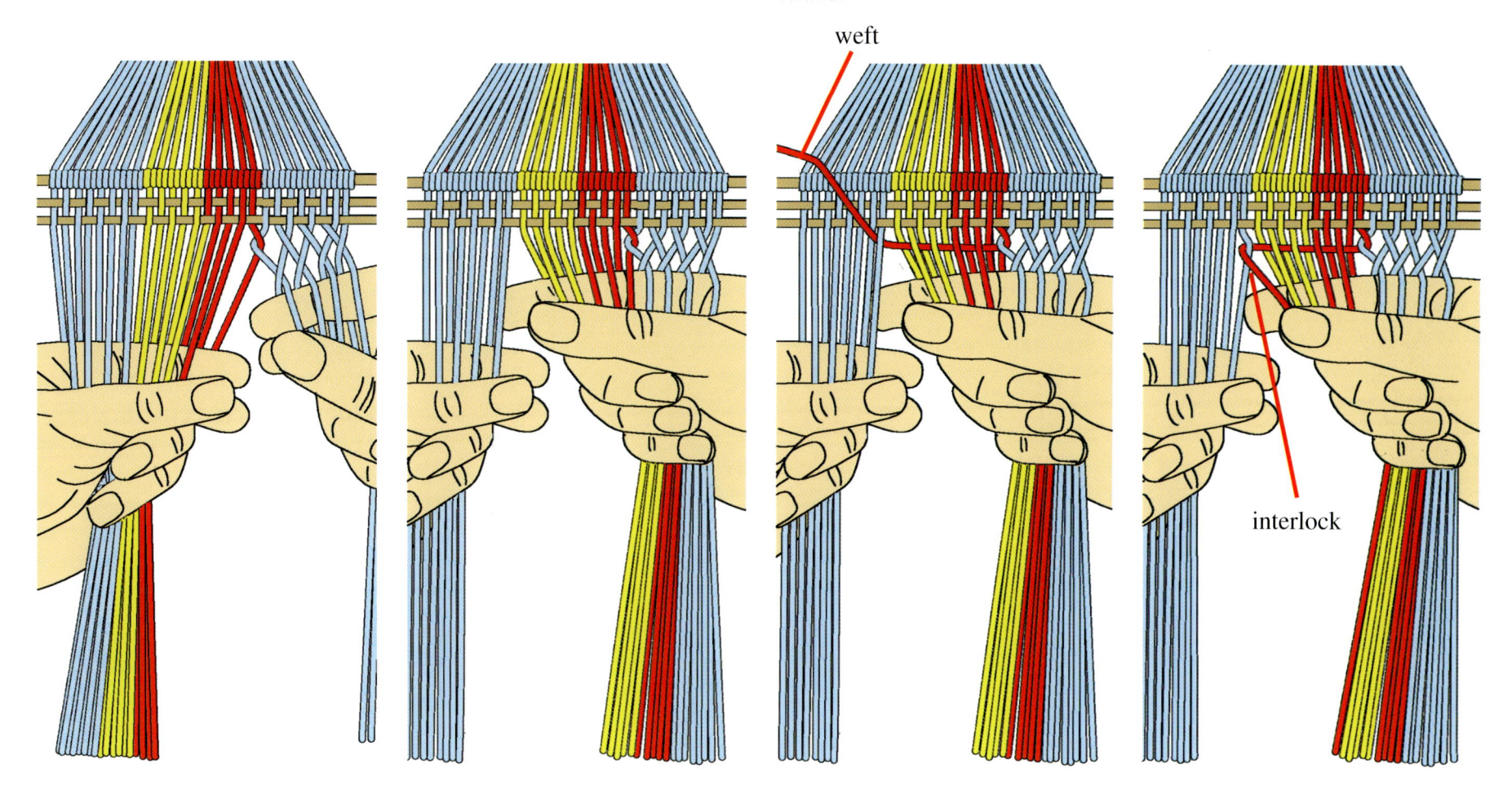

interlock

[103]

[STEP 10(R/L)]
Reverse the shed of the warpface portion of the work piece.

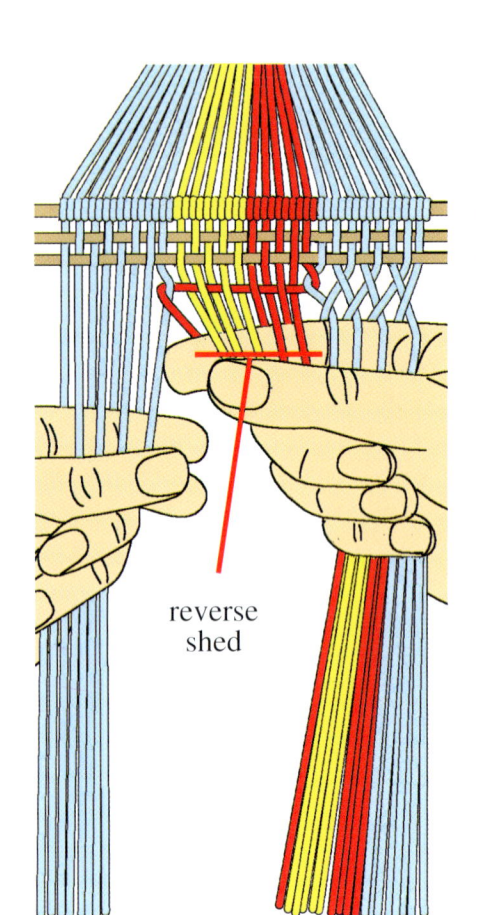

[STEP 11(R/L)]
Use openface weaving to weave the first row of the left hand border.

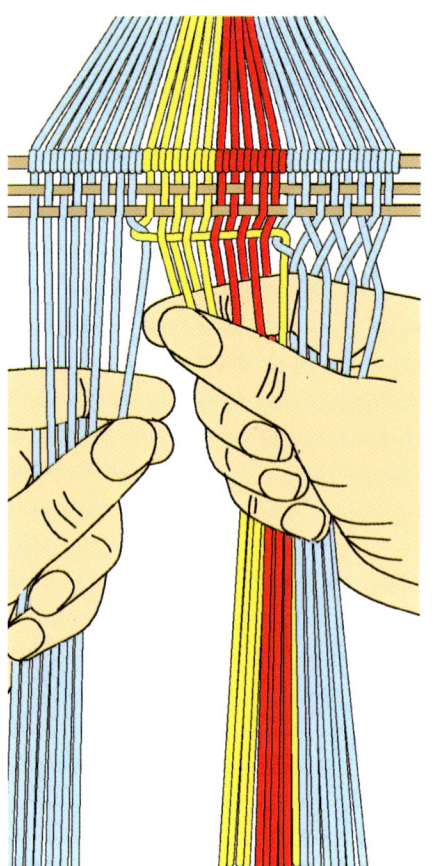

[STEP 12(R/L)]
Continue to weave in this manner until the desired length is reached.

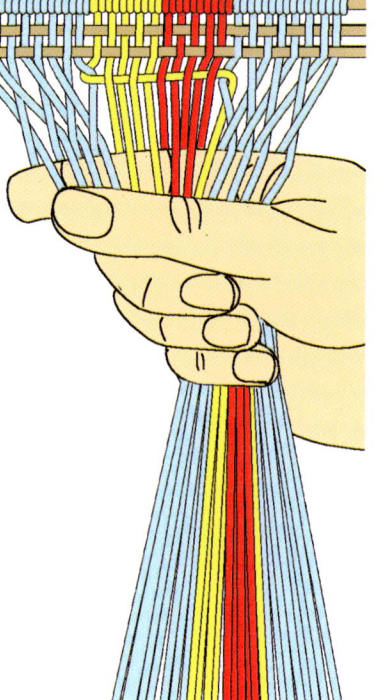

reverse shed

Openface Woven Borders On Left to Right Diagonal Warpface Example:

Openface Woven Borders On Right to Left Diagonal Warpface Example:

Openface Weaving
Adding Bead Accent

One way of decorating openface weaving is to weave beads into the solid color bands to form geometric patterns. The patterns take two forms; zigzag and diamond. The patterns are formed by stringing beads on one or more of the strands and weaving the beads in place as the work progresses.

Accent Beads
Carrier Strands

The carrier strands are usually more tightly spun and smaller in diameter. The carrier strands are the only strands that are strung with beads.

When using a carrier strand to form a zigzag pattern, the direction of the strand with the beads is changed by interlocking the bead carrier strand with a strand from the opposite diagonal.

The advantage of using carrier strands is that smaller beads can be used. Example: When 4-ply yarn is used, #8 beads can be used on a carrier strand. If #8 beads are strung on 4-ply yarn they are difficult to position because they do not slide along the yarn easily.

The disadvantage of using carrier strands is that the beading pattern must be made up of continuous lines of beads.

Accent Beads
Over/under Only

When a zigzag pattern is formed using an over/under pattern of weaving (without interlocking strands), the beads are strung on two or more strands of yarn. The over/under pattern of the weaving is uninterrupted.

One advantage of using the over/under method is that the beads can be added to any number of strands to create a pattern. Also the lines of beading do not have to be continuous.

The disadvantage of the over/under method of adding beads is that the beads must be larger so that they can slide along the yarn easily. Example: #8 beads work with 3-ply yarn but do not slide well on 4-ply yarn. #5 beads slide easily on 4-ply yarn but look bulky.

Accent Beads
Diamond Pattern

The diamond pattern is made by working two zigzag patterns in opposite directions so that the patterns cross each other.

Accent Beads
Diamond Pattern
Carrier Strands
[STEP 1]

Set up the head stick as usual but replace the strands to be beaded with a carrier strands.

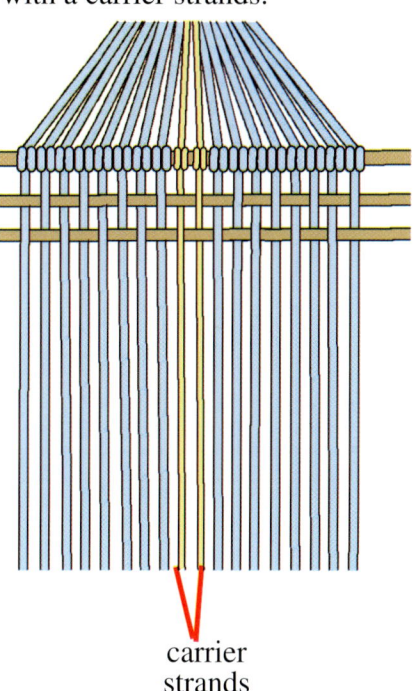

carrier strands

[NOTE] Either 4-ply or 3-ply yarn and #8 beads can be used when doing bead work with a carrier strand.
[NOTE] The carrier strand is a smaller sized strand that can be easily strung with beads. If you are using acrylic yarn for the main part of the work, a waxed nylon cord works well as a carrier strand.

[STEP 2]

String the beads on to the carrier strands.

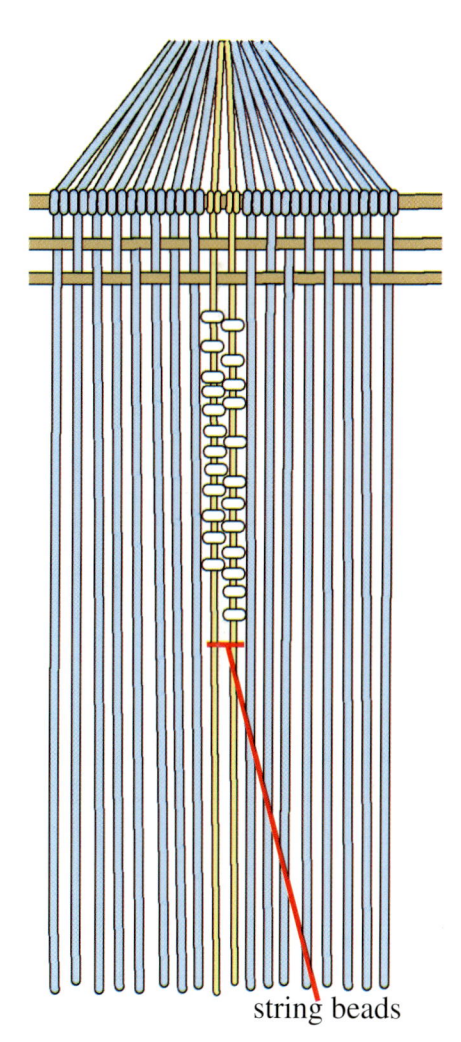

string beads

[NOTE] When 3-ply yarn is used the carrier strand can also be 3-ply yarn.

[105]

[STEP 3]
Tie slip knots in the carrier strands to prevent the beads from sliding off and to hold the beads close to the work area.

[STEP 4]
Follow the directions for openface weaving but place the beads as shown.

[STEP 5]
To change the direction of the carrier strand, follow the directions for openface weaving until you reach the point of change.

[STEP 6]
Interlock the carrier strand and the next weaving strand.

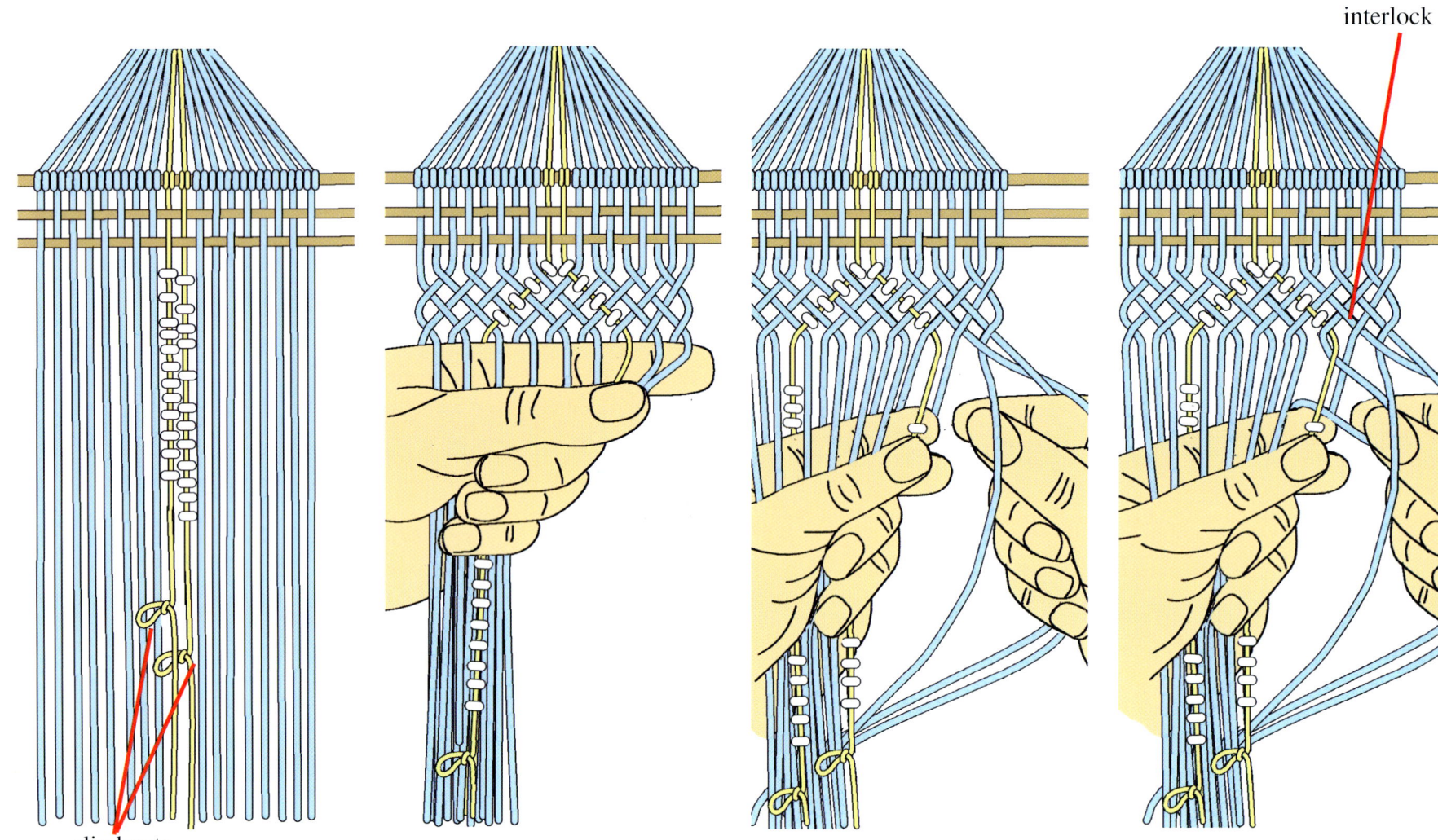

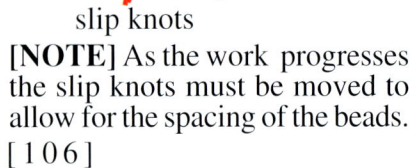

interlock

slip knots

[NOTE] As the work progresses the slip knots must be moved to allow for the spacing of the beads.

[106]

[STEP 7]
Transfer the strands to the right hand.

transfer

[STEP 8]
Notice that the carrier strand has moved from the top layer to the bottom layer and is on the opposite diagonal

[STEP 9]
Transfer the strands to the right hand as usual.

transfer

[STEP 10]
When the weaving reaches the next carrier strand, do a second interlock so that both carrier strands have changed directions.

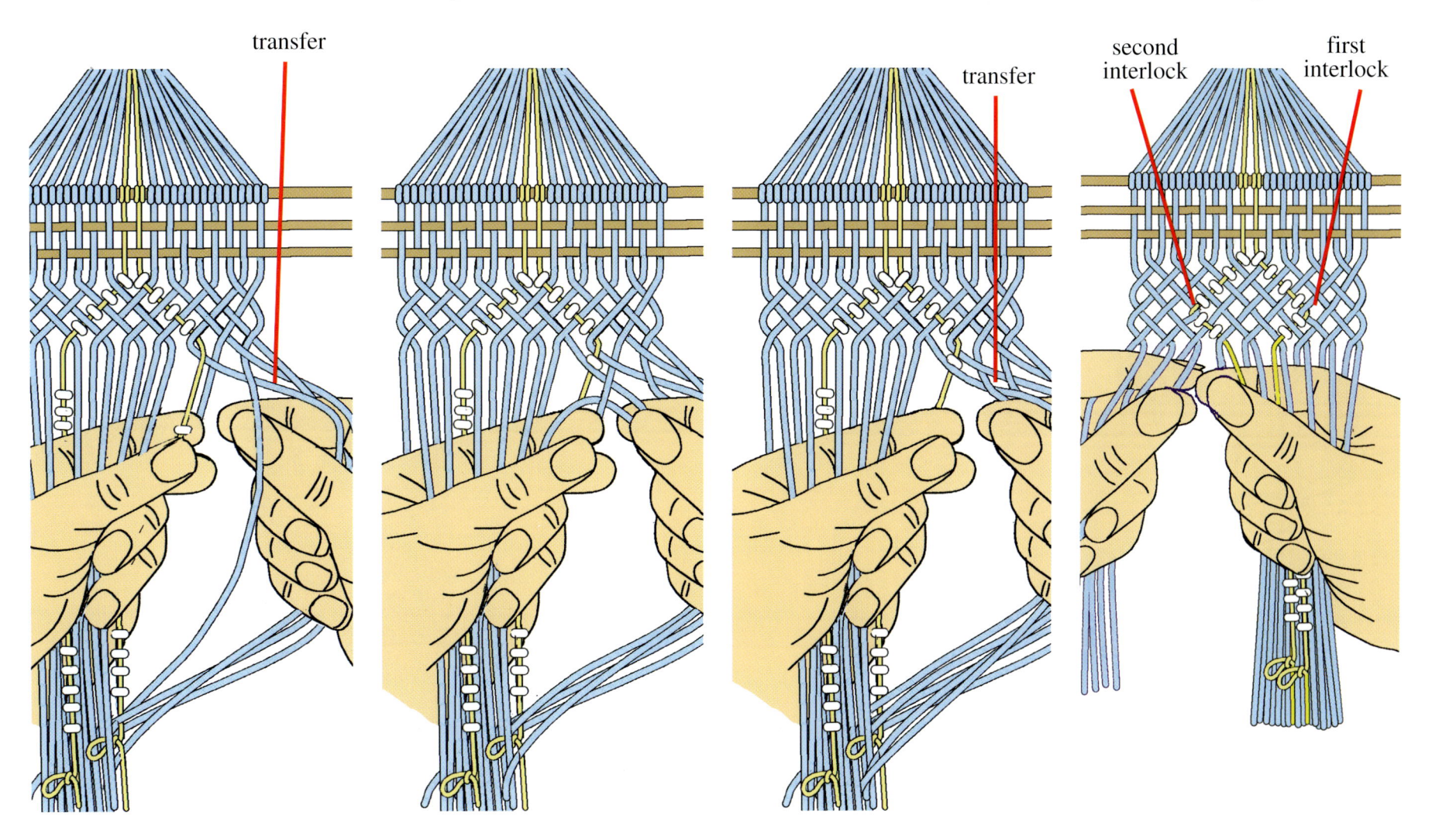

second interlock   first interlock

[107]

[STEP 11]
Finish the row of weaving by following the directions for openface weaving.

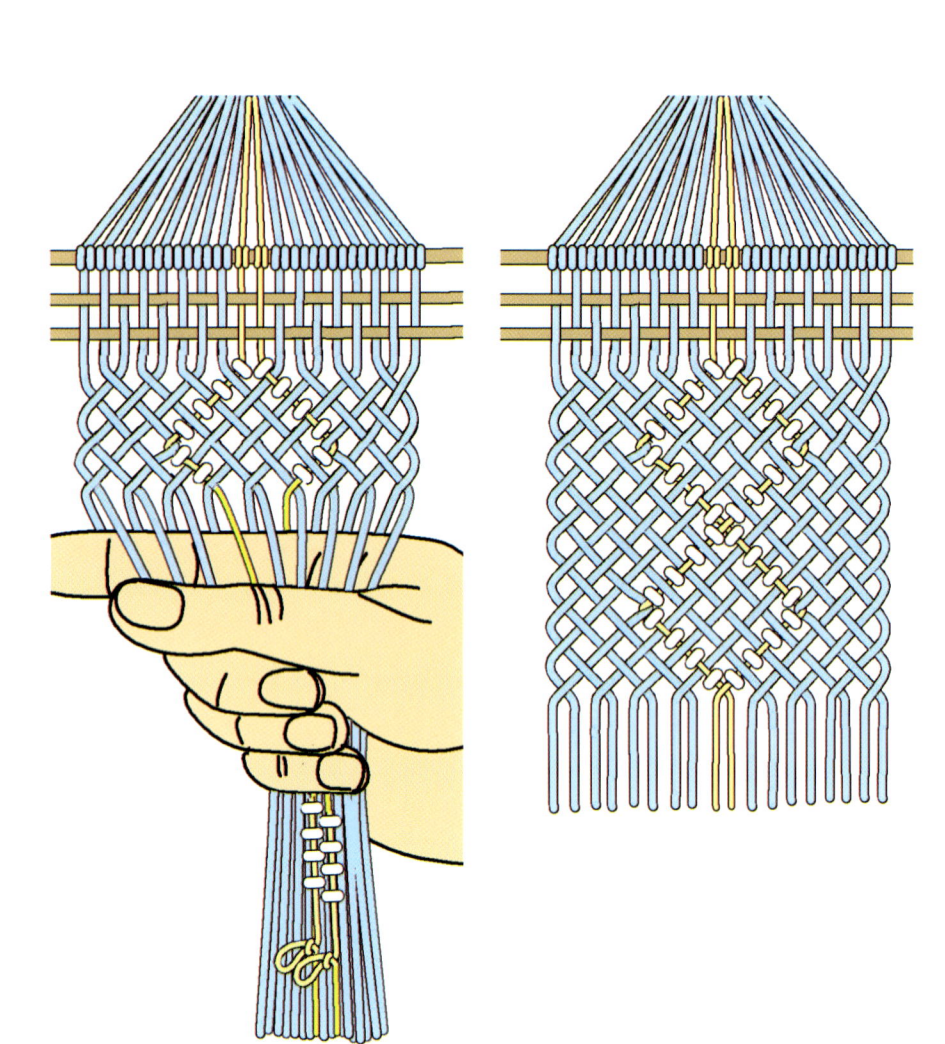

[STEP 12]
Continue weaving until the desired length is reached.

Accent Beads
Diamond Pattern
Carrier Strands
Example:

Accent Beads Over/under Only

Beads can be worked into open-face weaving by stringing beads on several strands and placing the beads into the work as needed. In this method the same type of yarn is used throughout the work and the over/under pattern is maintained at all times.

The diamond pattern can be planned so that a minimum number of beaded strands are used. When a strand is turned back into the work it will form the other side of the diamond pattern. The general rule to follow for this is that the number of beads on the side of the diamond must divide evenly into one half the total number of strands.

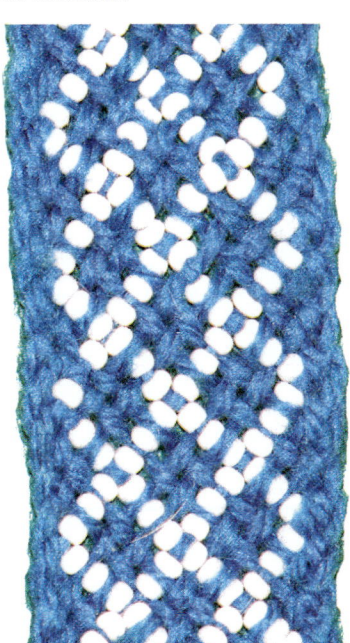

Accent Beads Over/under Only
Three Bead Diamond Mesh (1)

Diamond mesh with three beads in each side of the diamond can be formed by casting on a total of 18 strands. Beads are then strung on the center two strands and the 6th and 7th strands from the center on each side.

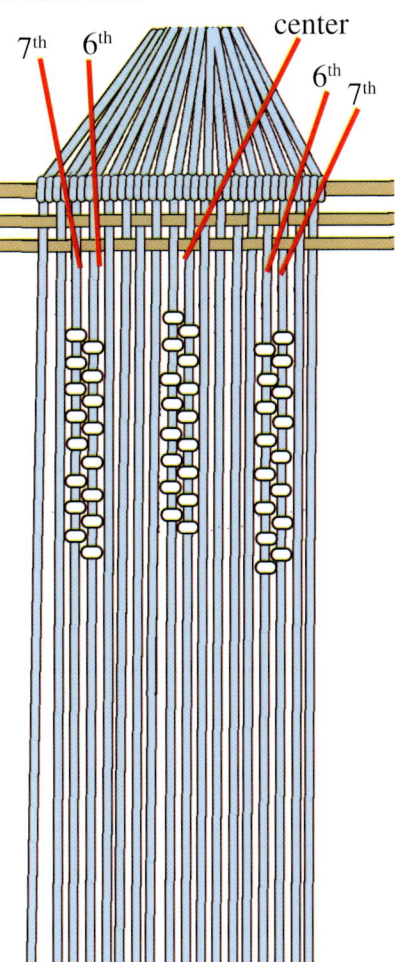

Accent Beads Over/under Only
Three Bead Diamond Mesh (2)

Follow the directions for open face weaving but place the beads as shown in the diagram.

Accent Beads Over/under Only
Three Bead Diamond Mesh (3)

The colored strands in this diagram are only to help visualize the position of the beaded strands in the completed work.

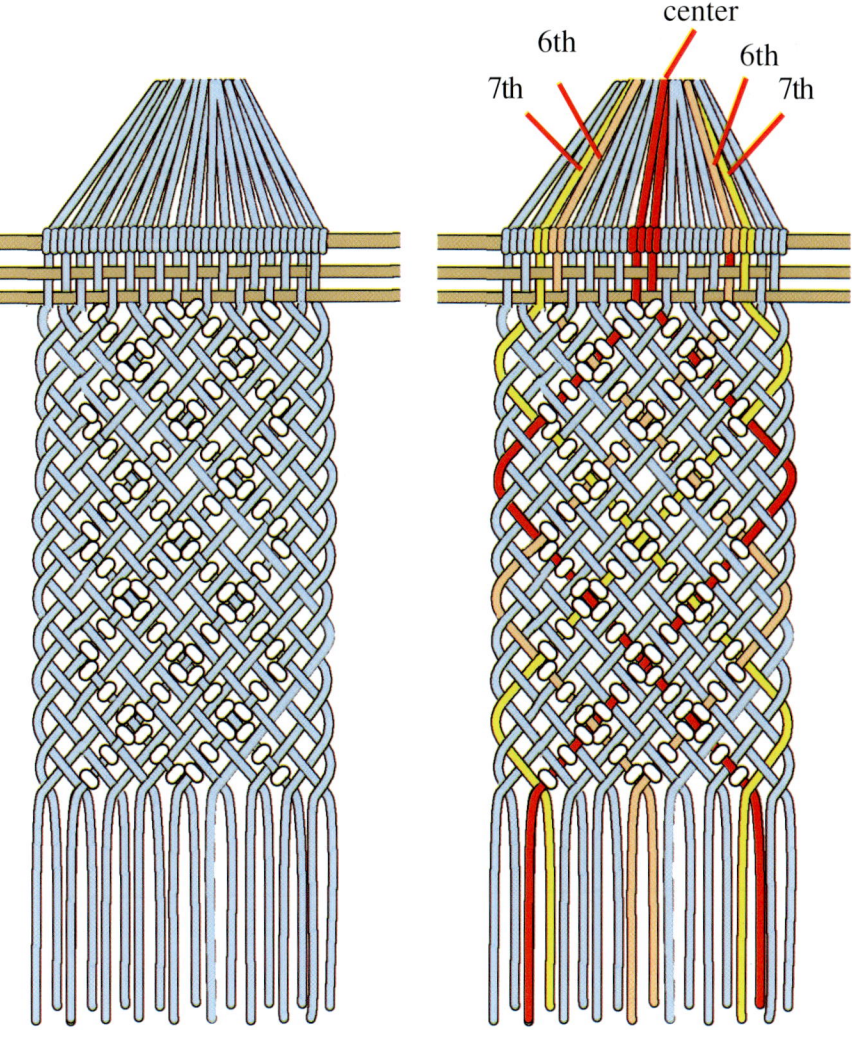

[109]

**Accent Beads
Over/under Only
Three Bead Diamond Mesh
Example:**

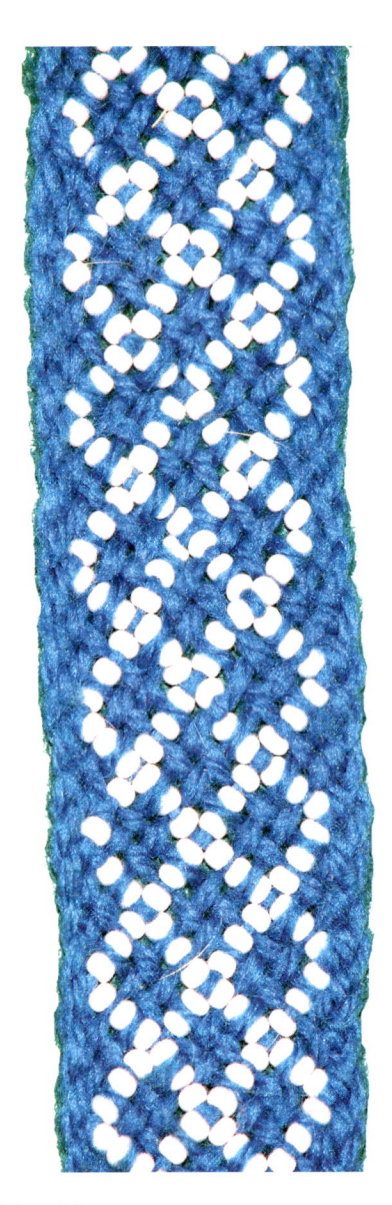

**Accent Beads
Over/under Only
Six Bead Diamond Mesh (1)**

Diamonds with 6 beads per side can also be achieved with this setup.

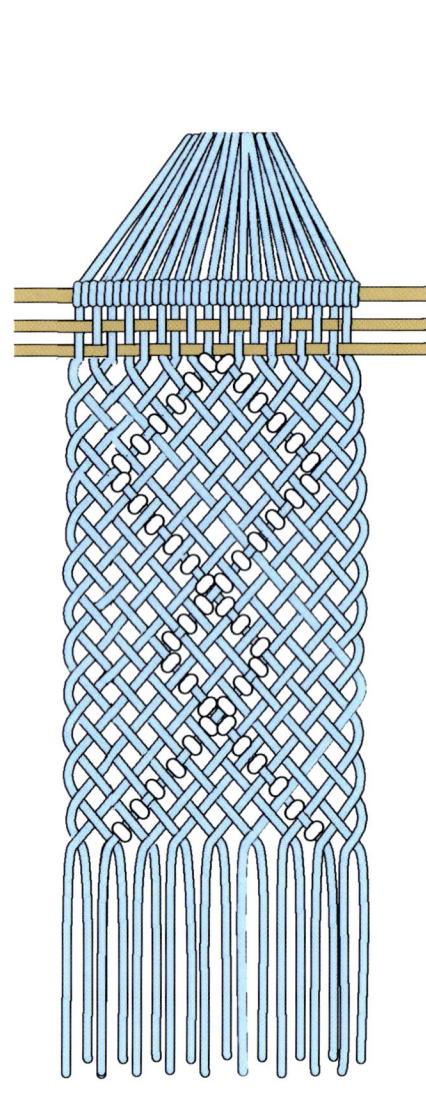

**Accent Beads
Over/under Only
Six Bead Diamond Mesh (2)**

The colored strands in this diagram are only to help visualize placement of the strands in the completed work.

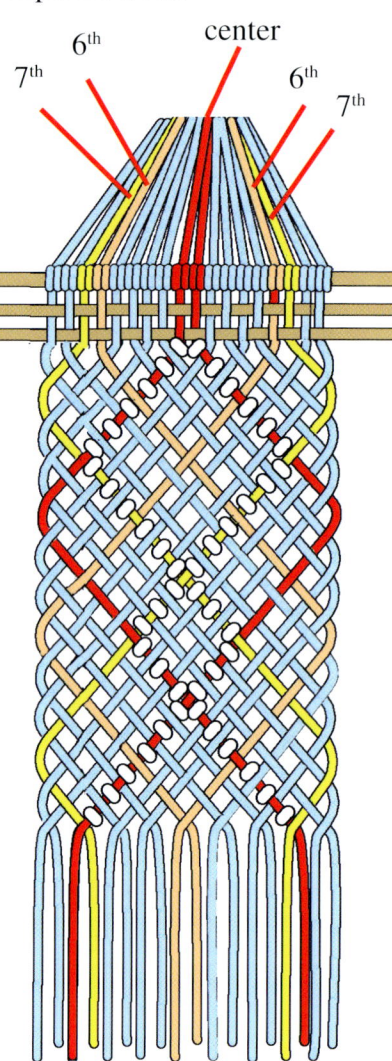

7th 6th center   6th 7th

**Accent Beads
Over/under Only
Six Bead Diamond Mesh
Example:**

[110]

Accent Beads
Over/under Only
Six Bead Zigzag (1)

A zigzag variation can be achieved by adding the beads as shown.

Accent Beads
Over/under Only
Six Bead Zigzag (2)

The colored strands in this diagram are only to help visualize placement of the strands in the completed work.

Accent Beads
Over/under Only
Six Bead Zigzag Example:

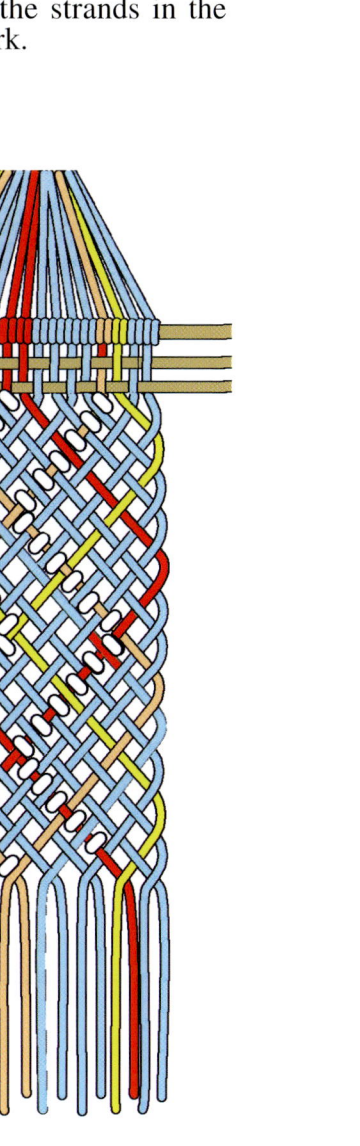

[111]

Accent Beads
Over/under Only
Four Bead Diamond Mesh (1)

Diamond mesh with four beads in each side of the diamond can be formed by casting on a total of 24 strands. Beads are then strung on the center two strands and the 8th and 9th strand from the center.

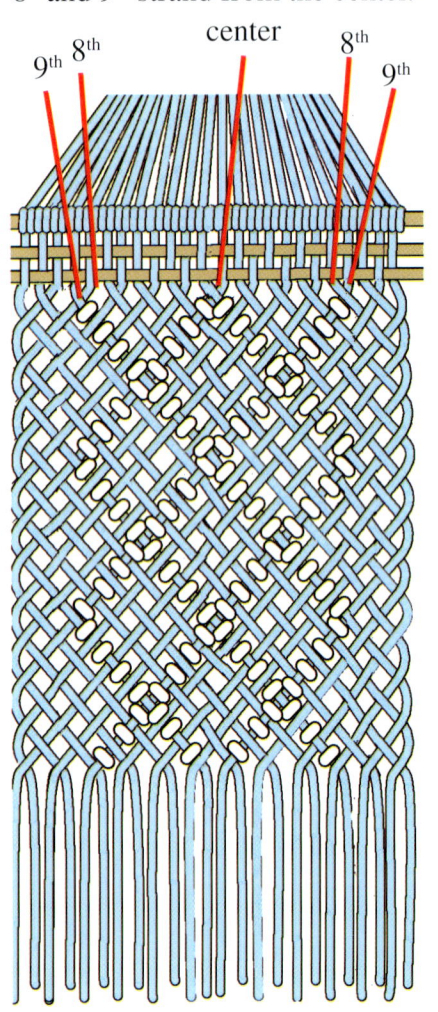

Accent Beads
Over/under Only
Four Bead Diamond Mesh (2)

The colored strands in this diagram are only to help visualize placement of the strands in the completed work..

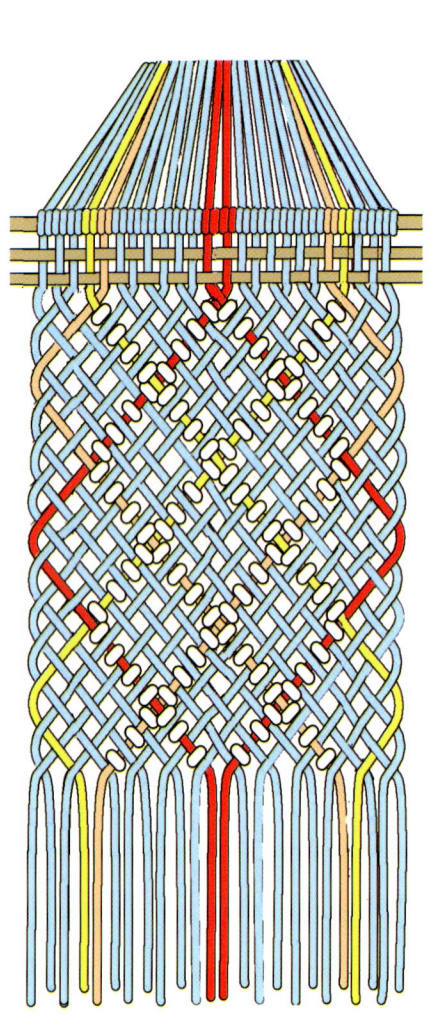

Accent Beads
Over/under Only
Four Bead Diamond Mesh Example:

Openface Weaving
Colored Strands Accent

Using colored strands of a contrasting color is another method of decorating openface weaving. A zigzag pattern can be produced by replacing several strands with strands of a contrasting color and following the over/under pattern of the basic weaving. The direction of the colored strands is changed by interlocking them with strands of the background color. Remember that the top layer of strands follows the diagonal angled to the right and the bottom layer of strands follows the diagonal angled to the left.

[NOTE] Bead accents can be combined with colored accent strands. Either method of adding beads can be used: carrier strand or over/under weaving.

[NOTE] A diamond pattern can be created by working two zigzag patterns at the same time.

[STEP 1]
Cast on the required number of strands. See (Part 1: Getting Started).

[STEP 2]
Set up the shed as shown.

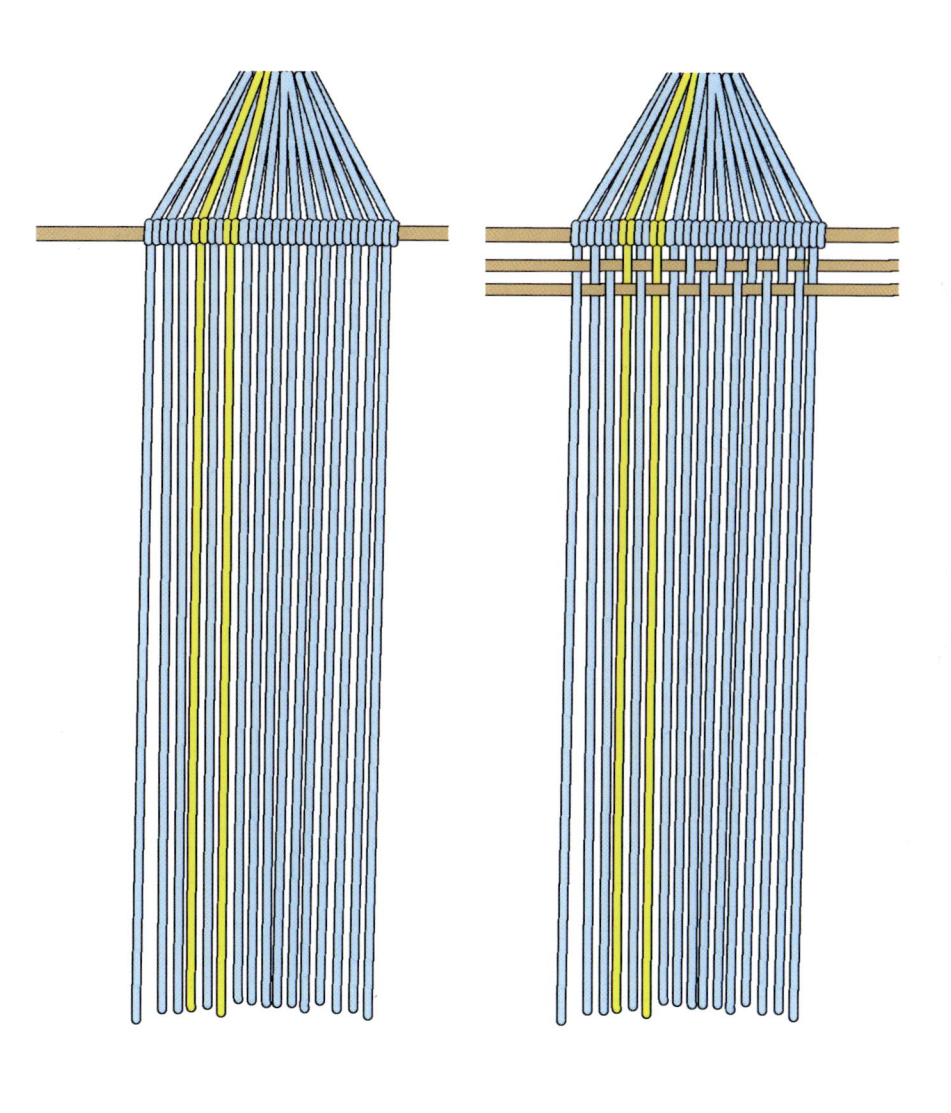

[113]

[STEP 3]

Pick up the shed. Use the index finger of the left hand to hold the shed open. Observe that the strands are now divided into two layers. The bottom layer is behind the index finger and the top layer is above the index finger.

[STEP 4]

Following the instructions for openface weaving, weave until you reach the row where the direction change will take place.

contrasting strands

two bottom layer strands

[STEP 5]

Interlock the first contrasting strand and the weaving strand next to it..

interlock

[STEP 6]

Move the next two strands to the right index finger.

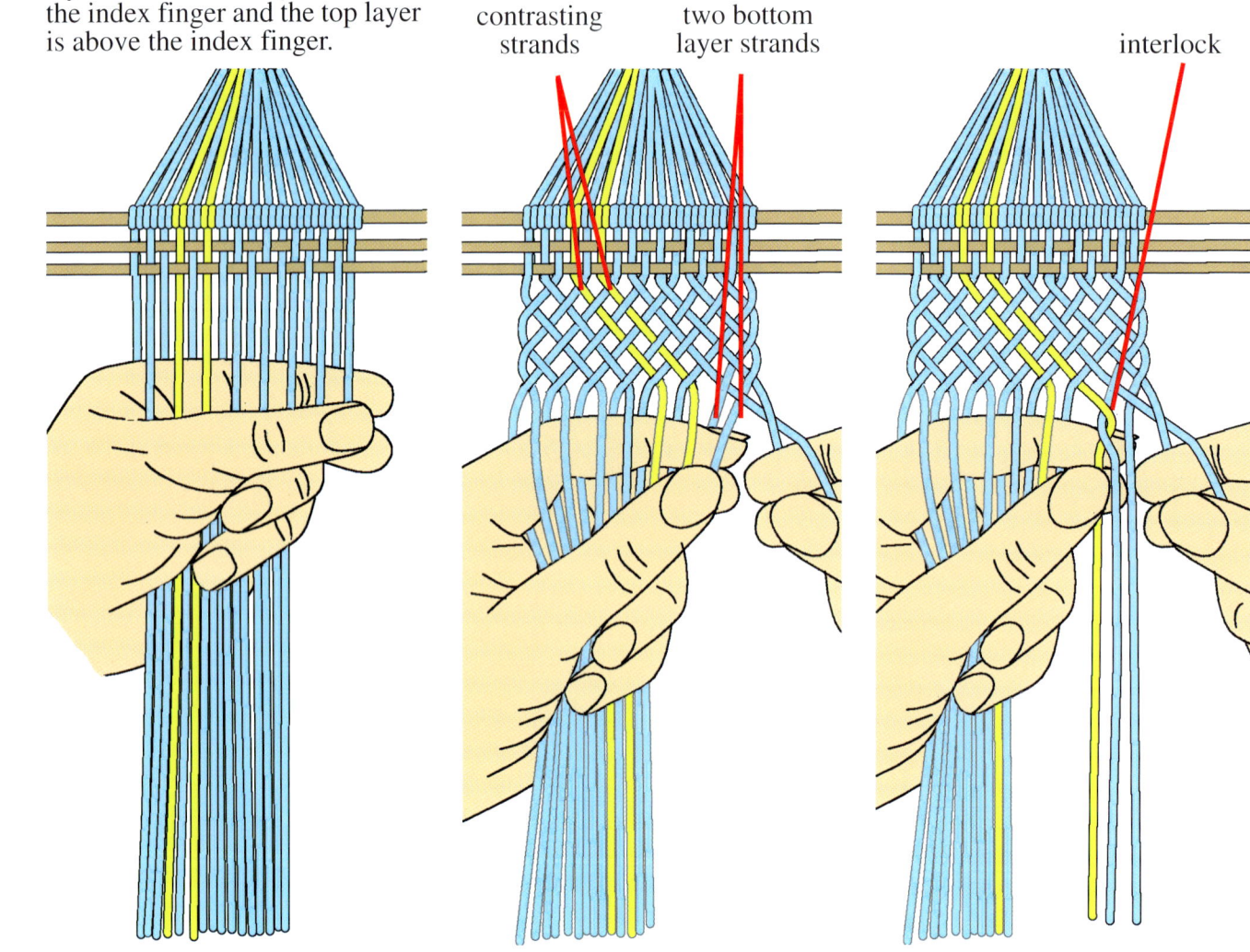

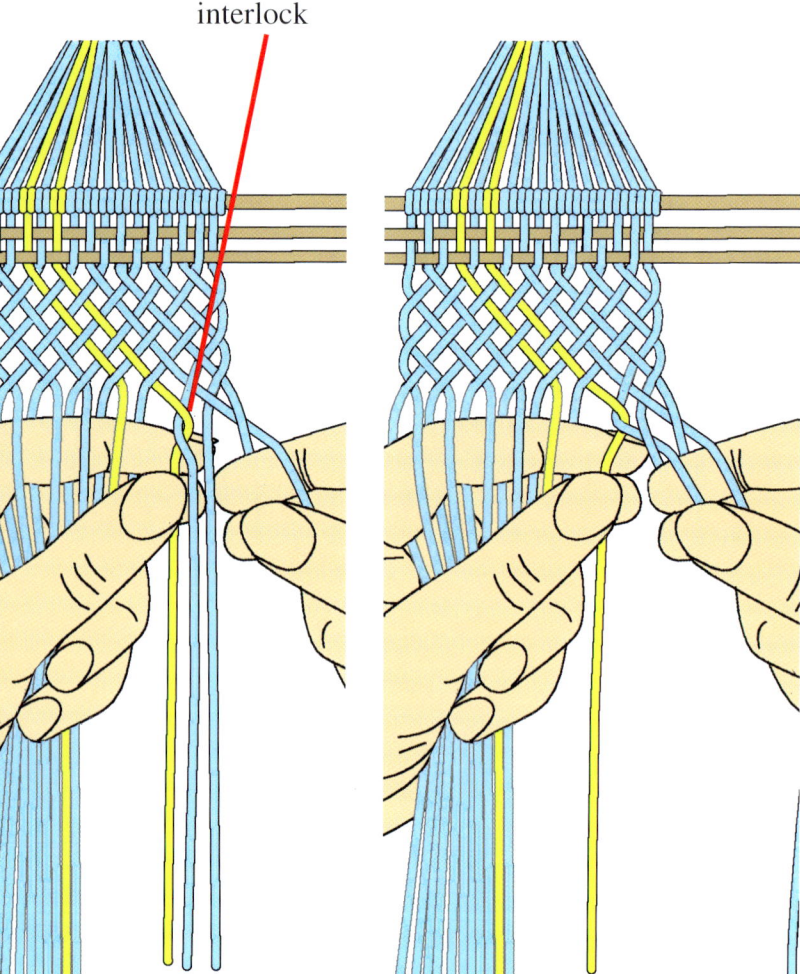

[114]

[STEP 7]
Interlock the second contrasting strand and the weaving strand to its right.

[STEP 8]
Move the right contrasting strand and background strand to the right index finger.

[STEP 9]
Weave the next top strand down between the bottom strand and the contrasting strand.

[STEP 10]
Move the left contrasting strand and background strand to the right index finger.

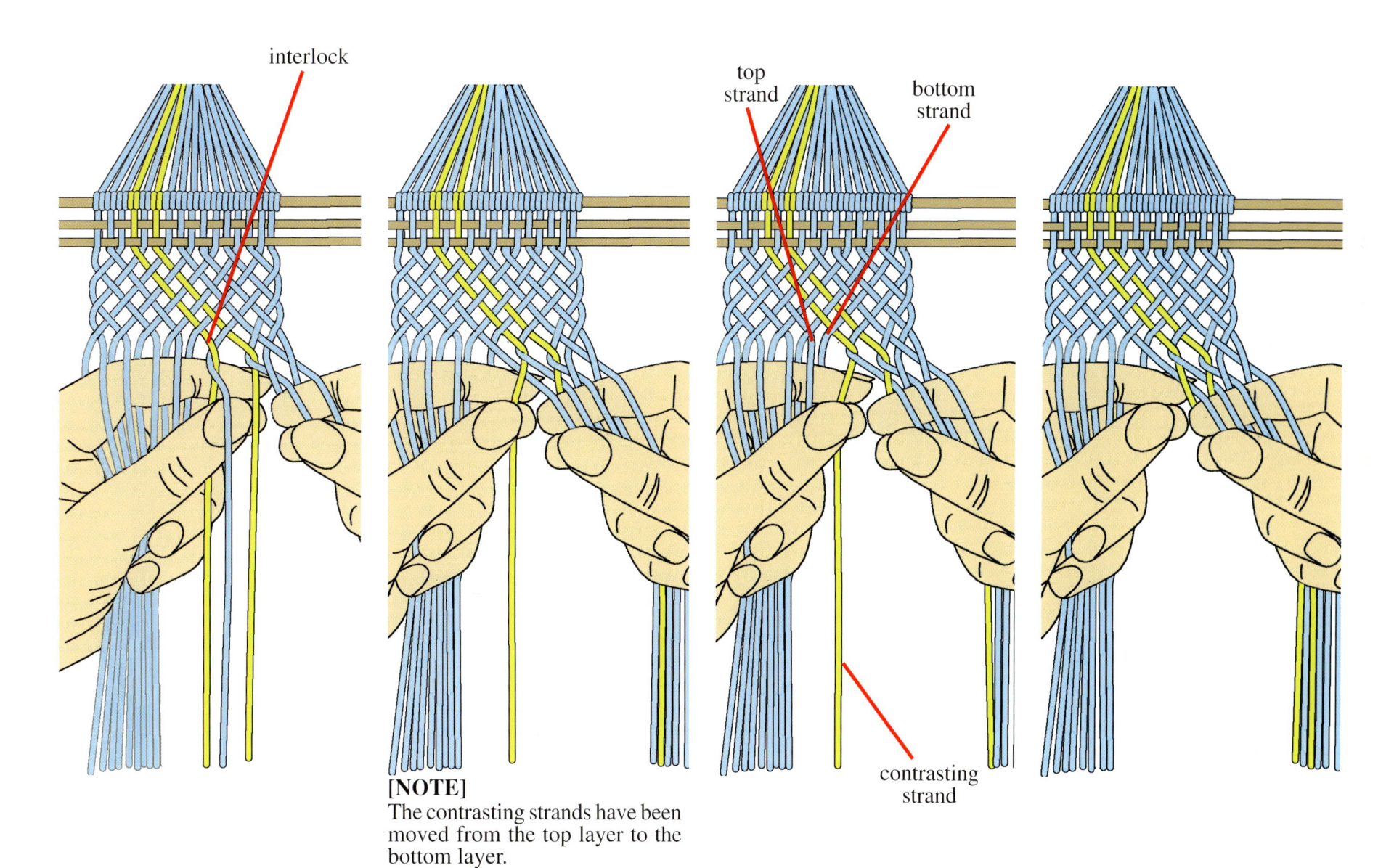

interlock

top strand

bottom strand

[NOTE]
The contrasting strands have been moved from the top layer to the bottom layer.

contrasting strand

[1 1 5]

[STEP 11]
Continue to weave in this manner until the desired length is reached.

Openface Weaving Colored Strands Accent Example:

Openface Weaving Colored Strands Accent with Bead Accent Carrier Strand

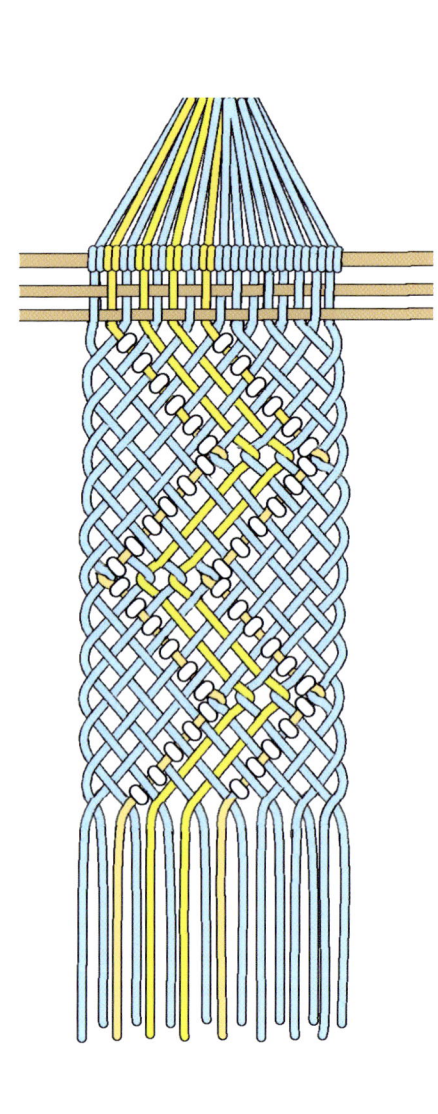

Openface Weaving Colored Strands Accent with Bead Accent Example:

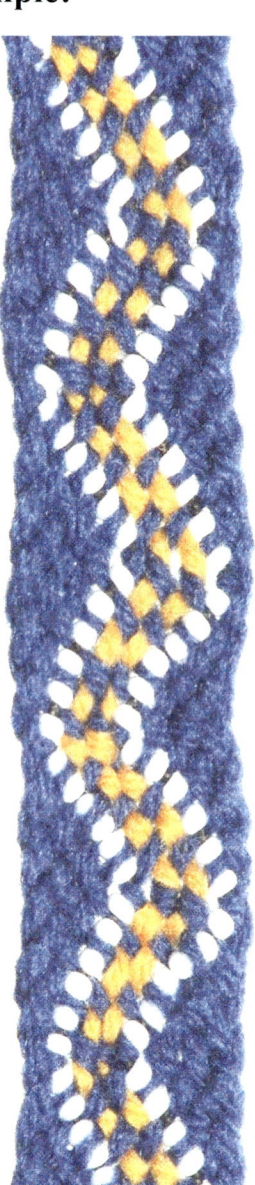

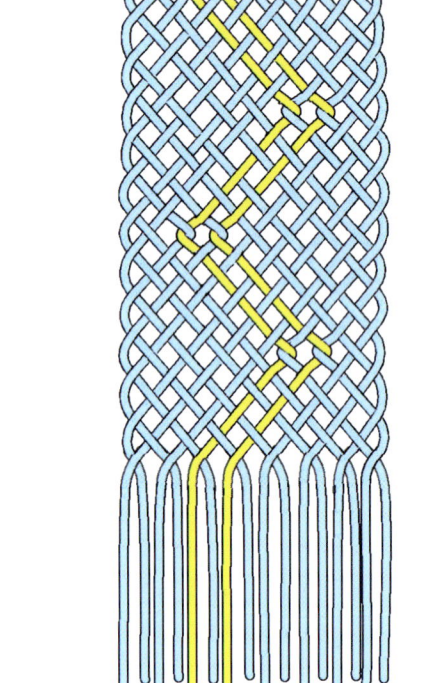

[116]

Openface Weaving Diamond Design

When two bands of different colors are used, a diamond design can be woven where the two bands meet. The diamond is formed between the two color bands by interlacing their strands. When the interlacing has formed half the diamond, interlock the strands of the two colors bands so that the strands return to their beginning color band.

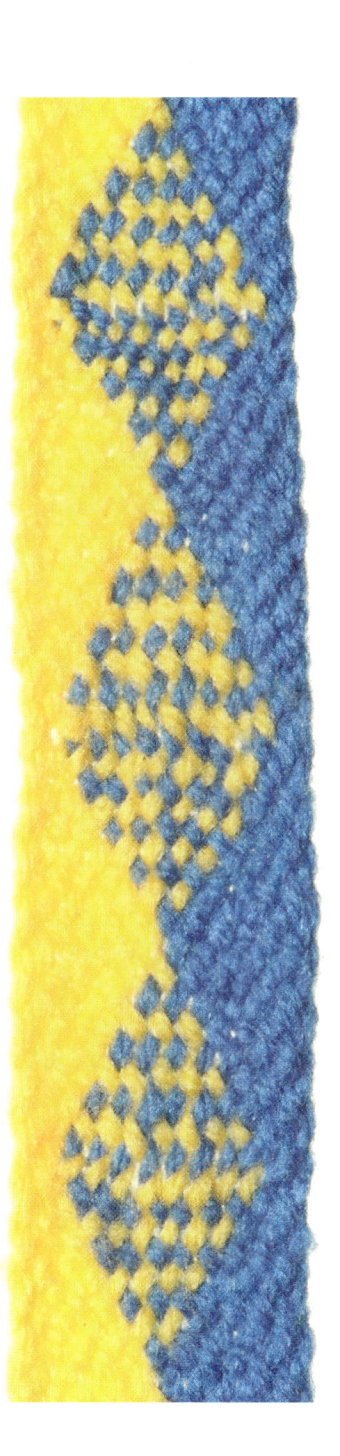

[STEP 1]
Set up the headstick. See (Part 1: Getting Started).

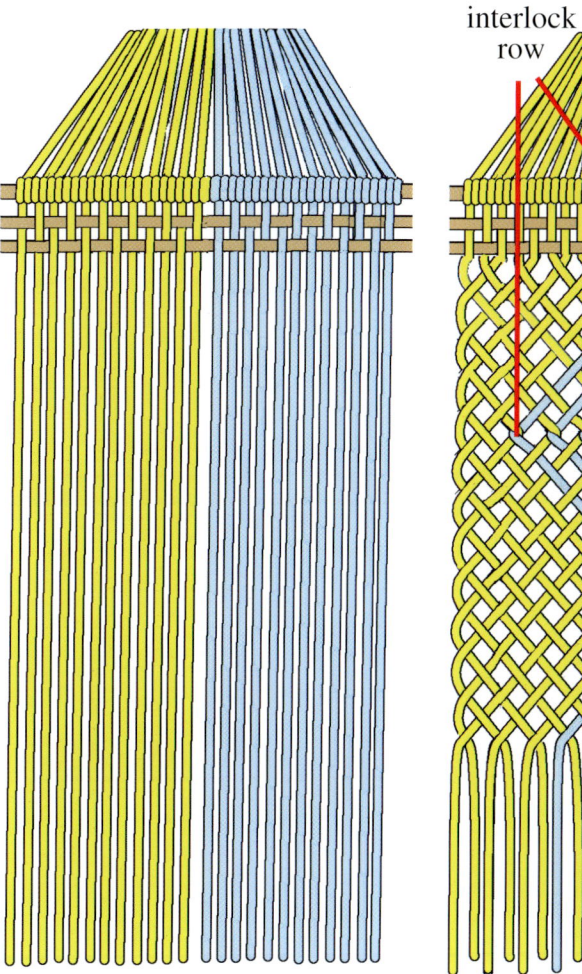

[STEP 2]
Interlace the two color bands by following the directions for openface weaving. When the top half of the diamond is formed, interlock the strands of the different colors.

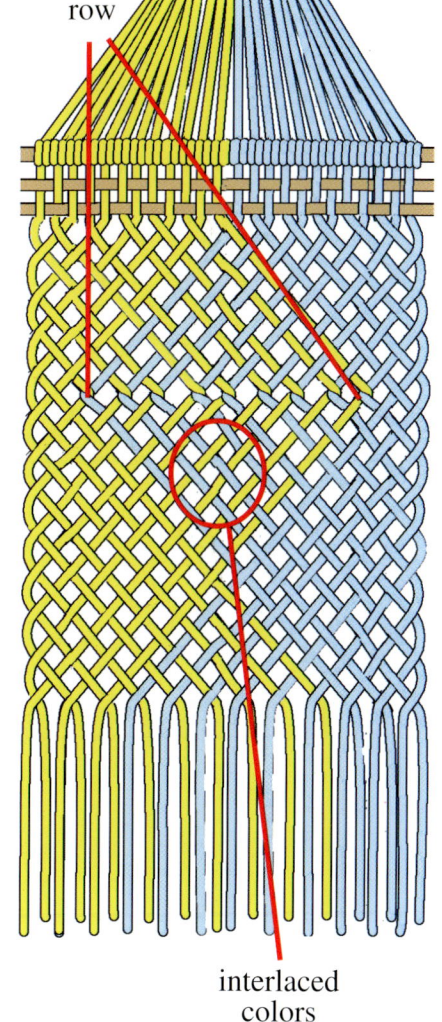

interlock row

interlaced colors

[117]

Openface Weaving Diamond Design with Bead Accent Over/under Weave

Openface Weaving Diamond Design with Bead Accent Over/under Weave Example:

Openface Weaving Diamond Design with Bead Accent Carrier Strand

Openface Weaving Diamond Design with Bead Accent Carrier Strand Example:

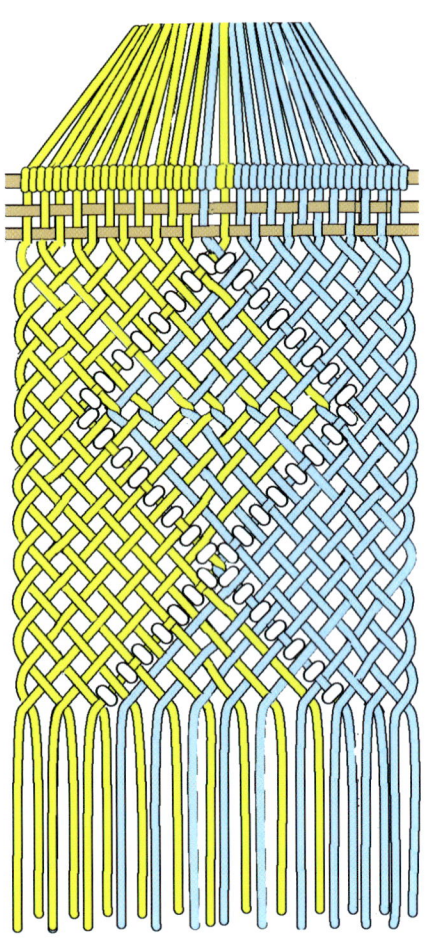

[NOTE]
Either method of adding beads to openface weaving can be used to add accent beads to the edge of the diamond pattern.

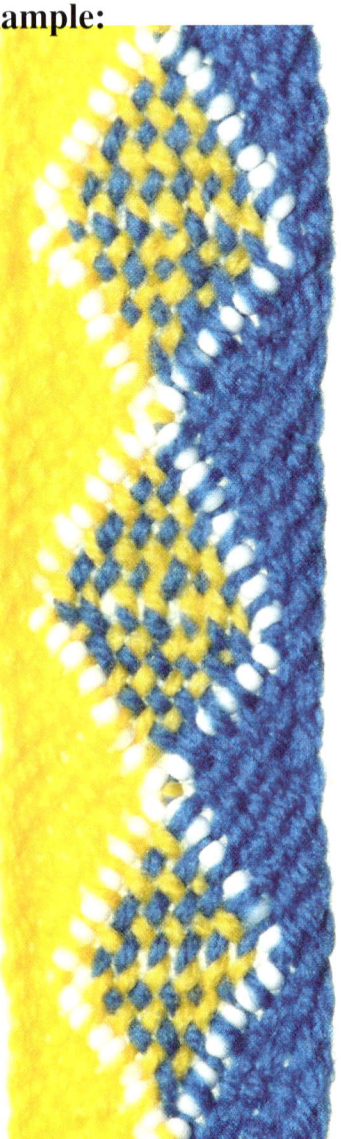

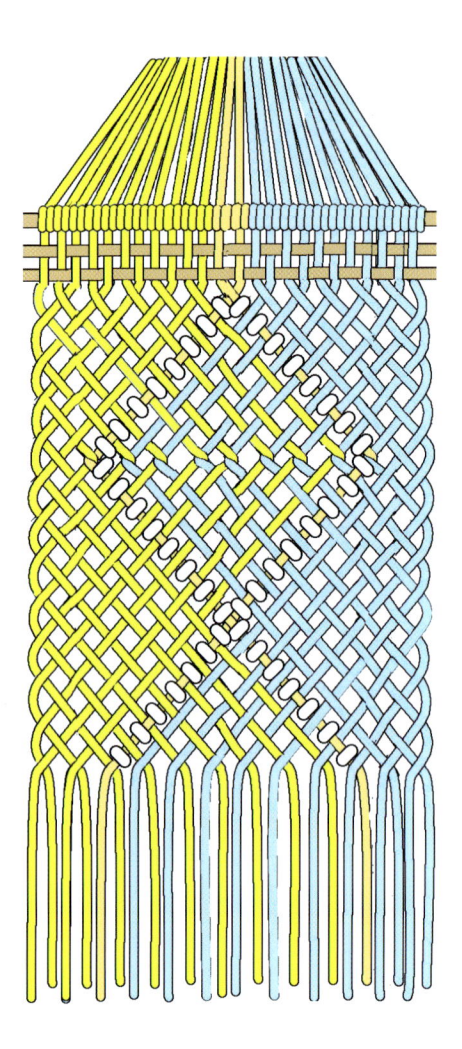

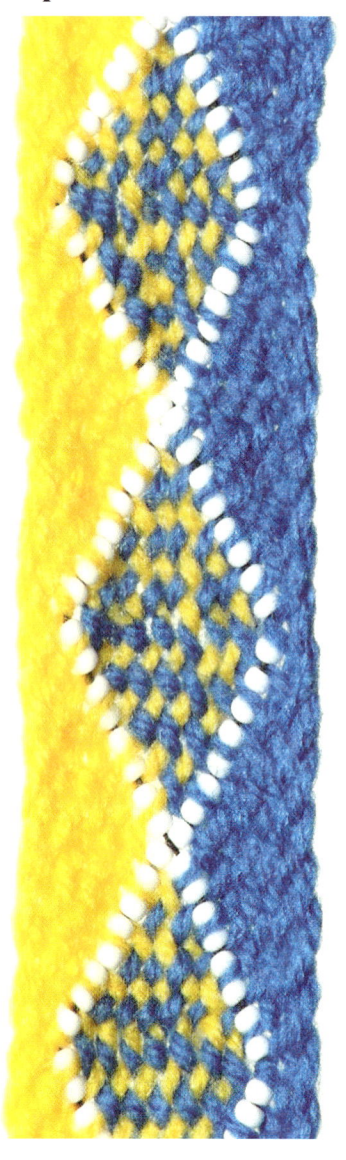

[1 1 8]

Openface Weaving Twining

Twining is another method of decorating openface weaving. Twining is done by replacing one strand with two strands of a contrasting color. Instead of following the over/under pattern of the basic weaving, the two strands are twisted between each pair of strands. This twisting results in a solid line of color. To change the direction of the design, the twining strands are interlocked with a background strand so that they both change directions. Remember that the top layer of strands follows the diagonal angled to the right and the bottom layer of strands follows the diagonal angled to the left.

[NOTE]
When setting up the pattern of the shed be sure to maintain the over/under pattern of the background color. The two twining strands are treated as one strand when the shed is picked up on the index finger of the left hand.

[STEP 1]
Cast on the required number of strands and set up the shed. See (Part 1: Getting Started).

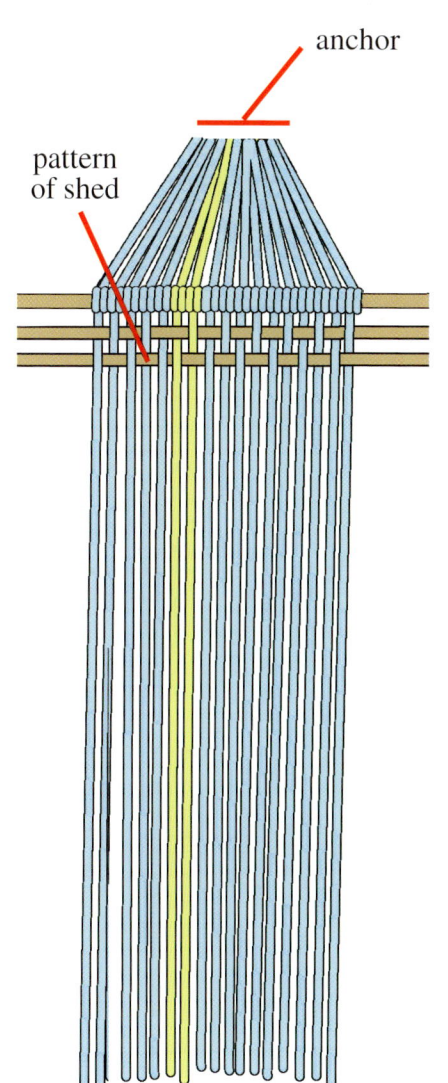

anchor

pattern of shed

[STEP 2]
Pick up the shed. Use the index finger of the left hand to hold the shed open. Observe that the strands are now divided into two layers. The bottom layer is behind the index finger and the top layer is above the index finger.

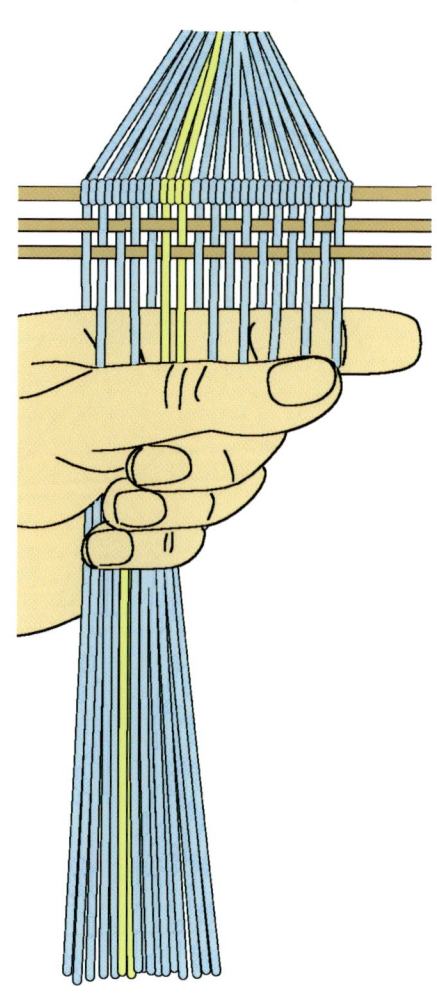

[119]

[STEP 3]
Follow the directions for interface weaving until there are two bottom layer strands left before the twining strands.

[STEP 4]
Pull the two bottom layer strands to the right.

[STEP 5]
Twist the twining strands together so that they cross each other once.

[STEP 6]
Place the adjacent bottom layer strand between the twining strands.

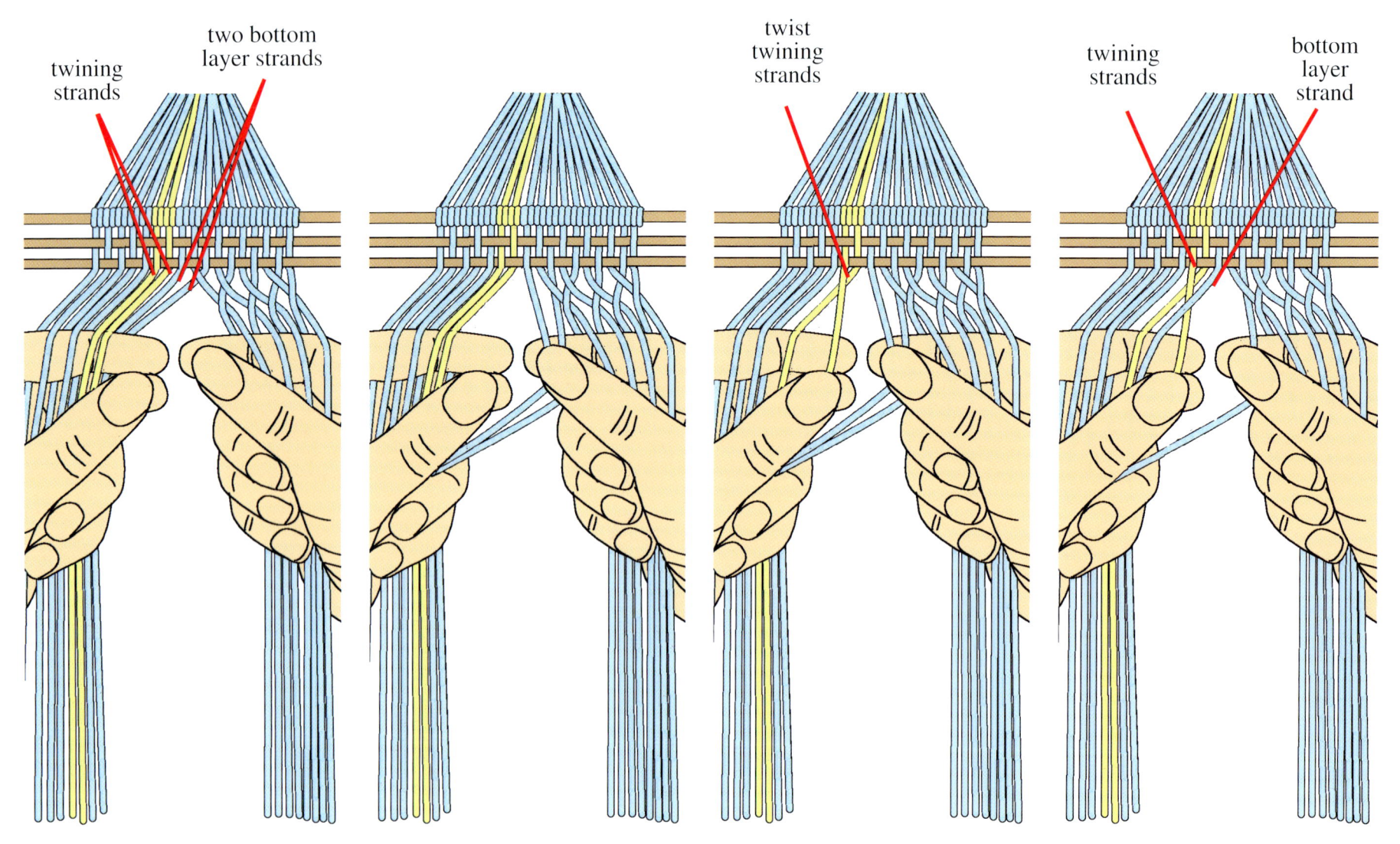

[STEP 7]
Twist the twining strands together so that they cross each other once.

[STEP 8]
Place the other bottom layer strand between the twining strands.

[STEP 9]
Pull the twining strands to the right.

[STEP 10]
Transfer the twining strands and the right bottom strand to the right index finger.

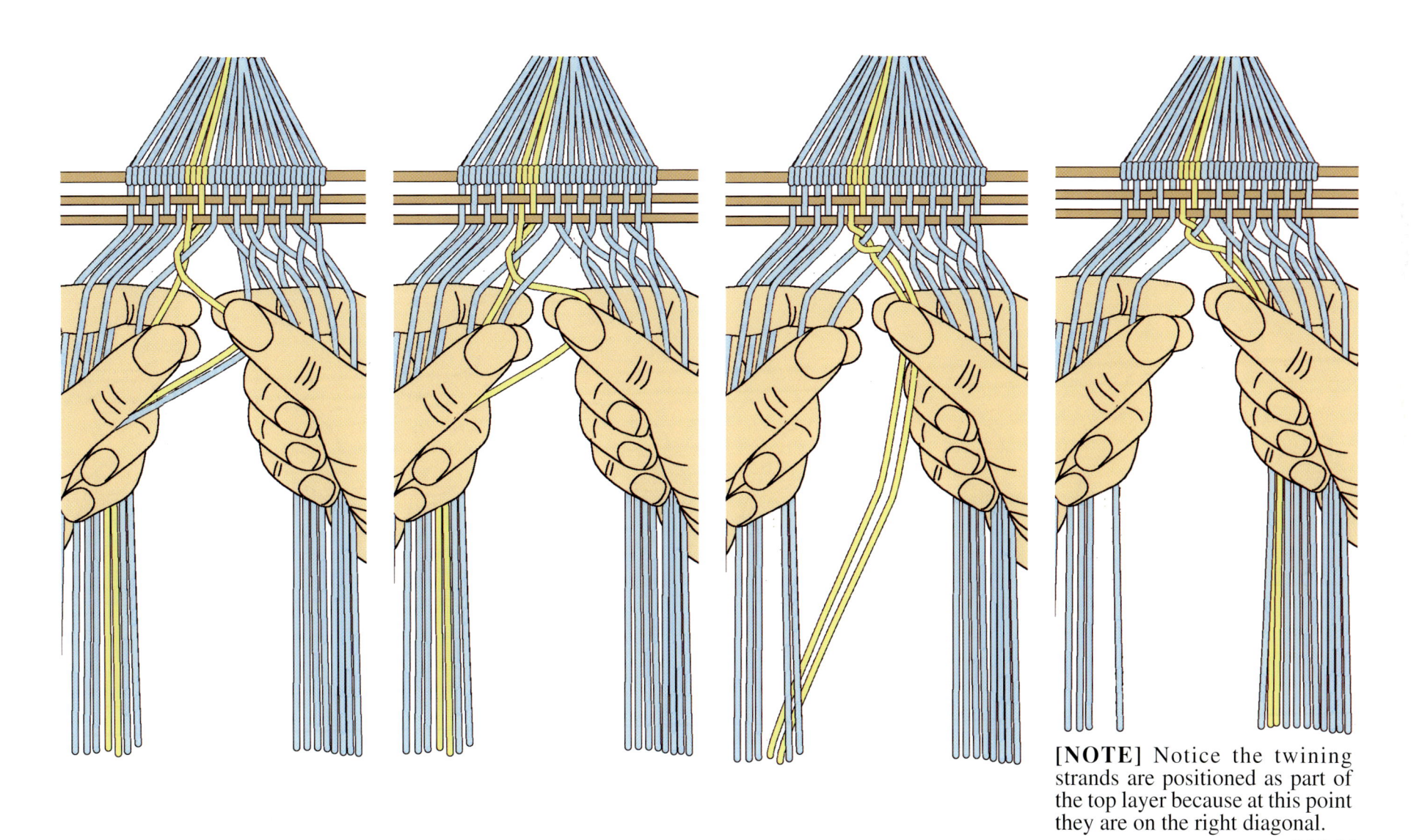

[NOTE] Notice the twining strands are positioned as part of the top layer because at this point they are on the right diagonal.

[1 2 1]

[STEP 11]
Continue weaving, follow these instructions and the instructions for openface weaving until you are prepared to change the direction of the twining strand.

[STEP 12]
Pull the two bottom layer strands to the right.

[STEP 13]
Twist the twining strands together so that they cross each other once.

twist

[STEP 14]
Place the left bottom layer strand between the twining strands.

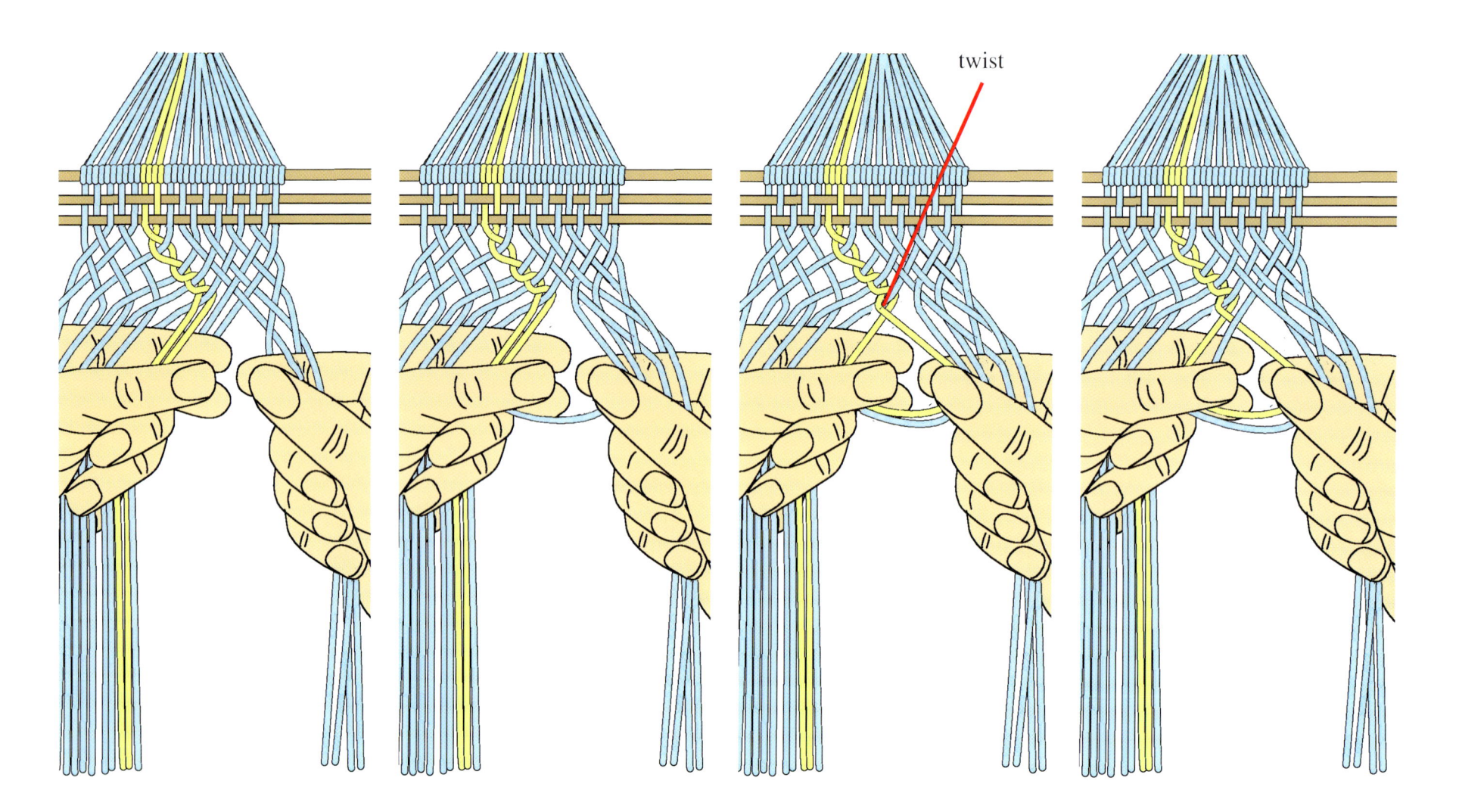

[1 2 2]

[STEP 15]
Pull the twining strands to the right and twist them together so that they cross each other only once.

[STEP 16]
Interlock the bottom strand and the twining strands by pulling the bottom strand between the twining strands.

[STEP 17]
Transfer the twining strands back to the left hand. The twining strands are now the first strand of the bottom layer.

[NOTE] The twining strands are now in the bottom layer of strands.

[STEP 18]
Complete the interlock by arranging the last two strands on the right index finger so that the over/under pattern is reestablished.

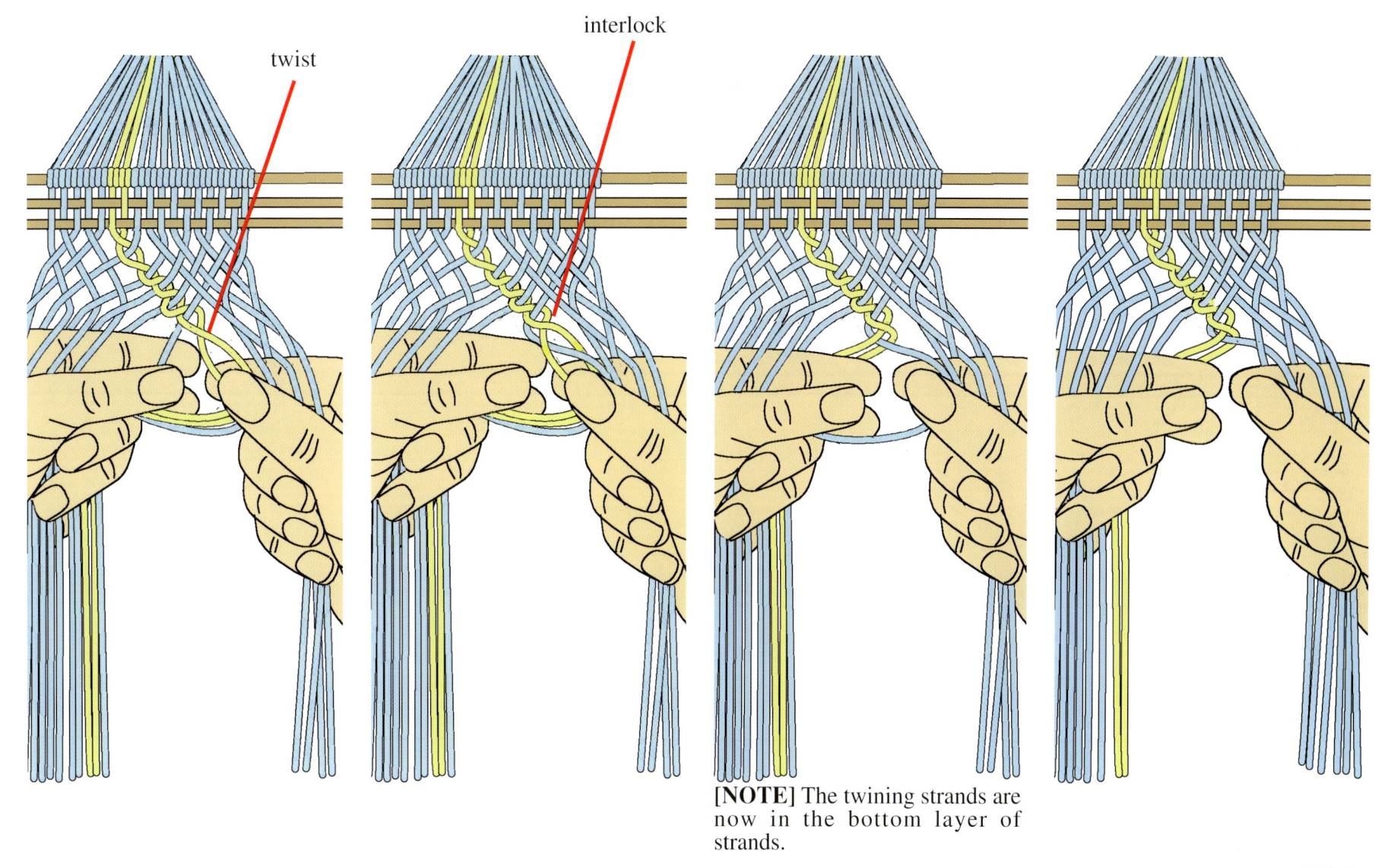

[1 2 3]

[STEP 19]
Continue weaving by twisting the twining strands.

[STEP 20]
Pull the next top layer strand between the twining strands.

[STEP 21]
Transfer the twining strands and the top strand to the right index finger.

[STEP 22]
Continue weaving in this manner until the work is the desired length.

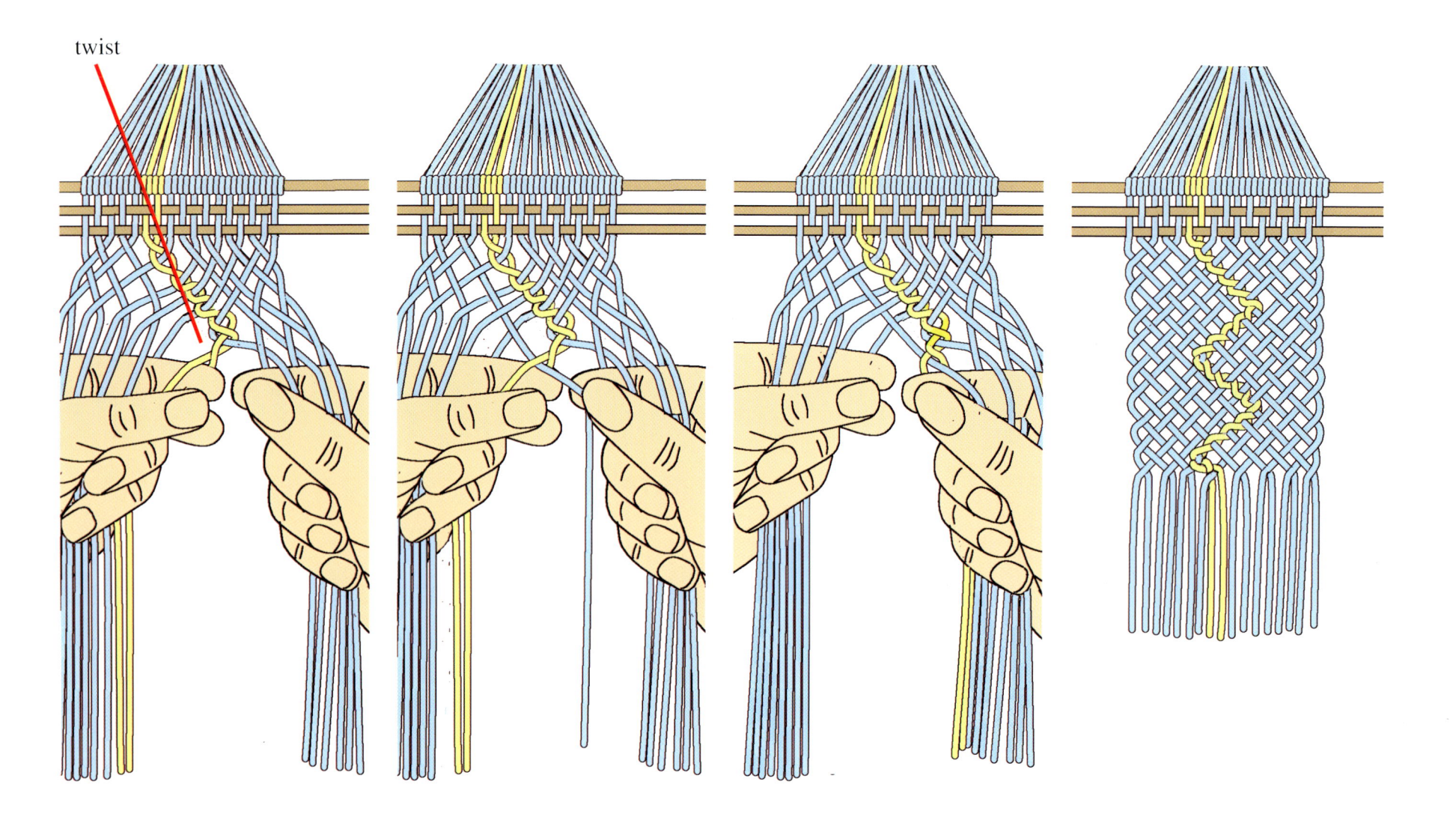

twist

[124]

Openface Weaving Twining Example:

Openface Weaving Twining and Beads Combined

Lines of beads can be added on either side of the twining. Since twining makes use of interlocking strands, it is easier to use carrier strands for the beads.

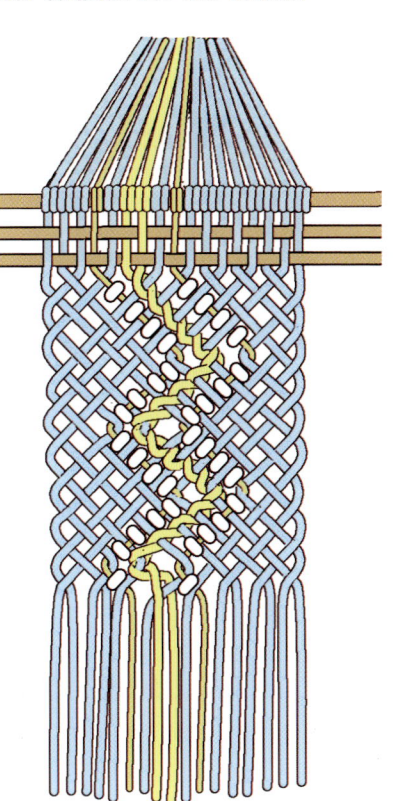

Openface Weaving Twining and Beads Combined Example:

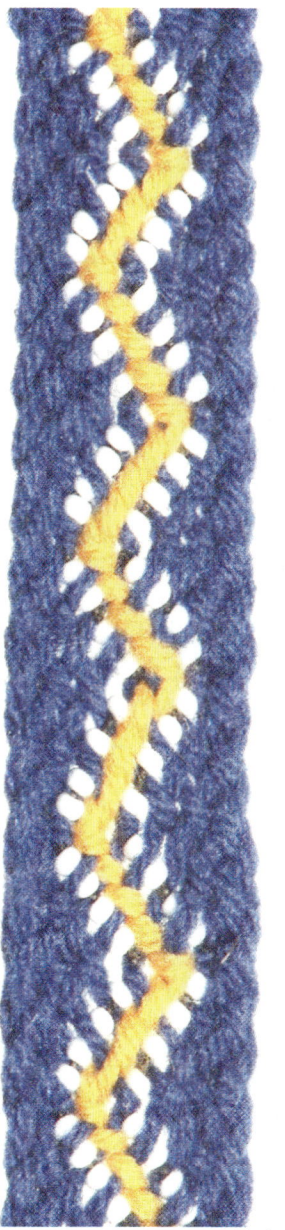

Openface Weaving Warp Accent

A combination of warpface and openface weaving can be used to produce zigzag strips of warpface weaving. The strips of warpface weaving can also be arranged to produce a diamond mesh.

The warpface portion of this form of weaving follows the diagonals of the open face portion of the work. The weft strands for the warp face portion of this design are the strands of the openface portion of the work.

The following directions are for two zigzag strips of warpface weaving combined to produce a row of diamonds.

[STEP 1]
Cast on the required number of strands and set up the shed. See (Part 1: Getting Started).

[STEP 2]
Pick up the shed. Use the index finger of the left hand to hold the shed open. Observe that the strands are now divided into two layers. The bottom layer is behind the index finger and the top layer is above the index finger.

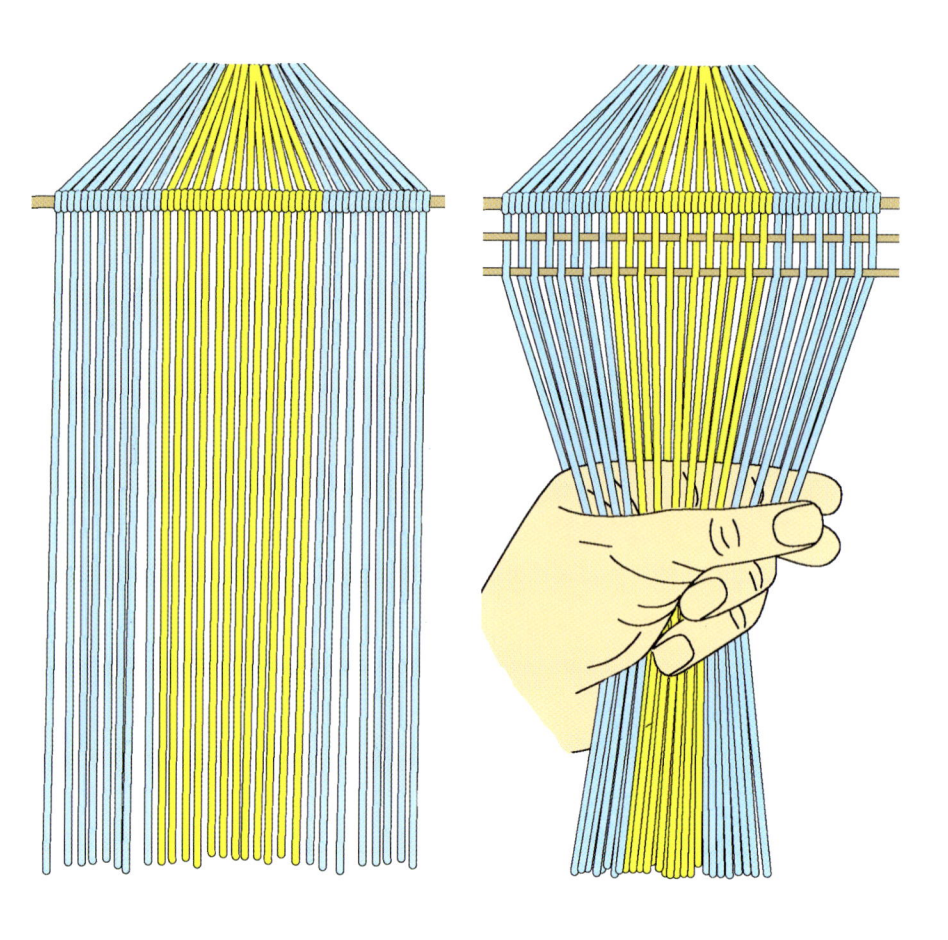

[126]

[STEP 3] Follow the directions for openface weaving until there are two bottom layer strands left before the warpface strands.

- warpface strands
- two bottom layer strands

[STEP 4] Move the right hand set of warpface strands and the two bottom strands to the right hand.

- left hand set
- right hand set
- two bottom layer strands

[STEP 5] The left bottom strand on the right acts as a weft strand when it is pulled to the left through the open shed of the warp strands.

- warp
- left bottom

[STEP 6] Reverse the shed of the warp strip and set the weft in place by pulling the two layers of the warp in opposite directions.

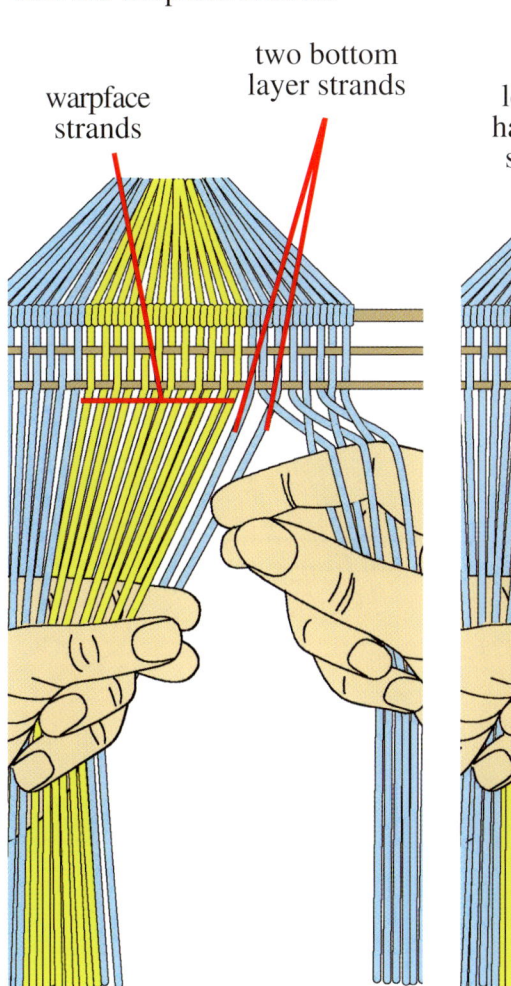

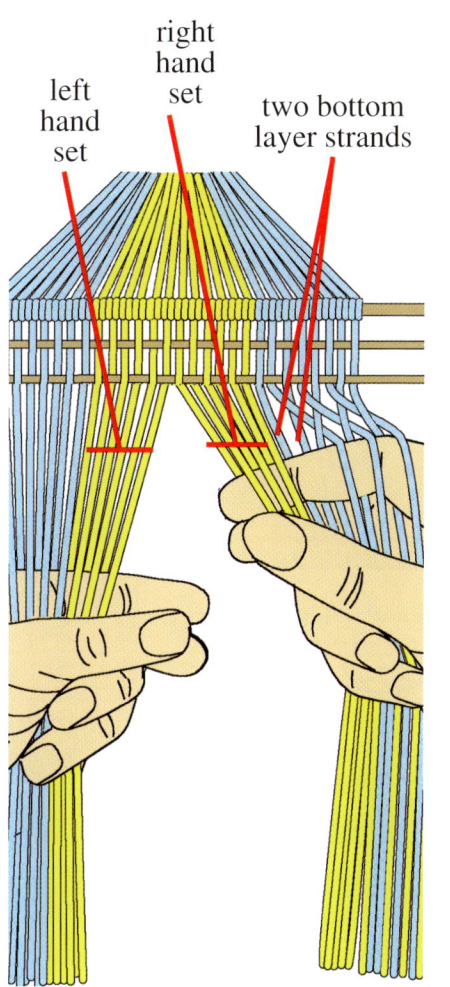

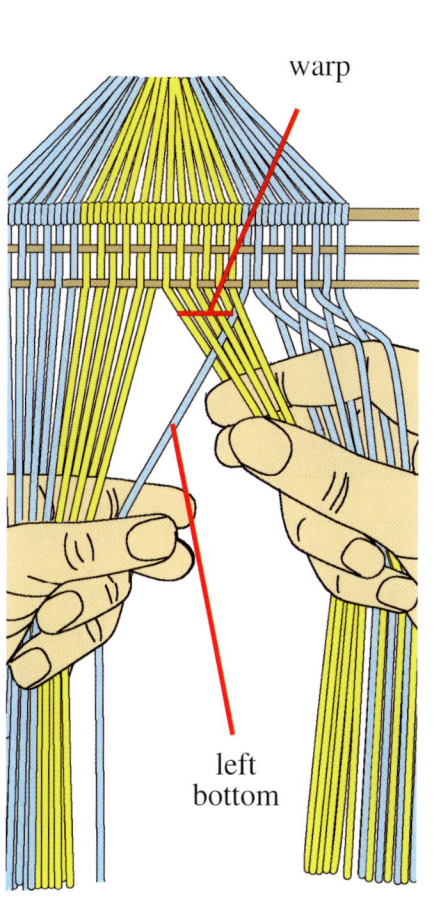

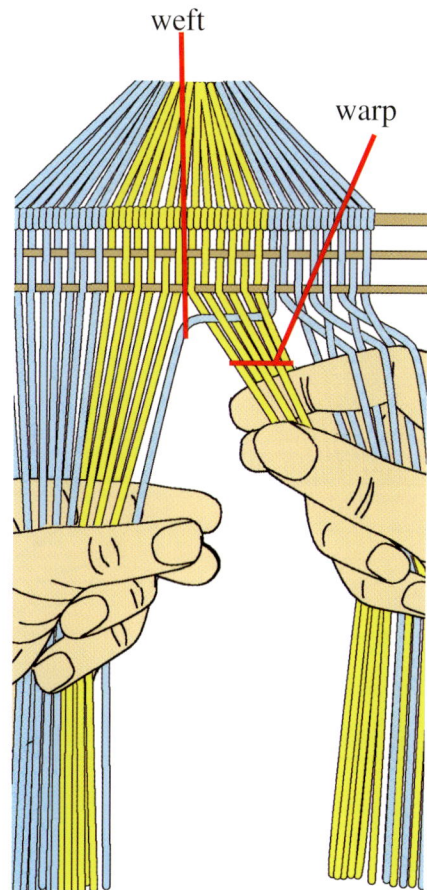

- weft
- warp

[127]

[STEP 7]
Pull the right bottom strand to the left through the open shed of the warp strands. The bottom strand is used as a weft strand for the warp face strip.

[STEP 8]
Reverse the shed of the warp strip and set the weft in place by pulling the two layers of the warp in opposite directions.

[STEP 9]
The first top strand on the left acts as a weft strand when it is pulled to the right through the open shed of the warp strands and down between the two bottom strands.

[STEP 10]
At the center, start the openface weave again by picking up the right two strands with the right index finger.

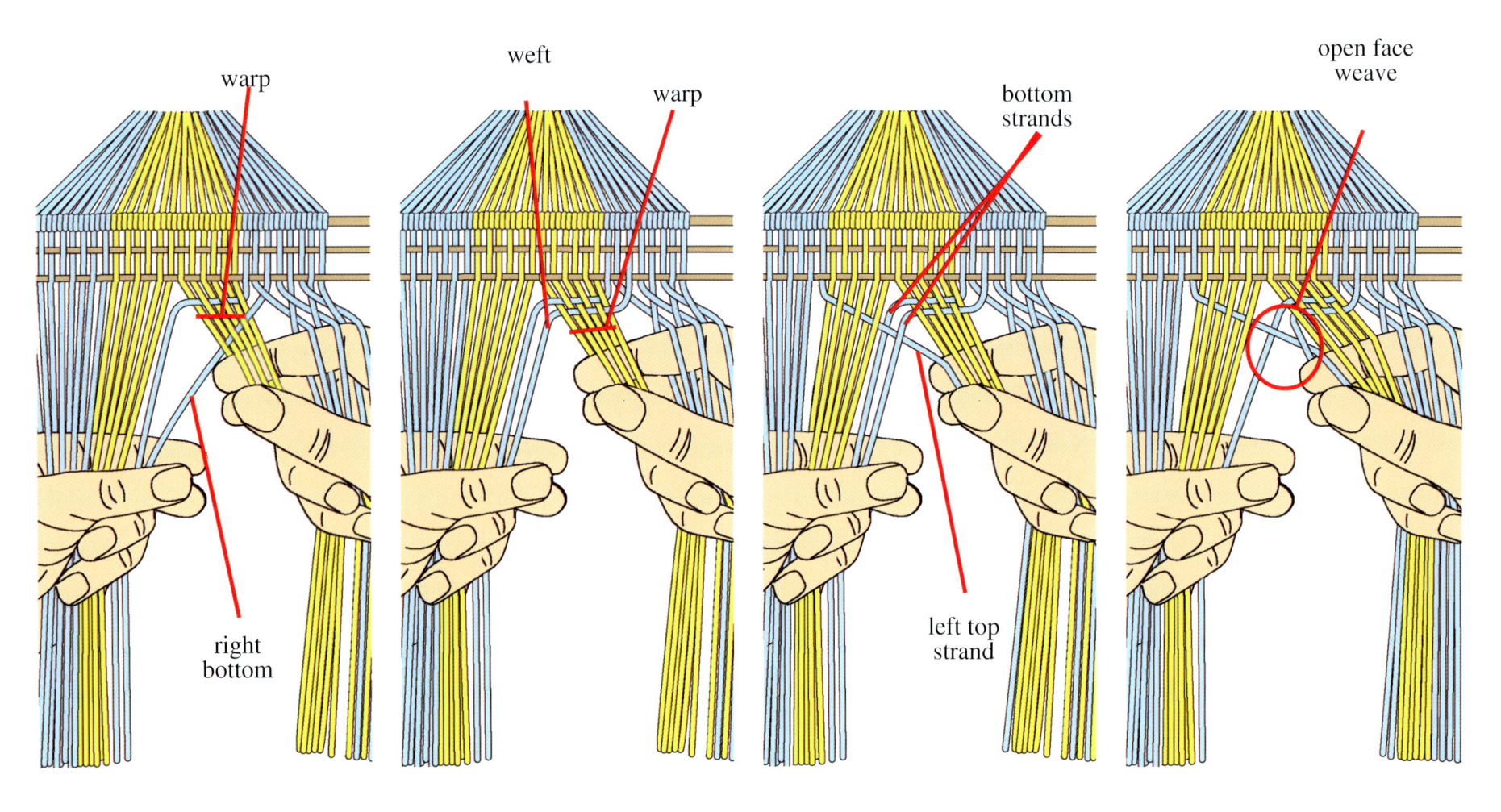

[128]

[STEP 11] Reverse the shed of the warp strip and set the weft in place by pulling the two layers of the warp in opposite directions.

[STEP 12] The second top strand on the left acts as a weft strand when it is pulled to the right through the open shed of the warp strands and under the remaining bottom strand.

[STEP 13] Reverse the shed of the warp strip and set the weft in place by pulling the two layers of the warp in opposite directions.

[STEP 14] At the center, continue the open face weave by picking up the left two strands with the right index finger.

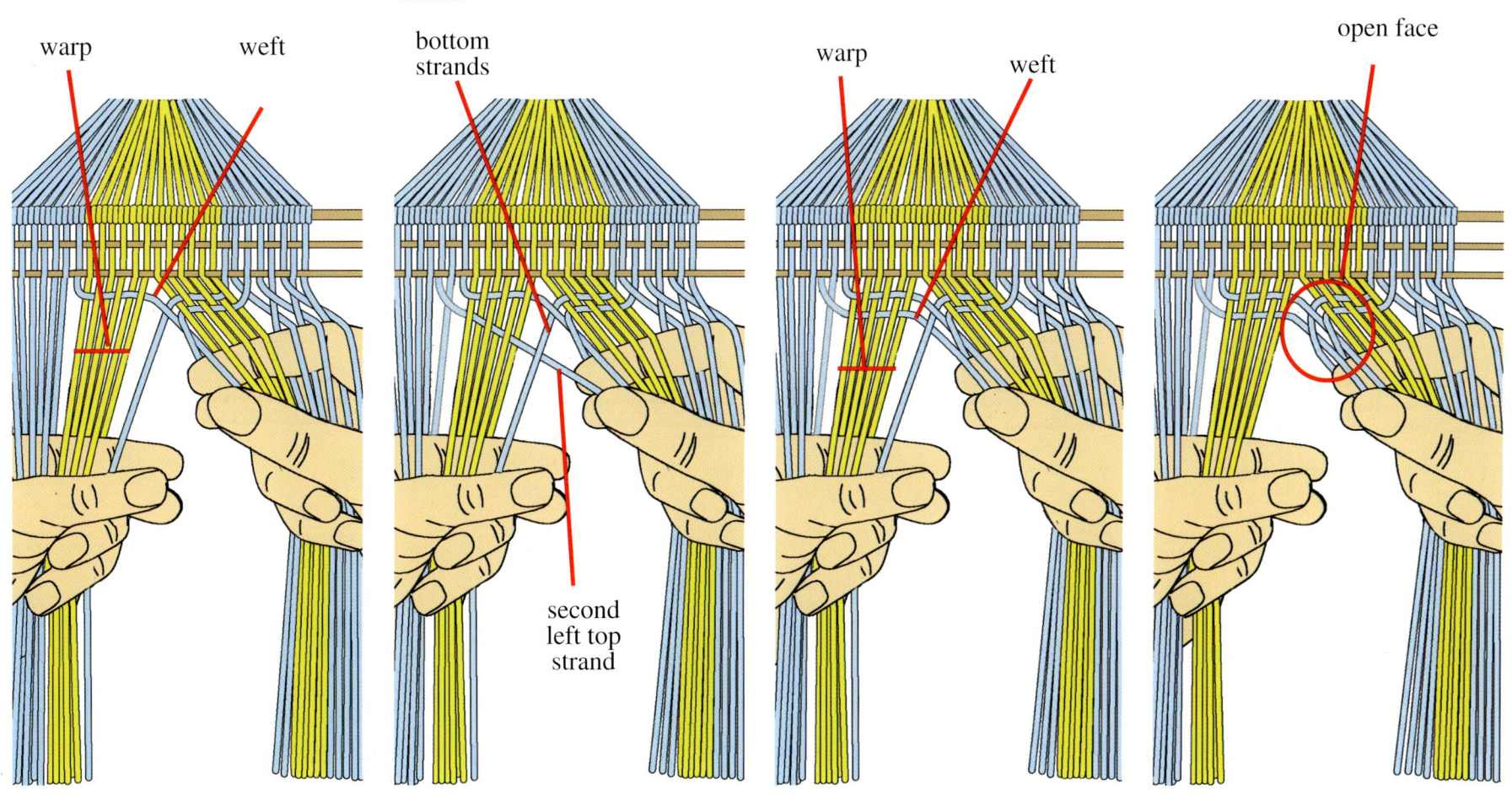

[129]

[STEP 15]
Transfer the left set of warp strands to the right index finger.

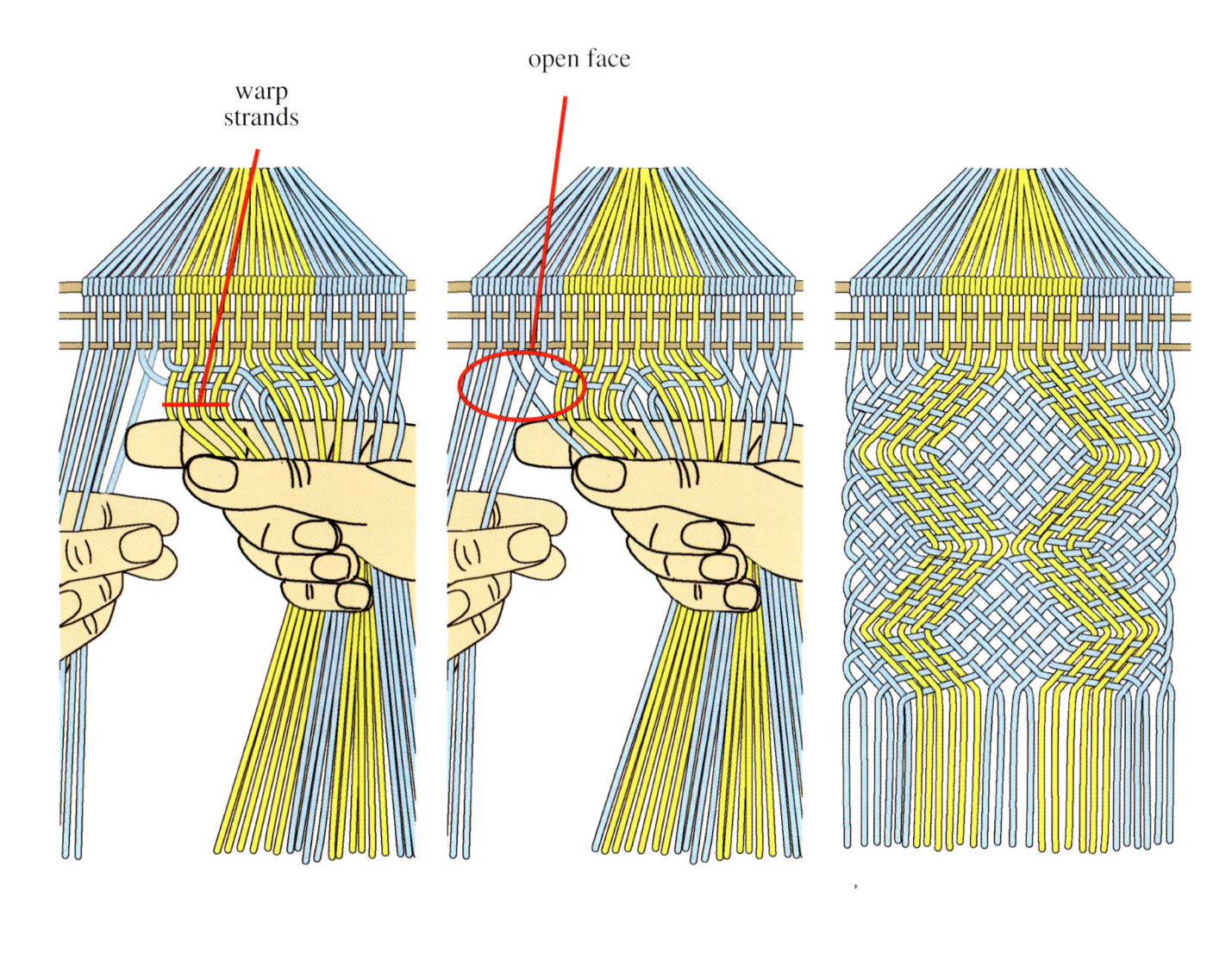

[STEP 16]
Finish the row by following the directions for openface weaving.

[STEP 17]
Continue weaving in this manner until the work is the desired length.

Openface Weaving Warp Accent Example:

warp strands

open face

[130]

Openface Weaving
Warp Accent With Beads

Beads can be added as shown below.

Example 1: **Example 2:**

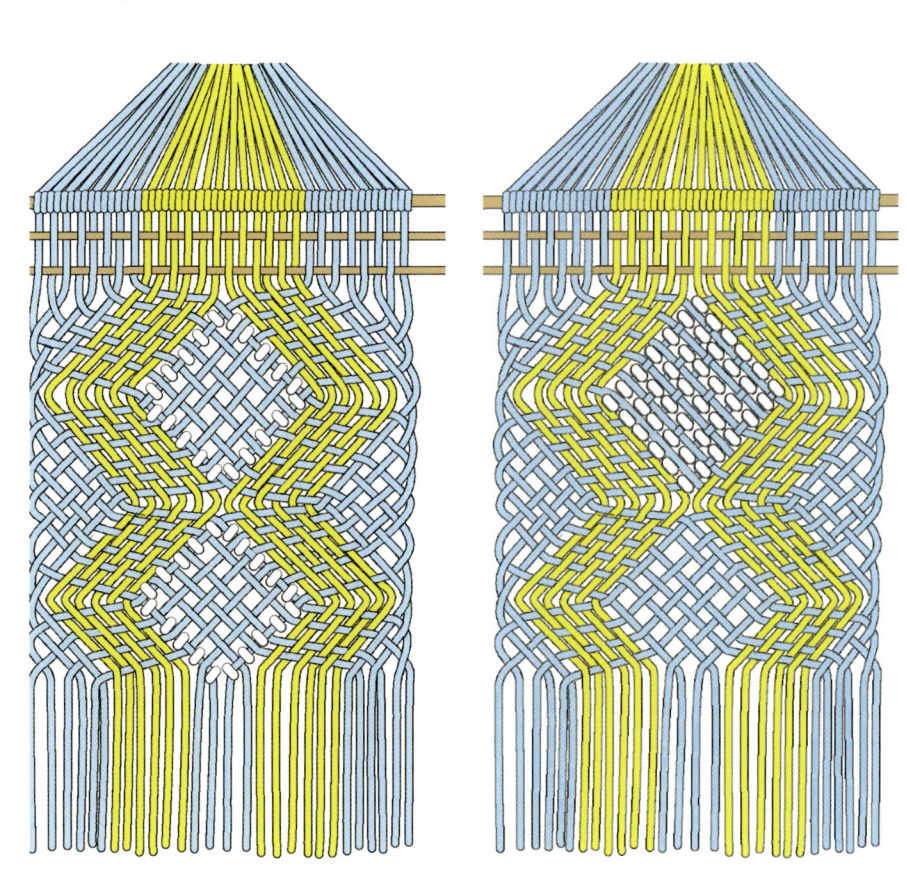

Openface Weaving
Warp Accent With Beads
Example:

[NOTE] Additional variations can be achieved by adding beads to more strands. Carrier strands for the beads can also be used.

[131]

PART 4: FRINGES

The work piece is usually ended by making the remaining part of the strands of yarn into a fringe. Fringes serve several purposes. The main purpose of the fringe is to prevent the woven portion from coming apart. Fringes can be used to tie a sash, a garter or other piece in place. Fringes also serve as decorative elements.

Fringes can take many different forms. Only three types of fringes will be dealt with here: tied, braided, and twisted.

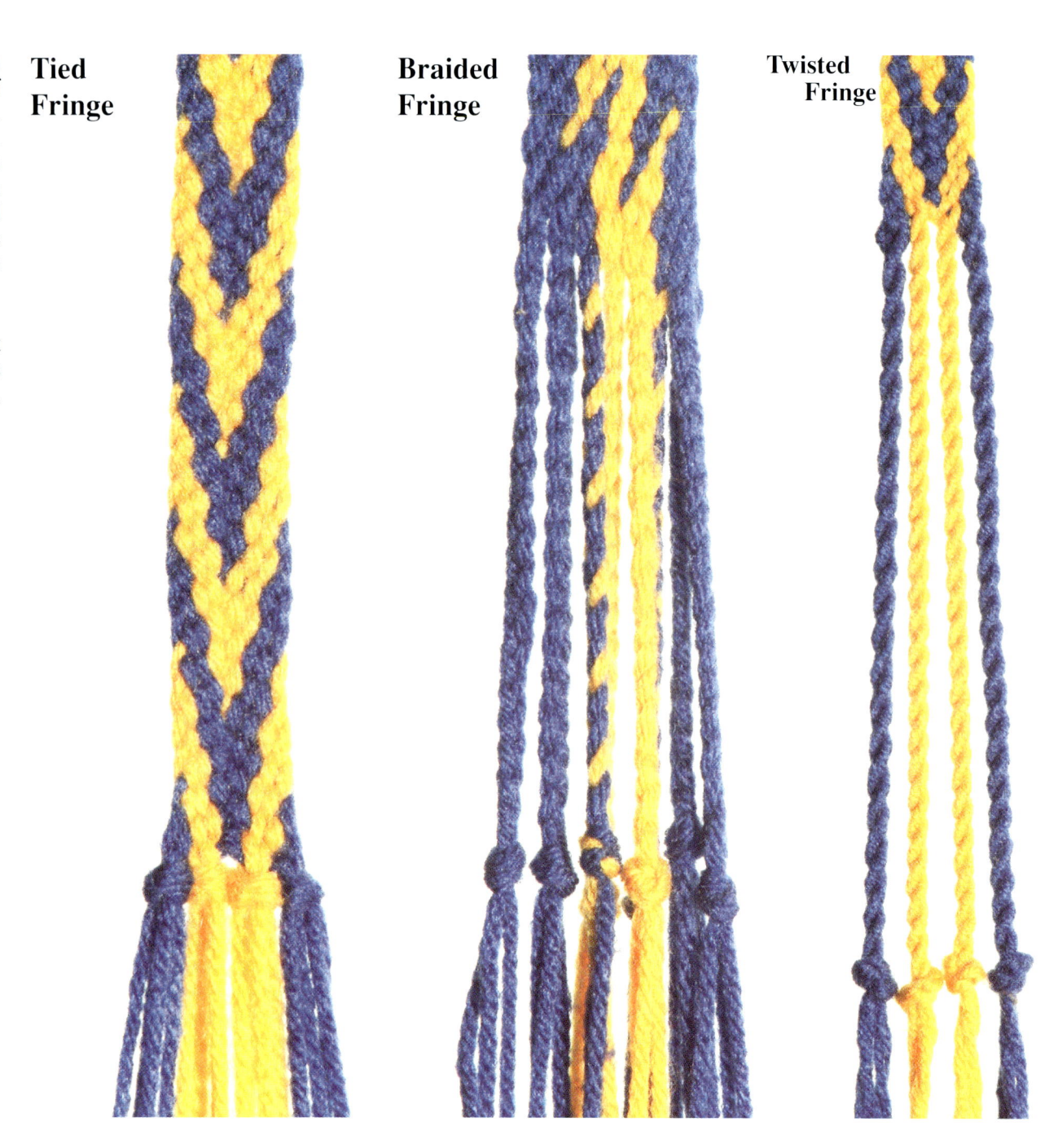

Tied Fringe

Braided Fringe

Twisted Fringe

Tied Fringe

The simplest form of fringe is to tie pairs or small groups of strands together. This can be done with an overhand knot, square knot or a wall knot. The overhand knot is not symmetrical and is difficult to tie close to the work piece. The square knot is easily tied close to the work, is symmetrical but the ends are not parallel to the work and the knot can be easily upset. The wall knot is symmetrical, the ends are parallel to the work and it is not easily upset. In addition, the wall knot gives the appearance of a small tassel when it is tied using several strands.

Two Strand Wall Knot
[STEP 1]
Select pairs of strands to be tied.

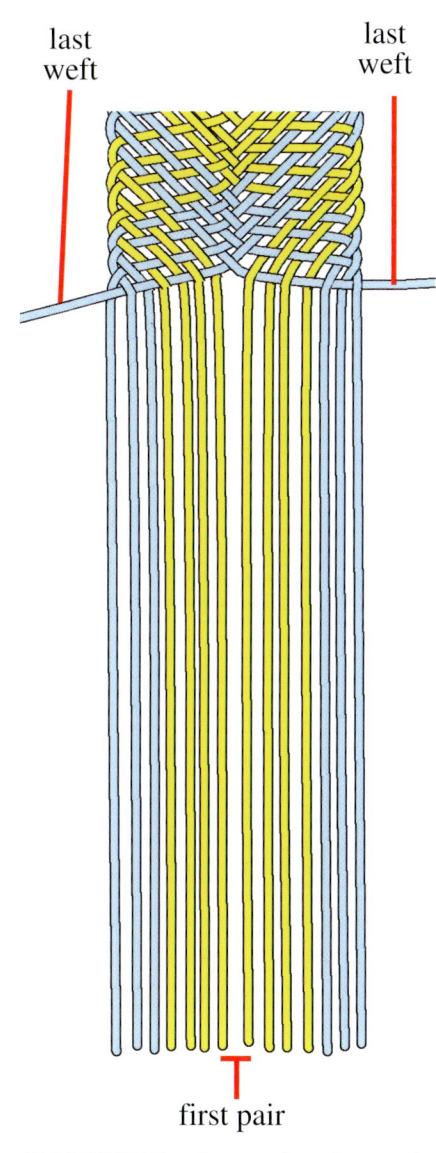

[NOTE] The last pair of strands tied should include the last weft strand. This ensures that the knot is drawn up snug against the work piece.

[STEP 2]
Form a loop in the right hand strand so that it passes under the left hand strand from left to right.

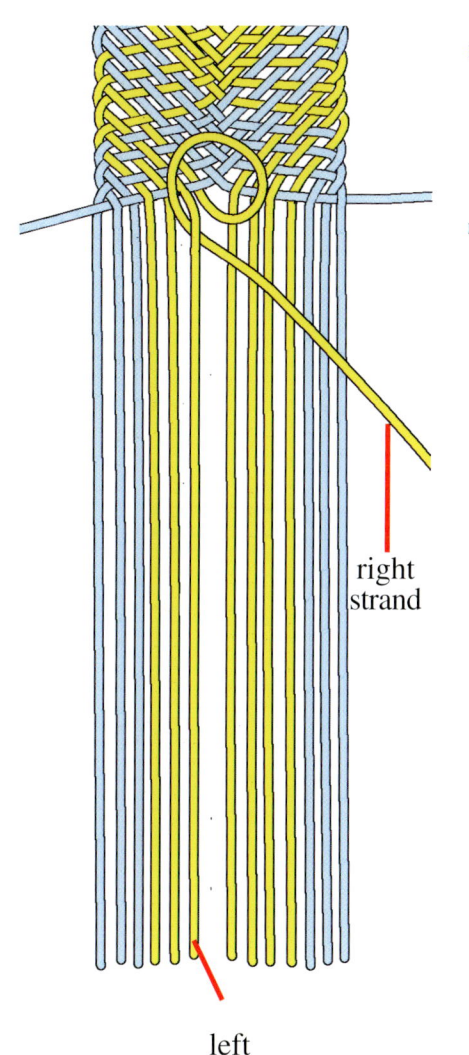

[STEP 3]
Pass the left hand strand under the right hand strand and reeve it up through the loop in the right hand strand.

[133]

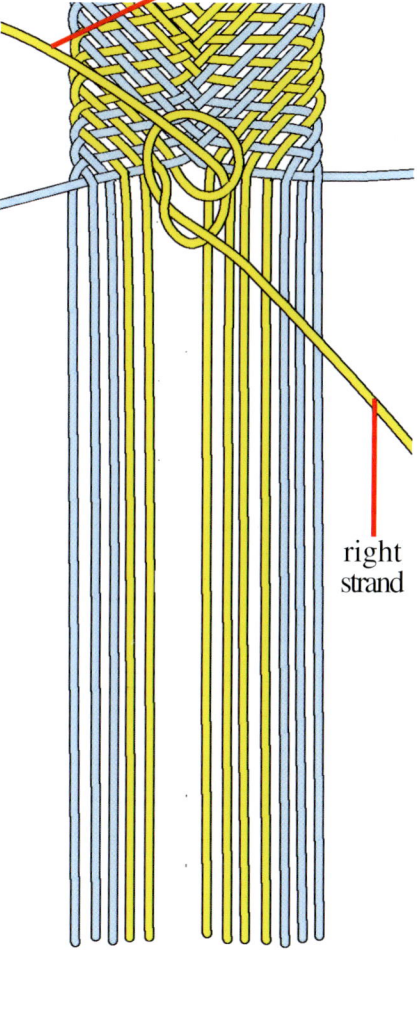

[STEP 4]
Pull the strands in opposite directions until the knot is snug and even.

[STEP 5]
Finish the knot by placing the strands parallel to each other and working it snug.

work snug

[STEP 6]
Tie the remaining pairs of strands following steps 2 through 5.

Tied Fringe Example:

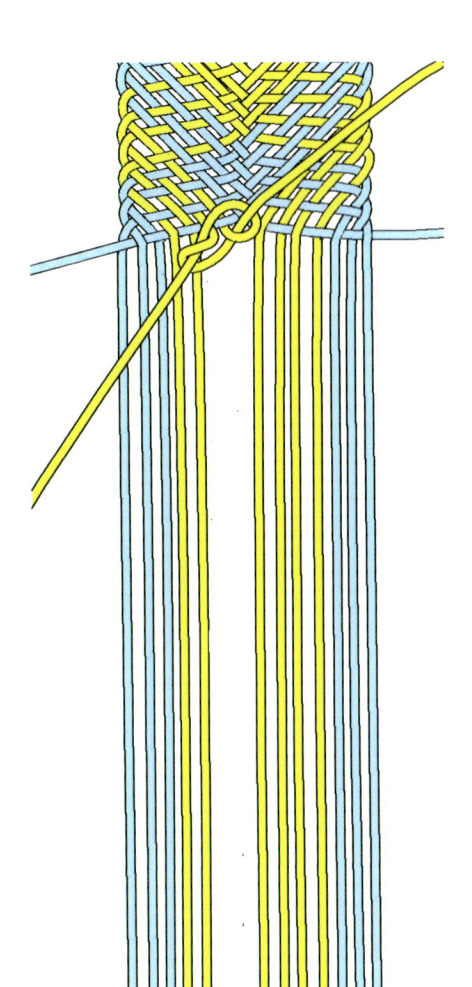

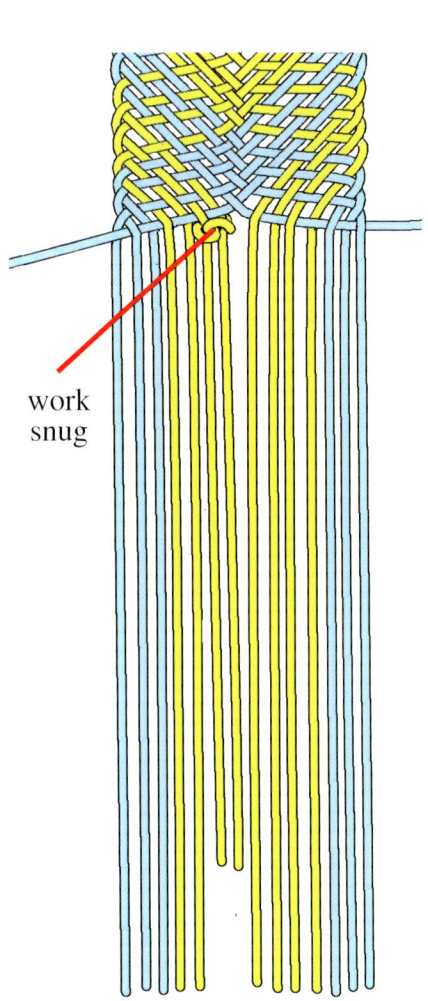

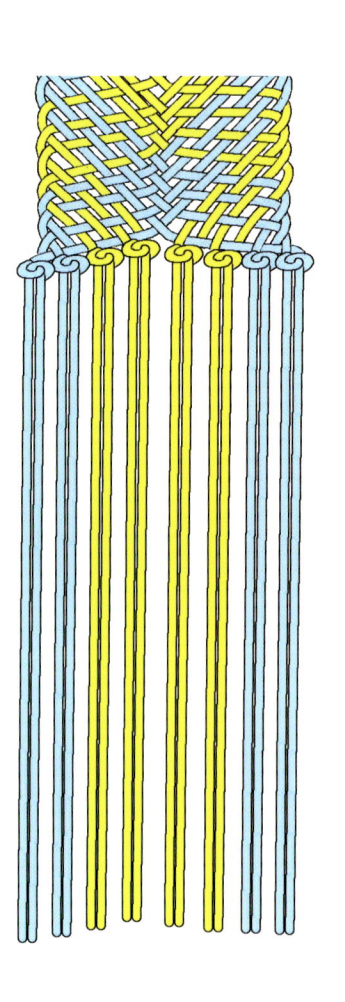

[1 3 4]

Braided Fringe

The easiest form of braiding to use to make a fringe is a three strand braid. Wider braids can be made by using openface weaving. Round braiding can also be used but will not be dealt with here.

[NOTE] One advantage of using a braided fringe is that beads can be worked into the fringe.

[STEP 1]

If you are planning to use a three strand braid for a fringe, the number of strands in the original setup should be divisible by three.

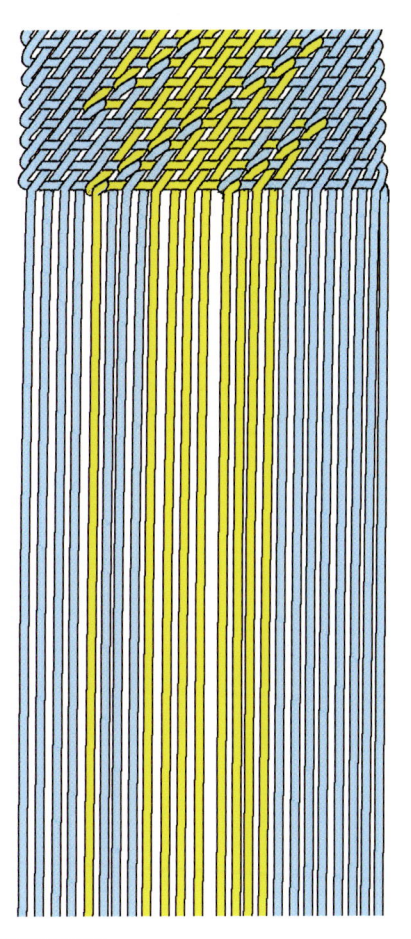

[NOTE] If you are planning to use 2 strands of yarn for each strand of the braid, the number of strands in the original setup should be divisible by six

[STEP 2]

Select a set of three strands. Move the left strand under the middle strand so that it is between the other two and becomes the middle strand.

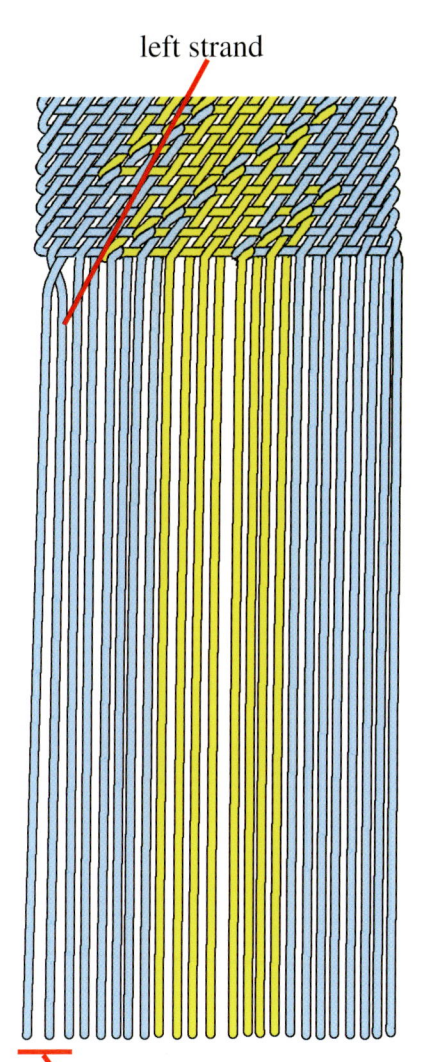

left strand

first three strands

[STEP 3]

Move the right strand under the new middle strand so that it is between the other two and becomes the new middle strand.

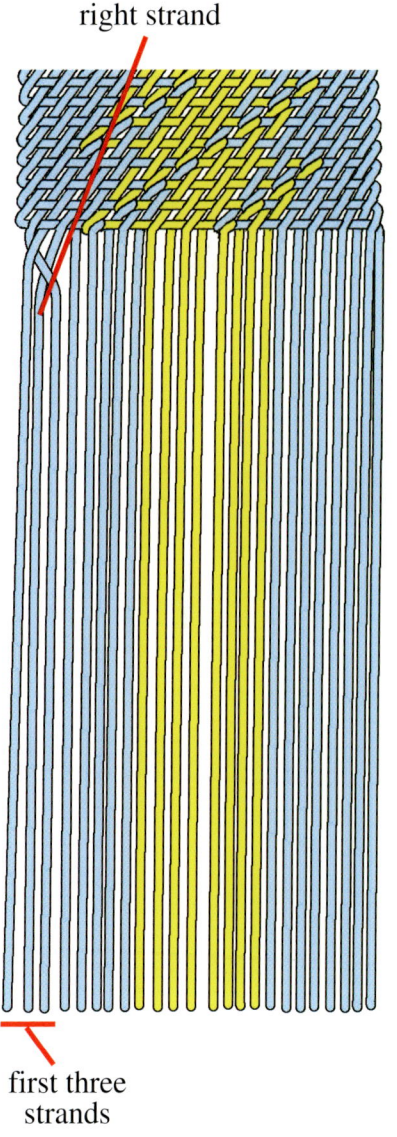

right strand

first three strands

[135]

[STEP 4]
Move the left strand under the middle strand so that it is between the other two and becomes the middle strand.

left strand

[STEP 5]
Move the right strand to the middle ....

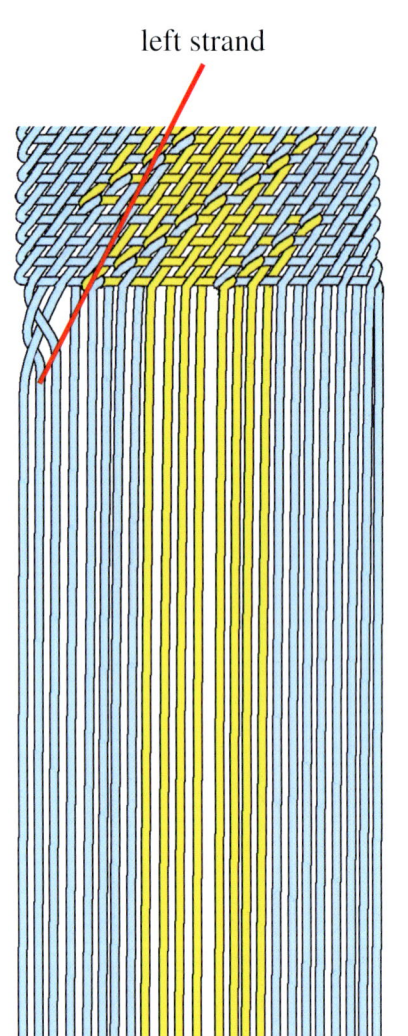

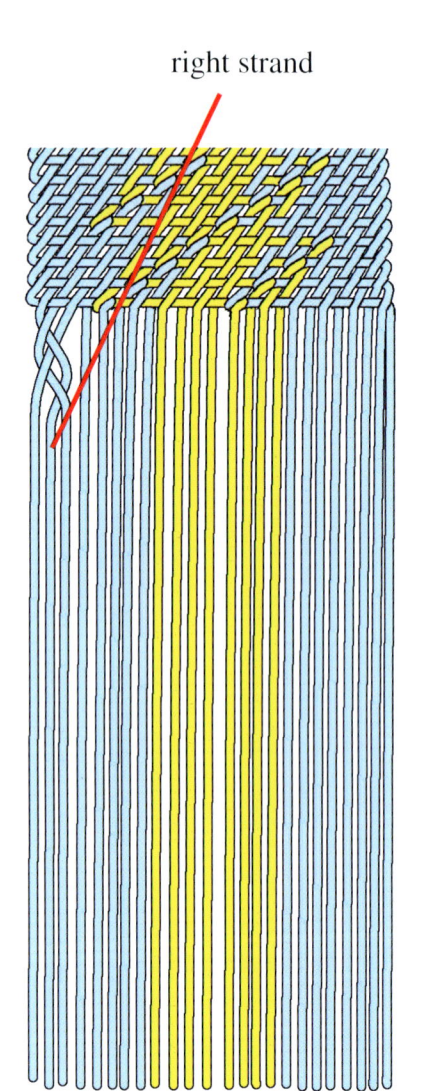

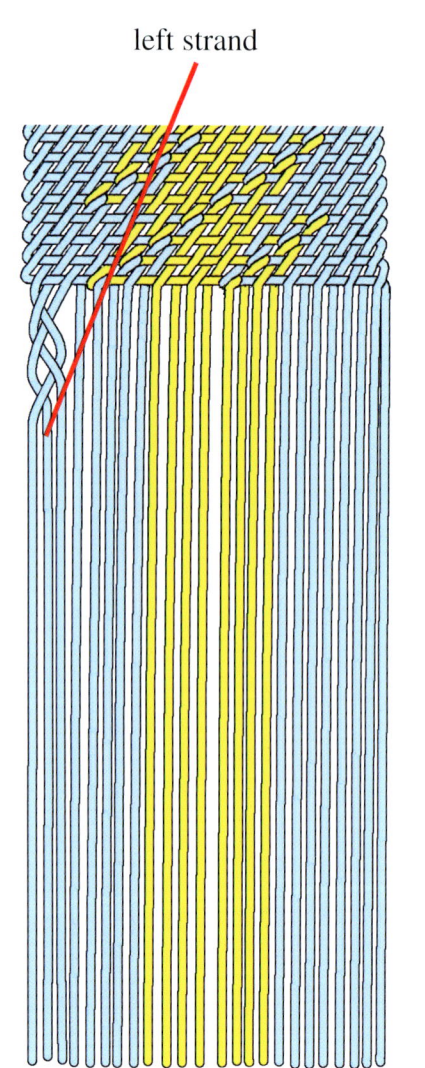

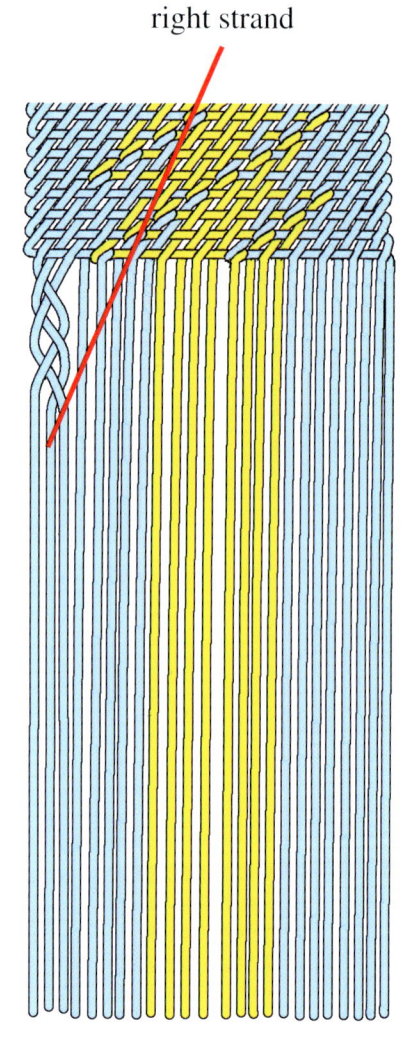

right strand

[STEP 6]
Move the left strand to the middle ....

left strand

[STEP 7]
Move the right strand to the middle ....

right strand

[NOTE]
This is the end of the first sequence. The strands are in their original order.

[STEP 8]
Move the left strand to the middle ···············

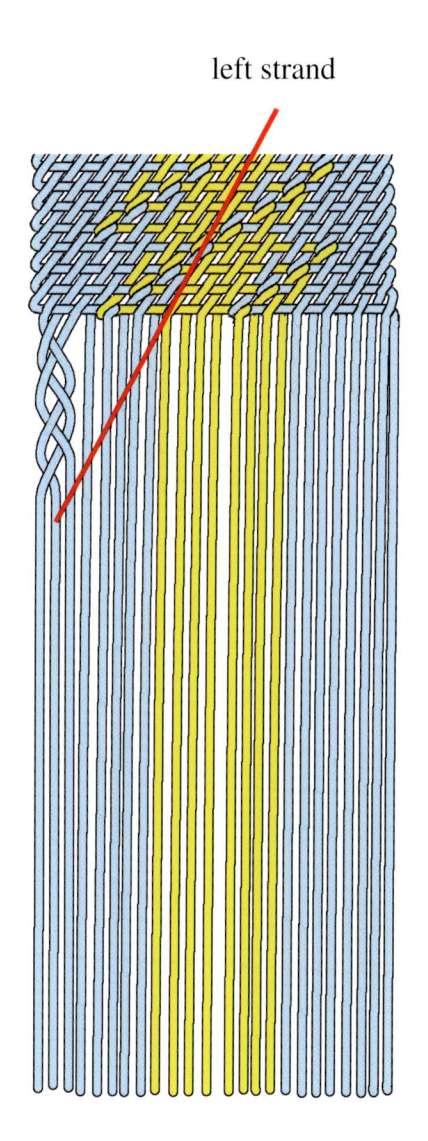

left strand

[STEP 9]
Continue to braid in this manner until the desired length is reached. End the braiding with an overhand knot.

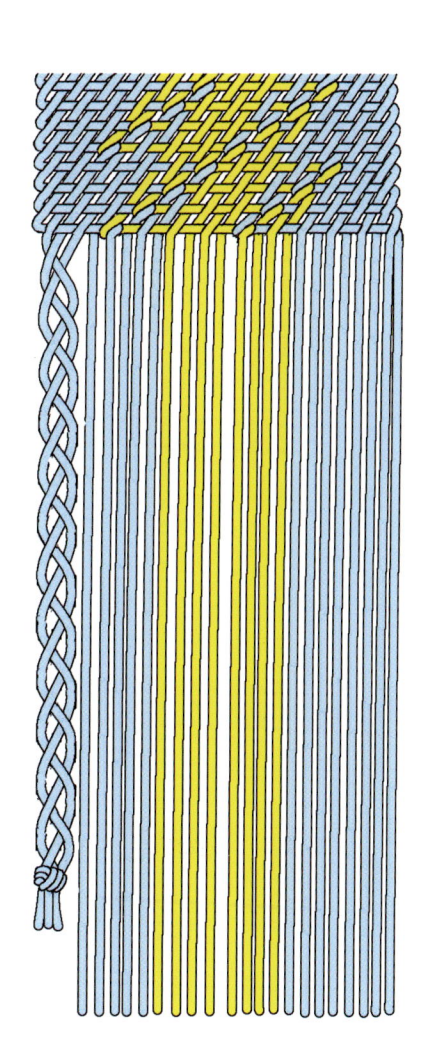

[STEP 10]
Braid the remaining sets of three strands. Follow steps 2 through 9.

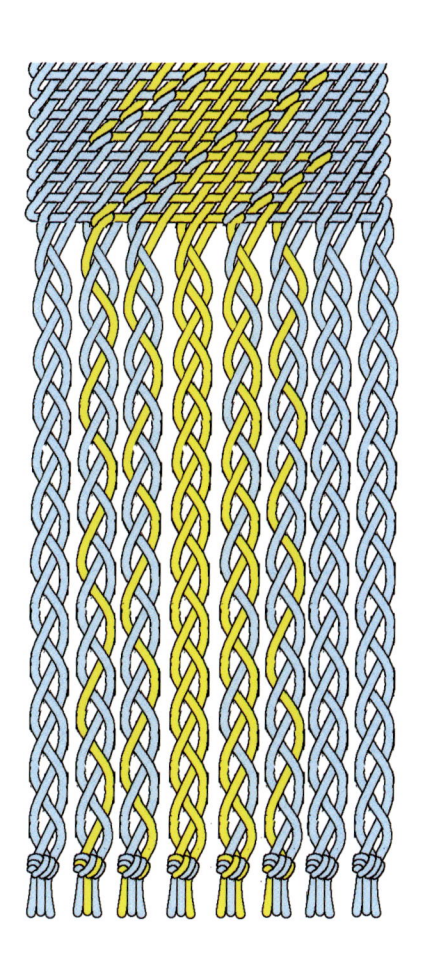

Braided Fringe Example:

[137]

Braided Fringe Bead Accented Example:

[STEP 1]
String beads on one or more of the set of three strands. See (Part 1: Adding Accent Beads).

[STEP 2A]
Follow directions for braided fringes steps 2 through 9 but place a bead in position before the strand is moved to the middle.

[STEP 2B]
Follow directions for braided fringes steps 2 through 9 but place a bead in position after the strand is moved to the middle.

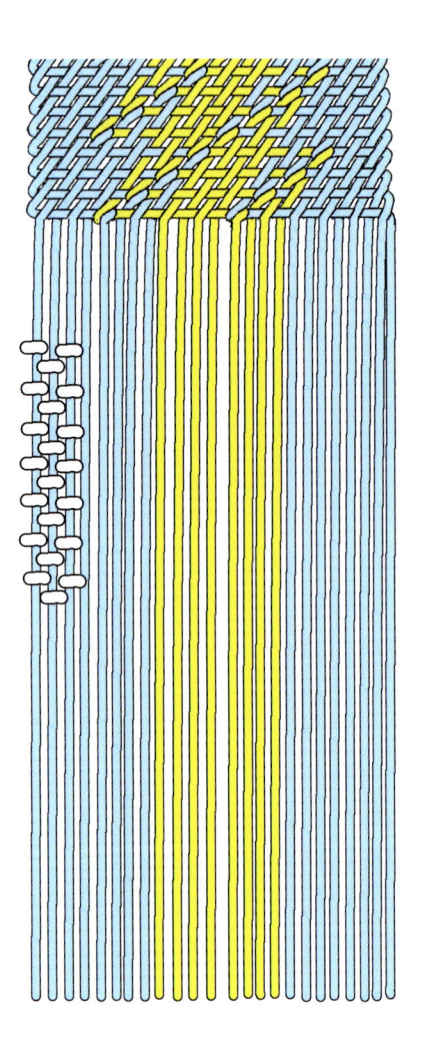

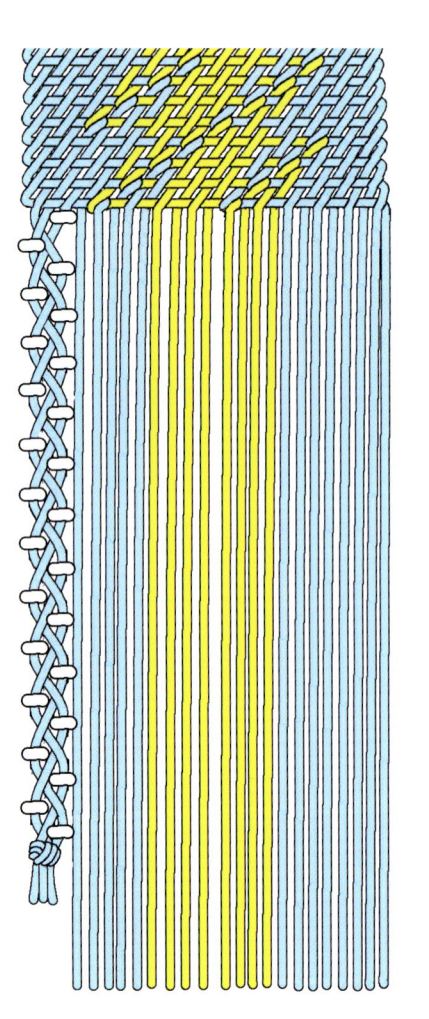

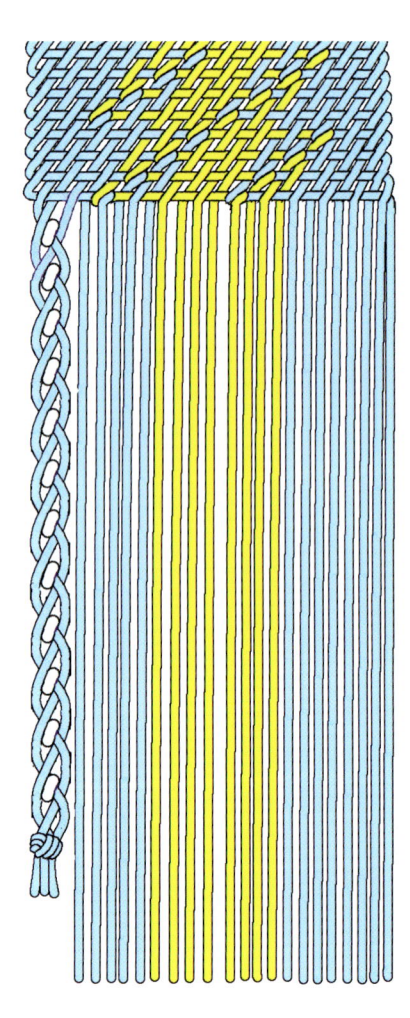

Twisted Fringe

Fringes of twisted strands are made by twisting two pairs of strands together. Then tie the twisted pairs together and allow the pairs of strands to twist together.

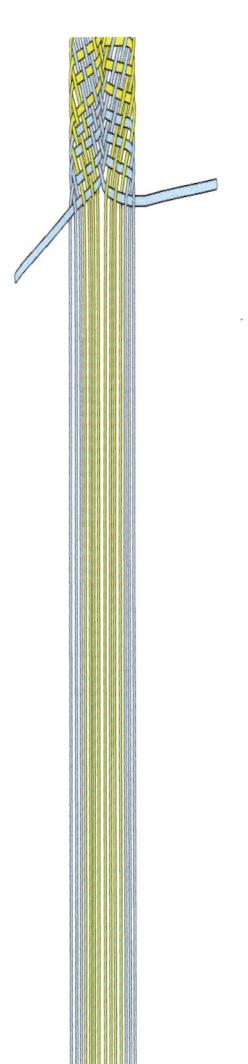

[STEP 1]
Set up the work piece so that the number of strands is divisible by four.

[NOTE] The last pair of strands twisted should include the last weft strand. This insures that the twisted fringe strand is drawn up snug against the work piece.

[STEP 2]
Twist two pairs of strands together.

twist

[STEP 3]
Tie the two pairs of twisted strands together.

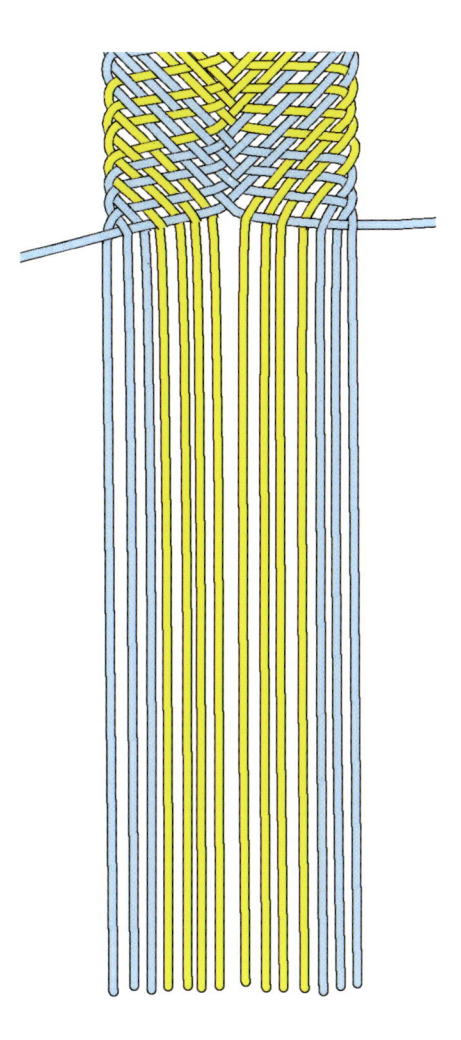

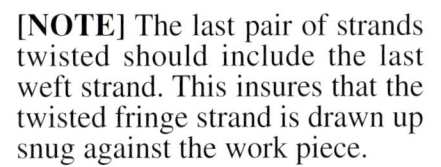

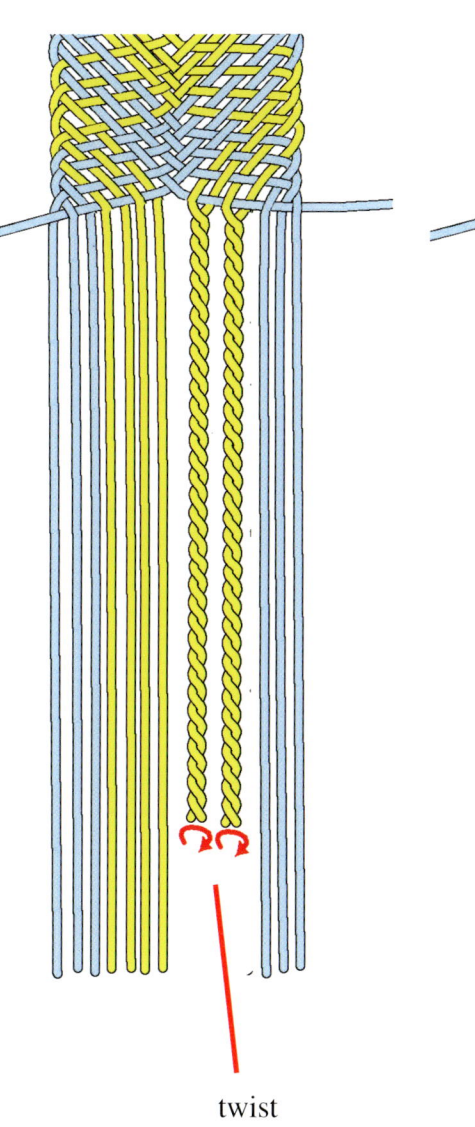

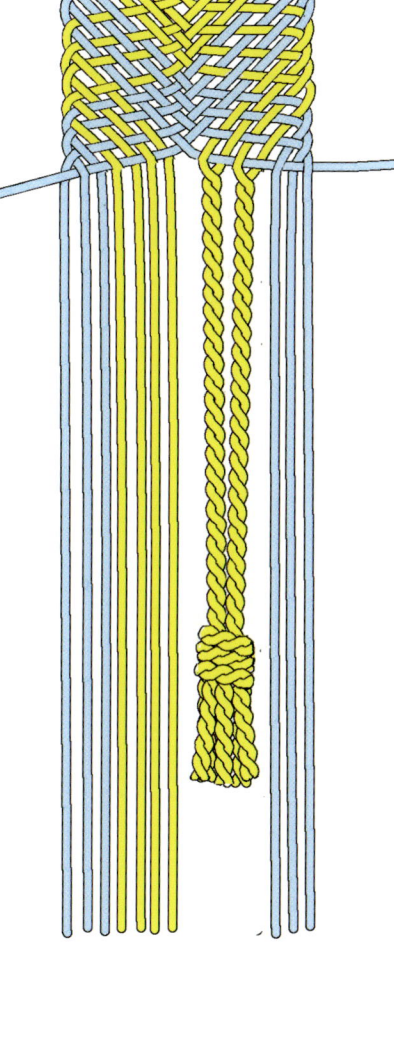

[139]

[STEP 4]
Allow the two pairs of twisted strands to twist together in the opposite direction.

[STEP 5]
Twist remaining sets of strands together following steps 2 through 4.

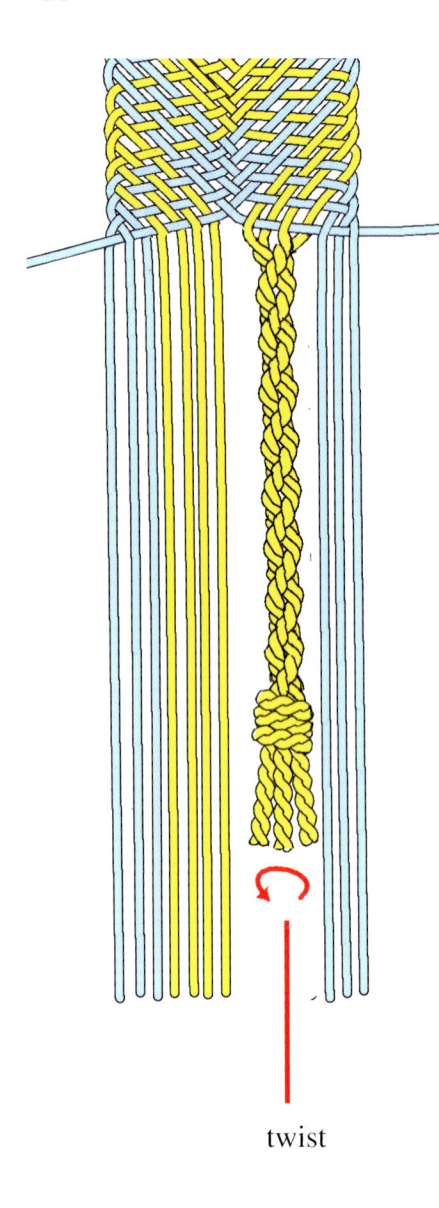

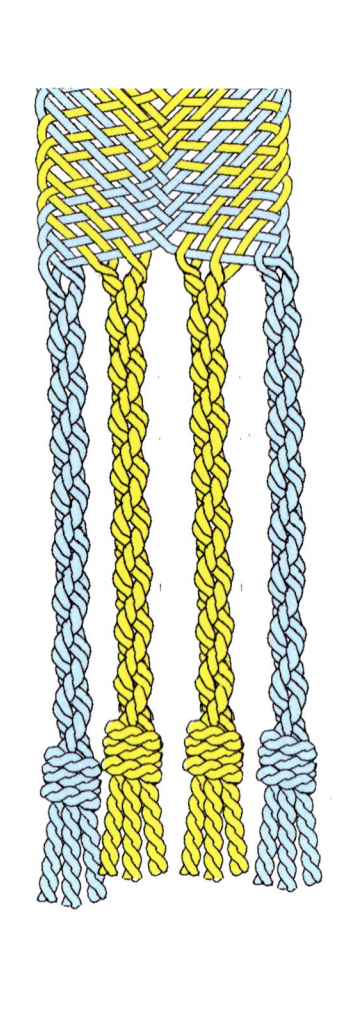

Twisted Fringe Example:

twist

[140]

GLOSSARY

anchor ---- Anything that the work piece can be fastened to so that proper tension can be maintained on the work piece. For example: a chair, a hook in the wall, a door knob, a pillow, etc.

braid ---- To interlace (weave) strands together to produce a textile when there are no clear warp and weft strands.

carrier strand ---- A strand of yarn of the same or different material used to "carry" beads while weaving.

casting on ---- Securing a strand to a headstick with a clove hitch.

chevron ---- A pattern that has the shape of a "V".

headstick ---- A small stick used to arrange and secure the strands when beginning a piece of finger weaving.

interface ---- See (openface).

interlock ---- the twisting together of two strands to change their position in the work piece. Change a warp to a weft or to change from the top layer of the shed to the bottom layer of the shed.

oblique weave ---- See (openface).

openface ---- A weaving technique that allows all the strands to be seen on the surface of the finished product.

plain face ---- See (openface).

ply ---- One of the threads in a strand of yarn.

shed ---- The open space between the two layers of warp strands.

twilling ---- A textile weave in which the filling threads pass over one and under two or more warp threads to give the appearance of diagonal lines.

twining ---- (1) A technique of weaving where weft strands are twisted together between warp strands. (2) A technique of adding an accent line by twisting two strands together as they are woven into the work piece.

warp ---- A series of strands that run the length of the work.

warpface ---- A weaving technique that allows only the warp strands to be seen.

weft ---- A strand that is pulled through the shed.

woof ----(weft) A strand that is pulled through the shed.

yarn ---- A strand of fibers made up of several threads.

INDEX

----- A -----

ACCENT BEADS
  CARRIER STRANDS - 105, 109
  DIAMOND PATTERN - 105, 109, 110
    CARRIER STRANDS EXAMPLE: 108
  OVER/UNDER ONLY
    ACCENT BEADS- 105, 109
    FOUR BEAD DIAMOND MESH - 111, 112
    FOUR BEAD DIAMOND MESH
      EXAMPLE: - 112
    SIX BEAD DIAMOND MESH - 110
    SIX BEAD DIAMOND MESH
      EXAMPLE: - 110
    SIX BEAD ZIGZAG - 111
    SIX BEAD ZIGZAG EXAMPLE: - 111
    THREE BEAD DIAMOND MESH - 109
    THREE BEAD DIAMOND MESH
      EXAMPLE: - 110
  YARN AND BEAD SIZE - 7

ANCHORING - 6

ARROWHEAD PATTERN
  OVER TWO/UNDER TWO
    (POINT DOWN) - 72
    (POINT DOWN) CENTER EXAMPLE: - 77
    (POINT DOWN) EXAMPLE: - 77
    (POINT UP) -78
    (POINT UP) EXAMPLE: - 78, 84
  OVER/UNDER WEAVE
    (POINT DOWN) - 53
    (POINT DOWN) BEAD ACCENT
      EXAMPLE: - 63
    (POINT DOWN) CENTER - 61
    (POINT DOWN) EXAMPLE: - 61
    (POINT DOWN) VARIATION 1 - 62
      EXAMPLE: - 62
    (POINT DOWN) VARIATION 2 - 62
      EXAMPLE: -62
    (POINT UP) - 64
    (POINT UP) CENTER EXAMPLE: - 71
    (POINT UP) EXAMPLE: - 71

----- B -----

BEAD SIZE, YARN AND - 7

BEADS
  BEAD SIZE - 7
  CARRIER STRANDS - 105
  DIAMOND PATTERN - 105
  OVER/UNDER ONLY - 105

BOARD, MEASURING - 4

BRAIDED FRINGE
  BEAD ACCENTED - 138
    EXAMPLE: - 138
  EXAMPLE: - 137

----- C -----

CARRIER STRANDS - 105

CASTING ON - 5

CHEVRON PATTERN
  OVER TWO/UNDER TWO - 32
    EXAMPLE: - 35
  OVER/UNDER WEAVE - 14
  POINT DOWN
    EXAMPLE: - 19
    VARIATION 1 - 20
    VARIATION 1 EXAMPLE: - 20

[1 4 1]

Variation 2 - 20
Variation 2 Example: - 20
Point Down (Center) - 19
Point Down (Center) Example - 19

COLORED BANDS - 85

COLORED STRANDS ACCENT
openface Weaving 113, 143

----- D -----

DIAGONAL PATTERN
Example: - 13
Over/Under Weave - 9

DIAMOND DESIGN
Openface Weaving - 117

DIAMOND PATTERN - 19, 105

DIAMOND WEAVE - 85, 117

DOUBLE CHEVRON
M Pattern -29
Example: - 31
W Pattern - 27
Example: - 29

DOUBLE LIGHTNING
Pattern - 47, 53
Added Color Bands - 56
Variation - 56
Variation Example: - 56
Example: - 55

----- F -----

FRINGES, TWISTED - 139

FRINGES, BRAIDED - 135

FRINGES, PART 4: - 132

FRINGES, TIED - 133

----- G -----

GETTING STARTED, PART 1: - 4

----- H -----

HEADSTICK - 5

----- I -----

INTERFACE - 85

----- J -----

JOINING BANDS, OPENFACE WEAVING - 93

----- K -----

KEEPING AN OPEN SHED - 7

----- L -----

LENGTH OF YARN - 4

LIGHTNING PATTERN - 40
Added Color Bands - 45
Variation 3 - 46
Variation 3 Example: - 46

Added Strands
Variation 2 - 45
Variation 2 Example: - 45
Example: - 45
Three Colors
Variation 1 - 45
Variation 1 Example: - 45

LIGHTNING PATTERN, DOUBLE - 47

----- M -----

MATERIALS AND TOOLS - 4

MEASURING - 4

MEASURING BOARD - 4

----- N -----

NUMBER OF STRANDS OF YARN - 4

----- O -----

OBLIQUE - 85

OPEN SHED, KEEPING AN - 7

OPENFACE WEAVING
Accent Beads
Carrier Strands - 105
Diamond Pattern - 105
Over/Under Only - 105

Colored Strands Accent - 113
Bead Accent Carrier Strand - 116
Bead Accent Example: - 116
Example: -116
Bead Accent Over/Under Weave - 116
Colored Strands Accent Example: - 1116
Diamond Design - 117
Example: - 117
Diamond Design with Bead Accent
Carrier Strand - 118
Carrier Strand Example: - 118
Over/under Weave - 118
Over/under Weave Example: - 118
Joining Bands - 93
Example: - 97
Plain Weaving - 96
Example: - 92
Twining - 119
Example: - 125
Twining and Beads
Combined -125
Combined Example: - 125
Warp Accent - 126
Example: - 130

OPENFACE WEAVING, PART 3: - 85

OPENFACE WOVEN BORDERS
On Diagonal Warpface Weaving -98
On Left to Right Diagonal
Warpface Example: - 104
On Right to Left Diagonal
Warpface Example: - 104
Warpface Weft Worked
Left to Right - 101
Right to Left - 98

[142]

OVER TWO/UNDER TWO
- Arrowhead Pattern - 72
- Chevron Pattern - 32
- Reversed Chevron - 36

OVER/UNDER WEAVE
- Arrowhead Pattern - 57
- Chevron Pattern - 14
- Diagonal Pattern - 9
- Reversed Chevron - 21

----- P -----

PART 1: GETTING STARTED - 4

PART 2: WARPFACE WEAVING
- Arrowhead - 8, 53
- Chevron - 8, 14
- Diagonal - 8, 9
- Lightning - 18, 40

PART 3: OPENFACE WEAVING
- Color Strand Accent - 85, 113
- Colored Bands - 85, 93
- Diamond Weave - 85, 117
- Solid Color - 85, 86
- Twining - 85, 119
- Warp Accent - 85, 126
- Woven Borders - 98

PART 4: FRINGES
- Braided Fringe - 132, 135
- Tied Fringe - 132, 133
- Twisted Fringe - 132, 139

PICKING UP THE SHED - 6

PLAIN FACE - 885

----- R -----

REVERSED CHEVRON PATTERN (POINT UP)
- Over Two/Under Two - 36
  - Example: - 39
- Over/Under Weave - 21
- Point Up - 26
  - Point Up Example: - 26
  - Point Up (Center)Example: - 26

----- S -----

SECURING A WEFT STRAND - 7

SETTING UP THE SHED - 6

SHED - 6

SHED, OPEN - 7

SHED, PICKING UP THE - 6

SHED, SETTING UP THE - 6

----- T -----

TIED FRINGE - 137, 138

Example: - 139

TOOLS, MATERIALS AND - 4

TWINING
- Open Face Weaving - 85, 119

TWISTED FRINGE - 132, 136
- Example: - 140

TWO STRAND WALL KNOT - 133

TYPE OF YARN - 4

----- W -----

WALL KNOT, TWO STRAND - 138

WARP ACCENT
- Open Face Weaving - 85, 126

WARPFACE WEAVING, PART 2: - 8

WEFT STRAND, SECURING A - 7

----- Y -----

YARN
- Length of - 4
- Number of strands of - 4
- Type of - 4

YARN AND BEAD SIZE - 7

----- Z -----

ZIGZAG PATTERN
- Colored Strands Accent - 113
- Bead Accent - 105

[143]

About the Author

Gerald L. Findley has had a life long interest in learning and teaching crafts. Some of his areas of interest are basketry; braiding (boondoggle and leather); bead work (loom, lazy stitch, gourd stitch, and applique); tablet weaving; inkle loom weaving; and wood carving.

Gerald's interest in crafts and his fifty five year membership in the Boy Scouts of America has provided him with many opportunities to encourage youth to expand their areas of interest. At present he is in his twenty sixth year as Scoutmaster of a troop in Northern New York State. In addition, Gerald serves as Ceremony Team Advisor for his local BSA council's Order of the Arrow lodge.

As OA Ceremony Team advisor, Gerald became interested in fingerweaving. Due to the lack of published material providing basic fingerweaving instruction, he began a series of drawings and crafted actual pieces to help his Ceremony Team members create their own costumes. Discussions with adults at National Order of the Arrow gatherings and with participants in reenacting groups prompted Gerald's decision to develop a basic fingerweaving book.

All photographs and diagrams in this book were produced by Gerald. The photographs represent some of the over 30 sets of fingerwoven pieces that he has woven and donated for use by members of the Order of the Arrow Ceremony team. Each set includes a pair of garters, a sash, and a bandolier.

Other works by Gerald include an article, "**Ladder Lashing**", which was published in the December, 1995 issue of the magazine, "Scouting". He is listed as a subject expert for the second printing and subsequent printings of the eleventh edition of The Boy Scout Handbook. Gerald is also the author and illustrator of a book on rope and knot tying titled **Rope Works** and an accompanying CD titled **Rope Works Animated**.